"Dr. Greggo has once again challenged us to think well about the work we do in Christian counseling and psychotherapy. A leading expert in the topic of assessment, he demonstrates both impressive breadth and depth in this important book. It is practical, current, well researched, and nicely written."

Mark R. McMinn, professor of psychology, George Fox University, author of *The Science of Virtue*

"In *Assessment for Counseling in Christian Perspective*, Dr. Stephen Greggo has provided the Christian counseling community a treatise that is exquisite in its quality of authorship and elegant in its graceful simplicity. His personal integrity is reflected in the quality of his work, a masterful demonstration of what he calls us to in this book. Dr. Greggo lays and maintains a biblical and theological bulwark for facing the challenges of assessment generally, but specifically for those uniquely applicable to counselors who are Christian. As such, *Assessment for Counseling in Christian Perspective* is a fundamental resource for counselors when thinking with biblical and clinical regard for those entrusted to their care. Christian counseling is better because of Dr. Greggo's contribution!"

David E. Jenkins, professor and director of MA in addiction counseling, Liberty University

ASSESSMENT

FOR COUNSELING

IN CHRISTIAN

PERSPECTIVE

STEPHEN P. GREGGO

IVP Academic
An imprint of InterVarsity Press
Downers Grove, Illinois

InterVarsity Press
P.O. Box 1400, Downers Grove, IL 60515-1426
ivpress.com
email@ivpress.com

InterVarsity Press® is the book-publishing division of InterVarsity Christian Fellowship/USA®, a movement of students and faculty active on campus at hundreds of universities, colleges, and schools of nursing in the United States of America, and a member movement of the International Fellowship of Evangelical Students. For information about local and regional activities, visit intervarsity.org.

All Scripture quotations, unless otherwise indicated, are taken from The Holy Bible, New International Version®, NIV®. Copyright © 1973, 1978, 1984, 2011 by Biblica, Inc.™ Used by permission of Zondervan. All rights reserved worldwide. www.zondervan.com. The "NIV" and "New International Version" are trademarks registered in the United States Patent and Trademark Office by Biblica, Inc.™

While any stories or case composites in this book are drawn from clinical experience, all names, identifying information, and descriptive details have been changed to protect the privacy of individuals.

Cover design: David Fassett
Interior design: Daniel van Loon
Images: pastel gradient: © Yuko Yamada / Moment Collection / Getty Images
grunge background: © in-future / iStock / Getty Images Plus
gold textured background: © Katsumi Murouchi / Moment collection / Getty Images
gradient spheres: © MirageC / Moment collection / Getty Images

ISBN 978-0-8308-2858-6 (print)
ISBN 978-0-8308-9711-7 (digital)

Printed in the United States of America ∞

InterVarsity Press is committed to ecological stewardship and to the conservation of natural resources in all our operations. This book was printed using sustainably sourced paper.

Library of Congress Cataloging-in-Publication Data
A catalog record for this book is available from the Library of Congress.

P	25	24	23	22	21	20	19	18	17	16	15	14	13	12	11	10	9	8	7	6	5	4	3	2	1
Y	37	36	35	34	33	32	31	30	29	28	27	26	25	24	23	22	21	20	19						

FOR BRIAN FAST

and the extraordinary staff who

co-labor with us to nurture hope

Soli Deo gloria

CONTENTS

ACKNOWLEDGMENTS

Trinity Evangelical Divinity School (TEDS) provided support through a sabbatical leave and wonderful teaching assistants. Many counselors-in-training made contributions to my research, writing, and supervision on the use of assessments. Special thanks to Sasa Mo Chan, Lucas Tillet, Karen Lawrence, Rainey Ray Segars, Danielle Whitaker, Amanda Geels, Camille Andress, Lauren Fisher, Angela Wessels, Tyler Hudson, Amanda Lai Wai Kuen, and Jenna Metcalfe. Appreciation is also due to TEDS faculty from the Deerfield Dialogue Group, who critiqued select chapters.

These chapters merge assessment technology, Christian theology, and counseling practice. Defining assessment in mental health counseling with a Christian emphasis requires venturing into territory where precedent is limited. Conference presentations and publication along the way generated useful feedback. This enabled fine-tuning of concepts such as redemptive validity, layers of wisdom, clinical application of rapid assessment instruments (RAIs), and corrective emotional relationships (CERs). It is important to thank anonymous reviewers from the *Journal for Psychology and Christianity*, the *Journal of Psychology and Theology*, *Christian Psychology: A Transdisciplinary Journal*, and *Journal of the Evangelical Theological Society*. Sections of these articles are incorporated here.

Insight was inspired by colleagues, counselor educators, students, and clients. The ideas stimulated by these dialogue partners were absorbed into these pages. The confidence of Andy Le Peau and Jon Boyd from InterVarsity Press was essential. In short, this project benefited from the input of many who are remembered with much gratitude.

Finally, thanks to my pastor, the Reverend Terry Breum. As he prays for me, often when celebrating the Lord's Supper, he explicitly intercedes by asking the Lord to bless my "teaching and writing ministry." This effort is indeed an answer to those persistent prayers.

ABBREVIATIONS

16PF	16 Personality Factor Questionnaire
AA	Alcoholic Anonymous
AACE	Association for Assessment in Counseling and Education
AARC	Association for Assessment and Research in Counseling
ACA	American Counseling Association
ADHD	Attention Deficit Hyperactivity Disorder
AERA	American Educational Research Association
APA	American Psychological Association *or*
APA	American Psychiatric Association
ATGS-9	Attitudes Toward God Scale
ASERVIC	Association of Spiritual, Ethical, and Religious Values Issues in Counseling
BAI	Beck Anxiety Inventory
BDI-II	Beck Depression Inventory II
Brief RCOPE	Brief RCOPE
BSI	Brief Symptom Inventory
CAD	Clinical Assessment of Depression
CAGE	CAGE Substance Abuse Screening Tool (Cut down, Annoyed, Guilty, Eye-opener)
CAICEF	Clinical Assessment Instrument Christian Evaluation Form
CCSM	*DSM*-5 Level 1 Cross-Cutting Symptom Measure
CERs	Corrective Emotional Relationships
CLOSE	CLOSE Therapy Graduation Dialogue Outline (Change, Lessons Learned, Openness to Others, Spiritual Practices/Support, Expectations)
CPAC	Counseling Partnership Alliance Check
CPE	Clinical Pastoral Education
CR	Celebrate Recovery
CSRI	Clinically Significant Religious Impairment
CUD	Character-Under-Development
DAG	Disappointment and Anger with God Scale
DRI	Duke Religion Index

DSM-5	*Diagnostic and Statistical Manual of Mental Disorders*-5th edition
DWI	Driving While Intoxicated
EBP	Evidence-Based Practice
EMRs	Electronic Medical Records
FFM	Five-Factor Model
FACT	Spiritual History-Assessment Tool (Faith, Activities, Coping, Treatment)
FICA	Spirituality Questionnaire (Faith, Importance, Community, and Address)
FIT	Feedback-Informed Treatment
FS	Flourishing Scale
GAS	Goal Attainment Scale
GRID-HAMD	Hamilton Rating Scale for Depression
HAM-A	Hamilton Anxiety Rating Scale
IC	Initial Consultation
ICD-10	Classification of Mental and Behavioral Disorders
ISS	Intrinsic Spirituality Scale
JCOPE	Jewish Religious Coping Scale
MBTI	Myers-Briggs Type Indicator
MCCI	Millon College Counseling Inventory
MCMI-III/IV	Millon Clinical Multiaxial Inventory-III/IV
MHPs	Mental Health Professionals
MMPI	Minnesota Multiphasic Personality Inventory
MMPI-2-RF	Minnesota Multiphasic Personality Inventory-2-Restructured Form
MMY	*Mental Measurements Yearbook*
NEO-PI-3	NEO Personality Inventory-3
NCME	National Council on Measurement in Education
NRC	Negative Religious Coping
O&A	Orientation and Assessment Session
PACE	PACE Treatment Progress Dialogue Outline (Partnership, Affinity, Collaborative Conversation, and Experience)
PAG	Positive Attitudes toward God Scale
PASS	Procrastination Assessment Scale-Students
PBE	Practice-Based Evidence

PCL-C	PTSD Checklist-Civilian Version
PHQ-9	Patient Health Questionnaire Depression Scale
PI	Perfectionism Inventory
PID	Personality-in-Distress
PRC	Positive Religious Coping
PS	Procrastination Scale
PSSI	Pinney Sexual Satisfaction Inventory
PTSD	Post-Traumatic Stress Disorder
QVW	Quickview Social History
RADS II	Reynolds Adolescent Depression Scale
RAIs	Rapid Assessment Instruments
RAPS	Rapid Alcohol Problems Screen
RCI-10	Religious Commitment Inventory
RSS	Religious Support Scale
RV	Redemptive Validity
SAI	Spiritual Assessment Inventory
SCL-90-R	Symptom Checklist 90 Revised
SCOFF	Eating Disorder Screening Questionnaire (Sick, Control, One stone, Fat, Food)
SCSRFQ	Santa Clara Strength of Religious Faith Questionnaire
SDS	Zung Self-Rating Depression Scale
SLA	Spiritual Life Assessment
SMQS	Sacred Moment Qualities Scale
SRF	Session Rating Form
SRS	Springfield Religiosity Scale
START	START Initial Consultation Outline (Story, Therapeutic Alliance, Assessment, Recommendations, and Treatment Plan)
SUDS	Subjective Units of Distress Scale
WAI/WAI-SF	Working Alliance Inventory (or WAI-SF, short form)

PART 1

REASON FOR

ASSESSMENT

ASSESSMENT TO

NAVIGATE CHANGE

And whatever you do, whether in word or deed, do it all in the name
of the Lord Jesus, giving thanks to God the Father through him.

COLOSSIANS 3:17

THEOLOGICAL THEME

Virtue and Vocational Excellence

PICTURE THE DESTINATION

Assessment starts by listening to someone's life story, dream, or personal experience and hearing the yearning underneath. The counselor listens earnestly
for the key challenge that must be explored. From this point forward, each
decision, instrument, and inquiry flows out of the rationale for launching the
investigation. The destination for change emerges as a response to the cry of a
heart. Assessment then guides the journey.

Mental health evaluations by tradition are descriptive and technical. The
scientific legacy of psychological measurement has produced objective means
to investigate unique personal characteristics. Polished instruments identify
symptoms, gauge functioning, or detect personality patterns. Interviewers
probe for detail and take notice of the full range of immediate behaviors.
Results are merged into formal reports. This documentation outlines the reason
for referral, summarizes background information, lists the measures applied,
consolidates findings, and builds to a conclusion with recommendations. Such
evaluations rely on expert judgment to generate insight into the essence of the
presenting problem. The purpose is to pinpoint an accurate diagnostic profile
that tracks smoothly with the treatment options.

Descriptive assessment remains a necessity. For example, health systems allow for care to treat a disease, condition, or injury. The evaluation at the outset justifies eligibility for treatment by establishing the state of the patient. Further, the severity of the detriment dictates the treatment setting, frequency, format, and duration. Nevertheless, although important, this mainstream style of assessment contains a clinical hazard. Professional documents take on the tone of official pronouncements. The findings have power to inadvertently become limitations. The objective survey of the client's past and present detects a location on a psychiatric map of mental illness. A pin is dropped; a monument is erected.

There is a way forward that embraces the methodology of assessment yet reduces the risk that it will hinder growth. Counselors would do well to view assessment as a real-time navigational system that can expedite the route to a place of flourishing. Instruments can do more than describe; they can estimate proximity to the achievement of change. Or, when treatment is underway, measures may reveal aimless wandering or warn of the dreaded dead end. Awareness of the need to reroute the care plan is far more beneficial than pushing on as if all were well. Assessment, like its biblical counterpart, discernment, needs to be an ongoing and dynamic routine to encourage movement in a productive direction, toward what is truly best (Phil 1:9-10).

This book will explore flexible and vibrant ways to gather and apply information. Assessment informs both counselors and clients. It can tighten the focus of the conversation, reveal the presence of obstacles, stabilize risk from nonproductive expectations, and safeguard good will in the helping partnership itself.

The intersection of psychotherapy and Christian ministry is primed for reconstruction. There are numerous shifts occurring in cultural and spiritual values. Clergy who care for constituents via counseling must reflect on their priorities and purposes. Pastors and congregations will determine an acceptable balance of care implementing interpersonal discipleship, group instruction, or intercessory prayer. Is ministry counseling to be a comprehensive service, an entryway to mental health intervention, or a referral route to formation exercises with a spiritual director? Professional roles and expectations are in flux as specializations continue to evolve. Christians with credentials in mental health settings are prepared to serve diverse clients without imposing faith values. Such neutrality may not be appealing to those with deep Christian convictions. Obviously, the stakes in counseling are high, both personally and socially. Resources continue to fall far short of critical needs. Clinicians, ministry leaders, and medical professionals will continue to explore the potential for teamwork. Clinicians who follow Christ and have eyes to see those who are hurting, hiding, or seeking will feel the compassion of our Lord awaken. The crowds appear harassed and helpless (Mt 9:36).

When educating others, the challenge is to teach forward—that is, to teach with an eye on what is on the horizon. There is little benefit accomplished by merely looking back on what one has come to understand as valuable in the field and then passing that along. Those perceptions may be accurate, insightful, explanatory, and perhaps even entertaining. But unless guidance anticipates, it is functionally and pedagogically useless. The upcoming generation of people helpers and pastoral caregivers will not serve clients under the field conditions that existed five or more years ago. Experience generates knowledge, and this becomes wisdom when combined with vision to prepare learners for what's looming on the horizon. The next generation needs to be ready to embrace the questions of their day.

Here's the proverbial good news and bad news. The good news is that counseling is effective; therapy is a valid pathway for clients to resolve issues and pursue change. Clients who complete treatment generally improve. The supporting evidence for this claim is compelling (Lambert, 2013; Nielsen et al., 2004; Wampold & Imel, 2015). Furthermore, when therapeutic methods are accommodated to fit the faith traditions and commitments of religiously oriented clients, these approaches are generally effective (Worthington, Hook, Davis, & McDaniel, 2011). For those in the Christian tradition, there is a variety of therapeutic approaches available (Worthington, Johnson, Hook, & Aten, 2013).

However, despite much evidence for the effectiveness of therapy, there are still opportunities to improve the discipline. This desire for improvement has led to the call for standardization and customization. Standardization is uniformity in how counseling is delivered, while customization refers to how counselors fit approaches to unique clients. Additionally, there is a call for evidence that articulates the potential impact of specific models of treatment. The challenge, though, is that the reliability (e.g., consistency) of success is less predictable than those in the field might hope. Multiple factors contribute to the intricacies of delivering effective service, in particular the fact that no two clients are the same. Each client represents a specific background, family configuration, and cultural community, and skillful counselors recognize subtle distinctions in client presentation and openness. Adept counselors adjust interventions accordingly (Wampold & Imel, 2015). But the impediments to success are real.

How many mental health professionals (MHPs) does it take to change a light bulb? Only one, but the light bulb must want to change. The joke may be stale, but the myth it extols is worth exposing. Failures in counseling are not solely a matter of counselee factors or an unwillingness to commit. A motivational force brings a client in for that first appointment. It takes embracing that impetus to promote success. Extensive research into counselor actions offers insights into what's likely to go right or wrong (Castonguay & Hill, 2017; Marini, 2016; Swift & Greenberg, 2015). Counselor behavior matters. How will MHPs address uncertainties regarding the reliable delivery of care? Counselors are challenged to recognize and employ information on how the collaboration is proceeding. This is a formidable responsibility. There is much to consider, and there are many aspects to observe—all constrained by limitations on time.

THE HOPE OF PRACTICE-BASED EVIDENCE

Still, there is reason for hope. A robust movement is building momentum in the field of counseling and psychotherapy, described by phrases such as "preventing treatment failure," "feedback informed therapy," "patient-focused assessment," "psychotherapy quality assurance," and "outcome monitoring" (Prescott, Maeschalck, & Miller, 2017; Duncan, Miller, Wampold, & Hubble, 2010; Lambert, 2010; Swift & Greenberg, 2015). These labels can be summarized by the term "practice-based evidence" (Green & Latchford, 2012). Practice-based evidence (PBE) involves systematically collecting information at all phases of treatment through the use of assorted assessment procedures. Using assessment to monitor and inform the process of change can strengthen the quality of service and increase the likelihood that the desired outcomes will be reasonably achieved. This style of assessment will increasingly inform and empower clients, demonstrate progress, and maximize success by clarifying expectations and focusing on tangible outcomes.

This form of assessment is not about making a diagnosis or discovering an elusive underlying pattern. Rather, this is doing assessment seamlessly, with ease and comfort for the sake of the client. Approaching a clinical case is similar to conducting a research study: even though there is only one subject, it is essential to define the problem, develop a hypothesis, propose an intervention, deliver care, refine the plan as necessary, and review the evidence to see how successful the outcomes are (Glicken, 2005). And rather than diminishing the interpersonal nature of the work, these assessment procedures can contribute to the durability and endurance of the human aspects of care.

The past few decades have seen the establishment of evidence-based practice (EBP) in mental health care. This is typically defined as the implementation of the best current research into explicitly tailored methods to fit client characteristics, culture, and setting. EPB requires clinicians to engage clients with significant interpersonal skill (APA Presidential Taskforce, 2006). Using targeted approaches and adapting them to unique clients requires the application of assessment procedures posing these questions:

- What are the options?
- What's the best plan?
- Will this work?
- How should we proceed?

In contrast, PBE shifts the focus to consider how things are working in a live, multifaceted therapeutic effort. PBE is a complementary undertaking that extends the principle of relying on evidence to determine the direction of care by mapping the progression of the change experienced by the client. PBE prefers these questions:

- Is this option working?
- What's our best plan?
- Are we working?
- How can we adjust to improve our plan or partnership?

Both EPB and PBE seek improved quality of service, but the distinction between the two is that although EBP looks to researchers to demonstrate efficacy, PBE turns the spotlight on the counseling dyad, making the argument that quality care will provide the evidence that treatment was indeed effective. PBE is collected, calibrated, and interpreted in the counseling room, not in the laboratory.

We live in an era when customers rate everything, from the burger they ate at lunch to a new piece of luggage to their medical services. It's common sense to check with clients *before* they depart our offices to ascertain if our procedures and services were close to their expectations. In fact, this sort of evaluation can help shape counselee expectations, even from the earliest contact. Incorporating practice-based evidence allows counselors to evaluate progress alongside clients so that accomplishments and the ongoing strategy for growth are understood and agreed on mutually.

This form of assessment becomes a means to sharpen our craft while improving the connection and tracking results in real time. My goal in this book is to equip clinicians to come to terms with the necessity and advantages of bringing a productive blend of assessment strategies into our interpersonal helping conversations.

TOWARD A THEOLOGY OF ASSESSMENT

When I began teaching counseling in a seminary, my core assignment was to teach two psychological testing courses for future counselors with pastoral ambitions. However, each course encountered ample resistance: "Loving God and listening to others has no resemblance to statistics, standardization, or psychological surveys!" The force of the impasse prompted me to wonder, is there a definitive theology of assessment practices?

This question led me to consult with a well-regarded and published expert on the merger of assessment and Christianity. He explained that psychological testing is where the field relies on scientific methods. Christian theology is religious activity and has its own structure. In this curricular area, it's best not to conflate the two.

The consultant continued with his assertion. There are two subjects where it does not matter if the instructor is a person of faith: research and assessment. The methodologies rely on science, evidence, and systematic interpretation. These are not domains for theology. As jarring as this was, his central contention does remain sound. Given the demands on MIIPs to grapple with special terminology and statistical material, courses in assessment must require learners to press hard into matters of technical import. Fluency in the language of test construction and proper implementation is indeed a requirement (American Educational Research Association, American Psychological Association, & National Council on Measurement in Education, 2014).

Yet while instrument construction may be a methodology of science, its application raises issues related to worldview, values, and religious tradition. When assessment procedures are used in ministry, there is value in pondering how theological thinking can contribute to right speaking and doing. From the standpoint of Christian anthropology, there may be risks that arise from the promotion of instruments devised to reduce complex human characteristics into comprehensible, discrete quantities. Can these measures be put to use in ways that continue to respect the agency and holistic nature of human beings?

The serious reminder delivered in that consultation has not been forgotten. People helpers must grasp the power and risk embedded in assessment before bringing any measure to a client, and this requires mastery of basic concepts and the language related to psychometrics. Still, my passion follows the charge of another mentor who reminds that no matter the activity, the process of people helping is a means for the Lord to accomplish his perfect will through imperfect people (Collins, 2000). Therefore, selecting and applying assessment technology is not exactly value neutral or a venture in pure objectivity.

These pages do not offer a comprehensive theology of assessment. However, a theocentric foundation, supported by sound biblical theology, should guide the application of any and all applied technology. Scripture provides the basis for this theology as it addresses themes such as stewardship, discernment, wisdom, hospitality, the kingdom of God, sanctification, and the redemptive activity of the Holy Spirit. These theological domains can be addressed through the use of assessment. After years of interacting with future Christian and pastoral counselors on how to apply standardized psychological instruments, I offer these pages to share my attempt to bring biblical directives into this clinical discipline.

MAXIMIZING ASSESSMENT WITHOUT MINIMIZING CHRISTIANITY

When assessment furthers the planning of the helping effort, goals, and exit strategy, it enhances communication. Assessment procedures can establish a built-in mechanism to evaluate how the partnership is progressing toward the goals. Viewed in this light, assessment becomes the pursuit of excellence in counseling and pastoral care.

Assessment in clinical practice is nothing new, but it is currently being rethought. However, this is not an exhortation to simply comply with the latest trends. There are reasons why it may be particularly important for Christians in the field of mental health to become proficient in demonstrating practice-based evidence. Counseling committed to a ministry orientation can utilize assessment to confront several unfortunate contemporary pressures.

Medicalization. An unrelenting tendency in our day is to categorize matters of human experience hastily and exclusively in medical terms. A young child who places inedible items in his mouth may automatically have this behavior tagged as *pica*. The term denotes a legitimate medical condition with mental health associations. This language classifies the behavior as a craving, compulsion, and disease. But there are normal alternatives to a medical diagnosis, alternatives such as boredom, curiosity, rebelliousness, or hunger. Assessment determines when and if the line of disease is crossed. Ordinary human experiences such as feeling down, anxious, restless, fatigued, excited, or dissatisfied can be a symptom of an extensive array of issues, but a disease model with medical causes and cures tends to be the default route.

Without a doubt, the range of medical treatments in behavioral healthcare has removed needless and unnecessary suffering. The challenge for Christians who counsel, however, is to recognize the blessing of medical advances while still acknowledging a holistic view that includes existential, religious, and spiritual matters. Counselors are often in a prime position to sit with clients and consider the psychological, behavioral, relational, and cultural domains. Christian therapists may also wish to raise awareness regarding lifestyle, family priorities, ethics, values, and spirituality in conjunction with exploring a stated concern.

The key to distinguish when a behavior or experience lies within the normal or atypical range is to investigate its frequency, severity, and duration. Such analysis is fundamental in assessment. Comprehensive and systematic assessment encourages practitioners to resist the urge to close in on a physical or biological explanation too readily or absolutely. To be certain, there are times when medical concerns are legitimate, and well-rounded assessment makes this evident. But routine and targeted data collection with quantification directs client treatment toward holistic care.

Makeover madness. Reality shows bring the fantasy of a complete makeover within the range of plausibility. Home makeover shows often portray a run-down, money-pit of a house being transformed into the neighborhood sweetheart in a matter of weeks. Dramatic and nearly instantaneous makeovers are all the rage.

Buoyed by these makeover stories, clients may show up for that first appointment with the unspoken expectation that a magical phrase or savvy advice is going to rock their world. Counseling can be transformative, and there are occasions when a homework assignment leads to a series of outlook-altering revolutions. The norm, however, usually involves contemplation of change over time; rarely does it happen so completely or rapidly as the makeovers in media accounts. Our mission in helping, therefore, is to stir hope. The dialogue work will entail getting a good picture of the present scenario and resources in order to help clients turn wishes for change into realistic and recognizable goals.

Assessment can be critical in this process of helping clients set a reasonable outlook on what can be accomplished in the counseling journey. For Christian counseling, assessment can also provide insight in how to pray for the courage to heal, grow, and transform. This can temper clients' hopes for miraculous change with the recognition that the Lord will provide daily bread to sustain them on their sojourn toward wholeness.

Marginalization. The embrace of spirituality and religion by the broad therapeutic community over the past two decades is a radical shift. Whereas spirituality and religion were once viewed as irrational defenses or as an irrelevant rabbit trail in psychotherapy, faith is now viewed as a central individual, cultural, and transcendent resource.[1] The counseling profession has integrated spirituality and religion into its helping process and produced its own resources (Cashwell & Young, 2011), and in 1993 the Association of Spiritual, Ethical, and Religious Values Issues in Counseling (ASERVIC) became a division within the American Counseling Association (ACA). This moved a formerly Catholic organization into a broad and diverse community of over four thousand counselors within the ACA who express an interest in spiritually sensitive counseling. Spiritual competencies were established in 1995 and updated in 2009 (Cashwell & Watts, 2010).

This new enthusiasm regarding spirituality is confirmation of the important place that transcendence has in human experience. There is also a profound recognition that in times of turmoil, clients are open to exploring their spiritual/religious perspectives and practices (Young & Cashwell, 2011). Yet this shift has resulted in a growing uneasiness among those committed to the vital and historic Christian tradition. The discomfort arises from indications that, as a generic and individually defined spirituality is on the rise, orthodox Christianity with its grounded moral code and religious authority may be marginalized or rejected completely. Christianity speaks to the immediate and eternal salvation of broken persons, not to the humanistic fulfillment of an autonomous individual (Rom 1:16-17). According to the Christian tradition, human beings are dependent on an external source for renewal. This perspective can be viewed by some as primitive, judgmental, and archaic.

Christians who counsel need to develop a thoughtful perspective to clinical assessment. Counselors who represent ministry traditions need not be hesitant in supplying credible evidence for the value of a distinctly Christian therapeutic approach. One way to confront the cultural pressure to marginalize authentic Christian approaches is to demonstrate their effectiveness via practice-based evidence. This will require that counselors reach routinely for instruments. Doing so will affirm for Christian counselors that their work is effective and worthy of recognition.

---

[1]The American Psychological Association (APA) has published volumes on the topic (Pargament, 2013; Aten, McMinn, & Worthington, 2011; Walker & Hathaway, 2013; Aten & Leach, 2009; Plante, 2009).

Mediocrity. Counselors may be torn in trying to address the expectations of the mental health system, the professional guild, and Christian ministry. There can be a reluctance to adopt procedures that appear secular, trendy, or overtly scientific. Or, alternately, there may be hesitation to make biblical themes or Christian discipleship a central focus in counseling. The trouble with seeking a middle ground between competing expectations is that it can lead to mediocrity.

Strategic assessment is a means to examine a client's experience, expectations, and views. This can be done not only to enhance therapeutic alliance but also to discern openness to the direction of the Holy Spirit. This allows for agreement about what determines quality service as well as a means to evaluate outcomes.

For clients who come with fervent Christian commitments of their own, there is an opportunity to chart a course for care that brings best practices together with the conventions of Christian discipleship (Vanhoozer, 2014). Counselors can make wise use of what is known about fostering excellence in a therapeutic encounter in a manner that is thoughtful, respectful, and thoroughly Christian. This moves away from the middle ground to higher ground.

PLANNING THE APPROACH

The purpose of this book is to enable counselors to put assessment into practical use, particularly with clients who are looking to grow their identity with Jesus Christ. It seeks to bring the best of assessment into counseling that reflects the true essence of the Christian faith. The main goal is to display how to implement measures in treatment for the sake of a mutual therapeutic relationship. As a Christian perspective on assessment, this book is designed to complement and supplement. This is not intended to be a comprehensive text on assessment in counseling.[2]

The four parts of this book, purposefully titled *Assessment for Counseling in Christian Perspective*, follow the typical outline of an assessment report: (1) reason for assessment, (2) background information, (3) assessment selection and administration, and (4) results and interpretation. Here are the central questions and topics to anticipate.

---

[2]Readers need to consult popular references to refresh awareness and place this material into a broader context. Consider this short list of select choices: *Assessment in Counseling: Procedures and Practices* (6th ed.; Hays, 2017); *Principles and Applications of Assessment in Counseling* (5th ed.; Whiston, 2017); *Assessment Procedures for Counselors and Helping Professionals* (8th ed.; Drummond, Sheperis, & Jones, 2016); *Essentials of Testing and Assessment: A Practical Guide to Counselors, Social Workers, and Psychologists* (3rd ed.; Neukrug & Fawcett, 2015); *Assessment for Counselors* (Erford, 2013).

Reason for assessment. How can a counselor clearly and uniquely formulate a strategy to assess with purpose in the throes of a genuine helping relationship? Part one identifies the value of assessment. Chapter two defines key terms and clarifies the purpose of assessment in therapeutic partnerships in contrast to a full psychological evaluation. The role of a mental health professional as both client advocate and ally becomes the overarching value when introducing measures into the helping process. Assessment done right can bring necessary past and present details to the surface, increase awareness of the dynamic interpersonal forces that are in play, and establish a means to speak with precision to invested parties about treatment progress.

Does a Christian worldview offer distinguishing parameters for assessment practice? Scripture has a good deal to say about gaining understanding on the inner ways and leanings of the heart. The pursuit of wisdom is the central frame of reference that governs counseling with Christian intentions. Thus, chapter three connects the search for wisdom with discerning the desires of the heart. In Christian counseling, Scripture is the ultimate "norming norm"; therefore, this chapter addresses customs for counselors to implement in order to "interrogate" the Word.

Background information. Can clinical proficiency in assessment bring glory to God? Part two lays the foundation for a theology of assessment. A response to the question of how systematic data collection can be an act of worship begins by expanding the theological layers for wisdom in counseling (chap. 4). Wisdom is intricately bound to artisanship. A craftsperson is one who is "wise" in the use of hands when demonstrating handiwork. Counselors are encouraged to use the finest tools available with well-executed artisanship for the benefit of clients.

Will counselors promote social justice as they come alongside their clients? The goal of developing standards to construct measures is not only to build better measures but to ensure that these measures are used justly across various cultural groups and diverse populations. Chapter five challenges counselors to personalize the core value of using honest and fair scales in ways that keep righteousness central in their own heart. Chapter six continues the press to account for cultural identity and diversity with unique clients by using illustrations from important biblical commands (Heb 12:14; Jas 2:9). The challenge to Christian clinicians to adopt specific disciplines as clinical habits is suggested to accomplish open-minded, holistic, and impartial assessments.

How can the crucial psychometric construct of validity be translated into our Christian faith? Chapter seven then builds the case for an explicit review of all measures through the lens of redemptive validity (RV). RV offers a way for clinicians to evaluate how a measure will function when applied to clients who value the Christian faith. RV is not a concern for those who develop measures, so this term will not show up in any test manual or prominent assessment text. Rather, RV goes beyond looking at an instrument's items, construct, or predictive criterion; it extends validity considerations to the renewal taking place in a client's life. Instrument evaluation, selection, and utility must first be viewed through a psychometric lens. Then, a theological perspective may be advantageous when a Christian viewpoint is desired.

Assessment selection and administration. In what ways can the intrusion of objective procedures in therapy be transformed into a message of hospitality and affirmation? Part three, "Assessment Selection and Administration," lays out practical applications. Chapter eight explores the assessment aspect of two vital elements of counseling: interviewing and dialogue. These skills are put to use in a tailored approach to reveal a client's faith orientation along polarities such as extrinsic or intrinsic, seeking or dwelling, Scripture or experience. Chapter nine follows by making the case to employ both subjective and objective assessment. The START model for initial consultations is introduced: story, therapeutic alliance, assessment, recommendations, and treatment plan. This rubric for a semi-structured interview provides an approach to demonstrate hospitality to a stranger with the hope of becoming an ally.

How can counselors maximize the benefits of a therapeutic alliance to attend to immediate concerns and foster spiritual formation? Chapter ten explores the concept of the therapeutic alliance and how to assess it. For clients who want counseling that is both restorative and spiritually transformative, the therapeutic partnership takes on special meaning. This is done through the lens of viewing the self as striving to live out one's role in God's great Gospel narrative— that is, the self that performs as a child who images God by displaying divine characteristics and enacting God's redemptive story. There are efficient ways to monitor the alliance and progress in therapy. This helps to address both a client's chief request while seizing the opportunity to cultivate character. The PACE rubric for ongoing progress evaluation of the therapeutic process is offered: partnership, affinity, collaborative conversation, and experience. This treatment review procedure can assist the dyad to stay true to both its clinical and formative mission.

Can assessment measures be implemented that enhance the precision and potency of the counseling conversation? There is a world of opportunity to access assessment instruments that are short, sweet, and tightly targeted (chap. 11).

This brings the use of semi-standardized measures to the attention of clinicians. Selective therapeutic assessment is defined as a strategy for combining instruments into a unified package that covers the critical areas for diagnosis and treatment planning. Selective assessment can expand by uncovering and evaluating credible resources. Rapid assessment instruments (RAIs) can be overlooked by MHPs as these are not commercially marketed or comprehensibly normed. The use of RAIs is a way to affordably and purposefully enlarge one's assessment toolkit. There are even measures of religious commitment and spirituality that can be applied to foster formation.

Results and interpretation. Part four shows how these measures can contribute not only to good counseling but also to conversations that are distinctively Christian.

What are the best practices to assess a client's spirituality or specific Christian tradition? Chapter thirteen provides interview techniques and measures to conduct a spiritual assessment. Clinicians are shown how to adopt a stepwise procedure to grasp clients' spiritual commitments, practices, and history as a means of ascertaining clients' desire for counseling that ultimately influences their spiritual journey.

How can counselors incorporate formal personality measures to add depth and substance to the counseling experience? Chapter fourteen transitions to explore well-established, self-report personality measures, namely, the NEO Personality Inventory-3 (NEO-PI-3); Sixteen Personality Factor Questionnaire (16PF); Minnesota Multiphasic Personality Inventory-2-Restructured Form (MMPI-2-RF); and the Millon Clinical Multiaxial Inventory IV (MCMI-IV). Measures such as these are definitely worth considering. Each one can bring light and language to enrich a clinical dialogue aimed at resolving immediate concerns and can also have a lasting impact on how the self relates to others. This is a key priority—to restore health while increasing conformity to the image of Jesus Christ.

How can assessment done well contribute to client retention, treatment completion, and aftercare planning? Chapter fifteen challenges the common closure terminology for counseling (termination) and offers a productive alternative (graduation). The chapter highlights lessons learned from the literature on how best to reach the graduation milestone and what steps counselors can take to prevent treatment failure. The CLOSE model is explained as an outline to recollect and remember the key events of treatment: change in chief concern, lessons learned, openness to others, spiritual practices (or support), and expectations. Bringing therapy to a meaningful close allows for a retrospective review of the relationship. Treatment concludes with plans for postgraduation maintenance, development, and fellowship (aftercare).

A VISION OF QUALITY CARE

The phrase *quality care* is often associated with mission statements and organizational mottos. This provocative term is far easier to claim than it is to demonstrate. What does quality actually look like in counseling? Care, respect, empathy, empowerment, restoration, and mutuality are lofty ideals. These need a firm grounding in client-friendly enactments. Further, for the disciple of Christ who counsels, we have a heavenly partner whom we wish to honor with the fruit of our labor. Service to clients is our service to him.

Through the promotion of an active, practice-based evidence approach to care, quality is cultivated in each conversation and in each session. There will be clearly defined benchmarks to set the course, to check for a good-enough partnership, and to track progress. In the chapters ahead, counselors will be shown ideas to synthesize a standardized program of assessment rituals. The result should fit your style, setting, and clientele. Further, the beauty and kindness of bringing grace into each counseling experience flows through the way treatment is customized to match the special features of the client on an exacting journey.

Catch this vision. Quality in care can be demonstrated. It is on display when we establish a plausible starting point to begin the work. It shines on when there is a readiness to share informed insights into the challenge of the moment. Quality prevails in the courage to explore the intricate dynamics of the immediate helping partnership. Further, it is expressed by ease in adapting evidence-based interventions into practical helps to fit a client who is known and understood. It is to these ends that the benefits of assessment will connect. It is to this higher level of craftsmanship that clinicians will be called.

Here are clinical habits, techniques, and strategies to navigate the complexity of the therapeutic encounter. The intent is to employ assessment as a flexible activity to inform, focus, and enliven helping conversations. What follows is a way to make counseling conversations not only edifying but to make its outcomes transparent. Counselors can show clients, or even outside parties, evidence of the therapeutic work that the Lord has enabled.

Christian theology will be prominent in selecting and shaping the questions, not merely as an aid to make sense of a string of responses. This is what it means to be a follower of Christ who is ready to bring healing to others who may or may not hold to our convictions. Our deepest conviction is this: to serve the other as neighbor and to love God in each moment.

REFERENCES

American Educational Research Association, American Psychological Association, & National Council on Measurement in Education. (2014). *Standards for educational and psychological testing.* Washington, DC: American Educational Research Association.

APA Presidential Task Force on Evidence-Based Practice. (2006). Evidence-based practice in psychology. *American Psychologist, 61*(4), 271-285.

Aten, J. D., & Leach, M. M. (Eds.). (2009). *Spirituality and the therapeutic process: A comprehensive resource from intake to termination.* Washington, DC: American Psychological Association.

Aten, J. D., McMinn, M. R., & Worthington, E. L., Jr. (Eds.). (2011). *Spiritually oriented interventions for counseling and psychotherapy.* Washington, DC: American Psychological Association.

Cashwell, C. S., & Watts, R. E. (2010). The new ASERVIC competencies for addressing spiritual and religious issues in counseling. *Counseling and Values, 55*(1), 2-5.

Cashwell, C. S., & Young, J. S. (Eds.). (2011). *Integrating spirituality and religion into counseling: A guide to competent practice* (2nd ed.). Alexandria, VA: American Counseling Association.

Castonguay, L. G., & Hill, C. E. (Eds.). (2017). *How and why are some therapists better than others?: Understanding therapist effects.* Washington, DC: American Psychological Association.

Collins, G. R. (2000). An integration view. In E. L. Johnson & S. L. Jones (Eds.), *Psychology & Christianity: Four views.* Downers Grove, IL: InterVarsity Press.

Drummond, R. J., Sheperis, C. J., & Jones, K. D. (2016). *Assessment procedures for counselors and helping professionals* (8th ed.). Upper Saddle River, NJ: Pearson.

Duncan, B. L., Miller, S. D., Wampold, B. E., & Hubble, M. A. (2010). *The heart & soul of change: Delivering what works in therapy* (2nd ed.). Washington, DC: American Psychological Association.

Erford, B. T. (2013). *Assessment for counselors* (2nd ed.). Belmont, CA: Brooks/Cole.

Glicken, M. D. (2005). *Improving the effectiveness of the helping professions: An evidence-based approach to practice.* Thousand Oaks, CA: Sage.

Green, D. & Latchford, G. (2012). *Maximizing the benefits of psychotherapy: A practice-based evidence approach.* West Sussex, UK: Wiley-Blackwell.

Hays, D. G. (2017). *Assessment in counseling: Procedures and practices* (6th ed.). Alexandria, VA: American Counseling Association.

Lambert, M. J. (2010). *Prevention of treatment failure: The use of measuring, monitoring, and feedback in clinical practice.* Washington, DC: American Psychological Association.

Lambert, M. J. (2013). Outcome in psychotherapy: The past and important advances. *Psychotherapy, 50*(1), 42-51.

Marini, I. (2016). Enhancing client return after the first session, and alternatively dealing with early termination. In I. Marini & M. A. Stebnicki (Eds.), *The professional counselor's desk reference* (2nd ed., pp. 99-104). New York: Springer.

Neukrug, E. S., & Fawcett, R. C. (2015). *Essentials of testing and assessment: A practical guide to counselors, social workers, and psychologists* (3rd ed.). Stamford, CT: Cengage Learning.

Nielsen, S. L., Smart, D. W., Isakson, R. L., Worthen, V. E., Gregersen, A. T., & Lambert, M. J. (2004). The *Consumer Reports* effectiveness score: What did consumers report? *Journal of Counseling Psychology, 51*(1), 25-37.

Pargament, K. I. (Ed.). (2013). *APA handbook of psychology, religion, and spirituality* (2 vols.). Washington, DC: American Psychological Association.

Plante, T. G. (2009). *Spiritual practices in psychotherapy: Thirteen tools for enhancing psychological health.* Washington, DC: American Psychological Association.

Prescott, D. S., Maeschalck, C. L., & Miller, S. D. (2017). *Feedback-informed treatment in clinical practice: reaching for excellence.* Washington, DC: American Psychological Association.

Swift J. K., & Greenberg, R. P. (2015). *Premature termination in psychotherapy: Strategies for engaging clients and improving outcomes.* Washington, DC: American Psychological Association.

Vanhoozer, K. J. (2014). *Faith speaking understanding: Performing the drama of doctrine.* Louisville, KY: Westminster John Knox.

Walker, D. F., & Hathaway, W. L. (Eds.). (2013). *Spiritual interventions in child and adolescent psychotherapy.* Washington, DC: American Psychological Association.

Wampold, B. E., & Imel, Z. E. (2015). *The great psychotherapy debate: The evidence for what makes psychotherapy work* (2nd ed.). New York: Routledge.

Whiston, S. C. (2017). *Principles and applications of assessment in counseling* (5th ed.). Belmont, CA: Cengage.

Worthington, E. L., Jr., Hook, J. N., Davis, D. E., & McDaniel, M. A. (2011). Religion and spirituality. *Journal of Clinical Psychology, 67*(2), 204-214.

Worthington, E. L., Jr., Johnson, E. L., Hook, J. N., & Aten, J. D. (2013). *Evidence-based practices for Christian counseling and psychotherapy.* Downers Grove, IL: InterVarsity Press.

Young, J. S., & Cashwell, C. S. (2011). Integrating spirituality and religion into counseling: An introduction. In C. S. Cashwell & J. S. Young (Eds.), *Integrating spirituality and religion into counseling: A guide to competent practice* (2nd ed., pp. 1-24). Alexandria, VA: American Counseling Association.

CHAPTER TWO

DEFINING THE ASSESSMENT TASK

But the Lord *said to Samuel, "Do not consider his appearance or his height,*
for I have rejected him. The Lord *does not look at the things people look at.*
People look at the outward appearance, but the Lord *looks at the heart."*

1 Samuel 16:7

THEOLOGICAL THEME
Affections of the Human Heart

ENVISIONING BEST PRACTICE

Every story has a beginning. The story of my work in clinical practice begins
with an ordinary decision with a receptive client. At the time, it seemed like
nothing—a ridiculously basic intervention decision: I determined to build
more, not less, standardized assessment into my therapeutic services. In retro-
spect, this marked the start of an irreversible journey toward the integration of
assessment procedures into counseling for the purpose of enhancing the quality
of care and encouraging Christ-glorifying spiritual growth. This decision
continues to define any counseling care that I undertake personally or influence
via supervision.

One particular case displays how this commitment to assessment was solidified in my practice. Dan was a typical client who openly claimed Jesus
Christ as Lord.[1] Despite our common faith, we were often deadlocked in a
bewildering struggle to achieve and maintain a mutual alliance. In our initial
meeting Dan presented as a well-functioning individual with marked success

---

[1] Clinical examples throughout this text are formed from case composites. All identifying features,
particularly the demographic elements, presenting concerns, and treatment settings are combined,
altered, or exchanged. "Dan" and all other names are fiction; these are not actual clients. The features
under consideration are genuine and flow from clinical experience.

in multiple spheres: career, marriage, friendships, and the church. He had an accomplished career as an engineer and had recently been promoted. The board of elders at his church was making inquiries to bring him into a leadership role. This father of two had a schoolteacher wife who adored him. His depictions of her devotion could make other husbands groan with envy. The recognition of these blessings heightened his sense of shame. Despite all appearances, crippling anxiety would overtake him, and he sought relief in dark outlets. There were extensive compulsive, self-destructive patterns that his outward success could easily mask. Furthermore, each behavioral tactic that Dan used to gain relief was defeated by his own actions before its effectiveness could be realized. In ordinary conversation, Dan exuded self-assurance. When alone, however, hypocrisy and self-doubt would explode out of him. His anxiety and shame could leave him weeping like an inconsolable infant.

After ten therapy sessions, only modest gains were evident to justify the benefit of our work together. My erroneous prediction early on was that counseling with Dan would be complete in less than three months. Now there were glaring indications that an entrenched lifestyle concern and chronic, self-defeating propensities reflected an inward, fragile identity. The impetus to take a closer look came from the novel requirement to submit a formal treatment plan. This client had a top-quality insurance plan that included external managed-care review procedures in order to request additional sessions. As Dan left that tenth session, I was utterly perplexed. It was as if checkmate had been declared in an arduous game of relational chess. During our very next meeting, I administered a standardized, self-report personality measure. I gave Dan an orientation to the assessment and made a commitment to discuss how the results would be useful for his care.

A nagging discomfort provoked me to introduce the use of assessment methodology. In schools and social service settings, assessment expertise was central to my work; conducting bio-psycho-social-educational evaluations was my primary function. At community agencies, I would routinely generate formal evaluations prepared with extensive reliance on standardized measures to inform special education teachers, caseworkers, psychiatrists, child-care staff, and court personnel when making care decisions. Beyond a clinical interview, the comprehensive battery would be informed by collaborative discussions, behavioral observations, projective tests, interest inventories, ability measures, and standardized questionnaires. By design, the reports used the insight generated to formulate a care plan, prepare a prognosis, and establish benchmarks for success. In stark contrast, when it came to my own outpatient mental health practice, with its unique ministry orientation, assessment instruments were kept in their cases. Could it be that I was leading a double professional life? In Christian counseling, where I bore the sole responsibility for client care, my case files contained information gleaned exclusively via interview. There was not a shred of data from formal, standardized assessment procedures.

The striking inconsistency in my role and function was troubling. Did it make sense to tout the value of formal psychological measures in educational and community agencies but then set those identical tools aside for the very clients whom I was eager to offer my very best knowledge and skill? Were secular assessment measures irrelevant when engaging in Christian-oriented, ministry-enhancing, counseling care? And could my slow therapeutic movement with Dan benefit from selecting measures to answer pointed questions, clarify symptom severity, identify behaviors, and decipher interpersonal patterns relevant to his troubling bouts of anxiety?

Dan was not merely searching for relief and increased intimacy; he was eager to grow in his Christian faith. Sinful behavior and obstructive interpersonal patterns were stubborn cords tying him down and holding him back. Our helping relationship became too easily tangled. So, Dan completed a single, broad-based personality measure. We also took a deliberate pause to fill in the essential details regarding his bio-psycho-social history. Upon careful review, the patterns of his customary style of relating were no longer so mysterious. In fact, his unique profile characteristics were strikingly pronounced. The resulting personality sketch confirmed my subjective observations. The assessment results yielded an explicit language to describe his interpersonal tendencies and external scores to highlight the pervasive patterns.

Engineers respect data, and Dan was invested in the findings. Using ordinary language and relevant illustrations from our ongoing dialogue, Dan and I strove to make sense of the puzzle pieces. His traits, relational leanings, and action-oriented trends were considered in light of his calling as a Christfollower, father, husband, and church leader. Confession began to flow into the clinical setting as candor and transparency gradually increased. Dan postponed taking a leadership position with his congregation with the full support of his pastor. Critical clinical explorations began to center on traumatic losses and underlying fears. He faced these from the safety of our steady therapeutic relationship and his awareness of his position within the family of God. It was beautiful to acknowledge strengths, potential, and, most of all, his experience of the Lord's grace.

I will say more regarding the therapeutic use of self-report personality measures in chapter fourteen. What's important to observe here is that we had breached the barriers between psychological assessment and Christian counseling. The assessment measure itself did not supply the breakthrough or ignite change. It yielded nothing mysterious, magical, or miraculous. But those results did raise my confidence in recognizing the deeply rooted interpersonal ploys already evident in our relationship. We were able to find words to describe these actions, which helped to strengthen the therapeutic bond and focus our mission. We experienced joy as we predicted, named, and dismantled disabling behaviors and relational roadblocks. The therapeutic process fortified my awareness that good tools should never be left untouched when they can provide information that will improve a clinical connection.

A hard look at trends in practice reveals that too often mental health professionals are willing to offer outpatient therapy without tapping into the available array of assessment measures. For most, this avoidance stems from system mandates to contain costs. For others, this omission is linked to suspicion of the measures themselves or a lack of competence in interpretation.

My practice partner and I made hard choices over the years regarding the allocation of resources, initial procedures, and the use of technology. There is a cost to clients and the practice when including formal assessment in the helping process. We firmly agreed to use assessment tools discriminately, strategically, and, without question, cooperatively. Our decision flowed from the confidence that purposeful investigative procedures provide tangible evidence of our calling to offer quality mental health services with a distinctively Christian approach. Those who provide counseling from within a Christian worldview will recognize that it is a shared venture with the great Comforter, whether a client is striving to grow, struggling to overcome adversity, or following the Holy Spirit's leading through the sanctification process.

After three decades of implementing selective assessment into counseling relationships and learning from others who have taken a similar path, the opportunity is ripe to share lessons learned. It's exciting to see the benefit of having comprehensive information for making clinical decisions and understanding how best to come alongside clients with empathy, love, and dedication. This is the backstory to this theological and practical consideration of assessment use by Christian counselors.

COUNSELING: IN SEARCH OF A DEFINITION

Before exploring the purpose and principles of assessment it's important to have a firm understanding of what is meant by the broad term *counseling*. The label is applicable in numerous settings, can refer to an infinite range of discussion topics, and can reflect an assortment of roles and helping arrangements (ACA, 2018; Rollins, 2010). For starters, ponder this official, twenty-one-word definition established by thirty renowned counseling experts who invested a year in this communication exercise using a systematic, Delphi research procedure to arrive at consensus: "Counseling is a professional relationship that empowers diverse individuals, families and groups to accomplish mental health, wellness, education and career goals" (Kaplin, Tarvydas, & Gladding, 2014, p. 366).

Three features of this definition are worth exploring. First, the counseling relationship has clear boundaries and assigned roles. The phrase *professional relationship* recognizes that a set of ethical boundaries and procedures govern the undertaking. Second, counseling by design is intended to benefit, equip, and increase the recipient's experience of personal power. One or more participants in the counseling arrangement are on the receiving end of the pact. Third, counseling aims to accomplish a particular purpose.

No matter how these essential components are organized or where one places the emphasis, a counseling relationship ultimately depends on quality assessment. For the sake of simplicity, and to provide a definition that works for both ministry and generic counseling, we will use the following definition in this text: *Counseling is strategic dialogue within a defined relationship for the purpose of cultivating growth.*

COUNSELING THAT IS CHRISTIAN

The aim throughout these chapters is to consider information collection procedures as they apply to a variety of counseling settings and as practiced by mental health professionals (MHPs), including credentialed counselors, social workers, psychologists, marriage and family therapists, and other healthcare providers. In addition, *Christian counseling* functions as an umbrella term to reference talk-based care offered by pastors, biblical counselors, chaplains, and ministry leaders (Collins, 2007; Malony & Augsburger, 2007; Powlison, 2010). Churches and other organizations with conservative roots and evangelical commitments tend to favor the use of this identifier over that of a close cousin, *pastoral counseling* (McMinn, Staley, Webb & Seegobin, 2010). Of course, the label *pastoral counseling* is used informally to reference any supportive service conducted by clergy or lay leaders functioning in a pastoral role. It also can have a more restricted meaning. Those within the helping professions associate this phrase with a specific approach that has a lengthy history dating back more than half a century (American Association of Pastoral Counselors, 2018; Snodgrass, 2015).

The Reverend Anton Boisen (1876–1965), founder of the clinical pastoral education (CPE) movement, sought to reverse the unwavering secular trend in psychiatry (Vacek, 2015). He was once a patient with mental illness, and his pain and struggle meant he couldn't imagine psychiatric care without the incorporation of one's faith. Boisen envisioned that CPE would equip ministers to provide clinical assistance that addressed moral, religious, and spiritual matters. Faith was to be esteemed as an asset, not as a liability, an indication of pathology, or a reflection of personal weakness. Notice the implication for assessment in this shift of perspective. For those who provide pastoral counseling services, a prescribed training sequence and necessary supervised field experience are required. Pastoral counselors seek to provide sound psychological therapy that is thoughtfully combined with a spiritual and religious dimension. Across its history, pastoral counseling has been predominantly associated with mainline denominations, with less conservative theological positions, and with the medical, psychiatric establishment. The label is not popular within the evangelical wing of the Protestant spectrum.

Another important categorization to highlight is biblical counseling. This is the contemporary identifier for nouthetic counseling, a long-respected, ministry-oriented approach prevalent in church settings. This significant movement is associated with Jay Adams, a Presbyterian minister and author of many books such as *Competent to Counsel* (1970). The nouthetic movement sought to dispense admonishment derived from Christian theology and a strong biblical platform via pastoral authority sanctioned by the church. Over the years, biblical counseling expanded and clarified its strategies. Despite ongoing advancement, two central premises remain firm: (1) to bring the truth of Scripture to everyday life (2) through the ministry of a local church (Lambert, 2016; MacDonald, Kellemen, & Viars, 2013; Powlison, 2010). Biblical counselors hone expertise in applying truths of the Bible to life problems and assisting clients to mature in their relationship with Jesus Christ (Powlison, 2000).

When it comes to describing their helping approach, MHPs and pastors have a variety of preferred identifying labels along with specific models (Greggo & Sisemore, 2012; Johnson, 2010). The Christian tradition is richly complex, reflects cultural rootedness, and includes a range of theological priorities. Therefore, we should acknowledge at the outset that Christians counsel under a range of credentials, practice in diverse settings, and offer services that purposely vary in how explicitly the goals are framed in traditional faith terms or discipleship categories. Christian counseling thus broadly refers to a relationship between clients and counselors in which both parties expect to operate with biblical values. There are counselors who are dedicated Christ-followers who engage with clients professionally without bringing faith into the relationship. The assessment principles for counseling here should apply, but the label Christian counseling does not. This term is reserved for those distinct occasions when (at the client's request) the counselor and client openly bring Christian perspectives, resources, and interventions into the conversation. For the purposes of this book, the generic label *Christian counseling* will be used to identify counseling that takes place in a clinical or ministry setting that encourages clients to grow in their identity as Christ-followers (Greggo, 2014). The intent is to explore theological perspectives and practical techniques that are useful to those in the Christian tradition who engage in counseling. If a narrower term is a better descriptor for your practice role, you are encouraged to use terminology that more accurately fits your context.

When *counseling* is paired with the momentous qualifier *Christian*, assessment becomes an especially weighty activity. Assessment in Christian counseling adds a dimension beyond basic problem solving. Counseling that is Christian strives to stimulate relational experiences that foster spiritual growth, further sanctification, and promote faith development. The intention in these chapters is to demonstrate that these assumptions flow from a firm theological framework into counseling activity that promotes heart health psychologically, relationally, and spiritually.

CLARIFYING TERMS

Assessment is theoretically understood as the combination of observations from psychological measurement tools with clinical judgment. We'll focus here on how the adoption of tools and techniques and select use of psychological tests can provide a multidimensional perspective on a client's situation. Some of the questions I'll explore include the following:

- How will counselors adapt to advances in assessment technology?
- What assessment practices are compatible with a thoroughly Christian theological worldview?

- Are there steps that can be included in assessment protocols to foster hope and to open the way for the Spirit of wisdom to enlighten the eyes of seeking hearts (Eph 1:15-23)?

Before we dive deeper into these questions, though, I need to define some terms in order to clarify what constitute the tools, the outcome, and the process. For the sake of consistency and ease of aligning this discussion with material from complementary sources, the definitions used are drawn from *Standards for Educational and Psychological Testing* (American Educational Research Association [AERA], American Psychological Association [APA], & National Council on Measurement in Education [NCME], 2014). *Standards* is now in its seventh edition, and over its long history it has become a well-established reference and authoritative resource for defining terms in this domain (teststandards .org). Multiple professional organizations such as the American Psychological Association (APA) and the American Counseling Association (ACA), along with credentialing boards, government agencies, educational institutions, and test publishers, have contributed to the formation of these definitions and operational principles. So with that in mind, let's turn our attention to a few key terms.

The first term we must define is, of course, *assessment*. According to *Standards* (AERA, APA, & NCME, 2014), *assessment* is the broad umbrella term that describes the overall practice of combining findings from tests with information gathered from other resources for the purpose of drawing inferences. A representative list of potential data sources outside of the interview would include direct behavior observation, self-report inventories, rating scales, checklists, story-telling, projective tests, and, obviously, psychological tests. Whiston (2017) helpfully distinguishes formalized assessment techniques as either tests or instruments. Tests aim at evaluation, such as measuring achievement or determining pathology. Instruments offer a structured means to organize information in ways that illustrate. In making this distinction, she separates tools that quantify from those that qualify.

On the other hand, the separation of tests from instruments is often ignored because both are used for the purposes of evaluation. Specifically, the data from tests and instruments will contribute to conclusions that classify, categorize, or make one eligible for treatment. An instrument may be developed with the aim of being descriptive, but when findings contribute to the overall evaluation, the results will function in a manner similar to a test.

For example, at the outset of a therapeutic encounter MHPs are often in a position to consider whether a recognizable disorder is present as defined within the *ICD-10 Classification of Mental and Behavioral Disorders* (World Health Organization, 1992) or the *Diagnostic and Statistical Manual of Mental Disorders* (*DSM*-5; American Psychiatric Association, 2013). If the identified disorder adversely affects overall functioning, it becomes a healthcare concern, and medical treatment is required to improve the client's condition. Treatment would be eligible for insurance reimbursement because the presenting concern has symptoms that mark it as a disease that encumbers. If functioning capacity is significantly compromised, the disorder meets the criteria under conventional guidelines for medical intervention. Beyond establishing medical necessity, an accurate diagnostic profile will simultaneously identify the range of potential interventions. For instance, measures may help to narrow the chief complaint and name it as a panic disorder. The suggestion would follow to make use of cognitive behavioral techniques and applied relaxation. The main purpose of diagnosis is to match a known remedy with the condition. Therefore, both tests and instruments can yield useful information to contribute to this evaluative diagnostic and treatment decision.

While defining terms, we also need to consider two closely related terms: *psychological testing* and *psychological assessment*, as there is potential for confusion regarding how the general heading of *assessment* is applied to therapeutic endeavors. *Psychological testing* refers to any procedure where tests or inventories are employed to secure information on the particular psychological characteristics of an individual. These tests are standardized, which means they have established ground rules and detailed instructions for gathering a behavior sample accompanied by a prescribed method to classify observations (Gregory, 2014). The behavior sample is assembled and quantified according to a meticulous calibration procedure. The resulting score or descriptive category is then used in making predictions about future behavior.

Psychological assessment, on the other hand, includes the use of tests but expands data-collection procedures to include collateral information and reports about an individual. This may include the solicitation of ratings or descriptions from third parties, such as family members, teachers, or peers, as well as medical, educational, forensic, or occupational specialists. Interviews and behavioral observations are also customarily included in a psychological assessment where the objective is a comprehensive evaluation of psychological functioning. The results of psychological tests have substantial social importance and significant individual impact so meticulous training, supervision, credentialing, and ethical constraints are required for the application of these measurement tools. *Psychological assessment*, therefore, is too restrictive and specialized to capture the appraisal interests of the full range of human service professionals.

Psychologists are not intended to be the only audience for this book. To be sure, psychological characteristics are of great interest in helping conversations. But given that outcome goals across a broad variety of MHPs and pastoral care providers may be spiritual, ethical, social, or biological in nature, it is preferable to think of assessment in an inclusive manner. The intention behind collecting, categorizing, and weighing information is not solely to perform an evaluation of psychological functioning.

Assessment in Christian perspective. Christian clergy and counselors provide services in a wide variety of settings. Assessment has an additional focus when counseling is conducted in a ministry context with clients who take their Christian faith seriously. Certain clients seek out counselors who are explicitly committed to working within a Christian theological framework. In such cases, the counselor considers the orientation of the heart toward self, others, and the Lord (Deut 6:5; Mk 12:30-31). This focus on the spiritual attitudes, relationships, and behaviors associated with the heart overlaps but is not synonymous with evaluation of psychological functioning. Those who seek to offer guidance and solace within a Christian framework have interests that transcend what is customarily defined in secular perspectives as personality. The specific facets of personality may be parsed according to one's theoretical leanings, but the generic definition of personality is an individual's distinctive and consistent pattern of thinking, feeling, and behaving. Those working within a Christian framework attempt to hear and discern the spiritual affections of the heart (1 Sam 16:7; Prov 4:23; Ps 51:10). Thoughts, attitudes, and behavior are important indicators of the relational center, with its core motivations and connections.

According to the biblical narrative, the human heart is the center of relational orientation, emotional health, and spiritual well-being (see Deut 4:29; Ps 73:26; Lk 6:45; Rom 1:21; Greggo, 2011; Saucy, 2013). This metaphor is not conceptually precise enough to function as a technical term in modern psychology (e.g., personality, pathology, disorder, attachment, intelligence, cognition, emotional state). However, in what follows, my hope is to show that what is lost in its precision is more than made up for by the appropriateness of its fit within a Christian worldview.

Tools for clinical care. During this exploration we must keep in mind three features of assessment: (1) assessment is an orderly method of processing information; (2) assessment merges data from multiple sources; and (3) assessment is a procedure designed to establish working assumptions. Placing the pieces of a client's story and presenting concerns into a framework for treatment is typically referred to as formulating a case conceptualization (McMinn & Campbell, 2017). Our interest is identifying the best methods and procedures to further the purposes of a counseling relationship. The goal is to encourage proficiency in the selection and use of clinical tools—an assortment of assessment techniques that contribute to a comprehensive case conceptualization and guide the use of counseling interventions.

Gregory (2014) supplies a succinct definition of assessment as the appraisal of the magnitude of one or more personal attributes. He goes on to make an important qualification. Assessment demands that the one undertaking the assignment compile information by comparing and combining data to establish a composite portrayal of an individual. Data must be weighed, conflicts addressed, and assumptions made to fill in missing puzzle pieces. This implies that while assessment employs an impartial methodology, it is an intrinsically subjective enterprise. The tools, including tests and instruments, may contribute data deemed objective. Nevertheless, there is an inherent element of subjectivity in the overall undertaking as the dots of data are connected into an unambiguous explanation of trends and patterns. The subjective element is intentionally mitigated through the application of rigorously outlined interpretive guidelines, established classification criteria, extensive examiner training, and formal supervision during a sustained apprenticeship. These requirements are designed to develop sufficient expertise in the one who conducts the assessment and provides the formulation.

In more recent years, as technology has improved, a host of tools has been developed to aid in assessment. "Computer-assisted administration" refers to methods that are streamlined to move rapidly from administration to interpretation. Traditional psychological measures, particularly those that are self-report in nature, are reformatted so that instructions, item presentation, answer selection, scoring, and report generation are completed digitally rather than mechanically. These efforts are remarkably efficient and user friendly, and the general consensus thus far is that electronic presentation does not detract from the validity of the administration (Garb, 2000; Groth-Marnat & Wright, 2016; Whiston, 2017). In certain applications, a digital presentation even improves the quality of data by encouraging frank disclosure to an impersonal source (Garb, 2007). Digital presentation also reduces transmission and examiner errors in scoring.

In addition to the migration of standardized tests into digital formats, other data collection procedures have become automated as well, including common record-keeping templates such as information forms, questionnaires, problem checklists, developmental histories, behavioral descriptions, and risk assessments. Given the demand for social service and medical providers to document diagnostic impressions and contact details, the combination of these templates with information technology is a welcome development that helps providers spotlight specific areas of human functioning and interaction. There is vigorous discussion in the literature regarding checklists, forced choice items, response fields with word limits, and brief rating scales (White, Hall, & Peckover, 2009). Assessment technology has replaced narrative reporting to improve documentation and efficiency. This saves time and effort, though nuances of description regarding motivations and behaviors may be compromised, collapsed, or lost. Controversies associated with labor-saving devices in counseling are far from settled, and the criticisms found in the literature show that greater attention is being given to the relationship between technique, communication, and effective helping as assessment procedures merge with technological innovations.

The attempt to capture, describe, and quantify the complexity of human persons and processes is central to any mental health undertaking. For ease of reference, in this book I use hybrid terms such as *assessment techniques*, *tools*, and *technology* as general concepts to indicate any psychological test or information-cataloging method in digital or manual versions. The elements that unify these procedures are standardization, streamlined documentation, communication exchange, orderly procedures, and free-flowing to semi-structured processes. I use *assessment* and *appraisal* synonymously as is common in the supporting literature.

CONTRASTING APPLICATIONS

The topic of assessment is extensive. Thus, our discussion will be narrowed to how measurement tools are applied within therapeutic partnerships. In order to make sense of this limitation, let's contrast the aims and purposes of general psychological evaluation with mental health appraisal to pursue change. The emphasis here is on measurement as a means to further development, remediation, and change. This sets the stage for consideration of assessment in counseling as a search for wisdom. We should acknowledge that the boundaries between these types of evaluation are not particularly precise, and there is often overlap between them. Nevertheless, this distinction can contribute to a deeper appreciation of the purpose of assessment procedures in counseling scenarios where spiritual growth is a desired outcome.

Psychological testing is typically aimed at evaluation, and each instrument gives extensive consideration to specific characteristics. The goal in choosing which instrument to use is to facilitate well-rounded evaluation with research-grade precision. The scores reflect the exact ranking of the individual within a specifically defined population. Results typically blend classification, prediction, or selection with recommendations centered on preserving or achieving optimal functional capacity in areas related to the reason for referral. For example, one can conduct an evaluation on a person having difficulties performing routine employment responsibilities or abiding by legal mandates. The psychological evaluation will address personal factors to elucidate the chief complaints or referral issues. The next step is to offer potential directions for remediation or management. This involves the generalization of test findings to make predictions about the factors contributing to the stated concerns. After gathering the data and compiling everything into a profile, one can detect behavioral patterns. These evaluations can then be used to inform forensic proceedings, address competency dilemmas, determine educational deficits, guide career choices, or tailor medical treatment.

Broad-based psychological tests such as occupational surveys, personality inventories, projective measures, or sophisticated cognitive and neurological batteries are traditionally the exclusive domain of psychologists or educational specialists with advanced assessment training. The applicable ethical standards may not explicitly restrict the use of these evaluations to credentialed psychologists. Nevertheless, ethical use of such tools requires significant training and a firm foundation in psychological testing so that these evaluations are conducted only by those with advanced competency. This is a core focus within the academic curriculum for psychologists. The production of comprehensive psychological evaluations is a demanding and specialized activity. Tools that require a high level of proficiency to administer and interpret rightly require corresponding professional credentials and educational degrees. Therefore, this type of advanced psychological evaluation for the purpose of writing confidential, stand-alone reports is outside and beyond the scope of the current undertaking.

It is important to distinguish between the necessity for an extensive toolkit to investigate broad functioning and the focused use of select measurement devices. In medical, mental health, or social service settings, select measurement instruments can assist in arriving at an accurate diagnosis. If diagnostic identification were the sole objective, there would be extensive overlap with traditional testing due to the emphasis on identification and categorization.

In treatment settings, however, arriving at a proper diagnosis is a critical but limited initial undertaking. This is only one bridge that must be crossed to reach the desired goal: entering a relational process that will foster change in the area of identified concern; that is the primary aim of any assessment activity. Assessment results highlight individual differences and needs, which can then be used to determine optimal therapeutic methods.

For the sake of setting up the sharpest possible distinctions, *psychological testing* here is defined as a detached process of evaluation for the purpose of determining how a person functions in domains such as cognitive ability, neurological performance, personality characteristics, and other defined behavioral areas. The main consumer of the formal psychological report is not typically the person undergoing evaluation. In contrast, *mental health appraisal* is a collaborative undertaking for the purpose of locating the factors contributing to an individual's life disturbance and identifying reasonable options for a remedy. While certain information may be released to a third party to secure funding or to comply with accountability procedures, the main recipients benefitting from assessment in a clinical setting are the MHP and the client, who will embark on a partnership. Formal evaluations or reports for outside parties are not routinely produced. Instead, the material gained from assessment becomes part of the confidential clinical record.

We can summarize the distinction between psychological testing and mental health assessment along the following lines. Psychological evaluations result in formal, comprehensive reports utilized by external parties to make decisions about the subject(s) of the report. The independence of the specialist and the research orientation may lead to relational barriers. This is not a substantial concern for expert consultants who tend to have limited contact with the person being evaluated beyond the delivery of the results. This type of evaluation yields weighty, authoritative recommendations to inform verdicts, make pronouncements, or establish a diagnosis.

On the other hand, mental health appraisals generate treatment plans to mitigate expressed concerns with a client in ongoing care. The MHP may offer expertise from assessment tools similar to that of a psychological consultant, but there is a deliberate effort to cultivate an atmosphere of advocacy and to identify a common agenda. This collaboration is best described as a therapeutic partnership that directs its attention toward solving problems and promoting growth.

The notion of assessment for therapeutic purposes is nothing new or unusual (Krishnamurthy, Finn, & Aschieri, 2016). In fact, there are those who advocate using assessment as the only or principle therapeutic strategy. Finn (2007) recommends a consultation procedure that takes the idea of using assessment in counseling care to an extreme. He advises MHPs to conduct full-blown, in-depth psychological evaluations using all the high-power instruments common to a psychological test battery. In between the phases of standardized testing, the consultant pauses to join forces with a client to consider how the results shed light on relational or personal concerns. Finn's model of therapeutic assessment performs formal evaluation step by step to generate findings that have direct therapeutic benefit in the form of insight and objective understanding. This is an intriguing suggestion. Nevertheless, such a specialty service would only be feasible for those with extensive expertise in psychological evaluation.

LOCATING TARGETS FOR CHANGE

Counseling begins by defining the helping relationship and initiating conversation to prompt change. Regardless of the model or helping technique, assessment is a crucial activity. Whether exploring career possibilities, urgently addressing an addictive pattern, or embarking on a quest for spiritual vitality, helpers use strategic inquiries to formulate an approach. Consider the following sample assessment questions:

- What recent event, life transition, or inner change initiated this important conversation between us at this time?
- These disturbing episodes of crying, kicking, and yelling behavior by your two-year-old are challenging and frightening. Consider the past twenty-four hours. Let's inventory exactly how many of these tantrums occurred, how long they lasted, and the intensity of each one.
- Imagine that curiosity compels you to pick up a strange, antiquated bottle you find while walking along a white, sandy beach. Upon opening its seal, a genie emerges and issues the fantastic offer to grant three marvelous wishes that will change your life. What possibilities emerge as you ponder this?
- Think back to a recent disagreement with your fiancée. The churning in your gut is awful. This is one of those dark moments that convinced you to make this appointment. Close your eyes. Verbalize aloud a list of expressive words that capture what you hear, see, sense, and feel.
- Let's identify workplace incidents over the past five days. What stirs your sense of personal accomplishment, Christian fruitfulness, peace, energy, or human connection?

- Bring to mind a recent experience of refreshing spiritual worship. Stay in that gracious blessing for a moment. Now share recollections of the surroundings, sounds, people, voices, your inner experience, and the most memorable message.

The intent in each inquiry is to initiate conversation on topics such as interpersonal conflicts, spiritual blessings, dreams of the future, and problem behaviors. Strategic probes to launch targeted explorations are common at the outset of help-oriented talk. The MHP uses descriptive metaphors, vignettes, or behavior samples to characterize the client's unique human experience. Assessment in counseling is the process that turns generalities into tangible experience as it aims to transform hope into realistic goals.

Collecting background information is a routine exercise that can be accomplished orally via interview, in a survey administered electronically, or through a fill-in-the-blank paper form. Clients may put their problems into words using stories, or they may be asked to compile concerns by completing a checklist with bulleted symptoms or complaints. Any of these procedures is an assessment undertaking. The success of a counselor's ministry to others will depend on what is done with each response. By listening to a client's request and distress, the counselor can detect what direction is necessary to effect change. The recognition of these clues and the organization of them into a helpful framework will influence a client's satisfaction with care and bond with the counselor. Furthermore, the range and focus of assessment procedures can shape how a client's Christian faith and quality of spiritual life are embraced, neglected, or diminished.

ASSESS FOR THE SAKE OF DIALOGUE

In summary, counselors too often leave useful tools on the table. The argument in this chapter is that therapists need to look beyond the limited utility of instruments to define and diagnose. Employing assessments solely for evaluation too often restricts the benefits to stakeholders or external reviewers. Since our intent is to serve our clients, we turn the purpose of assessment to informing them.

Counseling is strategic dialogue within a carefully constructed therapeutic relationship to stimulate growth. Appraisal furthers this collaboration. The information gained is made transparent to enhance the precision and focus of the dialogue. Assessment is not for outsiders; rather, its results enlighten client and counselor alike.

When a disciple of Christ seeks counsel, the priorities of spiritual growth, holy living, and faith enhancement are fused into the helping agenda. For these clients, assessment becomes a way to increase awareness of the heart's condition. It contributes to a wisdom quest to further one's heavenward journey. Counselors harness technology for the sake of this worthy dialogue.

This book is written for those who are dedicated to conversational helping and who desire to expand the assessment resources in their technical toolbox. Those with Christian convictions may require encouragement to ponder these options. Thus, the next step is to propose a broad theological perspective on assessment.

REFERENCES

Adams, J. E. (1970). *Competent to counsel: Introduction to Nouthetic Counseling*. Phillipsburg, NJ: Presbyterian & Reformed.

American Association of Pastoral Counselors. (2018). Retrieved June 21, 2018 from http://aapc.org/page/WhyPastoral?

American Counseling Association (2018). 20/20: Consensus definition of counseling. Retrieved June 21, 2018 from https://www.counseling.org/knowledge-center/20-20 -a-vision-for-the-future-of-counseling/consensus-definition-of-counseling

American Educational Research Association, American Psychological Association, & National Council on Measurement in Education. (2014). *Standards for educational and psychological testing*. Washington, DC: American Educational Research Association.

American Psychiatric Association. (2013). *Diagnostic and statistical manual of mental disorders* (5th ed.). Arlington, VA: American Psychiatric Publishing.

Collins, G. R. (2007). *Christian counseling: A comprehensive guide* (3rd ed.). Nashville: Thomas Nelson.

Finn, S. E. (2007). *In our clients' shoes: Theory and techniques of therapeutic assessment*. Mahwah, NJ: Lawrence Erlbaum Associates.

Garb, H. N. (2000). Computers will become increasingly important for psychological assessment: Not that there's anything wrong with that! *Psychological Assessment, 12*(1), 31-39.

Garb, H. N. (2007). Computer-administered interviews and rating scales. *Psychological Assessment, 19*(1), 4-13.

Greggo, S. P. (2011). Internal working model as heart: A translation to inspire Christian care groups. *Edification: The Transdisciplinary Journal of Christian Psychology, 5*(1), 4-13.

Greggo, S. P. (2014). Counseling case and evangelical pastoral leadership: Implications for seminary education. *Trinity Journal, 35*, 275-292.

Greggo, S. P., & Sisemore, T. A. (2012). *Christianity and counseling: Five approaches.* Downers Grove, IL: InterVarsity Press.

Gregory, R. J. (2014). *Psychological testing: History, principles, and applications* (7th ed.). Boston: Pearson.

Groth-Marnat, G., & Wright, A. J. (2016). *Handbook of psychological assessment* (6th ed.). Hoboken, NJ: John Wiley & Sons.

Johnson, E. L. (Ed.). (2010). *Psychology & Christianity: Five views* (2nd ed.). Downers Grove, IL: InterVarsity Press.

Kaplan, D. M., Tarvydas, V. M., & Gladding, S. T. (2014). 20/20: A vision for the future of counseling: The new consensus definition of counseling. *Journal of Counseling & Development, 92,* 366-372.

Krishnamurthy, R., Finn, S. E., & Aschieri, F. (2016). Therapeutic assessment in clinical and counseling psychology practice. In U. Kumar (Ed.), *The Wiley handbook of personality assessment* (pp. 228-239). Malden, MA: Wiley-Blackwell.

Lambert, H. (2016). *A theology of biblical counseling: The doctrinal foundations of counseling ministry.* Grand Rapids, MI: Zondervan.

MacDonald, J., Kellemen, B., & Viars, S. (2013). *Christ-centered biblical counseling: Changing lives with God's changeless truth.* Eugene, OR: Harvest House.

Malony, H. N., & Augsburger, D. W. (2007). *Christian counseling: An introduction.* Nashville: Abingdon Press.

McMinn, M. R., & Campbell, C. D. (2017). *Integrative psychotherapy: Toward a comprehensive Christian approach.* Downers Grove, IL: InterVarsity Press.

McMinn, M. R., Staley, R. C., Webb, K. C., & Seegobin, W. (2010). Just what is Christian counseling anyway? *Professional Psychology: Research and Practice, 41*(5), 391-397.

Powlison, D. (2000). Affirmations & denials: A proposed definition of biblical counseling. *Journal of Biblical Counseling, 19*(1), 18-25.

Powlison, D. (2010). *The biblical counseling movement: History and context.* Greensboro, NC: New Growth Press.

Rollins, J. (2010). Making definitive progress: 20/20 delegates reach consensus on definition of counseling. *Counseling Today.* Retrieved from https://ct.counseling .org/2010/06/making-definitive-progress/

Saucy, R. L. (2013). *Minding the heart: The way of spiritual transformation.* Grand Rapids, MI: Kregel.

Snodgrass, J. L. (2015). Pastoral counseling: A discipline of unity amid diversity. In E. A. Maynard & J. L. Snodgrass (Eds.), *Understanding pastoral counseling* (pp. 1-15). New York: Springer.

Vacek, H. H. (2015). *Madness: American Protestant responses to mental illness.* Waco, TX: Baylor University Press.

Whiston, S. C. (2017). *Principles and applications of assessment in counseling* (5th ed.). Belmont, CA: Cengage.

White, S., Hall, C., & Peckover, S. (2009). The descriptive tyranny of the common assessment framework: Technologies of categorization and professional practice in child welfare. *British Journal of Social Work, 39*(7), 1197-1217.

World Health Organization. (1992). *The ICD-10 classification of mental and behavioural disorders: Clinical descriptions and diagnostic guidelines.* Geneva: World Health Organization.

CHAPTER THREE

ASSESSMENT BASICS FOR CHRISTIANS WHO COUNSEL

All Scripture is God-breathed and is useful for teaching, rebuking,
correcting and training in righteousness, so that the servant of God
may be thoroughly equipped for every good work.

2 Timothy 3:16-17

THEOLOGICAL THEME
Scripture as "Norming Norm"

FROM TECHNOLOGY TO CONVERSATION

The counselor pauses. Phillip, a withdrawn and discouraged college student, shifts in his seat, twists to get comfortable, and eventually makes eye contact. The counselor meets his gaze and smiles softly to engage him. Reaching toward Phil, the counselor passes over an iPad open and ready. This is the third week that the duo has met, so Phil accepts the device with a readiness for this opening routine. "It is good to have you back, Phil. As we have done in each session thus far, I would appreciate if you would show me how you have been feeling the past few days. Use the touch screen to complete this scale. This will direct us on where to focus our discussion." Phil slides his finger with intentionality over the face of the screen to select his responses. Despite the deliberate attention that he gives to each item, the procedure takes less than a minute. When he's finished, the app immediately produces a graph of the ratings for each session.

The counselor accepts the device back from Phil and immediately glances at his ratings. "Thanks, Phil, for sharing so honestly with me. It looks like it's been an uncomfortable, distressing week, particularly as you interact with others. Good work showing attentiveness to this trend of feeling pretty miserable in social settings. We'll certainly explore those heavy experiences. At the same time, you're aware that you didn't feel as ragged within yourself as you reported last week. Tell me what is happening to give you that boost. You actually shared last week that your walk with the Lord was stirring courage. Any connection?" In response to this invitation, Phil now returns the counselor's delicate smile and begins to share his story.

Combining assessment technology with interpersonal communication is common in today's helping relationships.[1] It is crucial to monitor progress in ways that are clear and accessible to everyone involved. Being able to see progress toward desired outcomes can be very beneficial to the relationship. In addition, clients like Phil value being given opportunities to articulate what may not come naturally in ordinary conversation. Active assessment enables them to express how they are feeling physically, emotionally, socially, and spiritually.

The development of practical tools such as these is enormously exciting because they enable us to serve clients even more effectively. The possibilities are nearly endless. Nevertheless, in any and all helping relationships, opportunity brings responsibility. Key criteria and cautions need to be made clear. This equips practitioners to make the best possible decisions about assessment applications. Most importantly, when assessment technology becomes part of the counseling conversation, counselors in Christian ministry must not lose sight of God's role in the process. Considering these concerns to the fullest extent and preparing clinicians to serve well into the future is the passion that drives this project.

ASSESSMENT: HEARING THE CRY OF THE HEART

Applying assessment technology requires both prudence and proficiency in order to minimize risk, enhance benefit, and prevent worldview distortions. Let's begin by visualizing the entire assessment process in conjunction with a search for wisdom.

Central assumptions: the search for wisdom.

1. Assessment is the means to activate effective therapeutic conversation (Prov 1:7).

2. Assessment is the diligent search utilizing systematic techniques to secure insight, understanding, and skills for living (Prov 2:1-5).

---

[1]Electronic applications for screening and outcome management are constantly expanding. Check out the medical applications in the app store for your device or explore these options: https://www .myoutcomes.com/, http://www.psychlops.org.uk/, or http://ebasis.org/index.php.

3. Assessment activity is the gateway to communication that enables the
heart to hear (Prov 3:1-6).

These three statements capture the central claims about assessment that, if embraced, will help us both to achieve our expectations and to ensure quality in
our work.

Counseling within the Christian faith is, at its essence, a search for wisdom
within a unique interpersonal dialogue that nurtures the whole person. Its
kingdom purpose is to condition the heart to love God unconditionally and
self in such a fruitful way that a Christlike love for others is sustained (Ps 4:1-9;
51:10-17; 61:1-4; Mt 22:37-39). The first eight chapters of Proverbs define wisdom
as the primary virtue for informing our inner being so that our outward actions
display a life that honors God. By placing each assessment premise alongside
a corresponding message from Proverbs, we connect the purpose of assessment
to spiritually formative heart care.

Assessment and therapeutic conversation. Assessment activates effective therapeutic conversation (Prov 1:7). As a therapeutic relationship initially develops,
the conversation seeks to identify where change is required. In this case, assessment and discernment run parallel to each other. Proverbs depicts discernment as a heart open to instruction and yearning for wisdom (e.g., Prov 1:5;
15:14; 18:15). Counseling is similarly a collaborative effort to uncover the hidden
matters of the heart and use the grace of insight to adjust attitude and actions.

The beginning of wisdom is no mystery in Scripture. The prerequisite for
knowledge and comprehensive understanding is repeatedly declared to be a
deep conviction regarding the fear of God (Job 28:28; Ps 111:10; Prov 2:5; 8:13;
9:10; Eccles 12:13; Hughes & Laney, 2001). Such "fear" is not a passing emotional
state. It is a foundational, solemn declaration of utter dependence on the Lord
God—the sovereign source of absolutely everything. The starting point for at-
taining wisdom is a posture of awe, namely, an awareness of being in the
presence of a majestic, heavenly Father. Fear of the Lord inspires reverence for
his will because his ways are recognized as true and just. What the Scripture
goes on to assert is beyond remarkable (Rom 8:15-23; Eph 1:5; 1 Jn 3:1): in return
for our acknowledgment that the Lord is our divine Creator, we are adopted as
children—becoming family, friends, and co-laborers in his creation.

What does this have to do with contemporary counseling and sophisticated
assessment techniques? A helping relationship makes inquiries into life's details,
stories, priorities, expectations, and relationships. In doing so it sparks contemplation, ignites a desire to grasp what is unknown, and prompts one to revise

misconceptions. Assessment not only looks at the client's external situation and attitude about these conditions but untangles the intricacies of the therapeutic relationship itself to foster an effective and credible alliance. The hope for an idealized, affirming relationship is exchanged for one where misunderstandings naturally occur. Quality assessment can give the therapeutic relationship a razor-sharp edge. It offers a ready means to identify disruptions and focus repair before a hurt or misunderstanding begins to harden. Christians who counsel recognize that this helping relationship is designed to represent a connection to the only true source of strength and stability. After all, wisdom may flow through the counselor, but it is the Lord who provides. All blessings and good gifts are the redemptive benefits of the gospel.

Assessment is a strategic and systematic search. Assessment is a diligent search that makes use of the best systematic techniques to secure insight, understanding, and skills for living.

> My son, if you accept my words
> > and store up my commands within you,
>
> turning your ear to wisdom
> > and applying your heart to understanding—
>
> indeed, if you call out for insight
> > and cry aloud for understanding,
>
> and if you look for it as for silver
> > and search for it as for hidden treasure,
>
> then you will understand the fear of the LORD
> > and find the knowledge of God. (Prov 2:1-5)

There are powerful instructions and striking images packed tightly into these verses. Each unique phrase identifies a characteristic of people who seek wisdom. They are to soak up good teaching, treasure compassionate direction, conform to divine commands, turn an ear to attend to wisdom, condition the heart to comprehend, cry aloud for insight, and examine matters thoroughly in order to investigate their motives diligently.

Locating the hidden cache of wisdom is somewhat like the process of mining the earth for silver. There is nothing superficial about such an expedition. Mining can be strenuous, sweaty, and disciplined work. Locating valuable ore from within a mass of surrounding material requires accomplished systems and sturdy tools. The mining metaphor provokes images of intensive work conducted in close quarters, under adverse conditions, while coping with elements of risk. The endeavor takes effort, strategy, dedication, and diligence. Similarly, adverse life circumstances often motivate a client to initially obtain assistance. In order for the partnership to be productive, there must be agreement on the level of effort required. Formulating wisdom involves active and focused examination. This explains the routine invitation that jumpstarts many counseling sessions: Where would you like to direct our work today? Assessment is a means through which the helping partnership focuses its efforts on unearthing valuable ore. Wisdom is a priceless resource that brings rich benefit to those in need.

Assessment is communication to open hearts. Assessment is a gateway activity to communication that enables the heart to hear (Prov 3:1-6). These instructions from Proverbs accentuate the value of godly teaching and guidelines. The offer within these verses is no stingy, symptom-only, superficial relief. When internalized, living wisely produces prosperity and peace. This is genuine shalom—peace that surpasses all understanding. It reflects health, wholeness, and well-being. The heart—one's inner thoughts, emotional ties, will, and center of being—must be penetrated until saturated with the Lord's insight and perceptions. In counseling, helping conversation is pursued with an extraordinary effort to provide customized care. Such personalized nourishment makes use of dynamic relational resources to soften the heart, open the mind, and move holistically toward shalom. By grace, wisdom compels us to honor the relationship at the center of our heart and soul. This is done by loving the Lord our God with our whole heart, soul, mind, and strength.

PREPARING THE HEART OF THE COUNSELOR

It would not be appropriate to equate modern assessment technology with the ancient prescription to discern and secure wisdom without acknowledging how meaning is formed. "For the LORD gives wisdom; / from his mouth come knowledge and understanding" (Prov 2:6). In the opening chapters of Proverbs the mandate to search for wisdom is proclaimed. There is a contextual assumption that the seeker will devote utmost attention to the collected teachings on the way of the Lord that have been passed along through faithful community and godly parents (Prov 6:20-23). The Bible, a divinely originated and timeless text, is the authoritative record of the Creator's activity, mercy, redemption, justice, and instruction on the way of salvation. Scripture unites past to present and thrusts our perspective forward with hope toward a future that is nothing short of eternal! Scripture brings finite human understanding into connection with God's limitless perspective. Thus, all insights are evaluated according to the redemptive movement of the gospel outlined in Scripture.

There is little value in examining the benefits of using cutting-edge assessment technology for soul care if we're not clear on this premise. Those who conduct investigations into the resources, issues, conflicts, and personal patterns of others need a guide to help them make sense of the data that will eventually be obtained. Without a doubt, there are numerous psychological, medical, and spiritual frameworks to facilitate understanding. But Christians have a way to evaluate the system itself—namely, the revealed Word of God. J. I. Packer (1993), in *Concise Theology: A Guide to Historic Christian Beliefs*, declares the following:

> Christianity is the true worship and service of the true God, humankind's Creator and Redeemer. It is a religion that rests on revelation: nobody would know the truth about God, or be able to relate to him in a personal way, had not God first acted to make himself known. But God has so acted, and the sixty-six books of the Bible, thirty-nine written before Christ came and twenty-seven after, are together the record, interpretation, expression, and embodiment of this self-disclosure. God and godliness are the Bible's uniting themes.
>
> From one standpoint, the Scriptures (*Scriptures* means "writings") are faithful testimony of the godly to the God who they loved and served; from another standpoint, through a unique exercise of divine overruling in their composition, they are God's own testimony and teaching in human form. The church calls these writings the Word of God because their authorship and contents are both divine. (Packer, 1993, p. 3)

These words appear at the beginning of Packer's summation of basic theology because Scripture is the very source of our doctrines. These doctrines are the sanctified teachings or tenets of Christianity drawn from a reasoned, attested, and shared understanding of Scripture (Vanhoozer, 2005). The Bible is how God declares himself.

Any counselor who desires to serve others through participation with the Holy Spirit must maintain ongoing engagement with Scripture. According to Christian tradition, Scripture is the authoritative criterion against which other criteria are measured because it is the "norming norm" ("Westminster Confession of Faith," 1646/1982); it is the "standard" God has given to instruct his people on acting with discernment. For those who seek to make sense of all forces and factors that influence human growth, maintaining contact with God's revelation of himself through Scripture is a necessity.

Counselors who wish to offer services under the banner of Christianity need to maintain what Kevin Vanhoozer calls "canon sense" (Vanhoozer, 2010), meaning the sound judgment derived from a profound appreciation for the full range of biblical literature.

> The canon is far more than a mere list of books in the Bible. It is a measuring or even *divining rod* that enables us to discern what we should say and do today in order to continue and correspond to the way, truth, and life made known in Jesus Christ. As such, it is both source and norm of the disciple's individual identity as well as the church's corporate identity. In short: the canon is the Christian framework for knowing who you are and what you are supposed to do *coram Deo* ("before God"). (Vanhoozer, 2010, p. 12)

Stated plainly, canon sense is having the essence of Scripture so central in our convictions, so crisp in our thought, and so steadfast within our hearts, that what flows from our lips reflects the mind of Christ (Phil 2:5).

Ultimately our faithfulness in the pursuit of canon sense—not our professional affiliation, denominational background, preferred therapeutic approach, service location, or clientele—will determine if our insights and healing presence are unequivocally Christian. Anyone who yearns to serve others in the name of the Lord must recognize that Scripture is God's very breath, and as such it is always relevant and useful for those who seek to spread life in how they teach, correct, rebuke, or guide in righteousness (2 Tim 3:16). Preparing one's heart in this way is important even if Scripture is never directly cited or spoken aloud in a clinical appointment.

Counselors who aspire to provide soul care would therefore do well to establish practices for maintaining a robust canon sense. These practices allow Scripture to configure our automatic, underlying thoughts. With this in mind, I offer five practical activities that can help cultivate wisdom. These five recommendations are not intended to dictate a Bible-only approach to helping; rather, they provide a template to help followers of Christ condition their own hearts to conduct assessment with an inner awareness of the Lord's role in the process. Through Scripture we enter into a divine discourse in which the Holy Spirit converses with our soul and so prepares us to care for others.

Enter Scripture devotionally. Reading Scripture devotionally means entering the Bible as an act of worship. This may be the most elementary area for counselors to evaluate in their own lives. Nevertheless, this customary practice remains one of the most potent ways that the Holy Spirit penetrates our inner being. Typically, a period of devotional reading—whether brief or extended, light or intense—begins with a childlike prayer: "Speak[, Lord], for your servant is listening" (1 Sam 3:10). For centuries, Christians invested in renewal and, being spiritually formed, have promoted the practice of *lectio divina*, sacred reading. This is attentive and consecrated reading in which one proceeds slowly and deliberately through each phrase to acclimate to the voice of the Holy Spirit. At its core, this is the act of approaching Scripture with an open heart in humble anticipation that the God of heaven is ready to dialogue with his children through the Word.

Most churches, discipleship ministries, and fellowship groups are eager to provide a worthy assortment of dependable plans or suggested sequences for devotional reading. These may tie to the ongoing liturgy for worship or follow a daily regimen to accomplish reading the Bible through in a specified period of time. One popular approach for devotional material is to meditate on a chapter of Proverbs each day of the month. There is also a plethora of devotional guides, from classic to contemporary, that juxtapose a Scripture passage with an uplifting message.[2] My intent here is not to define how often, long, traditional, or trendy one's approach to devotional reading should be. The goal is to consistently worship, read, encounter, and listen. Followers of Jesus Christ— the Word made flesh to dwell among us—access the written Word and welcome the Holy Spirit, who in turn increases awareness of the presence of Jesus.

The first step for counselors is to take note of personal expectations for devotional practice based on faith tradition, cultural heritage, discipleship experience, role models, and intimate conversations with the Lord. Second, in light of your counseling ministry and professional role, consider what devotional habits would be realistic, suitable, and sustainable. Once there is a fresh awareness of your personal, private, thoughtful, and committed values, take the third, most challenging, step: evaluate your own satisfaction with recent devotional reading experiences. Finally, bring any discoveries and decisions from this review before the Lord and prayerfully discern whether to maintain your current practice or develop a new plan.

Explore Scripture in community. Regularly receiving instruction and challenging messages in corporate settings is another important component of our faith journey. Pastors, mentors, and spiritual leaders speak from Scripture with wisdom and maturity. When Jesus left his disciples on earth, he gave explicit instructions that his representatives were to make disciples, baptize, and teach others to obey all his commandments (Mt 28:18-20). Since the outpouring of

---

[2]For example, https://odb.org; www.biblegateway.com/devotionals.

the Holy Spirit at Pentecost, believing Christians have made it their custom to gather, break bread, fellowship, pray, and sit under the teaching of spiritual leaders (Acts 2:42). Whether we have extensive clinical experience or are apprentices under supervision, we all do well to submit to the authority of one who has accepted the high calling to teach God's Word (Jas 3:1).

On the day I wrote this paragraph, I participated in congregational worship. The pastor dedicated a sizable portion of his sermon to a selection of phrases from the Sermon on the Mount. He pressed firmly on teaching that cautioned against judging, measuring, and taking specks of dust out of our brother's eye (Mt 7:1-4). The passion in his delivery was accompanied by tenderness in his voice. As counselors we must seek fellowship where the Word of God is rightfully admired and proclaimed. The Holy Spirit will do the rest.

Examine Scripture to develop fluency in biblical theology. One who desires to counsel others "Christianly" needs to make a concerted effort to examine Scripture both thoughtfully and systematically. This is not a one-time excursion. Pondering the text of Scripture to know its meaning in part and as a whole is critical, not only for ongoing growth as a disciple of Jesus Christ but in terms of one's ability to come alongside others as counselor. The purpose of studying Scripture for professional development is to gain a clearer understanding of our faith and biblical norms. Assessment techniques compare findings about our clients to established population customs, practices, and standards. Making sense of those comparisons from the vantage point of our Christian faith requires keen alertness to what God describes as normative. The Word sheds light on his expectations for his people—those called to be holy (e.g., Mt 5–7; Rom 12; Col 3:1-10).

Scripture includes an assortment of literary genres—history, law, wisdom, narrative, poetry, prophecy, letters, and apocalyptic—but together they communicate an essential unity. Biblical theology is acquiring a holistic understanding of the sayings, stories, and message of Scripture while attending to its cultural background, stylistic trends, linguistic intricacies, and central author (Bromiley, 1960). Counselors may not all be biblical specialists who have advanced linguistic competencies or have the background of a scholar who can produce a detailed analysis of complex passages. Nevertheless, awareness of biblical norms is important for counselors if they aim to help clients deepen their identity as children of God.

Examining Scripture to increase understanding has been described as "interrogating" the text (Scharf, 2005). The intent of such dedicated investigation is to press beyond what immediately comes to our minds when Scripture is read in order to uncover, with help from the Holy Spirit, what God as its divine author had in mind. What is the grammatical, historical, logical, and contextual message? Interrogating the text compels us to methodically probe a passage of the Bible to discern its meaning and application. In practical terms, this implies reading select passages intently, with an eye toward subtleties of each passage while not neglecting its overt message. Get to know the passage as you would get to know a patient—by listening to words, statements, and stories while looking below the surface for themes, implications, and patterns. Studying the Bible this way is not out of reach for the ordinary student and professional counselor given the range of accessible print and electronic resources.

Make note of key words or phrases. Use a Bible dictionary or word-study guide to get into a word's usage and associations. For example, pore over the ways God's wonderful activity and characteristics are revealed in Psalm 139. Pause at the statement in Psalm 139:13 regarding how humans are "knit . . . together," woven or issued a covering before physical birth ever occurs. A word study on this term will yield a portrait of God as the master artist who has made each person with ingenuity, resolve, and meticulous attention to detail. Having a rich theology of God's creation of each person paints a beautiful picture to carry with us into the counseling room. This allows us to truly see what may only appear at first as a broken and damaged human life.

Consult biblical commentaries to gain an appreciation for hidden images, the ancient cultural setting, political-historical background, and even personality descriptions. Look up related references to compare how parallel passages shed light on the meaning of the one under consideration. Read the passage deeply enough to (1) be able to paraphrase its intent, (2) recognize its contribution within a particular book, and (3) place it within the larger scope of biblical revelation.

Practicing scriptural examination in this way can cause our assumptions to be fortified, refined, or flatly rejected. "For the word of God is alive and active. Sharper than any double-edged sword, it penetrates even to dividing soul and spirit, joints and marrow; it judges the thoughts and attitudes of the heart" (Heb 4:12). This is the result when we expand our biblical theology, that is, our understanding of how God is at work in human history and our lives as informed by Scripture. This type of scriptural interrogation enables us to describe what the Bible actually says. This is one level of understanding. An even better outcome is when such study becomes prescriptive. Scripture then speaks into how we live and relate. This level of contemplation turns our attention from what we can say about Scripture to what Scripture says about us and our entire perspective of the created universe. In summary, we counselors seeking to help produce change in others need a routine that allows the message of Scripture to change us.

Expand access to biblical passages relevant to client concerns. When a counselee seeks assistance, those who listen with empathy may identify a predominant theme that characterizes in ordinary terms the chief complaint and concern. This is more an emotional and biblical impression than it is a clinical assessment. Words such as *discouragement, fear, anger, self-control, relational security, grief, loneliness, parental conflict,* and so on are reasonable options. These simplistic labels are not diagnostic; they are not precise summaries that lead to treatment plans. Rather, these themes point to the essential barrier that the helping work will focus on or a characteristic to develop. Scripture often speaks to these concerns.

One practice counselors may find useful is to locate specific passages, stories, and verses that address the issues at the top of the list of concerns. A concordance and a topical Bible will help in assembling a list of relevant passages. A concordance is a Bible reference that functions as an index to locate all occurrences of a word (Kohlenberger, 2012; Strong, 2007). A topical Bible is quite similar, but instead of locating single words, it pulls together passages or verses that address the desired theme (Nave, 1997). You can also access similar tools online (biblegateway.com).

I am not suggesting turning a counseling conversation into a discussion of a specific Bible passage. Given that assessment aims to move counselors from quick impressions to more nuanced and detailed analysis, it would be counterproductive to suggest that a simple pairing of passages to a particular need is an appropriate action step in an actual client intervention. Instead, this exploration of Scripture is a more foundational activity. Locating and meditating on a handful of key passages or verses related to a specific concern is for our benefit, not the client's. The list can inform and guide our prayer as we prepare to meet with a returning client or when praying through treatment reviews or a perplexing roadblock.

For an extended season in clinical practice, I would prepare a short list of appropriate passages for weekly clients using an electronic Bible. I then printed the lists and placed them loosely in the patient's chart. Whenever I reviewed the client's material before the start of a session, I would see the list of passages, and it would guide petitionary prayer on their behalf before the session ever commenced. I don't always adhere to this practice, but the association of biblical texts with the needs of clients helps to keep their struggles, setbacks, and victories in proper perspective.

Imagine the counselor who attempts to do this exercise for select clients on her caseload. Over time, she would have a substantial repertoire of Scripture passages coming to mind in conjunction with significant needs. The intention of this exercise is to attune our hearts and attend to a client's cry for mercy (Ps 10:17; 18:6; 84:2). Using tools to locate passages and placing Scripture in a position where it functions as a prayer guide is an effective method to increase biblical fluency. Moreover, it enables us to bring Scripture to mind when our hearts are drawn to pray for our clients.

Exhibit suitable scriptural expertise in special presentations. Christians who counsel are in a position to conduct psycho-educational workshops, to teach, or to train other helpers through supervision. Opportunities to invest in prevention or to consolidate clinical experience into lessons that promote growth could initially appear to lean on experience and not assessment. This is a beginner's error. Skilled presenters rely on assessment to learn about their audience, recognize messages implicit in inquiries, and observe group dynamics so as to maximize learning opportunities for the participants. This is assessment in action. Counselors who teach toward outcomes will consider where learners are before directing them where to go. Thus, we continue to engage in assessment when we step outside the counseling office. As we anticipate how learners may benefit from information or guided experiences, we consider what we have to share and how it coheres with Scripture.

When we are called on to prepare a psycho-educational presentation, it can be helpful to dig deep into a cross section of Scripture passages. These should speak to the theme, premise, or concern under consideration. A sensible cross section of Scripture would pull from a relevant historical account, a psalm, and the teaching of Jesus in the Gospels. Drawing from three or more distinct points in Scripture whenever possible reduces the risk of twisting the meaning of a select verse to fit one's desired teaching point. Working from a cross section of genres and passages establishes a secure biblical theology for our presentation. Related passages often connect to one another to form a sturdy web of meaning.

Whether speaking to a cohort of weary mothers raising energetic kids through the terrible twos or coaching engaged couples on the top ten strategies to resolve unexpected conflicts, it is useful to press fervently into Scripture. This is how we secure wisdom before dispensing lessons gleaned from the counseling room or clinical literature. Check yourself and your material by asking the following questions: (1) What hope or promise does Scripture offer related to my theme? (2) Does Scripture specifically name a sin pattern to avoid or a character trait to cultivate that connects directly to the topic? (3) Is there a biblical figure referenced in Scripture who faced similar circumstances or trials whom the Lord offers as a model for faith?

I recommend asking these questions even if the material is based on concepts written by a Christian authority. Examine the author's key concepts against Scripture. Our own study in the Word combined with the subject material is what generates confidence in the material we present. In order to meet the multitude of expectations that arise when speaking to an audience, thoroughly study the Word for how it deals with the key matters at hand. Combine the best from your clinical expertise with the solid foundation found in Scripture.

REFERENCES

Bromiley, G. W. (1960). Biblical theology. In E. F. Harrison (Ed.), *Baker's Dictionary of Theology* (pp. 95-97). Grand Rapids, MI: Baker.

Hughes, R. B., & Laney, J. C. (2001). *Tyndale concise Bible commentary*. Wheaton, IL: Tyndale House.

Kohlenberger, J. R., III. (2012). *NIV Bible concordance*. Grand Rapids, MI: Zondervan.

Nave, O. J. (1997). *Nave's topical Bible*. Peabody, MA: Hendrickson.

Packer, J. I. (1993). *Concise theology: A guide to historic Christian beliefs*. Wheaton, IL: Tyndale House.

Scharf, G. R. (2005). God's letter of intent: Six questions that reveal what God meant to say in a text. In H. Robinson and C. B. Larson's (Eds.), *The art and craft of biblical preaching: A comprehensive resource for today's communicators* (pp. 230-233). Grand Rapids, MI: Zondervan.

Strong, J. (2007). *Strong's exhaustive concordance of the Bible: Updated and expanded edition*. Peabody, MA: Hendrickson.

Vanhoozer, K. J. (2005). *The drama of doctrine: A canonical linguistic approach to Christian theology*. Louisville, KY: Westminster John Knox.

Vanhoozer, K. J. (2010). Forming the performers: How Christians can use canon sense to bring us to our (theodramatic) senses. *Edification: The Transdisciplinary Journal of Christian Psychology, 4*(1), 5-16.

Westminster confession of faith (1646/1982). In J. H. Leith (Ed.), *The Creeds of the Churches* (3rd ed., Vol. 1, pp. 10, 196). Atlanta: John Knox Press.

PART 2

BACKGROUND

INFORMATION

CHAPTER FOUR

FORMING A THEOLOGICAL FOUNDATION

The fear of the Lord *is the beginning of knowledge,*
but fools despise wisdom and instruction.

Proverbs 1:7

THEOLOGICAL THEME

Wisdom

A THEOLOGY FOR ASSESSMENT

Christian theology can actually give us a useful perspective on how information can be gathered and assembled under the guidance of the Holy Spirit. This chapter offers an excursion into biblical material that clinicians, novices, and veterans alike would do well to contemplate.

Artisanship. An *artisan* is a person who practices an art, trade, or handicraft by employing skills passed down as time-honored traditions. This describes one who hones a talent in producing limited quantities of particular top-quality items (e.g., bread, cheese, wine, jewelry, furniture, or pottery; *Merriam-Webster's Collegiate Dictionary*, 2003). The object produced reflects the artist. Each is uniquely and painstakingly handcrafted, unlike the mass-produced products pumped out using robotic, mechanical, or assembly-line procedures. The touch of the artisan gives the product or service its value. A related word would be *craftsmanship*, which expresses creative talent with skill, dexterity, and ingenuity. Both of these evocative terms stir images of persons who combine artistic vision, proficiency, and expertise to engineer commodities of merit with the utmost personal attention.

Like a carefully produced treasure, a search for wisdom also requires artisanship. Scripture describes skilled tradespeople as those who use tools responsibly, masterfully, and in service of the Lord. Christians who counsel operate as artisans, making expert use of tools for kingdom purposes and to establish a purposeful relational connection.

In the Genesis creation account, human beings were commissioned by God to represent him by stewarding resources as they populate the entire earth (Gen 1:27-30). The term for a skillful artisan appears early in Scripture where it depicts Tubal-Cain, only a few generations down the line from Adam, as one who worked metal with forge and hammer to manufacture fine tools (Gen 4:22). From making swords to bricks, perfume to bread, musical instruments to idols, those who combine expertise of mind and hand to generate art or crafts are mentioned with considerable respect throughout the Bible.

There is much to know before an inspired skill can be executed. First, artisans must understand the performance and pliability characteristics of earthly materials. Next, they must perfect tools, methods, and procedures to utilize materials effectively. Finally, the signature of a fine artisan is the transformation of a practical item into a piece of beauty and imagination. These traits are aspects of human workmanship that bring glory to a creative, personal God by illustrating the wonder of the human capacity to master elements in the environment.

Consider the prominent description of artists and tradespeople as God speaks at length to Moses regarding the tabernacle, altar of sacrifice, and garments for priests. The Lord chose Bezalel, son of Uri, and filled him with the Spirit to create an impressive setting so that his inventive designs in gold, silver, bronze, stone, and wood would distinguish the religious celebrations of God's people (Ex 35:30-35). The children of God were no longer in Egypt. The offering poured out by the work of their hands would now be lifted before a new master. The Lord commissioned a line of competent craftspersons to construct the sanctuary according to his commands. This arrangement was far more demanding than recording dimensions and specifications to assemble a building according to a generic blueprint. Artisans turn out items of loveliness that exceed utilitarian purposes. Handiwork displays intelligent design that honors the Creator of the universe. The Lord, who brought the physical universe into being from void and emptiness, left his imaginative handprint in incredible ways for human beings to behold. As human beings, we are the pinnacle of God's artistry, made *imago Dei*, in his image (Erickson, 2013). The central theological principle beneath the term *imago Dei* is that human beings mirror characteristics of the Creator. Men and women reflect the Lord of creation well when what emerges from our hands bears the mark of a devoted artisan. Artisans are wise with their hands. Image bearers offer the products of their hands back to the very same Lord who provides the materials and the means to create.

Scripture extends the application of expertise, skill, and creativity to those who exercise leadership or who advise regarding moral matters (Deut 1:9-18). The passage implies the existence of a dedicated capacity to direct and unify those who will offer the fruit of their hands in service. Notice the biblical unity between mechanical proficiency and mental competency. In contemporary use, physical handiwork is often distinguished from mental exercise associated with leadership, judgment, and management. For example, standardized intelligence tests focus on internal problem solving rather than performance or external manipulation. Verbal reasoning is separated from spatial and manipulative skills. In a biblical sense, work produced by hand or as the outcome of mental competence coheres through the process of practical implementation. Both artistry in productivity and the capacity for sage judgment exemplify wisdom when used in honor of the Creator.

Although *wisdom* cannot easily be defined, the term is abundant in Scripture. In most places it is used in reference to resourceful application of moral insight regarding right and wrong word and action. This requires intellectual understanding of how the world operates, along with social ingenuity, manifested in activities and decisions that lead to successful living. Scripture is consistent in teaching that wisdom is attainable as long as it is acknowledged as a gift from God (Ps 51:6-8; Prov 2:6). Wisdom mediates the relationship between physical creation, human social order, and the Creator (Dell, 2009). The foundation for wisdom is earnest respect for one's dependent status on the Creator (Job 28:28; Wilson, 1997). Therefore, artisanship in living wisely is displayed in ethical, virtuous living that honors God and reflects his divine, holy character suitably in the world.

Thus far, wisdom has been described as alive, practical, righteous, and relationally significant, not as peculiarly personal. Scripture will not allow such a division to stand, for wisdom calls aloud in the street and raises her voice in the public square (Prov 1:20). In the New Testament wisdom is associated with the Word made flesh who dwelled among us (Jn 1:1-5; 1 Jn 1:1-4). The craft of locating wisdom is not merely about knowing and doing but also about being in relationship. More specifically and significantly, wisdom is synonymous with knowing Jesus Christ. "Jesus Christ is the word and wisdom

of God, the revealer and the redeemer: the way, the truth and the life"
(Vanhoozer, 2005, p. 13).

In sum, artisanship encompasses handiwork as well as creative ethical activity. It is the finely attuned application of wisdom by those who carry *imago
Dei* in a manner that glorifies and reflects the triune God. It is the exhibition of
the Creator's characteristics in the stewardship of life by those creatures lovingly made in his image.

A discerning heart. No human person in Scripture is more associated with
wisdom than the son of David and Bathsheba, King Solomon. During his
reign, the nation of Israel experienced its grandest days, spanning four decades approximately one thousand years before the birth of Christ. Solomon's
expansive understanding is compared in Scripture to the grains of sands on
the seashore (1 Kings 4:29-34). Solomon was esteemed not only for compiling
wise sayings to guide action but also for his knowledge of botany, zoology,
political science, anthropology, and psychology. When Solomon ascended
to David's throne, the Lord granted him the opportunity in a dream to ask
for anything his imagination could possibly desire. Solomon openly acknowledged his limited grasp of leadership and his incompetency to rule
honorably over such a vast nation. His admission was paramount to
confessing a lack of the artisanship necessary to carry out his commission.
Revealing his humility and insight, Solomon implores the Lord for both a
discerning heart to separate right from wrong and the ability to govern an
entire nation as the Lord's chosen people (1 Kings 3:4-15). Scripture duly
records that the young king's response delighted the Lord (1 Kings 3:10). His
request for a heart that can truly hear, along with presence of mind to recognize righteousness, is a prayer that those of us who are helpers can imitate
without hesitation.

The remarkable passage that follows offers the link between assessment and
Solomon's gift of wisdom from on high (1 Kings 3:16-28). Two prostitutes who
had recently given birth petitioned the king. It was his responsibility to determine who held legitimate parental rights over a single infant. The case may
have already been reviewed in lower courts. The ability to ascertain which
woman was the rightful mother was a not a matter that could be readily resolved in any judicial proceeding of the day. The situation was further compli-
cated by a series of tragic events that affected the plight of these competing
women (Konkel, 2006). No mention is made of husbands or known fathers.
They, and others in their occupation, faced much scorn and lacked social status.
The women had given birth to fragile infants within three days of each other.

One newborn was accidently killed during the night, presumably by the mother inadvertently rolling on top of the little one, suffocating the infant. The accusation is that the grieving mother switched her deceased baby with the one still breathing. The second mother remained in slumber and did not detect the switch until she went to feed the child. The legal plea is one disreputable woman's word against another's (Farrar, 1893/1982). How could any respectable judge discern the sincerity of these women and thus determine proper custody? This case was heard thousands of years before any medical test would be available to solve such an atrocious human puzzle. But Solomon listens and hears their hearts.

He issues the order that the living child be severed into two. In the interest of fairness, each claimant would be given a bloodied half. The brutality of the ruling is striking. The pronouncement is vicious. Though utterly absurd, this decision was within the prerogative of a king of that period and culture. Further, this ruling was justified. The pitiful stubbornness of these women was insulting. They refused to resolve their own dispute. How dare such lowly harlots burden a king with these intractable positions and contradictory allegations? Solomon summons a sword to be brought speedily into the courtroom. Justice would be immediate and dramatic. These bickering women would come to know the power of the king. There was little doubt among those assembled in the court—this king had every intention of implementing his order.

Under these circumstances each prostitute turned mother issues a further statement. One spitefully applauds the impartiality of the death sentence (1 Kings 3:26). The other compassionately yields her parental rights in order to spare the life of the infant. From these declarations, the loving heart of the true mother becomes utterly transparent. Their responses separate grief-saturated bitterness from true maternal love. The one willing to sacrifice parenthood for the infant's life was the mother. The one suffering great loss was bound in mindless darkness, shock, denial, and mourning.

News of Solomon's judicial wisdom traveled not only across the known world; it has been preserved throughout the ages. This courtroom drama stands as an enduring testimony to his prowess in detecting the motives hidden in the recesses of the human heart. How did he arrive at his judgment?

Solomon may not have come up with this assessment technique as a ploy. He held the authority to carry out his decree. His motives are not unpacked in this ancient court transcript. No postsentence commentary is available. What Scripture does reveal is his recognition of the mother by her readiness to sacrifice her parental rights in order to protect the child's precious life. Consistent with the definition of a modern psychological test, Solomon's order elicits a sample of behavior that has relevance for the classification of interior motivations, relational attachments, and emotional state. The words spoken in that instant offer a graphic portrayal of the state of these desperate hearts. Overt behavior opens a window into the covert. The brilliance of his decision is not tied solely to subjective powers of discernment. Solomon's cleverness acquires what amounts to a confession through his radical pronouncement and the expectations associated with the courtroom practice of a formidable king. Authority, action, and speech proclaimed a violent sequence about to unfold; two women responded by exposing their hearts.

The collected sayings of Solomon throughout the Wisdom literature display further the intricate web connecting external behavior and inner affections. For example, a villain who harbors evil intent may make bold promises with his mouth while proclaiming contrary signals in his body language (e.g., eye, hand, and foot movement). Behavior, not speech, reveals the malicious plot in his inner being (Prov 6:12-15; 10:10). Further cases suggest that a heart full of rage and hate stirs dissension while love seeks to reduce or diminish the impact of careless, accidental, or improper actions (Prov 10:7; 15:18). A righteous person displays kindness even to a defenseless animal whereas a wicked man delights in perpetrating cruelty (Prov 12:5). A fool finds unceasing satisfaction in expressing his own opinion while a wise person opens his mind to receive understanding (Prov 18:2; 19:8). In collecting numerous pithy sayings of the wise, Solomon cataloged perceptive ties between behaviors and the inner motives they expose. Once brought to light, the matters of the heart are left open for interpretation. It is here we see Solomon's artistic creativity in unmasking the inclinations of human beings in crisis. Solomon's discerning emotional, relational, and ethical center were granted by God. He had the ability to link what is seen or heard with that which is hidden. This skill is the essence of assessment.

A counselor is an artisan of the heart. This specialization requires the examination of words and behavior to discern the intricate ties between what is conveyed on the surface and what lies within. We collect details regarding events, behaviors, and relationships in order to assemble a plausible explanation for what may be occurring on a deeper, more intimate level. Likewise, we may use a current behavior sample to make a prediction regarding subsequent actions. An artisan of the heart ponders and evaluates behavior in the light of a broader narrative and interpersonal patterns. An assortment of techniques and specialized assessment tools might be created or appropriated and applied. This allows us to form associations between readily observable behavior and unseen motives. Remember, for one in distress, the desire, depth, and deceptiveness of the heart may be concealed even from the self.

Discovering wisdom afresh. There is a downside to illustrating artisanship of the heart using the great Solomon. The risk is that inexperienced or overzealous helpers may mistakenly attempt to repetitively implement in formulaic fashion the golden principles located in biblical material. Statements pulled from their ancient context may serve as prescriptions to guide current decisions. In certain instances this can produce a favorable outcome. Nevertheless, the application of wisdom with success mandates submissiveness to the Lord and right relation with others.

"A gentle answer turns away wrath, / but a harsh word stirs up anger" (Prov 15:1). The interpersonal approach of using soft-spoken and cooperative speech in response to anger has near universal application. When this does not work, the failure is usually not in the inaccuracy of the statement but in the person-to-person recognition of emotional cues. In order to ascertain whether the biblical recommendation applies, we must decode the communication within the context of the specific relationship. Anger can be a natural response to a provocative statement. It can also be an emotion used to manipulate or intimidate. In difficult interpersonal interactions is the best answer always gentle submission? Is there a place for a firm challenge spoken softly but with resolve? Rigid adherence to a biblical principle from the Wisdom literature is not a sign of faith but a presumption of magical thinking. Those who seek wisdom need to be discerning and alert to layers of communication. This is the criterion for wisdom. As helpers we err when we enforce application of biblical principles without wise consideration of the relational dynamics. Rather, as we see with Solomon, dispensing wisdom happens in the moment as we discern the context.

Biblical principles have no expiration date attached to their relevance. Nevertheless, the situations in which we apply particular principles are never packaged so neatly that we must only select, unwrap, and dispense. If the metaphor for wisdom were a massive library, extensive database, or a mammoth warehouse, the necessity of spiritual dependency and constant abiding that Scripture so forcefully advocates would be irrelevant. Wisdom would be available for the taking instead of being realized as a God-honoring solution for fresh situations. Rather, as exemplified in the courtroom of Solomon, a more accurate metaphor for wisdom is the stage, where the drama of divine-human relationship, moral choices, and spontaneous decisions are on display scene by scene. Scripture asserts the necessity of searching and listening for wisdom in community and with divine consultation.

Cultures, ethical scenarios, and person-to-person interactions are consistently in flux, and will remain that way until the Lord's return. Thus, Word-based principles for living are best applied in innovative and original ways. Consider the theatrical ingredients that make Solomon's courtroom scene so compelling. The intensity of the conflict is brilliantly dispelled by a marvelous unveiling of truth. How is the truth brought to light? Solomon cleverly combines faith, exemplary use of authority, understanding of human nature, compassion, intuition, and quick thinking as he takes in the situation. Solomon does not resort to a rote formula. Wisdom emerges from his capacity for discernment. He recognizes the volatile, fever pitch of emotion operating in the immediate context.

The biblical account stands as a living testimony to this remarkable blend of objective observation, subjective awareness, and cognitive acuity. Like manna in the wilderness, God supplies wisdom to meet the demands of the day. As much as we may covet a storehouse of wisdom, it cannot be preserved or set aside to inform future actions.

Christian theology as revealed in the Word of God is essential for living in a manner that brings glory to God. This position is entirely consistent with Christian tradition and the Reformation priority of *sola Scriptura*. This Latin phrase refers to Scripture as sacred writings that stand alone, meaning that Scripture provides God's authoritative pronouncements regarding Christian faith and practice. The God of Scripture speaks and acts so that human beings are empowered to recognize, comprehend, and respond to God in the ongoing movement of creation, redemption, and restoration (Vanhoozer, 2002, 2005, 2010).

Vanhoozer (2002, 2005) contends that Scripture is not a storehouse of revelation but one of God's mighty speech acts. The Bible communicates the content of the gospel as it shows God in action drawing human beings into his ongoing enactments in creation and with his creatures. Christian tradition and faith rest on what God has done, is doing, and will do with words, the Word, and the Holy Spirit (Vanhoozer, 2010). "Theological competence is ultimately a matter of being able to make judgments that display the mind of Christ" (Vanhoozer, 2005, p. 2). Believers seek to obey or act out Scripture as they live in Christian community. The Holy Spirit enables Christ-followers to hear that "speech act" afresh and to obey in a manner that reflects the mind of Christ in the contemporary context. Wise living requires more than knowledge of a critical mass of abstract material, regardless of how spiritual or Word saturated that material may be. Information about God and his creation is necessary, but it is not sufficient to produce action that reveals mature faith or spiritual depth.

Wisdom that reflects sound theology and biblical allegiance flows from respecting, listening, and relating anew to the voice of God. Wisdom is made alive in humans when our dialogue invites God, who continues to communicate in speech and action. Believers are granted the power of the Holy Spirit to produce bidirectional outcomes; that is, inwardly, the mind of Christ is formed; outwardly his glorious grace is displayed to the surrounding world.

> The imagination is a cognitive faculty, however, and can be a servant of the truth. Indeed, only with an eschatological imagination can we see the reality of the "already" and the "not yet" of the kingdom of God in our midst. (Vanhoozer, 2010, p. 9)

Wisdom is the means to living virtuously and rightly. The search for wisdom may bring a counselor to encourage reflective contemplation, reasoning via dialogue, redirecting affections, or taking action (Treier, 2006). The following proposal portrays wisdom in layers. Assessment opens understanding to enable clients to move more firmly in ways that reflect the mind of Christ. This means relating to others naturally and realistically as the Holy Spirit directs.

DISCERNING WISDOM IN LAYERS

Posture: submissive to triune God. These five layers of wisdom surface in dialogue between Christians while listening for the Holy Spirit (Greggo & Tillett, 2010). See figure 4.1. Wisdom is the collective property of the community devoted to loving God. Counselors need to seek wisdom, not only for insight regarding particular dilemmas but for determining how to speak and act with clients. A client's cultural heritage, uniqueness, worldview, and values must be fully respected. This is a professional mandate for mental health professionals (MHPs), who function in a pluralistic culture. Nonetheless, those of us with Christian convictions recognize that in the same way that research guides therapeutic methods, the Lord reveals his wisdom to those who seek it by faith in prayer (Jas 1:5-8).

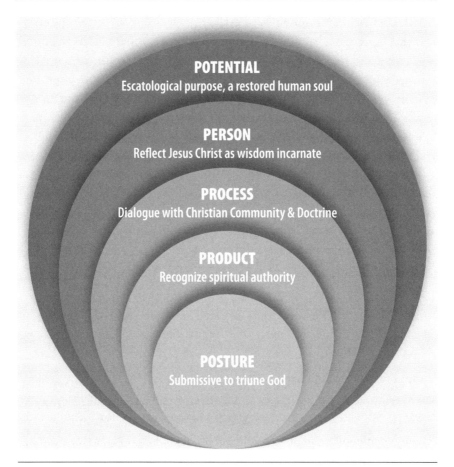

Figure 4.1. Layers of a wisdom search

The first layer in the wisdom search—an absolute precondition to any wisdom quest—is to assume a submissive posture toward the triune God. This means placing one's desires and volition before the Lord. The opening prayer of wisdom pursuit has one central plea: "thy will be done." This is an acknowledgment that the fear of the Lord is the foundation for wisdom.

Product: recognition of Scripture as authoritative. Second, a wisdom search can at times lead to a tangible result, or product, meaning that the Lord God has spoken with authority on this matter. Scripture may speak explicitly through a verse, historical event, or teaching passage that matches the need. Give to those who are in need (Mt 5:42). Provide for widows and orphans (Jas 1:27). Such verses form the basis for wise and direct recommendations for how to live. Seek the Scriptures to discover what they state directly and plainly. This search may provide perspective for our work, or it may lead us to a passage that the client needs to consider with a pastor or spiritual mentor, or in personal meditation.

Imagine counseling a woman who forthrightly professes a Christian faith and has done so for her entire engagement and eighteen-year marriage. You offer empathy and concern as she discloses her recent loss of appetite, sleeplessness, inability to focus, and an emergency room visit for chest pain, eventually diagnosed as a panic attack. The bigger story reveals turmoil, inner conflict, and intense agony over a growing infatuation for a coworker who, as soon as she is ready to step forward to declare her interest, reportedly has said he will reciprocate. The symptoms in her presenting profile may fit within the parameters of depression and anxiety, but as we learn more, we see a war going on within her. On one side are her feelings of loyalty for her husband of nearly two decades, and on the opposing front is awakening passion for a novel romantic interest. Speaking with biblically informed wisdom, we may point out that the inner war is actually about obedience to scriptural teaching.

Biblical references to adultery are pretty difficult to miss. The plain meaning is not subject to contentious hermeneutical dispute (Mt 5:27-30). Of course, issues related to personal happiness, marital satisfaction, or personality conflicts are likely to surface when considering application. Social standards and the reality of contemporary options may be explored. Eventually, seeking Word-based wisdom will lead to dialogue between the client and the Holy Spirit over her identity as a Christian. The client must come to acknowledge that Scripture contains a clear message about marriage as a sacred covenant. The drama under consideration is primarily about this client's relationship with herself, others, the Word, and God. Wisdom in this scenario could direct the client, who desires an explicitly Christian approach, to application of biblical chapters, verses, and themes. Assessment will track presenting symptoms, spiritual priorities, long-term interpersonal patterns, and broader themes of personal identity.

Process: dialogue with Christian community and doctrine. Wisdom searches are not limited to locating explicit statements in Scripture. The third layer of wisdom is penetrated when the difficulties that arise in counseling have no counterpart in a biblical text. There are human symptoms, choices, dilemmas, and interpersonal challenges for which instruction cannot be obtained neatly from chapter and verse. This does not make the Word irrelevant or unnecessary. The canon is not pushed aside in cases where there isn't a specific command, principle, or biblical story to match the identified concern. Scripture retains its authority. The search continues using Scripture to hear the voice of God and inspire theological reflection on what it means to have the mind of Christ. The pursuit of wisdom is an interactive process in which communication with others involves diligent, strategic, reflective, and prayerful contemplation.

We may not take on this type of search exclusively or in its entirety with clients. Encouragement to clients may take the form of a recommendation to converse with faith mentors, believing peers, pastors, and spiritual leaders. Seeking direction from credible books to grasp the perspective of the wider Christian community throughout the world and ages may be useful. Eventually, clients make decisions with hope that God will speak through his Spirit and that Jesus Christ will be honored in the implementation. Wisdom is not discovered as new revelation in community. Instead, God speaks through Scripture and in community, and the helping relationship becomes a process by which we can aid clients to comprehend the Spirit's way forward.

Assessment practices for seeking this layer of wisdom may involve the consideration of dispositional traits such as tendencies toward introversion or extroversion, solitary or group-oriented relational patterns, and passive or aggressive styles of resistance. Family relationships past and present, peer networks, support systems, and the range of community resources will all affect how the wisdom search proceeds when paying attention to how God speaks through others. What characteristics of the client may limit the impact of relational support? In this wisdom layer, Christian fellowship is the means to decode the path that honors the Lord.

Person: reflecting Jesus Christ as wisdom incarnate. Fourth, wisdom may center on how the person is significantly affected by prevailing character traits. What spiritual fruit not previously exemplified, such as love, joy, peace, patience, or self-control, does the client need to display more frequently (Mt 5:3-11; Gal 5:22-25)? Self-sacrifice, sanctification, and reflection of the image of Christ are the essential efforts in this layer of the wisdom search (Phil 2:5-11). As will be shown in a later chapter on personality screening, it is often extremely useful in clinical assessment to make apparent in plain language default patterns of behaving, thinking, speaking, and relating. The matter at hand is not likely to be resolved or drastically altered by simply implementing a plan of action. The client, by grace, must grow in awareness of long-established patterns that now must be curbed, managed, and submitted to the renewing ministry of the Holy Spirit. In this wisdom layer we see that movement forward is not about what one says or does; rather, it's about whom one becomes.

Potential: eschatological purpose, a restored human soul. The final layer in a wisdom search is coming to the point where the potential of eternity in the

Lord's presence is brought into view (Hiers, 1985). Scripture makes regular references to themes surrounding the Promised Land, the kingdom of God, heavenly dwellings, and the new Jerusalem (Is 2:2-4; Mt 16:27-28; Jn 14:1-3; 21:2–22:5). There are indeed counseling concerns that have no apparent resolution this side of death or prior to the Lord's return (Mt 24:42-44). A wisdom search may result in a realistic and profound awareness that the Lord will not restore well-being this side of heaven. Chronic disease, infertility, the death of a loved one, disability in a child, trauma associated with a natural disaster, random violence, and systematic injustice are only a few causes of intense suffering. Clients may grieve these deeply within a counseling relationship and find refreshment and comfort in the supportive relationship. Still, the core matter remains untouched since no remedy is within reach this side of eternity. The hope for bodily wholeness, relational security, restitution, justice, or freedom may not rest on an immediate redemptive act of God. Ultimate hope will be realized in that amazing place where the presence of the Lord makes all things new and where Jesus Christ personally wipes every tear from our eyes.

Understanding these layers of wisdom is intended to expand perspective. Solomon's courtroom drama may not be replayed in a counseling session. No breakthrough of insight or a way forward may appear in a sudden flash of inspiration or unleashing of the unconscious. As counselors we keep these layers in perspective while exploring matters of the heart. Understanding different layers of wisdom increases our awareness of how the mind of Christ may establish a new perspective on an ongoing concern.

In summary, the theological foundation for assessment is tied to the biblical theme of a search for wisdom. Counselors operate as artisans, using select tools and techniques to discern the movement and leaning of the human heart in conjunction with the leading of the Holy Spirit. Opening the Word is essential in developing the mind of Christ as we seek to walk with clients in the grand drama of redemption.

ASSESSMENT WITHIN A CHRISTIAN APPROACH

This discussion of clinical assessment and psychological instruments alongside the biblical theme of wisdom places front and center the ongoing controversy regarding counseling that is undeniably Christian. Positions vary on what constitutes an optimal model to manage the discourse between the disciplines of psychology and theology (Johnson, 2010). Christians who work in mental health systems rely on the conventional practices derived from the social sciences. They make circumspect use of corresponding theoretical, empirical, and clinical literature (e.g., levels of explanation and integration). Despite general reliance on evidence-based interventions, submission to the ultimate authority of Scripture is paramount. Other positions align counseling assistance closely with ministry objectives (e.g., Christian psychology, transformational, biblical counseling). Proponents of these views rely heavily or exclusively on faith sources, such as Christian tradition, spiritual experiences, and the applied exegesis of Scripture, for setting counseling direction.

The major disagreements across the different views stem in part from differing positions on the definition and scope of psychology. How the discipline is mapped depends on the degree of confidence placed in two sources of revelation. General revelation comprises the truths God has made evident about himself by grace in the forces and laws of nature, through the characteristics of humans who are made uniquely in the image of the Creator, and in the unfolding of salvation history (Ps 19:1-2; Rom 1:19-20, 2:14-15; Erickson, 2013). Those who value empirical evidence obtained through research on human behavior consider the social sciences to be a reflection of general revelation. Special revelation is the sole source of the salvation story and is composed of what God has spoken in Scripture and is revealed in the Song of God becoming flesh and dwelling among human beings (Ps 119; Jn 1:1-4; 2 Tim 3:16-17; Heb 1:1-3; Erickson, 2013). The authority ascribed to each source of revelation influences the parameters of professional practice (Beck, 1997; Hurley & Berry, 1997; Johnson, 2010; Welch & Powlison, 1997). Regardless of the explicit position on epistemology (i.e., how we know what we know), all positions have concerns about the impact of modern psychology on helping services because they all desire to respect a theological understanding of human flourishing.

The features that set apart counseling as Christian have to do with core theological commitments related to doctrinal matters of epistemology, anthropology, and ecclesiology (Greggo & Sisemore, 2012). Counseling by helpers who are Christian is shaped by factors such as vocational calling, occupational role, and educational orientation, as well as employment status in a healthcare, academic, social service, or ministry setting. The crucial matter for our consideration is how different definitions affect assessment technology. Will the assessment procedures in use enhance the promotion of a Christian worldview and the implementation of wisdom that flows from the Word? What facets of assessment as implemented might actually inhibit Christian maturation and sanctification?

This chapter is offered to establish common ground. Each of the contemporary views on the relationship between counseling and Christianity operates from a distinct framework of anthropology and human psychology. Thus, each champions a corresponding system for understanding behavior across a range of options deemed as dysfunctional, unhealthy, selfish, and sin-bound or normal, loving, and Christ-exalting (Eph 4:17-24). Each position has a different perspective on how to conceptualize concerns, and, therefore, each must come to terms with a set of assessment procedures. Christ-followers with views that are heavily skeptical of the modern psychological establishment will not be comfortable using theory-laden assessment batteries or instruments that rely on humanistic theories. Even evidence-based research may be suspect because it is based on procedures established by social science. Still, the need to conduct a suitable mental health appraisal to form a sound clinical, social, and spiritual perspective regarding presenting problems keeps the practice of assessment priorities front and center. If we issue a form to gather information, a rating scale to study severity of symptoms, or a set of credible inquiry questions, then we are using assessment procedures. Christian clinicians who are more comfortable incorporating social science methods may be more comfortable using a wider range of tools.

No matter what view on the relationship between counseling and Christian theology you adhere to, there is reasonable cause to consider information-gathering strategies that enhance helping services. The intent in this under-taking is less about promoting a single approach and more about applying biblical stewardship to the use of tools that contribute to efficient, quality as-sessment. All Christian helpers collect, sort, and assemble descriptions from life stories into broad portrayals of problems and character challenges. Thus, it is worthwhile to weigh appraisal options thoroughly from an informed bib-lical perspective. Clinicians must be theologically responsible in the use of assessment technology.

In an attempt to apply an inclusive framework for Christian counseling that contains enough doctrinal transparency to allow for a faith-based critique of assessment procedures, it is best to state a few biblical essentials plainly. The application of the label *Christian counseling* infers that helper and client ex-plicitly agree on and hold to the parameters of ultimate concerns, nature of reality, ethics, morality, and the destination of history (Hathaway, 2009). There is a unique connection in the therapeutic alliance between a professing Christ-following client and a counselor who is able to be transparent about her or his Christian faith. If the counseling framework is overtly Christian, Scripture is granted an evident position of authority, and we take steps to ensure the Word is not bent to conform to private interpretation. We acknowledge the gospel as the unchanging and still-unfolding storyline for all matters that are discussed and pondered.

Gospel is the English term for the Greek word *euangelion*, translated as "good news." In Scripture, the good news is proclaimed by Jesus Christ himself when he announces that the kingdom of God is at hand (Mk 1:14-15). Placing helping conversations in a gospel context declares at the very outset that God has accomplished his redemptive purpose for human beings through the life, death, and resurrection of Jesus Christ (Rom 1:3-5). The united message across the Old and New Testaments is one of hope. The poor and outcast are under the Lord's care, prisoners will be set free, the blind will see, the broken-hearted will be restored, and those who mourn will be comforted (Is 61:1-2; Lk 4:18-19). A gospel framework is one in which hope prevails even if present suffering is inevitable. The power of God brings redemption as it makes salvation a reality through the incarnation, crucifixion, and resurrection of Jesus Christ (Rom 1:16).

Now that we have explored the theological underpinnings for assessment, it is time to turn our attention to the matter of choosing the best assessment technology for the task. The challenge before us is to pray for discernment to become a hearer of hearts. The instruments employed must contribute to this objective. Further, we must develop skills like those of high-caliber artisans, to use the best available tools to understand as much as possible about the heart of the person seeking wisdom.

REFERENCES

Beck, J. (1997). Sola Scriptura: Then and now. *Journal of Psychology and Christianity*, *16*(4), 293-302.

Corey, G., Corey, M. S., & Callanan, P. (2019). *Issues and ethics in the helping professions* (10th ed.). Belmont, CA: Brooks/Cole, Cengage Learning.

Dell, K. J. (2009). Wisdom in the Old Testament. In K. D. Sakenfield (Ed.), *The new interpreter's dictionary of the Bible* (Vol. 5, pp. 869-875). Nashville: Abingdon Press.

Erickson, M. J. (2013). *Christian theology* (3rd ed.). Grand Rapids, MI: Baker.

Farrar, F. W. (1893/1982). The first book of Kings. In W. R. Nicoll (Ed.), *The expositor's Bible* (Vol. 2, pp. 213-335). Grand Rapids, MI: Baker.

Greggo, S. P., & Sisemore, T. A. (2012). *Christianity and counseling: Five approaches*. Downers Grove, IL: InterVarsity Press.

Greggo, S. P. & Tillett, L. (2010). Beyond bioethics 101: Where theology gets personal and pastoral. *Journal of the Evangelical Theological Society*, *53*(2), 349-63.

Hathaway, W. L. (2009). Clinical use of explicit religious approaches: Christian role integration issues. *Journal of Psychology and Christianity, 28*, 105-112.

Hiers, R. H. (1985). Eschatology. In P. J. Achtemeier (Ed.), *Harper's Bible dictionary* (pp. 275-277). San Francisco: HarperCollins.

Hurley, J. B., & Berry, J. T. (1997). The relation of Scripture and psychology in counseling from a pro-integration position. *Journal of Psychology and Christianity, 16*(4), 323-345.

Johnson, E. L. (Ed.). (2010). *Psychology & Christianity: Five views* (2nd ed.). Downers Grove, IL: InterVarsity Press.

Konkel, A. H. (2006). *The NIV application commentary: 1 & 2 Kings.* Grand Rapids, MI: Zondervan.

Merriam-Webster's collegiate dictionary (11th ed.). (2003). Springfield, MA: Merriam-Webster.

Treier, D. J. (2006). *Virtue and the voice of God: Toward theology as wisdom.* Grand Rapids, MI: Eerdmans.

Vanhoozer, K. J. (2002). *First theology: God, Scripture & hermeneutics.* Downers Grove, IL: InterVarsity Press.

Vanhoozer, K. J. (2005). *The drama of doctrine: A canonical linguistic approach to Christian theology.* Louisville, KY: Westminster John Knox.

Vanhoozer, K. J. (2010). Forming the performers: How Christians can use canon sense to bring us to our (theodramatic) senses. *Edification: The Transdisciplinary Journal of Christian Psychology, 4*(1), 5-16.

Welch, E., & Powlison, D. (1997). "Every common bush afire with God": The Scripture's constitutive role for counseling. *Journal of Psychology and Christianity, 16*(4), 303-322.

Wilson, G. H. (1997). Wisdom. In W. A. VanGemeren (Ed.), *New international dictionary of Old Testament theology & exegesis,* (Vol. 4, pp. 1276-1285). Grand Rapids, MI: Zondervan.

CHAPTER FIVE

MULTICULTURALISM AND
ASSESSMENT STANDARDS

Do not use dishonest standards when measuring length, weight or quantity.
Use honest scales and honest weights, an honest ephah and an honest hin.
I am the LORD your God, who brought you out of Egypt.

LEVITICUS 19:35-36

THEOLOGICAL THEME

Honest Scales

THE PURSUIT OF IMPARTIALITY

The assessment literature dedicates extensive attention to cultural fairness in test construction and norming procedures. The intent is to confront bias in all forms. This explains why those who administer instruments are required to demonstrate mastery of psychometric concepts (e.g., standardization, measures of central tendency, validity, reliability, and utility) prior to gaining access to sophisticated instruments. Measurement technicalities contribute not only to better tests but also to useful and impartial findings for those who take them. Typically such constructs are introduced through an overview of inferential statistics, normal distributions, and features of the bell curve. An alternate way to approach them is to recognize the relationship between psychometric essentials and core human values such as trust, justice, and fairness. These value-laden themes resonate well with New Testament priorities. Respect for all persons regardless of their diverse characteristics is consistent with the Great Commandment given by Jesus (Mt 22:36-40) and offers an ideal starting point.

"Teacher, which is the greatest commandment in the Law?"

Jesus replied: "'Love the Lord your God with all your heart and with all your soul and with all your mind.' This is the first and greatest commandment. And the second is like it: 'Love your neighbor as yourself.' All the Law and the Prophets hang on these two commandments."

Counselors who take Christianity seriously use their vocation as a service to the Lord. This means honoring each and every client as an act of loving one's neighbor. Paul charges Christ-followers to do nothing out of favoritism (1 Tim 5:21). Fulfilling this high calling requires multicultural insightfulness, that is, recognizing, respecting, and embracing a client's cultural identity. Culture represents a deeply embedded worldview that includes beliefs, values, customs, norms, traditions, family loyalties, and social structures. Applying multicultural insight requires clarity about how to do assessment ethically and with integrity. Fairness is not an abstract ideal; it is built into an instrument's design. We must be people with sharp moral vision and technical perceptiveness to recognize whether a measure is balanced, accurate, and true to its purpose for anyone it purports to measure. Artisans can explain how metrics and standards contribute to fairness in the tools they use. In this chapter we'll explore the link between multicultural attentiveness, fairness, and testing standards. In the following chapter we'll focus on greeting clients in all their uniqueness and cultural complexity. As counselors we conduct clinical assessments while strategically hearing and affirming diversity. Our ability to recognize nuances related to cultural identity and ethnic expressions within a client's story contributes to the formation of a deeper therapeutic connection.

Universal standards inform the development of psychological tools. When behavioral samples are gathered well, we can ensure that the comparisons made are never apples to oranges. Still, apples come in many varieties. It would not make sense to measure a McIntosh by the same criteria as one uses for a Golden Delicious. Further, guidelines and accountability requirements for use are essential when making high-stake judgments. The *Mental Measurements Yearbook* (*MMY*) publishes test reviews to promote transparency and formalize opportunities for critique (Carlson, Geisinger, & Jonson, 2017). Organizations such as the Association for Assessment and Research in Counseling (AARC; http://aarc-counseling.org/) offer guidance for users on best practice policies (e.g., Standards for Assessment in Mental Health Counseling; aarc-counseling .org/assets/cms/uploads/files/AACE-AMHCA.pdf).

The intense emphasis on training and accountability is driven by deceptive or incompetent misuse of tests over the past century. Striking historical controversies highlight ignorance of diversity or outright cultural bias. These missteps are regrettably associated with mental testing (Gould, 1981/1996; Samuda, 1998). In the chronicles of assessment history we can find dramatic attempts at social engineering through the use of measures unfair to ethnic subgroups. These events, now acknowledged as shameful, serve as the ongoing motivation for invested parties to hammer out elaborate yet appropriate protective ethical parameters. Human rights are at stake. Diligent integrity in assessment is warranted. This also reflects our responsibility as ambassadors of Jesus Christ.

During his ministry on earth, Jesus issued a sweeping command: "So in everything, do to others what you would have them do to you, for this sums up the Law and the Prophets" (Mt 7:12; cf. Lk 6:31). This is a fitting charge to launch our consideration of fairness in assessment. These memorable words come with the force of a divine command. As his disciples we must not settle for shallow or passive restraint from doing harm. Doing good is not merely avoiding wrong. Minimalistic moral instruction was commonplace in Jesus' day. The ethical bar that Jesus raises demands a vigorous pursuit of virtue. Disciples secure righteousness, goodness, and peace on behalf of others via advocacy. As mental health professionals (MHPs) and ministry leaders who utilize psychological instruments in counseling, we benefit from contemplating assessment ethics in personally meaningful ways. This enlivens our instincts for justice and stirs fervor to live out the high calling of the Great Commandment.

"GIVE ME YOUR TIRED, YOUR POOR, YOUR HUDDLED MASSES."

Mount Vesuvius, a volcano located on Italy's west coast, looms four thousand feet over the city of Naples. It's most famous eruption was in AD 79. In a sudden and vicious blast, toxic ash swiftly buried the cities of Pompeii and Herculaneum. Excavations unearthed graphic scenes of inhabitants baking bread or walking in the marketplace as the volcanic veil of death descended.

The repeated rumblings of Vesuvius in the early 1900s made the prospect for prosperity uncertain across the hills and farmlands surrounding the Bay of Naples. This was an era of strident class stratification. Peasant life in this harsh economic climate was precarious enough without a nagging fear of a looming, earth-scorching, geological peril.

Around the kitchen table on Sunday afternoons my grandfather often repeated tales of threat and struggle from his homeland of Italy. From the time I was a young child, this history lesson fed my inner sense of heritage. My maternal grandfather did not harbor a desire for adventure or express urges to leave the family farm. However, difficult economic forces pushed an ordinary teenager to leave his cherished homeland. He booked a passage on a steamer bound for a land he'd never seen. Paying his way to board the *Napolitan Prince*, my grandfather made the fateful journey—solo—to enter the land of opportunity.[1] This reluctant New World explorer, with less than twelve dollars in his pocket, left everything he knew to escape poverty and the spewing of Mount Vesuvius. Pasquale's hope was to secure a better future for the family he would one day have. The cost required saying goodbye to the love he'd known.

Upon his arrival in the harbor that Henry Hudson once explored, my grandfather sailed beneath the silent stare of Lady Liberty. The *Statue of Liberty Enlightening the World* is how French sculptor Frédéric-Auguste Bartholdi titled his creative masterpiece. The sculpture stands as a beacon to approaching ships. This symbol of a century-old republic welcomed generations of immigrants. Emma Lazarus, a female poet with a Jewish heritage, wrote "The New Colossus" to raise funds to construct the pedestal for that iconic statue. Read at its dedication ceremony, her poem became the stirring inscription on a Liberty Island plaque. Her inspirational phrases established the statue's symbolic association with hope, optimism, and freedom. This famous line proclaims America's bold invitation to the downtrodden: "Give me your tired, your poor, your huddled masses." Our nation called out to embrace all those who were inwardly "yearning to breathe free." The poem references Lady Liberty's grand torch lighting the path to better tomorrows. Displaced persons with no home, property, or fundamental human rights could secure a fresh beginning under the safe escort of her outstretched arm. Ordinary folks with meager resources could pass through this gateway with a profound anticipation of good fortune and an assured sense of place. Crossing the Atlantic provided an opportunity to realize one's dreams.

Beyond Lady Liberty, a very different French import draws our assessment attention. This transplanted implement is the Binet-Simon scale, an innovative psychological device formulated to appraise educational potential in children. The measure traversed the Atlantic to make its mark on the immigration process. Its appearance was not prompted by its creators. Rather, American ingenuity and our propensity for efficiency are to blame. The test was thought to have potential to temper the hospitality offered at America's gates. The ember

---

[1]The details described are a plausible match between available records on Ellis Island and family accounts. Not all factors fit with absolute precision. My grandfather's age was most likely fifteen, not seventeen, as recorded on the ship's manifest. These events occurred during a major influx of Italian immigrants. The core of this account rests on reasonable historical grounds.

of hope, held out to multitudes willing to undertake adventure, was in danger of fading under the shadow of a psychological test. This is the tale of a political experiment in social control with assessment at its center.

Immigrants who arrived in New York Harbor were subject to a detailed entry examination—that is, if the traveler was from one of the steerage decks. This interrogation step was unnecessary for those in first or second class (Richardson, 2003). This class-sensitive procedure reflects a selective screening policy based on a presumption of economic status. Passengers with funds to obtain upscale accommodations gained entry into the United States with a level of scrutiny that was nothing more than a formality. In fact, upper-class passengers did not even make the stop on Ellis Island. They would conveniently disembark directly on a New York City pier. The ship's manifest specifies that my grandfather proceeded through the more stringent receiving line on Ellis Island. Personnel for the review board were employees of the Department of Commerce and Labor, along with physicians in a newly formed government division that would eventually become the Public Health Service. Fortunately, my grandfather passed scrutiny. The box on the ship's record checked alongside his name pronounced him healthy—physically and mentally.

This story points to the danger of recklessly using psychological tools for bias and the impact that can have on vulnerable persons. Here is the thought-provoking question: Would my family genealogy be vastly different if my grandfather had been the target of further screening for mental ability? The occupation listed was laborer. It is unlikely that he could read, write, or converse in English. With little, if any, educational background, it's unreasonable to expect that he would perform well on an intellectual screening measure.[2] The intersection between this personal family account and the renowned historical testing event on Ellis Island makes me profoundly aware that decisions made using test results can markedly affect a person's life. In this case, misclassification could have altered an entire family tree! My grandfather's entry into the great American land of opportunity could have been blocked based on an irrelevant test. The tool was proven reputable for its intended purpose—educational placement of children. Its use with immigrants in its early format was not justified. The results obtained represent a tragic use of an objective procedure.

---

[2]The national park at Ellis Island in New York Harbor offers a tour that describes the medical, mental, economic, and political screening procedures. There is a room in this museum dedicated exclusively to "mental" testing. This is worth a visit for those who utilize standardized questions to inform critical decisions. My field trip while preparing this chapter was a moving experience.

SCIENTIFIC METHODS: TRIUMPH OR TRAVESTY?

Let's fill in the backstory to the experiment. Debate over an inclusive or exclusive immigration policy was heated in the opening years of the twentieth century. The discussion is not unlike that over undocumented immigrants in the present. America in that era was in dire need of strong backs and skilled hands for massive construction undertakings. But concern was widespread. Was the nation's population exploding rapidly and recklessly? Political pressure was mounting to tighten admission into the land of promise. The settled masses were fighting for higher wages. The prevailing mood was hostile toward newcomers who were willing to work for less.

This is the climate in which the proposal to use the Binet-Simon scale on new arrivals to the United States arose. The reception for modern novelties during this historical period was enthusiastic. The Wright brothers succeeded in manned flight at Kitty Hawk in 1903. The construction of the *Titanic* was completed in 1909. Optimism in human ingenuity was high, and so people were open to the promise of a scientific tool that could precisely measure human potential. The gate to America might narrow. Anyone labeled as a moron, an imbecile, or feebleminded (the terms of the day) could be excluded (Dorfman, 1982; Goddard, 1910/1991; Kamin, 1982). At that time, there was thought to be a connection between feeblemindedness (mental retardation) and the propensity to be socially degenerate. Further, people believed these traits to be hereditary. Evolutionary theory and notions of eugenics—good genes—were used to address social clashes. An Englishman and cousin to Charles Darwin, Francis Galton, was an unabashed proponent of eugenics and a pioneer during the Victorian era of psychometric testing (Murdoch, 2007). Eugenic assumptions prompted a movement insisting that safeguards be put into place to protect the biological fitness of the nation's gene pool. America's gates were open to the unwanted, undervalued, and unsupported. This policy was at odds with such a social evolutionary agenda. Psychological testing might hold an answer.

Compulsory education became a reality in the United States in the closing decade of the nineteenth century. Interestingly, this is the same period that produced psychological laboratories seeking methods to ascertain individual differences. Public awareness increased around the issue of mental deficiency. Students were required to attend school, but there were some who could not demonstrate the aptitude necessary to benefit from the formalized curriculum. Interest in techniques to evaluate student aptitude was at a fever pitch.

Early efforts to gauge mental ability focused on physical attributes, facial expressions, or physical deformity. One school of thought hypothesized cranium size as a tangible indication of intellectual potential. Others were captivated with phrenology, the study of the shape, bumps, and protrusions on the exterior of the skull. The next generation of measurement efforts moved from pure physical presentation to skills such as perceptual speed, visual recognition, or reaction thresholds. Researchers began to wonder if the five senses could be the means to quantify mental ability. Finally, models of assessment turned from physical prowess to mental problem solving. Tasks designed to test cognitive operations associated with higher reasoning, abstract thinking, language skills, verbal proficiency, and acquired knowledge grabbed top priority on the research agenda. Those investigating how to match children with the optimal educational programs realized that minds could not be measured in the same way as physical attributes. Techniques to quantify mental operations focused on precise observation of the accuracy, creativity, and speed of a solution generated for a specified problem. Researchers began to see how internal processes could affect behavior, speech, and reasoned response. The psychological test as a way to study a sample of behavior was born. The separation from its medical ancestor, the physical examination, was complete.

Henry Goddard was a prominent psychologist and director of research at a school for "feeble-minded," or difficult to educate, children in New Jersey. Through experience, he recognized that the prevailing devices to map individual differences, notoriously popular in laboratories, were not adequate to accomplish the task of measuring the inherent learning potential of struggling students. Goddard went abroad in 1908 to investigate options. In France, Alfred Binet and Théodore Simon had developed a novel scale to test mental capacity. This intelligence-gauging kit proved effective in clustering children into classifications that fit well with the enrollment requirements of educational programs. Goddard does not appear to have had any direct contact with the developers, but he did obtain a copy and undertook translation. As the scale crossed the Atlantic, its application broadened, and it became the basis for psychologists to diagnose mental retardation (Richardson, 2003).

Gregory (2014) raises a relevant point regarding this critical turning point in the history of assessment. For Binet and Simon, the tool was not a measuring device to pronounce detailed comparisons on a single human trait. Rather, it gathered samples of performance on problem-solving tasks to help determine placement in suitable educational contexts. At that point intelligence as a psychological construct was undefined. The measure, born out of respectable motives, was twisted to function as a diagnostic tool with implications for social control.

Political conjecture escalated regarding the costly care of those with cognitive capacity in the "moronic" range. The adoption of this descriptive term came from the Greek, *moronia*, meaning foolish (Gregory, 2014). The term itself contributed to the confusion of mental deficiency with morally undesirable behavior such as criminal activity, alcohol abuse, social maladies, addictions, and mental illness. Emerging psychological science didn't adequately differentiate levels of mental retardation and these social evils. Researchers did have awareness of the complexity of assessment and suspected that the available assessment options were not sophisticated enough to generate insight into such multifaceted concerns. Still, the nature-nurture debate reached a boiling point. Prejudice regarding underdeveloped mental capacity increased, along with political posturing.

This is the point at which questions began to be raised about whether the influx of immigrants was a plague or a blessing. As Goddard's research using his adaptation of the Binet-Simon scale became public, the plan surfaced to use this new device as a screening measure for adult immigrants. Goddard's assistants administered the scale to steerage-stowed immigrants whose sea legs were barely acclimated to solid ground. The majority of these subjects were reeling from the bleak and traumatic conditions aboard ship. The percentage of immigrants freshly arrived on US soil who were flagged as functioning in the "moronic range" was stunning. The prevalence rate among Jews, Hungarians, Italians, and Russians for extremely limited, moronic-level functioning ranged from 79% to 87%. Goddard presented his findings at the annual convention of the American Psychological Association in 1916 and published them a year later (Dorfman, 1982; Richardson, 2003).

These assessment results in this scenario were incredibly skewed because the application of the instrument was entirely unsuitable. First, it was not designed for that purpose. Second, the administration conditions placed every immigrant at a severe disadvantage. Traumatized by a long sea journey and without sufficient language mastery, subjects were frightened when confronted with these bizarre questions. Third, the assumption that any results could be generalized to the larger population of immigrants was flawed.

This spectacular example stands out as a classic illustration of an expectancy effect. That is, researchers formulate a bias and proceed to confirm precisely what they set out to prove (Kaplan & Saccuzzo, 2013). Gelb (1986) offers a balanced presentation, sorting myth from reality concerning Goddard's pronouncements on his research of Ellis Island immigration. The report of widespread, low intellectual capacity among immigrants was an outrageous exaggeration.

There was immediate recognition of the misapplication of the scale. This was plain in the comments of a physician assigned to conduct immigrant health screening (Richardson, 2003). Howard Andrew Knox, assistant surgeon at Ellis Island, raised questions about the measure, procedures, and results. Knox's objections went straight to the central concern. Any test designed for use with schoolchildren could not possibly be a dependable tool to detect mental retardation in illiterate adult immigrants. Many of those assessed had no formal education; thus, the relevance of a measure developed for use in the educational sphere was unfounded. Finally, Knox questioned the neutrality of the examiners and whether prejudices, political views, and personal motivations influenced the interpretation of responses.

Interestingly, his stand may be evidence of a jurisdictional turf war between physicians and those with the educational or psychological training to use these novel tools. A dispute between professional guilds over who was in the best position to ascertain mental competency may have been a factor. In any case, this friction was an ominous sign of the battle that lay ahead between medical physicians and mind specialists known as psychologists.

Regardless, Knox astutely spoke out about important concerns. His one-hundred-year-old commentary is worth reading today. Valid mental appraisal must use an individual's native language. A tool originating in French and subsequently adopted into English could not be of value in assessing immigrants who spoke neither language. Meaning is lost in each progressive translation! Knox concluded with a grave concern—the classification of immigrants had been based solely upon a single cognitive test, inappropriately applied. It was not surprising that application of this set of irrelevant items might classify the majority of such individuals in the moronic range of intellectual functioning. Knox contended that if the test items were adapted to reflect the actual conditions in the cultural *context* of these subjects, nearly all would classify as possessing average intelligence (Richardson, 2003). Knox's work sends an important message about the importance of those undertaking assessment developing a multicultural perspective.

Knox's critique regarding the flaws in Goddard's psychometric effort was a foreshadowing of the contemporary standards. The principles he articulated reflect (1) the rudiments of test development, item content, and measurement tool selection; (2) the necessity of objective administration; and (3) the evidence-based application of results. Knox proposed his own imaginative procedures as an alternative. He offered language-free, puzzle-style tasks, which would have been a far fairer method to screen for mental retardation. His techniques contributed to the development of the nonverbal performance elements in intellectual measures. The advanced distinction between verbal reasoning and a cognitive capacity to solve problems or adjust to environmental demands continues today.

Thankfully, my ancestor from Naples stepped into this country as one among the tired, poor, and huddled masses yearning for freedom. He was never required to demonstrate proficiency outside of his native tongue on a culturally biased intelligence test. Nevertheless, this family narrative is one I bear in mind to recall the historical controversies associated with assessment.

The erroneous application of any measure in educational, government, medical, or employment settings remains a legitimate concern to this day. Administration of unfair tests under unfavorable circumstances can still occur. This explains why measures in use are subject to heavy scrutiny to remove unintended and unfair cultural or ethnic bias. These historical events explain the strict training requirements stipulated for anyone who uses these potent measures. Allegations of ethnic bias or outright discrimination in assessment procedures raise justifiable discomfort and suspicion regarding the merits of assessment. There is complete agreement that those unfounded applications of intelligence measures produced a dark season in the early growth of the psychological profession. These were blunders and exploitive experiments. This was not a victory for scientific psychology. And yet, the publication of results launched the practice of peer review that brought erroneous assumptions to the surface. Lessons of justice are evident in these pioneering efforts at intellectual, mental health, and "moral" screening.

Assessment is powerful. Science can develop measures to serve and benefit. For this to be fair, it is essential to take every precaution when classifying and categorizing individuals according to results on a select sample of items. Psychological tools brandished destructively can isolate and discriminate. Conversely, when applied with compassion, understanding, and finesse, they can shed light on distinctions that can become a remarkable means for connection.

From a Christian worldview, Scripture offers principles that speak to matters of accountability and justice. The Lord God desires his honorable and fair nature to permeate the social order of creation (Ps 76; Mic 6:6-8). Scripture is consistent in expressing the Lord's special regard for the poor, oppressed, alien, and weak (Deut 10:18-19). The term for justice as referenced in Scripture is rooted in straightness, fairness, and balance. Ultimately, *justice* implies measuring up to the Lord's righteous standards. This premise follows. Measurement informs decisions that affect persons who are weak, exposed, or at risk. Those who implement these pronouncements are accountable to the Creator who treasures justice.

ESSENTIAL ELEMENTS OF MEASUREMENT SCALES

Assessments must have integrity at three levels: (1) internally, or within the test itself; (2) procedurally, or throughout the administration; and (3) externally, in the interpretation of results. The components for integrity within each level are articulated in professional ethical codes as well as in the agreed-upon standards for educational and psychological test development, credentialing procedures, and implementation (American Educational Research Association, American Psychological Association, & National Council on Measurement in Education, 2014). There are minimum competencies for the proper use of tests (Moreland, Eyde, Robertson, Primoff, & Most, 1995). In summary, here is an outline of five elements that solidify the strength of an instrument: a conceptual model, standardization, reliability, validity, and utility.

Conceptual models. Assessment is not feasible without hypothetical assumptions. A test collects samples of behavior under uniform conditions. The composition of the sample reflects critical assumptions between what can be readily observed and what one wishes to know. Each measure reflects a theory about how behaviors—whether overt or covert—can be operationalized and quantified. A behavior sample is given a numerical value with descriptive meaning. Counselors must come to recognize the assumptions beneath the test to explain its underlying mechanism, model, or motivation. In the historical example explored earlier, the Binet-Simon scale collected samples of problem-solving behavior on school-type tasks. If the expectation is to make a prediction about future educational performance in an academic setting, the conceptual assumption behind these items would make sense. As a means to estimate intelligence in adults with limited education in order to predict economic contribution to society, the model behind the measure is questionable.

In the field of mental health, each measure represents a conceptual model. The Minnesota Multiphasic Personality Inventory (MMPI-2) was built on a premise of dustbowl empiricism—seemingly random items were selected not based on a theory or line of logic but because they could readily distinguish between diagnostic groups (Nichols, 2011). The House-Tree-Person has its grounding in the projective hypothesis—given an unstructured or ambiguous stimuli, a person will draw on his inner unconscious needs, motives, and conflicts to respond (Wenck, 1977). There is an evolutionary-based personality theory beneath the Millon instruments (Jankowski, 2002). Even diagnostic categories rely on conceptual models. It is important to recognize that every subjective clinical judgment rests on a set of assumptions. The advantage of standardized instruments is that the underlying theory or assumptions have been subjected to professional scrutiny. They have been used in research trials and have undergone review and revision based on the results. Opportunities for review can promote multicultural fairness because numerous voices are invited to comment.

Assessments collect samples according to articulated, defined relationships. Clinicians should have a firm grasp of the underlying model central to the premise of the measure. As counselors, we must understand the connection between what is observed and the insights that can be drawn from that. A client may give informed consent, but we are responsible to provide the rationale for implementing the assessment.

Standardization. The broad heading of standardization includes the features related to psychometrics, statistics, and norming, or control, population. Tests undergo rigorous procedures to collect information on an initial, well-defined population. The expectation is that every psychometric measure will come with an operational manual with complete disclosure of how the control group was gathered and its demographics. Commonly researchers will diversify the sample using participation ratios from a recent census. It is critical that we be familiar with the research sample that an instrument used—particularly the developmental stage, cultural background, and socioeconomic status of the group—in order to consider whether it is a reasonable match for our client. We must ascertain how well the standardization sample reflects our client, and we can only proceed to make inferences about a client if he or she fits within the norms of the instrument.

Information on test development includes detailed descriptions of how each item was formed, reviewed, and revised. This will reveal if there was any statistical investigation on differential item functioning, that is, if the difficulty of certain items varies depending on ethnic background. In other cases, instruments may be screened by experts for language clarity and vernacular that reduce comprehension by select participants. Looking at how the items actually perform not only results in a better measure; it further reduces cultural bias.

Finally, the manual or guidelines for the assessment tool that one chooses must include instructions for use, scoring, interpretation, and reporting results. These procedures are crucial. The clinician must attempt to do everything that can reasonably be done to replicate the exact conditions used with the norming sample in order to obtain a fair comparison. This gives us a meaningful way to discuss traits, conditions, or patterns with clients who are trusting us to be informed, fair, and just.

Reliability. The term *reliability* refers to the consistency and stability of a tool. Reliability procedures reduce the degree of error in a measure and specify the anticipated consistency between repeated administrations at specific intervals under identical or equivalent conditions. The internal consistency of a measure can be determined through a variety of statistical procedures. Reliability findings are automatically included in all contemporary test manuals.

We meet clients with unique characteristics. Yet each time a measure is administered, we can trust from our review of the reliability data that the score produced is reasonably free from error that could influence our understanding.

Inter-rater reliability is the reliability subtype that focuses on the potential score variability when the measure is administered by different users. Good measures yield consistent results no matter who puts them into use or when that is done.

Validity. *Validity* refers to the degree to which the test measures in real life what it was intended to measure when developed in the laboratory. Validity determines the parameters around what can be derived from a measure. Establishing validity involves considerable complexity. In addition, there are several subtypes of validity to examine. The chapter on redemptive validity (chap. 7) will discuss the major validity categories and add another. This expansion of validity relates directly to the Christian worldview. We must consider how the behavioral area investigated by the measure can be viewed though the redemptive sacrifice of our Lord and the comforting ministry of the Holy Spirit.

Utility. Utility has to do with how a measure will be put to use and whom it will be applied to. Utility encompasses all of the potential pragmatic details: Can a client read the questions, comprehend items, communicate information, and perform up to his potential? What does it demand of a counselor to administer, score, and comprehend? Essentially, utility answers questions regarding feasibility, effort, investment, risk, and cost. When it's time to incorporate the results into a report, communicate them to another professional, or tuck them away in a file, will the enterprise be worthwhile for the client, who submits to participation at our request?

These psychometric areas are necessary topics in comprehensive assessment texts assigned in counseling courses (i.e., Hays, 2017; Whiston, 2017). Mastery of these concepts by all who use instruments is essential. Let's conclude with an additional charge from the Word of God that we must take to heart.

HONEST SCALES

In the book of Leviticus, we read the following:

> Do not use dishonest standards when measuring length, weight or quantity. Use honest scales and honest weights, an honest ephah and an honest hin. I am the LORD your God, who brought you out of the land of Egypt. (Lev 19:35-36)[3]

This statement speaks to the unique responsibilities of Christian MHPs. The biblical principle of justice has been a means to distinguish people who honor God from those who do not recognize the lordship of Jehovah. The context of the passage is primarily commerce and marketplace ethics, so those of us who use psychological tools could inadvertently miss the relevancy of this principle. But this admonition has something important to say about assessment integrity.

A parallel passage appears in Deuteronomy:

> Do not have two differing weights in your bag—one heavy, one light. Do not have two differing measures in your house—one large, one small. You must have accurate and honest weights and measures, so that you may live long in the land the LORD your God is giving you. For the LORD your God detests anyone who does these things, anyone who deals dishonestly. (Deut 25:13-16)

This is not an isolated charge or an obscure biblical declaration. The core message is apparent within the wisdom of Proverbs (11:1; 16:11; 20:10, 23). Even the prophets reference the importance of justice when conducting any activity of measurement (Amos 8:5; Mic 6:11). Stated in the vernacular of our day, there is to be no cheating in any form among God's people. Fairness is essential. A fair trade requires items be sold by weight or apportioned into set amounts. In regulated transactions, the Lord will not tolerate the deliberate, deceptive shortchanging of consumers. This is not a pragmatic recommendation given purely to fortify a respectable business reputation. This is a declaration of how God's people are to reflect holiness in the public square. These commands reference an essential attribute that is to set apart God's people. Honesty in measurement is a reflection of God's justice.

Being shrewd in a business deal or when making a trade in the ancient world was not a matter of shame. Instead, it was a point of honor and a demonstration

---

[3]The ephah is a means to quantify dry materials, such as a bushel of grain, and a hin is a container that measures liquid (Porter, 1957).

of cleverness. The general rule for a market transaction was "let the buyer beware." If a customer lost on a business transaction, it was attributed to his lack of diligence or prudence. When a seller prevailed, all the better for the seller! Negotiation was the rule. In real terms, it was good practical strategy not to turn your back when your merchandise was being sorted, weighed, or packaged. Merchants were not required to be accountable to a local official to calibrate the scale periodically. There was no government regulation or seal of approval. Imagine the complaints that would ensue in our day if the media broke a story that the pumps at a chain of gasoline stations intentionally delivered fewer gallons than the pump indicated! By contrast, when the Lord gave these instructions to his people, it was not considered uncommon or deceptive for a merchant to have different scales or weights as a means to stretch profit. The message of Scripture is unmistakable: display God's holiness by using fair weights. The Lord makes his insistence plain and repeats it for good measure.

Can this biblical principle apply to the assessment of human characteristics? Undoubtedly. In the New Testament, we see Jesus' anger at corruption in the temple courts. He condemned money-changing fees for pilgrims who came to offer sacrifice. Jesus cried out against exorbitant pricing within the walls of his Father's house. He prohibited preying upon those with burdened hearts who were on a mission to worship. These practices were not out of character for the dominant culture. In fact, they might be sound business practices. But in the Lord's house, they were not acceptable.

The essential biblical message is this: the truthfulness and fairness we may or may not display in our interactions and transactions are reflections of our heart. A righteous and holy God, the one who will eventually weigh all things, attends to such matters with an eye toward justice. After all, he has numbered the very hairs on our heads and sees even the smallest of sparrows. Does it not follow that he knows the condition of our hearts (Mt 10:30; Lk 12:7)? The Lord does not have admiration for his followers who engage in deceptive schemes; he has only judgment and reproof. The servants of the Lord are called to conduct business according to kingdom ethics, no matter what typically prevails in the common marketplace.

When it comes to counseling, assessment tools help us remain objective. An external point of reference brings integrity to the interpersonal exchange and accountability to an otherwise subjective exchange. In the same way that honest use of the scales reflected a merchant's integrity and earned customers' respect, using assessment tools effectively can increase trust and mutuality in our relationships with clients. Those committed to honoring God are held to a higher level of accountability. Beyond the standards of professional practice, Christ-followers operate in obedience to the Lord. Referencing stable, scientifically valid measure is a matter of walking rightly and justly before the Lord (Mic 6:8). Thus, Christian MHPs strive to use honest scales in a manner that brings glory to God.

PERSONALIZE ASSESSMENT RISK

As helpers we must personalize the risk associated with the application of assessment measures. This will help us increase empathy and concern for clients while staying alert to issues of partiality and fairness. Objectivity is the professional stance most valuable in assessment. Nevertheless, reviewing part two of the Great Commandment can stir caution and sensibility: "love your neighbor as yourself "(Lev 19:18; Lk 10:27). As counselors we assume the role of neighbor to those in need, so it's imperative for us to take these words of Jesus into helping conversations. We are to love our clients as we love ourselves.

When I am contemplating care for my clients, I have to imagine how I would feel if a beloved family member of mine sought counseling from an MHP whom I supervised, instructed, or encouraged to use assessment. My hope is that the tools chosen for use would be worthwhile, that they would be administered with diligence and skill, and that the assessment application would help my family member grow as a person. I remember my grandfather, who sacrificed much for a voyage to America and whose dream could have been blocked by the equivalent of a psychological inquisition. This is my private reminder to maintain a highly sensitive ethics meter whenever I reach for a suitable assessment tool, to grant my clients the extraordinary care I would wish for those precious to me. Work out a personal scenario that will exercise your own imagination to promote fairness.

THE GREAT INVITATION

The poem by Emma Lazarus invited those with paltry resources from across the globe to come to America. This core value is essential to the heritage of multicultural openness in this country. Her words gave meaning to an icon that declared hope to a needy world (Lazarus, 1883). The Statue of Liberty stands to welcome the "wretched refuse," the "homeless," and "tempest-tossed." In this controversial assessment experiment at Ellis Island, the greatness and the vulnerabilities of American values are evident. Fortunately, this was only a research venture, and the faulty application did not become policy.

There are other assessment incidents recorded in the history of psychology. There were allegations that schoolchildren across America were inappropriately placed in special classes based on tests that were culturally unfair. In World War I, African American military recruits may not have been given an optimal opportunity to display their capabilities on group-administered intelligence tests. Prejudiced assumptions and unfair procedures thus affected assignments and placement. Assessments and the persons who use them are prone to bias. This explains why the profession has standards to ensure fairness and justice through transparency, training, and accountability. Stories of family members from ethnic and cultural groups who experienced adverse consequences of cultural bias can awaken deeply held grief and indignation. Our country may have a grand symbol of welcome to those seeking asylum, but it is not a perfect place of refuge. Therefore, Christian helpers must attend to a more remarkable kingdom. Jesus Christ issued the finest words of invitation:

> Come to me, all you who are weary and burdened, and I will give you rest. Take my yoke upon you and learn from me, for I am gentle and humble in heart, and you will find rest for your souls. For my yoke is easy and my burden is light. (Mt 11:28-29)

We greet clients on a small island along the journey of life. Our support and caring presence are an extension of the ministry of the Great Comforter (Jn 14:16-27). Clients come to address feelings of danger or fear provoked by trauma or discrimination experienced along the way. We use subjective interpersonal experience combined with objective assessment techniques to yield insights into the hidden places of the human heart. Integrity and multicultural fairness must guide our approach and decisions. Our mission is to connect with others to realize the benefits and security of this invitation from our Lord.

REFERENCES

American Educational Research Association, American Psychological Association, & National Council on Measurement in Education. (2014). *Standards for educational and psychological testing.* Washington, DC: American Educational Research Association.

Carlson, J. F., Geisinger, K. F., & Jonson, J. L. (Eds.). (2017). *The twentieth mental measurements yearbook.* Lincoln, NE: Buros Institute of Mental Measurements.

Dorfman, D. D. (1982). Henry Goddard and the feeble-mindedness of Jews, Hungarians, Italians, and Russians. *American Psychologist, 37*(1), 96-97.

Gelb, S. A. (1986). Henry H. Goddard and the immigrants, 1910–1917: The studies and their social context. *Journal of the History of the Behavioral Sciences, 22*(4), 324-331.

Goddard, H. (1910/1991). Four hundred feeble-minded children classified by the Binet method. *Journal of Genetic Psychology: Research and Theory on Human Development, 152*(4), 437-447.

Gould, S. J. (1981/1996). *The mismeasure of man.* New York: Norton.

Gregory, R. J. (2014). *Psychological testing: History, principles, and applications* (7th ed.). Boston: Pearson.

Hays, D. G. (2017). *Assessment in counseling: Procedures and practices* (6th ed.). Alexandria, VA: American Counseling Association.

Jankowski, D. (2002). *A beginner's guide to the MCMI-III.* Washington, DC: American Psychological Association.

Kamin, L. J. (1982). Mental testing and immigration. *American Psychologist, 37*(1), 97-98.

Kaplan, R. M., & Saccuzzo, D. P. (2013). *Psychological testing: Principles, applications, and issues* (8th ed.). Belmont, CA: Thomson Wadsworth.

Lazarus, E. (1883). *The new colossus.* Retrieved from Statue of Liberty & Ellis Island Website: http://www.libertystatepark.com/emma.htm

Moreland, K. L., Eyde, L. D., Robertson, G. J., Primoff, E. S., & Most, R. B. (1995). Assessment of test user qualifications: A research-based measurement procedure. *American Psychologist, 50*(1), 14-23.

Murdoch, S. (2007). *IQ: A smart history of a failed idea.* Hoboken, NJ: John Wiley & Sons.

Nichols, D. S. (2011). *Essentials of MMPI-2 Assessment* (2nd ed.). Hoboken, NJ: John Wiley & Sons.

Porter, H. (1957). Weights and measures. In J. Orr (Ed.), *The international standard Bible encyclopedia*, (Vol. V, pp. 3079-3081). Grand Rapids, MI: Eerdmans.

Richardson, J. T. E. (2003). Howard Andrew Knox and the origins of performance testing on Ellis Island, 1912–1916. *History of Psychology, 6*(2), 143-170.

Samuda, R. J. (1998). *Psychological testing of American minorities: Issues and consequences* (2nd ed.). Thousand Oaks, CA: Sage.

Wenck, L. S. (1977). *House-tree-person drawings: An illustrated diagnostic handbook.* Los Angeles: Western Psychological Services.

Whiston, S. C. (2017). *Principles and applications of assessment in counseling* (5th ed.). Belmont, CA: Cengage.

CHAPTER SIX

CULTURAL IDENTITY AND HABITS
FOR HOLISTIC ASSESSMENT

But the wisdom that comes from heaven is first of all pure; then peace-loving,
considerate, submissive, full of mercy and good fruit, impartial and sincere.
Peacemakers who sow in peace reap a harvest of righteousness.

JAMES 3:17-18

THEOLOGICAL THEME

Peacemaking

ASSESSMENT TO EMBRACE DIVERSITY

The prevailing ethical codes and standards issue a consistent declaration, namely, that the responsibility for fair and proper use of assessment measures rests on the counselor (American Counseling Association, 2014; Association for Assessment and Counseling, 2003). Furthermore, best practice, according to the Standards for Multicultural Assessment, entails accounting for the impact of age, culture, ability, race, ethnic group, national origin, gender, religion/spirituality, sexual orientation, linguistic background, socioeconomic status, or any other personal characteristics (e.g., disability or health condition; Association for Assessment in Counseling and Education, 2012). This list of individual attributes and group associations captures an extensive range of diversity factors. Counselors must carefully weigh these features with skill to further their understanding of clients and their stories. What makes this diversity challenge so stimulating is that these descriptors do not represent discrete or uniform categories. Instead, each factor occurs along a continuum—a gradient of intensity—in terms of its contribution to personal and collective identity.

Diversity contributes much to our personhood, commonality, and exceptionality. Further, cultural orientation is valuable in comprehending and predicting relational patterns. In initial contacts with clients we inevitably isolate and define the presenting problem. However, zeroing in on the problem itself is nearly useless unless we also become acquainted with how the client is embedded within a cultural system. Ample research validates the construct of ethnic, racial, and cultural identity (Burkard & Ponterotto, 2007; Paniagua & Yamada, 2013). The technical term to encompass both the critical importance of race and group affiliation is *ethnocultural identity*. There is variation in how ethnicity and cultural influences merge, overlap, or create tension (Marsella & Yamada, 2013). The ordinary language of cultural identity captures social-ethnic influences and group identification. Cultural identity includes our emotional connection to heritage, race, tradition, community, and family network. From these ties emerge socially constructed rituals and expectations that regulate the expression of traits. Thus, cultural identity influences behavior patterns, daily routines, and communication style.

Our social-cultural world instills values about time, self, and authority. In fact, culture even controls the meaning behind speaking with a therapist (Paniagua, 2014). Those from an Asian or African American culture might well classify a therapist as a type of physician. Hispanics may think of counselors as folk healers, and American Indians may envision a helper as a wise medicine person or tribal elder. Thus, the client's cultural lens turns on the therapist and launches expectations into motion from the earliest moments of contact. These may influence beliefs about the self, the collective, or the basis of mental illness as medical-scientific versus social-spiritual.

Assessment commences by gathering basic demographic descriptions (see fig. 6.1). Responses from survey items or checklists can quickly fill in those diversity-factor blanks on the counselor's need-to-know list. Categorical descriptors fit neatly and concisely on documentation forms. Yet there is a distinct disadvantage to having data that remain only at this simplistic level. Checked boxes cannot generate familiarity with a client's cultural identity. Answers on these items provide instant labels and quick identification. Meaningful gains and an increased understanding of the other are negligible; the lines of solidarity or tension are filled in via conversation. Naked demographic data are like vague coordinates that point only to a broad region on a map. These might take you near the destination city you wish to explore. Yet, without a specific GPS location, you are not able to visit a friend's new apartment, savor a local meal at neighborhood café, enter a museum, or attend a ball game. Demographic tags offer an obligatory starting point. They yield little when they leave attraction or empathy unstirred. This general informational input can be used to awaken our curiosity and prompt topics to explore in an interview. (Techniques to generate such a data trail will be highlighted in chap. 9.)

Client Demographic Survey

Sex: ◯ Male ◯ Female   **Age:** _____   **Birthdate:** _____/_____/_____

How do you describe yourself?

◯ American Indian or Alaska Native   ◯ Hawaiian or Other Pacific Islander

◯ Asian or Asian American   ◯ Black or African American

◯ Hispanic or Latino   ◯ Non-Hispanic White

Marital Status: ◯ Married ◯ Divorced ◯ Widowed ◯ Separated ◯ Never married
◯ Member of unmarried couple

Employment Status:

◯ Employed   ◯ Self-employed   ◯ Unemployed over 1 year

◯ Unemployed less than 1 year ◯ Homemaker   ◯ Student

◯ Retired   ◯ Unable to work

Religious Preference:

◯ Muslim   ◯ Seventh-Day Adventist   ◯ Mormon

◯ Roman Catholic   ◯ Christian Scientist   ◯ Protestant

◯ Orthodox (e.g., Greek, Russian) ◯ Jewish   ◯ Other: _____

Would you describe yourself as "born-again" or an evangelical Christian?

◯ Yes   ◯ No   ◯ Don't know

Are you a member of a church, synagogue, mosque, or other organized religious group?

◯ Yes   ◯ No

Have you attended a church, synagogue, mosque, or other organized religious service in the last seven days?

◯ Yes   ◯ No

Figure 6.1. Sample client demographic survey items. (Greggo, Stephen P. [2019]. *Assessment for Counseling in Christian Perspective*. Downers Grove, IL: InterVarsity Press.)

Cultural Identity Questionnaire

Describe how you identify yourself from a cultural or diversity perspective (e.g., ethnicity, race, nationality, religion, sexual orientation, age, or physical challenges).

Tell about the ways that your cultural network and family heritage shape your everyday life.

What is particularly important for me as your counselor to understand about your culture and family relationships?

Cultural communities and extended families tend to understand problems in ways that might not be recognized by mental health professionals. How would you describe your problem to someone in your circle of friends and family?

Are there ways that your relatives, friends, or members of your community have made your problem bearable (better)? What about pressure that makes this issue more difficult (worse)?

Share particular ways that you may relate to cultural expectations differently from others in your family. What do family members say about these distinctions?

Are there religious or faith perspectives from your cultural background that are important for us to take into consideration in our counseling conversations?

Figure 6.2. Sample inquiries into cultural identity[1]

[1]These sample questions are adopted from the Cultural Assessment Interview Protocol (Grieger, 2013) and the Cultural Formulation Interview (CFI) (American Psychiatric Association, 2013b). The full CFI from *DSM*-5 is available at no charge for research or use with clients.

The effective helper explores the depth and magnitude of social and cultural influences (see fig. 6.2). Our interest is not to establish an accurate label or to open a polite means to acknowledge customs.[2] This search is to discover the force of gravity that grounds a client to traditions, community, and a unique sense of self. How does the client experience interpersonal support or the rebuke of shame? What does she see, smell, and hear when she closes her eyes, taps her red slippers together, and whispers, "There's no place like home"? Who are the faces that he hungers to see with approving smiles when he does the "right thing"? What actions in a group setting feel normal, special, threatening, or immobilizing? We investigate cultural forces and diversity factors to recognize "ties that bind" and remarkable sources of hope located in the surrounding community. Cultural identity tells us about underlying pledges that maintain loyalty to community, family, and tradition.

MULTICULTURAL INSIGHTFULNESS AND PEACEMAKING

A mental health evaluation appraises how the client is functioning in his or her present life circumstances and social-environmental context. Awareness of cultural identity contributes to a holistic portrait. The pressures or comforts that a client experiences as a person in community must be brought to the surface. Understanding a client's worldview, inner narrative, and social interconnectedness opens the way for trust and partnership in the therapeutic relationship. Cultural awareness is important in choosing the appropriate assessment method and instrumentation as well as in administration of instruments and interpretation of results.

Earlier I defined multicultural insightfulness as an ability to recognize, respect, and embrace a client's cultural identity. The counseling profession depicts cultural competence along a continuum (Hong, Garcia, & Soriano, 2013). On one end of the continuum are interpersonal behaviors such as deliberate destructiveness, patronization, or cultural blindness. Marked by lack of insight and carelessness, these behaviors can lead to damaging microaggressions and cultural malpractice. At this end of the continuum behaviors stem from ethnocentric blinders causing people to confuse values and behaviors from the dominant culture with universal ideals. Obviously, this results in less than ideal client service. Counselor education and supervision ignite a progression from a self-limiting ethnocentrism toward clinician awareness of cultural identity

---

[2]A structured interview into cultural identity is available within *DSM*-5 (APA, 2013a, pp. 749-759). It can be retrieved free of charge (APA, 2013b): http://www.multiculturalmentalhealth.ca/clinical-tools/cultural-formulation.

and diversity. At the other end of the continuum is multicultural competence. This entails (1) awareness of the dimensions and relevance of culture; (2) knowledge of one's own cultural grounding, along with recognition of obvious or highly nuanced cultural differences; and (3) skill in reflective thinking, assessment, and intervention. Proficiency in cultural competence is considered a lifelong goal in professional development.

It is worth identifying how clinical cultural competence reaffirms the ancient Christian discipline of hospitality. The New Testament epistle of James gives considerable instruction acknowledging diversity. Believers are instructed to cultivate the habit of welcoming others as equals and to avoid subtle practices that display favoritism (Jas 2:1-13). Christians are called to act consistently and with honor toward others despite differences in status or culture. We are called to overcome the all-too-conventional human propensity to prejudice and partiality. "My brothers and sisters, believers in our glorious Lord Jesus Christ must not show favoritism" (Jas 2:1). James points out how easy it is to be impressed by another's looks, style, wealth, or social prominence. As our gaze is drawn toward those with much, we lose sight of those with less prominence, wealth, or familiarity.

Scripture exemplifies the behavioral principle of reciprocal inhibition, the idea that one cannot engage in two mutually exclusive behaviors simultaneously. We cannot show favoritism while sowing peace. Treating others fairly and with honor involves welcoming them in gentle, courteous, and peaceable ways. This is the means to demonstrating reconciliation that honors God. As Christian counselors we operate in faith as we attune to the differences and perspectives of others and accommodate religious and cultural identity, as well as differences in gender, sexual orientation, or age.

Becoming a person who sows peace requires prayerful examination. We must seek the Lord for grace to relate to others with pure motives, deliberate consideration, sincerity, an attitude of mercy, and humble submissiveness. This well-ordered honoring of others ultimately undermines the naturally occurring, destructive, ethnocentric flaw of showing partiality (Jas 3:17). Our upbringing and past experiences of violence or oppression may hamper this turn toward purposeful peacemaking. Nevertheless, with alertness and intention, these habits can become qualities that produce a harvest of righteousness. Our lives reflect this value through understanding, willingness to adjust communication to better engage others, and openness to people different from us. We exercise multicultural insightfulness not solely to meet ethical expectations or to display cultural competence in our professional role. Rather, we have a mandate to sow peace in relationships because that is how we imitate Jesus Christ (Mt 5:9; Jas 3:18). This becomes even more important when we remember that the therapeutic relationship is central to the promotion of growth and healing in our clients.

A faith commitment to engender peace will influence assessment decisions. Consider these provocative questions related to multicultural sensitivity on a practical level.

- Is the selection of an instrument a matter of convenience, availability, or fixed routine? Or is selection the result of a thorough review of its normative details and a deliberate decision that it is the right fit for this client's cultural background?

- Will screening measures or demographic surveys facilitate appropriate person-treatment matches? Could a response in one direction exclude a client from receiving the care he or she is requesting?

- Can clients incriminate or disqualify themselves for care by inadvertently revealing personality factors or personal history details?

- How are personal hunches and examiner bias recognized and checked?

- What safeguards surround the implementation of technology, particularly for those not at ease with personal disclosure to a computer-administered instrument?

- What precautions are in place to ensure best practice in regard to religious, cultural, and socioeconomic variables in the application of clinical assessment?

- Do diagnostic labels, functional pathologies, or demographic descriptors become taglines or nicknames that define clients in peer-to-peer conversations?

- Are client histories retold using stereotypical formulations? Is there a dedication to illustrate cultural depth, personal strengths, admirable characteristics, and future hopes, even when these are hidden behind suffering, hostility, or an air of entitlement?

The following strategies are intended to promote the establishment of systematic procedures that affirm diversity and multicultural insightfulness. We can begin to sow peacefulness long before hearing a client's story in all its cultural perspective.

Be informed of historical disputes on cultural fairness. Clinicians serve clients well when they are aware of the contentious disputes associated with measurement concepts or instruments. Academic instruction moves rapidly through the history of the profession. In the domain of assessment, linger a while on injustices and misappropriation of tests in material on multicultural assessment (Hays, 2017). These are cited within ethical considerations (e.g., litigation) or when evaluating validity of central constructs (e.g., group differences in intelligence; Whiston, 2017). Recognizing explicit concerns from the past can alert us to resistance from clients who have come to anticipate that these evaluations do not serve their ethnic community well. Direct and informative explanation of how assessment results will benefit a client's care meets the ethical expectation regarding informed consent (American Educational Research Association, American Psychological Association, & National Council on Measurement in Education, 2014). More pointedly, this transparency goes a long way toward building rapport across cultural lines and paves the way for a productive assessment process.

Mental health professionals (MHPs) need to stay up to date on the literature connected to measurement instruments in use. For example, imagine a new computer-administered instrument is developed to assess ability to sustain one's attention and impulse control. The test manual will explain the theory, etiology, and conceptualization of attention-deficit assumptions bound into the measure. We need to review the cited literature to understand how progression in the understanding of the concern itself has affected available appraisal methods. Once we understand that, we're able to consider how the definition of the construct applies across cultural groups.

Another important factor to investigate from a historical and client-risk perspective is how a given measure accurately measures the characteristic of interest. Clinicians should recognize the following concepts.

- True positive: the test indicates that a condition is present, and it is.
- True negative: the test reveals that a condition is not present, and indeed it is not a factor.
- False positive: the test may point to a condition being present even when it is not.
- False negative: the test may not detect the condition even though it is indeed present.

These terms describe the degree to which a scale reflects the actual state of affairs in a client's life. The history of assessment suggests that it is important for clinicians to know how well a test may predict a hit or allow a miss on the question at hand. The precision level of prediction determines what assessment steps must follow. Those familiar with the published information regarding a test's accuracy in prediction can use the measure to the best possible benefit of their clients. For example, it may not be an insurmountable problem if a screening measure for attention deficit hyperactivity disorder (ADHD) generates a few false positives along with true positives, as long as there are follow-up procedures that subsequently rule out the diagnosis in cases where the screening measure is oversensitive.

Evaluate novel methodologies and major instrument revisions. We must scrutinize new assessment tools and technological advancements with an alertness to multicultural implications. Responsible counselors conduct a thoughtful utility analysis with a specific clinical setting in view. What cultural groups are likely to seek out services in this setting? Think assessment purpose, clinical setting, and client cultural identity. Develop a thorough understanding of a measure's underlying assumptions. This requires one to acquire information beyond the endorsements supplied by the publisher. Seek out potential risks and predictable cautions from peer-reviewed journal articles and formal published reviews. *The Mental Measurements Yearbook* and database (unl.edu/buros) are longstanding, reputable sources for scholarly reviews (Carlson, Geisinger, & Jonson, 2017). Published reviews reference strengths, deficiencies, unknowns, and competing strategies. Typical reviews include commentary on how the norming sample was selected and how it compares to recent census data. If there are noticeable gaps in the ethnic distribution of the sample, this should be noted in the review.

Finally, we must stay alert to trends related to the larger questions bound to particular assessment methods; for example, the limits and advantages of self-reporting have long been a matter of interest. Therefore, while the measure itself may be solid, we need to consider the motivation of the client to cooperate with self-report questionnaires. Counselors have to contemplate in advance how the client might respond to the recommendations that could follow. Consider this scenario. Assessment results from ratings scales and behavioral inventories are highly influential in arriving at an ADHD diagnosis. This is the first step in initiating treatment with stimulant medication. Yet many students are well educated on ADHD symptoms prior to evaluation, and this advanced exposure, coupled with a particular desired outcome, can influence profile results (McCabe, Teter, & Boyd, 2006; Sollman, Ranseen, & Berry, 2010).

We also need an informed perspective on how our findings and recommendations could be applied in therapy. If symptom severity scales generate information that could later be shared with a health provider, this possibility should be revealed in the disclosure. It is essential to know not only the background of the measure we plan to use but the rationale for seeking this information. Be up front and candid with clients, particularly when addressing diversity and multicultural differences. Work from the outset to reduce suspicion regarding how a measure may invade privacy or be used as a means to pressure them into a decision they may resist because of cultural expectations.

Remain current on assessment ethics and standards. Making use of formal assessment in client service means grappling with the complete set of ethical codes and professional standards. Though the emphasis here is to begin forming a Christian perspective on the application of assessment techniques, this faith perspective does not diminish or reduce the basic responsibilities, ground rules, and ethical procedures articulated by each professional organization. Our call is to practice in accordance with the Lord's desire for justice. Clinicians enter careers in mental health as an expression of Christian ministry. This vocational awareness coupled with regular worship will help curb temptation to employ shortcuts that could have an adverse impact on clients. For example, it is essential to administer only instruments for which we're qualified. Use of certain measures may be restricted due to training and experience. Circumventing any best practice in the name of religious freedom or under the banner of Christian liberty is a serious pitfall. Ethical responsibilities demand careful attention.

Finally, it is vital to consult technical material and procedural manuals prior to administration. The internet can give us instantaneous access to an instrument and the results. This does not, however, mean that we are prepared to use those results with proper caution and with sensitivity to a client's cultural identity and well-being.

ASSESSING FOR ACCULTURATIVE STRESS

The term *acculturation* was once synonymous with *assimilation* (Iwamasa, Regan, Subica, & Yamada, 2013; Rivera, 2008). A cultural identity in conflict with the host context requires acclimating to the dominant language, dress, values, and social norms. Client distress was determined by the degree of difficulty required for the sojourner to make the shift from native orientation to mainstream expectations. In clinical terms, acculturation distress was a form of an adjustment disorder stemming from this transition. The assessment task was to ascertain how readily a client steeped in a minority culture learned the speech, customs, norms, and values of the mainstream. The terminology to describe the change process reflected the directional goal. *Integration* implies retaining a healthy sense of tradition coupled with interest and increasing fluency in the mainstream culture. Integration used to be viewed as the desirable approach to bringing together one's native culture and the present culture in which one finds oneself. *Separation* depicts clients who are struggling to accept or adjust to the host culture. *Marginalization* describes a cultural migrant who is lost or stranded between the culture of origin and the host environment.

This simplistic model of acculturation offers the benefit of following a linear direction and supplying categorical designations. Interventions used to accomplish the integration of cultural tradition with contextual demands appear on the surface to be relatively forthright to develop and implement. Further, each particular cultural group (e.g., Asian, Latino, African American/black) can be studied in order to uncover common points of tension with the mainstream. Information about distinct cultural identities can then be used to generate psycho-educational techniques to promote integration. Clinical intervention using the model of acculturation involves affirming appreciation of heritage and acceptance of current cultural placement.

Acculturation scales that align with this model (unidimensional) are available. They locate how respondents place themselves on the continuum between the culture of origin and the host culture. Items typically measure identification with a particular generation (e.g., first, second, fifth) as well as language and socialization preferences (e.g., I prefer to engage in social activity with . . .). These remain reasonable introductory items for exploring cultural connectedness.

There are also bidimensional or multidimensional instruments that map identification with the culture of origin and host culture (Paniagua, 2014). These measures offer a fuller appreciation of the dynamics of cultural adjustment. That is, the optimal outcome may not be cultural integration but bicultural or multicultural flexibility. The shortcoming of the basic style of acculturation model is that it fails to capture how the lines between host and home have become so permeable. Globalization is the current reality no matter what the locale. Increased travel, technology, communication, international higher education, multinational employment, and global migration create novel opportunities. Acculturation in this age is accomplished in varying degrees and with alternate strategies. The challenge for clients is often to navigate the complexities and fluctuations experienced as multiple cultural expectations collide.

The more viable and contemporary approach is to adjust our perception of acculturation and the subsequent assessment plan. Counselors do well to conduct assessment that identifies *acculturative stress* and *accountability pressures*. Acculturative stress is the reaction stemming from the requirement to function in the host culture while negotiating ongoing obligations to the culture of origin (Iwamasa et al., 2013). This is not reconciling past with present but openly acknowledging multiple cultural placements and simultaneous participation in real time. For example, the necessity to become fluent in the local language or dialect while speaking a native language in one's household can contribute to acculturative stress. Multicultural flexibility, like bilingual skills, may be applied daily to function in a mainstream workplace while continuing to interact with cultural traditions practiced by family, friends, and neighborhood merchants. Further, acculturative stress need not be deemed detrimental or unwanted. There may be positive associations with this challenge for students who come to the United States to secure an advanced degree. They embrace the acculturative stress necessary to become proficient in English and fluent in the customs of this country. On the other hand, for those seeking political refuge, acculturative stress may be overwhelming, causing feelings of helplessness, loss, and trauma.

Social ties and family demands to conform to habits and norms from the traditional culture generate accountability pressures (Iwamasa et al., 2013). There are also similar pressures in the host context. Approval and ongoing validation of one's narrative identity is linked to performing in a manner that maintains one's cultural priorities and connections. Accountability pressure may be imagined as an internal dialogue or experienced in conversation. The assessment task is to determine how well the client demonstrates flexibility, plasticity, and adeptness to manage differing expectations. This involves maintaining a secure cultural identity while moving between social systems that have different rules. Navigating this requires the formulation and use of advanced strategies. It requires the ability to tolerate varying degrees of ambiguity regarding social cues and risk taking when there is uncertainty in how to respond. Acculturative stress can be viewed as the disequilibrium that results from belonging to and operating within multiple cultural contexts.

There are productive uses for the concepts of acculturative stress and accountability pressure. For example, the search for ways to honor one's close attachments and community shares some parallels with the challenge of navigating cultural identity and Christian identity. There is a healthy form of acculturative stress that arises when we desire to please the Lord and act in ways that conform to membership within a redeemed fellowship of saints. As Christians we should strive for peace and holistic functioning without favoring or dismissing our home or host culture. Our hope is for the future glory where every tribe and every nation come together without hierarchical or competitive conflicts to worship the King of Glory (Rev 7:9). The intent is to prioritize cultural identity in the assessment process by accounting for acculturative stress and accountability pressures.

ASSESSMENT DIMENSIONS

In this section I outline a strategy for listening to a client's story with multicultural insightfulness. This calls for using a set of dimensional continuums. Counselors can practice listening in 3D, that is, by appreciating how *details* signal defining events, *dynamics* in relationships reveal patterns and pressures, and *dependencies* suggest priorities in one's identity.

Details: observe and recognize defining events. Assessment requires vigorous attention to detail. The details are where the particulars of what needs to change will emerge. We must notice both fine points of information and how the dots connect. We gather critical pieces of data in interviews and through instruments that eventually are assembled to tell the client's story with its plot, theme, and unifying threads. Scan the details to notice narrative motifs, significant behavioral incidents, and increases in symptoms to formulate diagnostic possibilities. Keeping track of tangents and story particulars can be a daunting task. Our attention must simultaneously "zoom in" and "pan out." The trick is to pay close attention to what the client is describing while keeping our perspective on the big picture in order to formulate a long-range, meaningful vision for change. We concentrate diligently on the unfolding client saga to pick up on subtle details. Again, this happens without ever losing sight of the overarching existential themes. Each informational fragment can only be understood when viewed in conjunction with the whole. Cultural and diversity features may stimulate acculturative stress in a new context. Situations that reveal tension or conflict often provide clues to the meaning that those have for one's identity.

Obtaining developmental or situational data is not done to chronicle change or to build a timeline. If a basic biographical recounting were the aim, we would be content with impartial and dispassionate fact gathering. True, the fundamental goals in sharing journalistic news are good starting points. Reporters retell the news using the essentials of who, what, where, when, why, and how. Assessment begins at the level of fact finding. Fortunately, unearthing gritty minutiae is not what a helping relationship is all about. The conversation moves from the particulars of history into commentary about expectations and motivations. The stories clients bring to a counselor set into motion the direction for change.

Counseling combines objective information gathering within an empathetic interpersonal encounter. Assessment does not end when the counselor can provide an accurate retelling of key events. This is because a client's personal and cultural narrative is not only heard; it is entered and joined. Counselors listen to a narrative with ears attuned to its life-giving undercurrents, tidal rhythms, and dangerous riptides. Helpers are passionate to enter into a client's experience. This means being with them in the grip of turmoil, weeping over the sorrow of loss, agonizing over injustices, and marveling at grace. The interpersonal core of helping alters the standard categories that an objective reporter employs to assemble facts. In supportive conversations, specific details are not points to dutifully accept at face value. Disclosures are recognized for what they represent: gifts that symbolize a willingness to trust. Pivotal story elements are examined with thoughtful and systematic scrutiny while empathy compounds understanding.

In a helping relationship, facts are not treated as neutral, cold, or concrete descriptors. Facts serve double duty. On the one hand, facts establish the realities of the client as a person and of their context. At the same time, these facts can pinpoint an explosion that sent emotional shockwaves throughout a client's soul. When an event causes eruptions within a person's inner being, it reverberates outward to impact interaction with family, community, and culture. Therefore, our job is to observe all the intriguing links between facts, feelings, and experience. It is not merely who, but who with, who will, and how well. Not what, but what for and what if. It is not about where, but where to, when, and when not. Appraisal in treatment settings is not a detective effort to decipher the single, simplistic solution to a mystery. Nor is it a mission to decode a captivating whodunit. At the end of the day, the helping enterprise puts its attention toward rearranging the connections between the objective facts of who, what, where, when, how, and why.

Assessment is not only to investigate data in the pursuit of insight; it is a means to earn loyalty as a trustworthy ally. A counselor must demonstrate skill in uncovering details along with prudence to weave a holistic picture of the person. The counselee is bathed in empathy and the security of being understood. As the counselor takes in the client's uniqueness and cultural community ties, the details are understood for the meaning they reveal.

Finally, the counseling dyad may jointly commit to place the conversation within a Christian theological perspective. This merges the understanding of cultural identity with what it means for the client to be a devoted follower of Jesus Christ, adding a transcendent perspective. There is excitement to hear how the Holy Spirit is bringing life experiences and the events of this personal history into the grand gospel narrative of creation, fall, redemption, and consummation. In essence, a uniquely Christian identity provides direction to cultural identity and to the daily experience of being a child of God. The assembly of facts and experiences into a comprehensive story in turn guides the ongoing details of living. Acculturative stress exposes the challenge of navigating not only the tensions between a native and host culture but also the tensions between belonging to an earthly culture and a multicultural heavenly community.

Dynamics: patterns with persons. The second listening dimension comprises the dynamic forces that coerce and constrain. Relational bonds can be stabilizing, dysfunctional, or both. These relational "ties that bind" are thus rightly labeled as accountability pressures, for they can directly contribute to a client's distress. It is also important to realize that the same forces of relationship, viewed from a health perspective, operate as attachments that anchor identity and foster security.

Being able to hear the emotion embedded in sharing of details is an important proficiency in becoming skilled listeners. Counselors develop sophisticated sonar to decipher subtle, characteristic patterns that clients use to manage pressure or to preserve social ties. The engrained and automatic patterns associated with feeling, acting, and behaving constitute one's personal traits. Recognizing the expression of a client's natural temperament within the intricate layers of relationship is critical. Social inventories or pulling together the names for a genogram help a counselor discern who is important to the client for security and support. Gazing at one's family tree may surface legacies that can unduly burden or undermine confidence. A relational bond and the patterns that play out in the social network can be sources of strength or shame. Noticing such dynamics will allow the counselor to pinpoint areas for more intensive consideration. Much emotional energy can be expended under the influence of key persons. Thus, these dynamics are worthy of our assessment effort.

There is an interesting twist to pondering the interpersonal ties between people and roles within the client's narrative. This inventory of social pressures—real and imagined—must be synchronized with a persistent monitoring of the relationship between counselor and counselee. Immediacy (i.e., "you-and-me talk") is the skill of imposing a status check on the current connection

(Egan, 2014). It involves a conversational assessment that ponders the question, how is our partnership performing in this very moment in striving to accomplish our mission? The practice serves as a strategically placed mirror to view the present interaction within the therapeutic dyad. This maintains the relationship as safe, protected, and goal-oriented. Immediacy allows for recognition of the relational and emotional patterns present that affect expectations in the helping relationship. If there are cultural barriers or diversity features that are creating challenging dynamics in this relationship, it is imperative to bring those to the surface for the sake of effective counseling.

Focused dialogue within the therapeutic relationship is what energizes storytelling. Counselor and client together face the past, realistically contemplate the present, and locate a reason for hope in the future. Two become better than one, and they have a good return for their labor (Eccles 4:9). This undertaking calls on its contributors to jointly consider expectations, trust, progress, and effort. Reflective examination like this is not common or comfortable. It can also require a rather large amount of multicultural flexibility. Therapeutic communication with an intense focus on the individual is not the norm or even socially acceptable in certain cultures. In counseling, this monitoring of the process is the means to secure a good-enough working alliance. Assessment in counseling takes a good look at how both participants cross the divide between them. We routinely check the relationship to ascertain how interpersonal patterns and cultural dynamics are being reenacted. This feedback loop is a unique feature of therapeutic dialogue because it separates the discussion from everyday conversation. It is rare in ordinary conversation to stop and consider the effectiveness of one's communication during a water-cooler chat or while catching up at a coffee shop.

Dependence: empowerment and submission. We have discussed how assessment entails gathering details while steadily learning how these promote insight into the client's personal narrative, as well as the intricate relational dynamics that tend to replay time and again in people's lives. The third dimension consists of the people or groups in the client's network who provide encouragement and empowerment. As stories unfold, we are introduced to the messengers of hope and their messages. This dimension searches for those the client depends on for strength, courage, and validation. The availability of those important voices confirms a client's personal and cultural identity.

Part of this dimension is listening for lifelines of affirmation. Pay attention to when these are intact or strained. This is key to the art of assessment, and here a counselor's awareness of traditions within major cultural communities can be useful. The role of parents, siblings, grandparents, relatives, community leaders, pastors, coaches, or mentors is often worth considering. There are more possibilities than those found in an immediate household. The mainstream culture in the United States emphasizes individual autonomy and thus gives limited attention to influential others. Ethnocultural communities outside the mainstream in the United States often have deeper, more intricate ties across extended family lines. These may continue to be significant even if a person lives a continent away. The assortment of supportive allies may not be limited to the living, as those from the past can continue to be sources of inspiration and challenge. A client who is invested in honoring the memory of a parent or a family legacy is dependent on them.

For clarity, the term *dependency* in this dimension refers to a resource for one's identity, security, and hope. These contributors to the formation and maintenance of the self can represent dysfunction or be a mixture of blessing and turmoil. Nevertheless, dependency in this dimension is generally viewed as healthy and normative.

Mental health professionals, including those who aspire to offer unequivocally Christian service, press toward depth in interpersonal connections to motivate growth. This includes the counseling relationship itself as a person-to-person collaboration. Each partner may have a distinct role, but mutual submission is practiced. The aim of any communication process associated with the Lord's name is to bring honor to him (2 Cor 5:14-15; Col 3:23). Consider how his presence is experienced by the client in the therapeutic alliance. Ultimately, the counseling relationship does not result in a long-term dependence on an expert adviser, caring supporter, or nurturing mentor. A Christian counseling experience produces a healthy reliance on the Creator of the universe. Whereas counseling in general targets autonomy or greater independent functioning as a goal, Christian approaches recognize that submission to the Lord of the universe is the only source of peace, security, and grace. This explains why Christian MHPs seek to sow peace in therapy by cultivating habits that honor the other. The focus is not merely on a problem to be solved but on a whole person, with all the splendor of diversity, heritage, and community.

REFERENCES

American Counseling Association. (2014). *ACA code of ethics: As approved by the ACA Governing Council.* http://www.counseling.org/resources/aca-code-of-ethics.pdf

American Educational Research Association, American Psychological Association, & National Council on Measurement in Education. (2014). *Standards for educational and psychological testing*. Washington, DC: American Educational Research Association.

American Psychiatric Association. (2013a). *Diagnostic and statistical manual of mental disorders* (5th ed.). Arlington, VA: American Psychiatric Publishing.

American Psychiatric Association. (2013b). *DSM*-5 cultural formulation interview. Retrieved from http://www.multiculturalmentalhealth.ca/clinical-tools/cultural-formulation

Association for Assessment and Counseling. (2003). Responsibilities of users of standardized tests (RUST, 3rd ed.). Retrieved March 12, 2018 from http://aarc-counseling .org/assets/cms/uploads/files/rust.pdf

Association for Assessment in Counseling and Education. (2012). Standards for multicultural assessment (4th rev.). Retrieved March 12, 2018 from http://aarc-counseling .org/assets/cms/uploads/files/AACE-AMCD.pdf

Burkard, A. W., & Ponterotto, J. G. (2007). Cultural identity, racial identity, and the multicultural personality. In L. A. Suzuki & J. G. Ponterotto (Eds.), *Handbook of multicultural assessment: Clinical, psychological, and educational applications* (3rd ed., pp. 52-72). San Francisco: John Wiley & Sons.

Carlson, J. F., Geisinger, K. F., & Jonson, J. L. (Eds.). (2017). *The twentieth mental measurements yearbook*. Lincoln, NE: Buros Institute of Mental Measurements.

Egan, G. (2014). *The skilled helper: A problem-management and opportunity-development approach to helping* (10th ed.). Pacific Grove, CA: Brooks/Cole.

Grieger, I. (2013). A cultural assessment framework and interview protocol. In L. A. Suzuki & J. G. Ponterotto (Eds.), *Handbook of multicultural assessment: Clinical, psychological, and educational applications* (3rd ed., pp. 132-162). San Francisco: John Wiley & Sons.

Hays, D. G. (2017). *Assessment in counseling: Procedures and practices* (6th ed). Alexandria, VA: American Counseling Association.

Hong, G. K., Garcia, M., & Soriano, M. (2013). Responding to the challenge: Preparing mental health professionals for the changing US demographics. In F. A. Paniagua & A.-M. Yamada (Eds.), *Handbook of multicultural mental health: Assessment and treatment of diverse populations* (2nd ed., pp. 591-607). Waltham, MA: Academic Press/Elsevier.

Iwamasa, G. Y., Regan, S. M. P., Subica, A., & Yamada, A. M. (2013). Nativity and migration: Considering acculturation in the assessment and treatment of mental disorders. In F. A. Paniagua & A. M. Yamada (Eds.), *Handbook of multicultural mental health: Assessment and treatment of diverse populations* (2nd ed., pp. 167-188). Waltham, MA: Academic Press/Elsevier.

Marsella, A. J. & Yamada, A. M. (2013). Culture and mental health: An introduction and overview of foundations, concepts, and issues. In F. Paniagua & A. M. Yamada's (Eds.), *Handbook of multicultural mental health: Assessment and treatment of diverse populations*. (2nd ed., pp. 3-23). Waltham, MA: Academic Press/Elsevier.

McCabe, S. E., Teter, C. J., & Boyd, C. J. (2006). Medical use, illicit use and diversion of prescription stimulant medication. *Journal of Psychoactive Drugs, 38*(1), 43-56.

Paniagua, F. A. (2014). *Assessing and treating culturally diverse clients: A practical guide* (4th ed.). Thousand Oaks, CA: Sage.

Paniagua, F. A., & Yamada, A. M. (2013). *Handbook of multicultural mental health: Assessment and treatment of diverse populations* (2nd ed.). Waltham, MA: Academic Press/Elsevier.

Rivera, L. M. (2008). Acculturation and multicultural assessment: Issues, trends, and practice. In L. A. Suzuki & J. G. Ponterotto (Eds.), *Handbook of multicultural assessment: Clinical, psychological, and educational applications* (3rd ed., pp. 73-91). San Francisco: John Wiley & Sons.

Sollman, M. J., Ranseen, J. D., & Berry, D. T. R. (2010). Detection of feigned ADHD in college students. *Psychological Assessment, 22*(2), 323-335.

Whiston, S. C. (2017). *Principles and applications of assessment in counseling* (5th ed.). Belmont, CA: Cengage.

CHAPTER SEVEN

THE CASE FOR REDEMPTIVE VALIDITY

See to it that no one takes you captive through hollow and deceptive
philosophy, which depends on human tradition and the elemental
spiritual forces of this world rather than on Christ.

For in Christ all the fullness of the Deity lives in bodily form,
and in Christ you have been brought to fullness. He is
the head over every power and authority.

Colossians 2:8-10

THEOLOGICAL THEME

The Authority of Jesus Christ

MEASURES OF CHOICE

Brice, a twenty-seven-year-old seminarian, speaks deliberately and maintains steady eye contact during this first consultation. A dry humor occasionally breaks through. Still, his predominant mood is subdued, his reflections are philosophical, and his tone is somber. Brice is not far into a master of divinity degree. His career objective is to become a pastor and preach the Word of God. The leadership role he had in a vibrant Christian fellowship on a large secular university campus contributes to his sense of calling.

Brice's counseling appointment was prompted by his request for a second extension on a major course project. His professor granted the first reprieve, but further exceptions require the involvement of the dean of students. Brice's ability is not the issue; his academic performance was exemplary in his pre-law undergraduate program. Procrastination, a lack of concentration, and an inability to complete tasks are the main culprits. Over the past month, his workload has predictably increased. Unfortunately, his capacity to complete assignments has withered. While the dean has granted the extension, she mandates that Brice meet with a counselor.

Six months ago, he experienced an abrupt and unanticipated breakup with his girlfriend of nearly two years. This was her decision, and it happened to coincide with the onset of his mood shift. Brice is verbal, insightful, and cooperative, but he talks about challenges and dilemmas. Mixed into Brice's comments to his counselor are memorable biblical phrases that refer to personal sin and a petition for a clean heart (Ps 51:10-11).

Three explanations for his struggle are bouncing around in Brice's head. Are his recent complaints—a lack of sustained attention, eroding confidence, and spiritual dryness—a temporary setback, a "dark night of the soul," so to speak? His academic adviser puts forward this suggestion, and, accordingly, the adviser recommends the involvement of a spiritual mentor. Brice's pastor knows Brice and his former girlfriend reasonably well. He raises the second possible explanation: Could his lackluster productivity indicate the withholding of the Lord's blessing due to concealed sin? The pastor poses a serious challenge. He wants Brice to reflect on how he may have taken the relationship for granted. Under the guise of spiritual leadership, had Brice dismissed her views, ignored requests, and dishonored her devotion to make this long-term companion feel more like a servant? The dean postulates the third possibility. Might Brice be in the midst of a mental health episode such as depression? Each of the three explanations offers a plausible account for why Brice is not able to invest energy in academic tasks related to his ministry calling. The counselor ponders each possibility as Brice reluctantly exposes his inertia and the details of his story.

This Christian counseling scenario illustrates the blurry boundaries between mental health concerns, matters of pastoral care, and ongoing faith development. Deciphering the collision of circumstantial, interpersonal, psychological, and spiritual forces within this client necessitates a well-balanced assessment plan. An informed strategy will investigate precedent-setting events (past), current stressors (present), and realistic avenues to resolve the immediate impasse as well as long-term strategies (future).

Counselors make calculated choices and incorporate assessment technology with an underlying strategy. Each discrete tool requires evaluation before it is enlisted into service. Will its findings reflect Christian values and theological priorities? Will the results sharpen our perception of the state of the client's heart as it pertains to faith? In this chapter I'll explore the premise that mental health professionals need a well-defined routine to evaluate tools and appraise techniques. First, it is essential to be fully aware of a measure's psychometric properties. Educated judgment of the advantages, risks, and goodness of fit represents the primary phase of measure selection. Second, a counselor needs to recognize worldview and faith implications embedded in the instrument. The final phase is to know how to collaboratively use the information generated to make worthwhile applications. Blending assessment options into a helping encounter that offers a thoroughly Christian approach requires putting one's instruments under theological scrutiny. Knowing the benefits and limitations of each one is a prerequisite to proper selection, use, and meaningful interpretation.

The Clinical Assessment Instrument Christian Evaluation Form (CAICEF) is a review protocol with a distinctive feature (see appendix 1). Its objective is to determine that each assessment option not only has respectable psychometric characteristics but also has advantages for Christian counseling relationships. Given our intentionality regarding worldview, I propose a novel validity subtype. *Redemptive validity* refers to the effectiveness of an assessment tool that samples behavior or attitudes to provide insight into living in greater conformity with the teachings of Scripture for those desiring to grow in reliance on the Creator.

The initial task is to establish a biblical platform for this term. The chapter then demonstrates how to determine RV in order to select a tool to build sustainable momentum in a productive direction for clients such as Brice.

BIBLICAL TERMINOLOGY: TESTING, PROVING, AND TEMPTING

Scripture conveys the unambiguous message that the Lord himself examines the righteous (Ps 11:5; Jer 17:10; 20:12). Implied in this attribute of God is his omniscience—the God of Scripture is all-knowing. This characteristic of the God of the Bible includes his awareness of himself, all things real, and all things possible. Thus, God immediately recognizes the motivations, affections, and intentions bound within the human heart (Ps 26:2; 94:11; 139:4; 1 Jn 3:20). The ultimate goal for any activity in Christian counseling is to discern God's vision of the interior of the person in order to pursue holiness with wisdom.

Unfortunately, finite and fallible counselors, even those prayerfully in touch with the Holy Spirit, are but fellow sojourners. Despite the stereotype of therapists as mystical mind readers, that ability does not come with the title. In fact, mental health counselors are never in an entirely detached or elevated position. This means it's impossible to detect with complete objectivity the inner workings of any human heart in a manner that mirrors what is seen by a perfect, holy, transcendent, and loving God. Helpers must cultivate keen intuitive skills to distinguish the affections of a client's heart. We begin assembling information by listening with empathy and clinical acumen to a client's self-report. We also gather behavioral observations and accounts of daily activities. Assessment techniques assist in this process by incorporating systematic methods to collect behavioral samples.

There is a beautiful Old Testament narrative where God conducts a matchless examination of a chosen servant. Bound into this ancient account are enduring messages that can inform a framework for the use of assessment as a redemptive enterprise. Genesis 22 relates the journey of Abraham to Moriah in obedience to the Lord's command. Upon arrival, the plan is to sacrifice his son Isaac. The chapter opens with an arresting statement: "Some time later God tested Abraham" (Gen 22:1).

Prior to this event, Abraham steadily exhibited devotion to the Lord and a willingness to obey his commands (e.g., Gen 12:1, 4; 13:4; 14:22; 15:18). God set Abraham apart to assume a privileged position as a leader among the nations. Genesis also records notorious incidents when Abraham regrettably relies on his own understanding. These actions reveal where earnest faith is absent, shaky, or deliberately withheld. Abraham does not uniformly manifest trust in the Lord's provisions. For example, despite God's incredible promise to grant him a son, he conspires with Sarah to conceive a son through her servant, Hagar. Further, Abraham publically speaks half-truths on several occasions about Sarah being his sister instead of acknowledging to those in authority that the beautiful woman in his household is actually his wife (Gen 16:1-16; 12:10-20; 20:1-18). He fears for his life, knowing that rulers with military power might desire to take Sarah as a wife and would not hesitate to remove him from the picture.

Although faithfulness to his calling is exemplary, Abraham did not live up to his status as the "father of many nations." He stumbled in his leadership role despite being the recipient of the Lord's covenant (Gen 17:1-14). These blatant failures are all recorded in Scripture. Yet God remained committed to fulfilling his word and did bless Sarah with a son, though Abraham had to wait until he was one hundred years old (Gen 21:1-7)! The very sign of God's provision, Abraham's son Isaac, birthed by Sarah when she was far beyond her child-bearing years, would be the prime target for this extreme test of faith.

Abraham unmistakably hears the voice of the Lord. The directive, however implausible in a modern context, occurs in an era and culture where a cult practice as horrible as child sacrifice is acceptable. The direction to Abraham is heart stopping: sacrifice Isaac as a burnt offering in the region of Moriah.

Abraham complies with these instructions and immediately commences with preparations for the journey. He convenes a caravan, gathers wood for a sacrificial fire, and sets out for the appointed location. He has ample opportunity to contemplate the magnitude of what he is about to do. The itinerary demands travel across fifty miles of desert along a three-day route with Isaac by his side. Scripture does not record any verbalized doubt or desperate attempt to negotiate with the Lord. Abraham advances every dusty step of the expedition in obedience to the Lord's authority (Dods, 1903/1982).

Further, Isaac was mature enough to grasp the intent of this mission and ascertain the lack of a sacrificial lamb. His devotion and trust in his father's directions were remarkable. The passage thus makes it evident that Abraham and Isaac were mutually obedient. Imagine the fortitude of Abraham's character when his precious and beloved son made this astute observation (Gen 22:6-8): "'Father? . . .The fire and wood are here,' Isaac said, 'but where is the lamb for the burnt offering?' Abraham answered, 'God himself will provide the lamb for the burnt offering, my son.'" It was not until the final seconds, when Isaac's death was imminent, that the Lord finally intervened.

The account vividly portrays the steadiness of Abraham's faith throughout this stressful journey. It's hard to imagine a more rigorous and faith-demanding experience, yet Abraham never wavers. His fingers grip the knife, the implement of death. Only in this dramatic climax does the Lord supply the genuine animal for the offering and affirm his covenant promise: *Yahweh yir'eh,* "the Lord will provide" (Ross, 1985). Abraham, with a resolute faith that will mark him for eternity, demonstrates his fidelity to the Lord. This testing constituted the defining moment in Abraham's life, and in his willingness to sacrifice his cherished son Abraham becomes the premier human model of our loving heavenly Father. In a fitting epitaph, Scripture declares that Abraham was justified by faith (Rom 4:1-3; Heb 11:17-19).

What was the purpose of this divine test? Who benefitted? What was accomplished? The Lord God, the Creator, orchestrated the divine plan of salvation for all eternity. It is implausible that he discovered anything original through Abraham's experience. The Lord Almighty already knows the heart (Ps 139:1-5). There are occasions in the Old Testament when the terminology associated with testing (*nasah*)—to put on trial or to tempt—refers to an intuitive sense of discernment. Other uses imply challenging a covenant partner to expose how well that person is living out the particulars of the agreement (Schneider & Brown, 1978). When God is conducting the testing, the connotation has more to do with formation than evaluation. The Mount

Moriah test was not an enactment to detect the interior affections of the heart but a dramatic pinnacle to affirm, purify, and cleanse. No shadow could hide any aspect of Abraham's inner being. God's transcendent perspective penetrates to the core of our self-protective psychological defenses. The designated patriarch of God's people had reached a remarkable level of spiritual maturity. Thus, he was competent to handle this difficult test and demonstrate the strength of his faith.

Building faith entails acting based on our certainty of the reliability of God. This demands behavior that exhibits trust despite the circumstances (Schneider & Brown, 1978). In this instance with Abraham, testing suggests proving, refining, or bringing an inner character trait to the surface for inspection and verification (Wilson, 1980). The experience is for Abraham a redemptive one; all his past failures faded in this successful walk of faith to the altar of sacrifice. After God intervenes and provides a lamb for the sacrifice, he declares to Abraham: "Now I know that you fear God, because you have not withheld from me your son, your only son" (Gen 22:12). Abraham hears these words and accepts that this indeed is an accurate pronouncement. Faith is recognition that the Lord is steadfast and dependable. At this juncture in his formation, Abraham has assurance that the Lord God is consistently trustworthy and acts accordingly.

Scripture gives clear indication that God tests human beings to reveal his purpose and to engender excellence. Nevertheless, it is not in the Lord's nature to tempt, condemn, or entice toward sin (Jas 1:12-15; Wiersbe, 1993). For example, in the book of Job we see that God permits Satan to test Job. This was not a punishment for Job; in the Lord's eyes, Job was blameless, upright, and submissive (Job 1:6-8). Though the trials were severe, Job was preserved by grace, and his faith stood. Likewise, God's testing of Abraham exposed the depth of this faith.

From the Abraham and Isaac narrative I have culled three lessons that will serve as guidelines to inform the redemptive practice of assessment in Christian counseling settings.

1. Tests in Scripture rely on behavior to reveal relational loyalties and inner convictions. Behavior flows out of affections, motivations, and complexities bound within the human heart.

2. Trials reveal an individual's understanding of divine direction and the way of wisdom. Pursuit or avoidance of virtue exposes genuine beliefs and values.

3. Tests make evident the uprightness of our heart (1 Chron 29:17).

It is important to recognize an obvious yet critical distinction between *test* as it's used in Scripture and the contemporary understanding of a psychological test, inventory, or instrument. The biblical terms associated with testing denote crossing over or passing through; they imply a period of transition. We reflect our commitment to the Lord when we're able to receive testing as a pilgrimage that strengthens our faith and our character. Experiences of testing reveal the internal affections of the heart. The validity of these tests is measured in the ethical, moral, and spiritual fruit detailed in Scripture. The tests in our lives are part of a Spirit-guided process of sanctification in our unfolding redemptive story. In this way, those who are born again and subsequently indwelt by the Holy Spirit are increasingly conformed into the image of Christ.

In contrast, the intent of mental health assessment is to yield observations on more modest, operationally defined, distinct slices from the behavioral spectrum to convey information on psychological constructs. The assessments are designed to empirically evaluate behavior based on socially constructed standards; there is no presumption of a uniquely Christian design. This is true even when the tool provides data on a person's spiritual perspective or resources or moral reasoning. The descriptions generated are essentially normative, reflecting the population used to determine the parameters of interpretation for the tool. These tests are helpful for uncovering information about affective patterns, interpersonal preferences, and automatic behavioral trends. In norm-referenced tools, results are measured against what is common, typical, and normal according to generally accepted cultural standards. Performance is understood based on its placement on a scale that anchors it within an appropriate standardization sample (Gregory, 2014).

Unlike norm-referenced instruments, criterion-referenced tools evaluate performance against precisely defined objectives. Criterion-referenced measures are customary in educational and occupational evaluation. They are less common in mental health applications, although certain checklists that treat health and optimal functioning as the absence of symptoms or problems may reflect this criterion format.

Measurement tools for counseling tend to offer objective statements about normally exhibited behavior. They rely extensively on statistical analysis of results as they relate to the bell-shaped normal distribution curve. The normal curve has mathematical properties that facilitate comparison and prediction regarding a range of human characteristics. Measurement technology associated with the normal curve contributes to the usefulness of norm-referenced tools. Essentially, this establishes a point of reference outside of the immediate, interpersonal counseling context. Its external perspective is what makes an assessment valuable and practical. Still, mental health professionals (MHPs) who desire to help their clients develop the mind of Christ must recognize that relative appraisals do not assess this type of growth.

Believers are not to conform to normality but are to press on toward a higher calling, that is, to emulate the perfect example set by Jesus Christ. Norm-referenced measures use calibrations that facilitate comparison with other human beings, not to the sinless Son of God as revealed in Scripture. Tailoring results to the pursuit of Christlikeness is the task of Christian counselors. We collaborate with clients by looking to Scripture to establish the criteria for God-honoring thinking, feeling, and behaving. Cultivating these criteria falls under the heading of redemptive validity. Mental health tools produce insights that we can apply to nurture a walk of faith.

Think back to the scenario with Brice. The crisis of faith and the difficulties Brice wants to overcome are examples of a test or trial as depicted in the epistle of James (1:2-18). Whether Brice seeks counsel with his spiritual mentor, his pastor, or a Christian mental health professional, the route toward healing will incorporate virtues such as perseverance, maturity, and wholeness into the treatment goals. Brice needs help on a practical level to figure out how to effectively meet the demands he's facing. But the counseling conversation may also encourage him to ponder his faith in ways that lead to lasting spiritual change.

Assessment instruments are selected for Brice that focus on differential diagnosis, personality characteristics, cognitive schemas, and behavioral habits. The data from these tools can contribute to the formulation of cognitive and behavioral targets for change, increase clarity on Brice's readiness to reach his career goals, or shed light on interpersonal patterns. Emphasizing specific targets for change helps bring formation objectives more clearly into view.

The purpose of this chapter is to consider the validity of tools theologically for counseling that is Christian. One reasonable assessment option for Brice would be use an instrument that gathers information on symptoms associated with depression. In the next section I show how a structured review locates the best measure to focus on depression. What follows is a template to implement theological discrimination and a procedure to conduct an assessment review that is redemptively oriented. That is, this is an effort to position clinical appraisal within a biblical perspective, and specifically to contemplate depression measures from a theological standpoint. The understanding gained from this assessment application can then be incorporated into a helping approach that takes closely related theological concepts under advisement.

TRENDS IN THE MEASUREMENT OF DEPRESSION

Over the past one hundred years, the modern therapeutic enterprise has produced nearly three hundred measures to detect and describe depression (Santor, Gregus, & Welch, 2006).[1] A busy clinician would find the obligation to cull through a list of that many tools overwhelming! Fortunately, it does not take extensive research to narrow potential choices. Assessment methods include self-report inventories, structured/semi-structured interviews, ratings from multiple sources, and direct observation. Goals and approach vary. Nonetheless, the bulk of these fall within the following categories: identification (i.e., screening, diagnosis, and classification); dysregulation (i.e., symptom description and severity); and intervention planning (i.e., clinical hypothesis testing, treatment approach, prediction of behavior, and treatment outcome; Nezu, Nezu, Lee, & Stern, 2014). The selection of the optimal measure for a particular application depends on the fit between the assessment goal and the traits measured by the instrument.

The starting point when searching for a specific tool is a comprehensive literature review (e.g., Groth-Marnat & Wright, 2016). For instance, the *Handbook of Assessment and Treatment Planning for Psychological Disorders* has chapters covering many common clinical categories (Antony & Barlow, 2010). My list for this example was influenced by reports of clinical usage in a comprehensive review of measures in the *Handbook of Depression* (Nezu et al., 2014). Whatever the application you're looking for, instruments that make the short list for possible use should be appropriate for the intended purpose, client population, and clinic setting. That is, there should be enough evidence to instill confidence that the results from each measure can be generalized to the client you're seeking to service.

After establishing a general list, the next step is to investigate the basic psychometric properties of the instruments in contention (Ayearst & Bagby, 2010). The primary criterion for selection is straightforward: a measure should meet generally acceptable guidelines regarding its psychometric qualities. There is no rationale to evaluating potential use if there are significant

---

[1]This section and the material on redemptive validity subtypes is adapted from Greggo & Lawrence (2012).

measurement flaws. Once an instrument is determined to be psychometrically credible, it is feasible to consider its suitability, both theologically and practically, for clinical application with Christian clients. Thus, each measure is evaluated in terms of its stated purpose, content within its internal structure, test development procedures, the representativeness of the norming population, and reliability before being assessed for theological appropriateness.

The tools included in this example are the revised and restructured Hamilton Rating Scale for Depression (GRID-HAMD), the Beck Depression Inventory II (BDI-II), the Zung Self-Rating Depression Scale (SDS), the Patient Health Question Depression Scale (PHQ-9), the Reynolds Adolescent Depression Scale (RADS II), and the Clinical Assessment of Depression (CAD). These instruments differ on psychometric qualities, but overall each offers sufficient reliability, validity, and utility to support extensive application. For full psychometric reviews of these instruments, see *The Mental Measurements Yearbook* (Carlson, Geisinger, & Jonson, 2017). The GRID-HAMD is predominant in psychiatric applications. The BDI-II is a scale widely accessed by MHPs. The SDS has extensive clinical popularity as well as international usage. The PHQ-9 has broad usage in primary-care settings. The CAD offers practical subscales to fine-tune treatment efforts. The RADS II targets early detection with its focus on an adolescent population and an academic setting, and while it warrants further evaluation for this redemptive validity illustration, it is evident that it would not be a match for Brice due to its restricted age range.

An assessment measure captures a discrete data sample, quantifies findings within a defined spectrum, and places results in a logical format to expand understanding. *Validity* is the psychometric term that refers to a test's capacity to provide information that is appropriate, meaningful, and useful (American Educational Research Association [AERA], American Psychological Association [APA], & National Council on Measurement in Education [NCME], 2014). An assessment tool is valid when it delivers on its claims. The three conventional categories of psychometric validity as described by Gregory (2014) are

1. Content: How well do the items reflect the overall domain?

2. Construct: How well defined and operationalized are the key assumptions underlying the measure?

3. Criterion: How well do the scores correspond to related variables or conditions?

More recently, validity is investigated by first exploring how comprehensively and accurately it represents its main construct. This requires conducting research into its internal empirical features. Validation efforts then consider its meaning, value, fairness, and clinical benefits by examining how well it performs in the field across differing clientele (AERA, APA, & NCME, 2014; Whiston, 2017).

There are additional validity subcategories that are of clinical interest. For example, *incremental* validity is the value that comes from a test's capacity to provide unique information compared to other similar instruments. If a scale captures information not readily obtainable elsewhere, it has incremental validity (Haynes & Lench, 2003). Another popular term, *conceptual* validity, refers to the contribution of a measure to the formation of a comprehensive and coherent description of the person (Groth-Marnat & Wright, 2016). A data source is conceptually valid when it contributes a distinguishing hypothesis about the individual (Maloney & Ward, 1976). Conceptual validity has to do with what a test reveals about the person whereas incremental validity has to do with the uniqueness of a test's data.

Christians who counsel need a validity subcategory to describe a test's ability to facilitate conversation and thinking about matters of worldview. This validity consideration is consistent with the recommendation to ponder how constructs from psychology cohere with historical Christian tradition and narrative (Roberts & Watson, 2010). *Redemptive validity* (RV) is a term offered to reflect the insights derived from particular measures that are beneficial to the pastoral and Christian counseling mission. According to our Christian worldview, the good news of the gospel is that all those who express belief in the person of Jesus Christ and in his atoning work on the cross are born anew. Through his death on the cross and resurrection, believers are free from the impact of sin because Jesus Christ paid the ransom owed. Through the shed blood of the second person of the Trinity, the resurrected Jesus Christ, human beings are liberated from the penalty of sin (1 Pet 1:18-19).

The definition of RV borrows from the language offered by Vanhoozer (2010) to summarize the mission of soul-care activity. The term describes the effectiveness of an assessment measure to provide insight into conforming one's life with the truth of Scripture and growing in dependence on the Creator. An assessment measure has RV if it encourages clients to ponder what it means to be crucified with Christ and to order their lives accordingly (Gal 2:20). In other words, does the assessment tool reveal aspects of a client's self-narrative and invite reflection from a gospel lens? RV is like conceptual validity in that it focuses on the subject, not the measure, and on derived implications, not the pure purpose of the tool. RV looks for a contribution to see patterns more accurately and pathways to sanctification more readily.

TEST CONTENT AND ITEM ANALYSIS
THROUGH A CHRISTIAN LENS

In reference to basic psychometric concepts, this review relies substantially on previous research. As clinicians we must consult the professional literature when considering the application of any tool. Santor et al. (2006) conducted a comprehensive investigation of over seventy depression scales developed over the past eighty years. Their goal was to determine how consistently internal psychological states relate to discrete sets of experiences, behaviors, and attitudes. These are the overt, external signs that a client in the midst of a depressive episode can readily use to communicate recent experience through realistic ratings. The content-representation aspect of their investigation identified specific symptoms included on these measures and established the proportion of items related to mood, behavioral, somatic, cognitive, and concentration symptoms.

A key finding from their work is that even though all these measures aim to quantify the same underlying construct, the number of items reflecting representative symptoms varies considerably. In a medical diagnostic context, depression is a classification of a legitimate illness. Depression reaches the threshold of being a medically defined mental health disorder when a person's low mood interferes with general functioning, physical well-being, and interpersonal relationships (American Psychiatric Association [APA], 2013). This prevailing APA definition of depression specifies that low mood and loss of the experience of pleasure (anhedonia) are core symptoms. Interestingly, numerous instruments for this construct target worthlessness in addition to depressed mood and anhedonia (Santor et al., 2006).

From a measurement perspective, this point is noteworthy. Instruments are designed to collect a sample of behavior that fairly represents the prescribed content domain. The weight granted to the subcomponent of worthlessness should prompt either a reconsideration of the item pool or the diagnostic criteria for depression. Further, from a theological perspective, items measuring worthlessness may have an embedded variable related to self-evaluation and self-esteem. Christ-followers from diverse traditions and cultural backgrounds may score lower on items that quantify how one values the self because of a desire to avoid any appearance of pride or self-aggrandizement. The point here is not to reject or dismiss such items that contribute to the psychological construct under consideration. Rather, it's important that we recognize how the population we're serving may misconstrue the intention of these items. In this example, the meaning of self-acceptance, humility, and pride in relation to self-esteem should be discussed with Christian clients (Cooper, 2003). Consideration of how a client's theological lens may influence responses to particular items demonstrates the importance of redemptive validity.

The next step is to perform a focused item analysis of a narrow sample of depression tools (BDI-II, CAD, GRID-HAMD, RADS II, SDS, and PHQ-9). Combining the items from all the measures allows for coding according the summary categories established by Santor et al. (see table 7.1). The following descriptions were applied: mood symptoms (e.g., depressed mood and irritability), behavioral symptoms (e.g., suicide and anhedonia), somatic symptoms (e.g., appetite disturbance, sleep disturbance, low energy, and psychomotor retardation or agitation), cognitive symptoms (e.g., hopelessness and worthlessness), and concentration symptoms (e.g., poor concentration and decision making). Sample items include "I feel downhearted and blue" (mood symptoms); "I feel like hurting myself" (behavioral symptoms); "I never have any energy" (somatic symptoms); "I feel my future is hopeless and will only get worse" (cognitive symptoms); and "I have great difficulty making decisions" (concentration symptoms).

Table 7.1. Item analysis of depression assessment tools

	BDI-II	CAD	GRID-HAMD	PHQ-9	RADS II	SDS	Total
Number of items							
Mood symptoms	4	14	11	1	10	5	45
Behavioral symptoms	4	9	13	3	6	3	38
Somatic symptoms	4	4	29	4	5	7	53
Cognitive symptoms	7	19	12	1	9	3	51
Concentration symptoms	2	4	0	1	0	2	9
Total	21	50	65	10	30	20	196
Percentages							
Mood symptoms	19%	28%	17%	10%	33%	25%	23%
Behavioral symptoms	19%	18%	20%	30%	20%	15%	19%
Somatic symptoms	19%	8%	45%	40%	17%	35%	27%
Cognitive symptoms	33%	38%	18%	10%	30%	15%	26%
Concentration symptoms	10%	8%	0%	10%	0%	10%	5%

The distinctive emphasis within each measure could be the key factor that makes it useful for selection. The assessment measure of choice would be one that offers the best complement to the clinician's conceptualization of depression. For example, assessment measures with proportionally more items in cognitive symptom areas would be the preference for counselors with a cognitive behavioral theoretical orientation (e.g., BDI-II, CAD, and RADS II). In another setting that emphasizes medication, clinicians would easily gravitate toward tools that specify the widest range of somatic symptoms (i.e., GRID-HAMD and SDS).

Now let's consider RV in conjunction with this item analysis. First, each measure directly assesses depression via specific content concerning the subject's current state of discontentment, discomfort, hopelessness, and physical distress. This indicates that the results represent a tangible description of life areas that are very much in need of the Lord's grace and restoration. A score in the clinical range on one of these measures signals to helpers how desperately the counselee is in need of basic psychological food, refreshment, rest, and companionship from the Great Shepherd (Ps 23).

Second, the cognitive items located in these measures address foundational beliefs to explore in counseling dialogue. Internalized schemas identified by the items may intersect with theological doctrine, scriptural principles, or a cultural adaptation of Christianity in community. Consider these cognitive items: "I feel my future is hopeless and will only get worse" (BDI-II) or "I feel that I am useful and needed" (SDS). The beliefs and the resulting emotions bound together with these statements have a bearing on how one's personal narrative flows from the grand gospel narrative of creation, fall, and redemption into the daily experience of being a child of God. The cognitive schema surfaced by the item alerts the therapist to matters for further exploration when these themes surface in session material. Conversations surrounding everyday assumptions and personal beliefs relating to biblical themes such as sanctification, stewardship, and the hope of eternal life may be appropriate and have therapeutic benefit.

Finally, each measure contains items that highlight emotional turmoil or safety concerns. A common procedure is to identify critical items that, when answered in a particular direction, necessitate immediate and specific follow-up. Typically an item is marked as critical because it may suggest suicidal thoughts or threats to harm self or others. In the interest of RV, counselors with Christian worldview convictions may identify items that signal a faith journey concern or a spiritual crisis. For counselors who desire practical strategies, identify these items as faith sensitive. Christian counselors who routinely use measures may come to recognize discrete items that tap into core convictions by addressing spiritually laden themes or concepts. Faith-sensitive items offer a gateway to discussing theological beliefs and faith practices. Consider the items in table 7.2.

Table 7.2. Faith-sensitive items

Measure	Item
BDI-II	I feel that I am a total failure as a person.
	I feel quite guilty all of the time.
	I feel I am being punished.
	I blame myself for everything bad that happens.
	I feel utterly worthless.
CAD	No one seems to care about me.
	It feels like no one loves me.
	I feel like I am being punished.
	My life has no meaning.
	It seems that there is no hope for me.
	I feel like a complete failure.
GRID-HAMD	How guilty have you been feeling this past week?
	Do you feel that your depression is a punishment for something bad you've done?
	Have you been hearing voices or seeing visions in the last week?
PHQ-9	You are a failure or have let yourself or your family down.
RADS-II	I feel that no one cares about me.
	I feel loved.
SDS	I feel hopeful about the future.

The standard guideline for responsible test interpretation is not to place undue emphasis on any single item or set of items not recognized as a distinct scale. Nevertheless, it is a common clinical practice to highlight items as productive dialogue starters to produce insight via expanded verbal processing after the measure is completed. Select items may stimulate conversation to detect theological distortions or practice applications. Christians using these tools may single out items for later query. Items that expose beliefs associated with scriptural concepts might be useful signposts to direct further exploration. Consider the potential of items that relate to themes of forgiveness, subjective versus objective guilt, the future, suffering, sin, and revelation (Collins, 2007). These could provide a channel to move counseling conversation, when clinically and ethically appropriate, toward further dependence on the Lord or a fuller understanding of the Word.

CONSTRUCT RELEVANCE: ALIGNING DEPRESSION AND
A HEAVY HEART

The transposition of Christian biblical concepts with psychological constructs is a matter for detailed consideration (Greggo, 2011; Johnson, 2007; Roberts & Watson, 2010; Watson, 2008). Counselors must be keenly aware of not only the construct a scale measures, but its technical definition in order to research the tool's effectiveness in quantifying what it is intended to measure. As Christian counselors we must also diligently examine Scripture for stories, metaphors, and instructions for living that apply to that construct. While it may be tempting to mix terms or ideas for the sake of convenience, such simplistic associations are rarely helpful in constructing a trustworthy, theologically grounded understanding. Determining RV requires pondering details and their meaning. The desired result of this consideration is the capacity to articulate a vision of God's intentions for a particular area of human experience. The following question provides the most helpful gauge of a tool's RV: Can I now communicate a common-sense explanation of the construct to clients in a way that will increase their curiosity and interest in the results?

While *depression* is a medical term, it is commonly used in everyday language to describe an emotional state of sadness and hopelessness, of living with a "heavy heart." *Depression* may not generate any hits in a biblical concordance, but Scripture certainly has rich depictions of a related condition of the heart. Proverbs 25:20 says,

Like one who takes away a garment on a cold day,

or like vinegar poured on a wound,

is one who sings songs to a heavy heart.

Proverbs 25:20 contains an idiom that is difficult to translate. The Hebrew word *ra'* is most commonly translated into English as "heavy." In this verse *ra'* is used as an adjective, but it can also be used as a noun or verb. In its adjective form, the most frequent translation is "bad" or "evil," sometimes in reference to specific actions, words, or thoughts, or more generally as immorality. Much less frequent is its reference to grievous or severe physical pain (Deut 28:35; Job 2:7). The translation of *ra'* in Proverbs 25:20 as "heavy heart" points beyond physical pain to emotional discontent or misfortune (see also Neh 2:1-2). This use denotes a dark covering that substantially alters the mind, emotions, rationality, inner consciousness, and will—a condition similar to our current medical condition of depression.

A heavy heart is a state in which sadness, grief, and ongoing suffering block anticipation of hope. The impact is so dramatic that one has a palpable sense of separation from God, others, and even self. The phrase "heavy heart" has a clear-cut connection to other undesirable heart ailments mentioned in the Bible such as sorrow (Prov 15:13-15), sickness (Prov 13:12), and suffering or affliction (Ps 22:24-26; Masri, Smith, Schaller, Smith, & Welch, 2000; Welch, 2000a). These conditions disturb the center of human affection. In Scripture, this may reveal the presence of sin in the corrupted creation or the effect of sin on the activities of fallen creatures formed in the *imago Dei* (Kilner, 2010). Nonetheless, any humanly contrived association between individual transgressions and a suffering heart is a serious matter that requires utmost care (Welch, 2000b). Specific causal associations to explain grief, hopelessness, or a heavy heart are often beyond the bounds of human understanding (Job 36–41). Cause-and-effect linkages can be blatantly reductionist and raise unnecessary suspicion in those enduring suffering and pain.

The terms *depression* and a *heavy heart* are admittedly distinct in derivation, usage, and precision. One is methodical and medical; the other is metaphorical and spiritual. Still, they represent overlapping psychological and affective states. The issue in construct relevance revolves around how this human experience is portrayed in the way these converge. For the sake of pursuing RV, pondering the theological implications is vital.

Medical terms have become a part of everyday language; as a result, terms such as *depression* and a *heavy heart* are viewed as synonymous. But as the language shifts from the general description of a metaphysical heart condition to a physical illness diagnosed through the application of scientific tools, the physical (or chemical/neurological) aspect of human distress becomes the emphasis. A client outspoken about spiritual concerns who manifests a corresponding dark affective experience is undergoing a crisis of faith due to the experience of depression.

Counselors with Christian worldviews do well to reverse conceptually the overlap between the constructs of depression and heavy heart. Depression as a mental health condition is a particular subheading of the broader experience of a heavy heart. The technical description of depression as a bio-psycho-social disorder is thus a subtype of a broader bio-psycho-social-spiritual condition. A client with a heavy heart may indeed be clinically depressed, but other conceptualizations may apply. This distinction is essential when exploring the RV of depression assessment because it maintains the integrity of these related and layered constructs.

Science explains the spiritual dilemma using a disease model. Thus, resolve the medical concern of depression, and faith will return. From the vantage point of RV, viewing the situation as predominantly medical may result in misguided interventions. Could the heavy heart experience be a disturbance not bound within neurochemistry that does not require direct physical treatment? The emotional pain may relate to a life transition or an adjustment of expectations in one's relationship with the Lord. This would reflect the phrase "dark night of the soul" (Coe, 2000, p. 293).

For centuries, Christians have recognized that there are seasons in a spiritual journey when the Holy Spirit instigates such a deep and profound work that the sojourner feels disoriented, as if traveling in mysterious and unfamiliar territory. The intent of this season is not to punish sin or wrongdoing. Instead, it provokes maturation in one's spiritual development through purgation or cleansing, illumination, or a tighter relational bond with the Almighty. In this instance, it would not be appropriate in Christian counseling to apply a treatment approach limited to medication or to target only somatic symptoms. This type of heart condition reveals a hunger to hear the Spirit and obey. There may be struggles with spiritual doubts that would benefit from Christian fellowship, pastoral support, and Spirit-directed, Scripture-saturated comfort. The affective experience may be unwanted, overwhelming, and dark, yet it could be the gateway to new life in one's relationship with the Lord.

Depression assessment supplies a quantitative description of an unwanted, disconcerting, and intense human experience. When the language of depression is rooted in a medically oriented worldview, there are assumptions regarding etiology and treatment that go beyond basic operational definitions (Welch, 2000a). It would be problematic to treat all experiences of a heavy heart as predominantly a mental health concern. Depicting depression as the overarching conceptual framework is an example of medical reductionism. Such a practice, no matter how subtle or well intended, favors treatments that primarily address physical symptoms. The clarification of language between these corresponding human experiences actually highlights the construct validity of the depression assessment tools in our example. These tools do indeed measure what they purport to measure: a medically relevant mental health condition. However, Christian helpers desire to resolve more than just medical concerns; under the ministry of the Holy Spirit, we seek to minister to hearts that are discouraged, despondent, and unnaturally burdened (Welch, 2000b). Regrettably, conceptualizing all experiences of a heavy heart within a strictly medical framework increases the risk of clients not getting the scope of help they need.

In terms of RV, Christians who rely on assessment measures must maintain a holistic and theologically consistent appreciation for the central condition of the human heart. The spiritual journey follows a path of longing to secure rest in the grace of our Creator. Our role is to consider whether the self-report data on a depression measure contribute to a deeper understanding of the central condition of the human heart or reveal core affections that point toward a need for further reliance on the grace of God.

EXPLORING MATTERS OF THE HEART

A Christian conceptualization of the condition of the heart will enhance treatment and result in effective care. This involves expanding the construct of depression beyond what these measures aim to capture and thus requires clinician initiative. Counselors must supplement available information to formulate a comprehensive, holistic, and gospel-oriented perspective. Clients who desire counseling within a biblically grounded framework deserve to have this magnified perspective included in any collaborative treatment plan.

Recognizing that a client's heavy heart may be connected to a turning point in spiritual formation, and not to brain chemistry, is an example of expanding the criteria. Interior calamity may precede spiritual advancement. Another possible explanation is that the unrest within is a sign of conviction, and the emotional repercussions are a press for repentance and renewal. The psalmist states that a "broken spirit" as reflected by a "broken and contrite heart" can be a desirable, favored condition. The Lord welcomes this attitude when offered as a sacrifice (Ps 51:17). Submission, dependence, worship, and adoration are the means to a clean heart, restored spirit, and rejuvenated joy. The context of Psalm 51 suggests that the internal suffering is associated with personal transgression.

Other wisdom passages attribute heart infirmities to the undermining, delay, or destruction of hope (Prov 13:12). Hope is central in promoting heart health and is shattered through loss, abuse, betrayal, abandonment, financial ruin, persistent stress, delayed or denied dreams, or the physical groaning of a decaying body. No matter what forces converge to provoke the onset of a heavy heart, movement toward wellness, or shalom, will require reliance on the Lord. When trust is strained, its renovation fortifies faith. When hope is shattered, suffering becomes a spiritual crucible that can produce sanctification and deeper faith. The mind is renewed as one conforms to the Lord's will.

Looking at validity in the light of the redemptive process reveals two veins of exploration. A psychological instrument focuses on what is occurring within the individual; measurement is descriptive. The Christian counseling process is one of engagement for a restorative purpose. It may involve pondering how the Spirit is moving or unpacking Scripture to provide meaning to an experience. The instrument supplies a point-in-time snapshot of one aspect of life experience. The counseling encounter puts that information to use by weaving it within the ongoing life story of a person participating in God's dramatic efforts to redeem humanity and creation. This is a formation process. RV considers how the description offered by a tool provides benchmarks that encourage conformity to the image of Jesus Christ. Describing the results of the test in concrete terms is one level of explanation; Scripture supplies the spiritual significance of those results.

REDEMPTIVE VALIDITY (RV) AND TOOL ADOPTION

The outset of the chapter introduced Brice, a seminarian struggling to stay the course to fulfill his ministry calling through the academic rigors of a divinity degree. What assessment tools would be appropriate for Brice? The answer is those that fit his concerns and the clinician's conceptualization, and that have potential for RV. The end result of a redemptive-validity application means that results from the measure contribute to conversations with Brice that furthers his grasp of how to live wisely in light of the full teaching of Scripture.

In Brice's case, under consideration are three conceptualizations of his lethargy and inability to concentrate on his academic assignments: (1) Is this a season of spiritual dryness that will eventually transition into spiritual growth? (2) Is there personal sin or character failings to confess and address? (3) Is Brice in the midst of clinical depression? A combination of assessment techniques could be productive in refining understanding regarding these options as well as others. A counselor consulting with Brice would need to gather more information to merge, separate, and eventually rule out other explanations that Brice has been contemplating. A standardized measure may aid in the assessment of depression according to accepted medical criteria. Insight derived from the implementation of a particular tool may facilitate communication with other professionals and interested parties such as the dean of students. Most importantly, obtaining tangible descriptions may be advantageous to Brice himself.

There is good reason to contemplate any normative information gained. Counselors with Christian convictions should not reject assessment results because of worldview differences. The adoption of measures may broaden understanding of a client's behavioral, affective, and physical experience. Christians who counsel should not succumb to the cultural trend of lumping the diverse experience of a heavy heart into the singular category of clinical depression. However, a well-formed medical perspective of depression may be instrumental in developing a plan for relief. Essentially, the theologically astute Christian helper focuses not only on the heart in agony but also on the Comforter's availability to refresh while guiding purposeful transformation in the midst of adversity. If the oppressed can no longer sense his presence, our helping function is to come alongside and minister his presence.

For the sake of illustration, let's assume that Brice was administered the Clinical Assessment of Depression (CAD). This can clarify a depression diagnosis across an extensive age range. The tool has three subscales built in to check the response style or attitude of the client toward the assessment experience (Inconsistency, Infrequency, and Negative Typical). The readings on those scales evaluate the quality of information that he supplied. This is good since Brice expressed frustration with the elementary format of the items. He was agitated that he could not qualify or add to the fifty "pathetically" basic statements and felt it restricted his freedom to express his position. Nevertheless, Brice communicated via the CAD.

The CAD total score (T = 62; mild clinical risk) suggests the presence of depressive symptoms at a level of concern but not as an alarming crisis. Intervention is indicated to relieve this distress, but it doesn't warrant undue pressure. Feedback of the main finding to Brice did appear to be useful in that it made the recommendation stick that further counseling would be a good investment of his precious time.

Two of the CAD's four subscales were significantly elevated, Depressed Mood and Diminished Interest, while the other two, Anxiety/Worry and Cognitive and Physical Fatigue, were in the normal to mild clinical range. Talk of these specific areas with Brice was productive in generating discussion on what is different about his life now and his current spiritual experience without the dynamic involvement he had with his former community. Brice made the observation that it's challenging for him to keep interest in his studies without the stimulation that he once enjoyed as a key leader in his college fellowship. Further exploration of the most telling scales made his current mood experience concrete.

Although not immediate, this trail of conversation brought him to confess that he underestimated and devalued the sustenance he once enjoyed from this girlfriend. He recalled how he wanted to stop the assessment at item seven,

"I do like myself." Through tears he blurts out, "It's hard to come out and admit how badly I treated her. I was so utterly caught up in my own importance. It was impossible to see past how the Lord was blessing my ministry. I never considered that she would stop loving me, but I gave her no reason to love me." Confession and cleansing did come in time. It seems that the pastor's insights that Brice failed to demonstrate respect and honor to his girlfriend may have been close to the movement of the Holy Spirit.

Christians who use assessments must become adept at drawing out faith implications from the test results. A measure may enhance understanding or it may detract from a theologically astute perspective. The category of RV offers a lens to incorporate and interpret results in order to realize the maximum gain for Christian clients. We accomplish this via an initial review of the recognized categories of validity—content, construct, and criterion. Then we move on to investigate these features using a biblical and theological grid (see appendix 1). RV involves examining the effectiveness of an assessment tool to generate useful information and promote wise living in conformity to Scripture. Stated differently, RV considers how information gleaned from a measure leads to a fuller understanding of the person as a bio-psycho-social-spiritual being from the vantage point of the good news of the gospel. The ultimate purpose is to ponder how quantified details about a slice of behavior can help clients participate in the holistic, redemptive work of the Holy Spirit in their lives.

REFERENCES

American Educational Research Association, American Psychological Association, & National Council on Measurement in Education. (2014). *Standards for educational and psychological testing.* Washington, DC: AERA.

American Psychiatric Association. (2013). *Diagnostic and statistical manual of mental disorders* (5th ed.). Arlington, VA: American Psychiatric Publishing.

Antony, M. M., & Barlow, D. H. (Eds.). (2010). *Handbook of assessment and treatment planning for psychological disorders* (2nd ed.). New York: Guilford Press.

Ayearst, L. E., & Bagby, R. M. (2010). Evaluating the psychometric properties of psychological measures. In Martin M. Antony & David H. Barlow (Eds.), *Handbook of assessment and treatment planning for psychological disorders.* New York: Guilford Press, pp. 23-69.

Carlson, J. F., Geisinger, K. F., & Jonson, J. L. (Eds.). (2017). *The twentieth mental measurements yearbook.* Lincoln, NE: Buros Institute of Mental Measurements.

Coe, J. H. (2000). Musings on the dark night of the soul: Insights from St. John of the Cross on a developmental spirituality. *Journal of Psychology and Theology, 28*(4), 293-307.

Collins, G. R. (2007). *Christian counseling: A comprehensive guide* (3rd ed.). Nashville: Thomas Nelson.

Cooper, T. D. (2003). *Sin, pride & self-acceptance: The problem of identity in theology & psychology*. Downers Grove, IL: InterVarsity Press.

Dods, M. (1903/1982). The book of Genesis. In W. R. Nicoll (Ed.), *The expositor's Bible* (Vol. 1, pp. 198-211). Grand Rapids, MI: Baker.

Greggo, S. P. (2011). Internal working model as heart: A translation to inspire Christian care groups. *Edification: The Transdisciplinary Journal of Christian Psychology, 5*(1), 4-13.

Greggo, S. P., & Lawrence, K. (2012). Redemptive validity and the assessment of depression: Singing songs to heavy hearts. *Journal of Psychology and Theology, 40*(3), 188-198.

Gregory, R. J. (2014). *Psychological testing: History, principles, and applications* (7th ed.). Boston: Pearson.

Groth-Marnat, G., & Wright, A. J. (2016). *Handbook of psychological assessment* (6th ed.). Hoboken, NJ: John Wiley & Sons.

Haynes, S. N., & Lench, H. C. (2003). Incremental validity of new clinical assessment measures. *Psychological Assessment, 15*(4), 456-466.

Hughes, R. B., & Laney, C. J. (2001). *Tyndale concise Bible commentary*. Wheaton, IL: Tyndale House.

Johnson, E. L. (2007). *Foundations for soul care: A Christian psychology proposal*. Downers Grove, IL: InterVarsity Press.

Kilner, J. F. (2010). Humanity in God's image: Is the image really damaged? *Journal of the Evangelical Theological Society, 53*(3), 601-617.

Maloney, M. P., & Ward, M. P. (1976). *Psychological assessment: A conceptual approach*. New York: Oxford University Press.

Masri, A., Smith, A., Schaller, J., Smith, B., & Welch, E. (2000). Christian doctors on depression. *Journal of Biblical Counseling, 18*(3), 35-43.

Nezu, A. M., Nezu, C. M., Lee, M., & Stern, J. B. (2014). Assessment of depression. In I. H. Gotlib & C. L. Hammen (Eds.), *Handbook of depression* (3rd ed., pp. 25-44). New York: Guilford Press.

Roberts, R. C., & Watson, P. J. (2010). A Christian psychology view. In E. L. Johnson (Ed.), *Psychology & Christianity: Five views* (2nd ed., pp. 149-178). Downers Grove, IL: InterVarsity Press.

Ross, A. P. (1985). Genesis. In J. F. Walvoord & R. B. Zuck (Eds.), *The Bible knowledge commentary: Old Testament* (pp. 64-66). Wheaton, IL: Victor Books.

Santor, D. A., Gregus, M., & Welch, A. (2006). Eight decades of measurement in depression. *Measurement, 4*(3), 135-155.

Schneider, W., & Brown, C. (1978). Tempt, test, approve. In C. Brown (Ed.), *The new international dictionary of New Testament theology* (pp. 798-808). Grand Rapids, MI: Zondervan.

Vanhoozer, K. J. (2010). Forming the performers: How Christians can use canon sense to bring us to our (theodramatic) senses. *Edification: Journal of the Society of Christian Psychology, 4*(1), 5-16.

Watson, P. J. (2008). Faithful translation, ideological perspectives, and Christian psychology beyond postmodernism. *Edification: Journal of the Society of Christian Psychology, 2*(1), 51-62.

Welch, E. (2000a). Queries & controversies: How valid or useful are psychiatric labels for depression? *Journal of Biblical Counseling, 18*(2), 54-56.

Welch, E. (2000b). Understanding depression. *Journal of Biblical Counseling, 18*(2), 12-24.

Whiston, S. C. (2017). *Principles and applications of assessment in counseling* (5th ed.). Belmont, CA: Cengage.

Wiersbe, W. W. (1993). *Wiersbe's expository outlines on the Old Testament.* Wheaton, IL: Victor Books.

Wilson, M. R. (1980). 1373 (*nasa*) test. In R. L. Harris, G. L. Archer, & B. K. Waltke (Eds.), *Theological wordbook of the Old Testament* (Vol. 2, p. 581). Chicago: Moody Press.

PART 3

ASSESSMENT

SELECTION AND

ADMINISTRATION

CHAPTER EIGHT

ARTISANSHIP IN
CONDUCTING INTERVIEWS

The wise in heart are called discerning,
and gracious words promote instruction.

PROVERBS 16:21

THEOLOGICAL THEME

Discernment

DEEP WATERS, RUSHING STREAMS: FROM WORDS TO WISDOM

Consider these lessons found among the riddles of the wise:

The words of the mouth are deep waters,

but the fountain of wisdom is a rushing stream. (Prov 18:4)

Before a downfall the heart is haughty,

but humility comes before honor.

To answer before listening—

that is folly and shame. (Prov 18:12-13)

For those of us with trouble-free access to water, the potency of the metaphor of words as deep waters might be lost.

Picture yourself in the arid desert climate in which these proverbs were produced. "Deep waters" alludes to water in a well in the depths of the earth. It requires exertion to pull it up bucket by bucket, but the water is necessary to sustain life so it must be lifted out of the well and carried home.

Communication can be a bit like this process of pulling water out of a well. Transparency and disclosure are not normal in everyday conversation; candor runs contrary to social sensibilities and survival instincts. People's words may contain inferences that are buried, diffuse, mysterious, and difficult to understand. Those who listen carefully learn to read between the lines of spoken words to discover more of the story. The hidden meaning becomes clear after disciplined inquiry, demonstrated compassion, and risky probes.

Conversely, conversation can resemble a gushing mountain stream. Melting snow becomes cool water that flows down the slope to revive and cleanse. Words can have the vitality and force of a gushing stream. When this happens, the meaning is plain, emotion is spontaneous, and wisdom is accessible. This type of dialogue is extemporaneous, refreshing, and alive.

The proverbs at the beginning of the chapter suggest sound tactics to guide assessment. Knowledge and technique about counseling should not evoke pride, superiority, or arrogance; rather, dedicated listening flows from a humble spirit. Christians who counsel must pray for open minds, careful listening, and anointed speech. When the words from our mouths proceed from hearts that have meditated on the Word, they will lead to understanding (Ps 49:3). When we listen well to our clients, we may uncover reservoirs of hope. Part of our role as counselors is to locate the underlying meaning and to open the door to conversations that revitalize. The interview is face-to-face assessment that tactfully secures pertinent information as it paves the way for a growth-directed encounter.

INTERVIEWING AND CONNECTING

It's useful to distinguish interviewing from typical dialogue. There is obvious overlap: both involve reciprocal interaction, for example. This means that both parties influence the tone, direction, and outcome. However, interviews are primarily directed by the person who is in the role of expert. It is imperative for counselors to be able to probe effectively. Mastering that skill allows us to obtain information that is not otherwise available or readily disclosed (Groth-Marnat & Wright, 2016; Mears, 2016).

The attempt to blend human communication with scientific investigation in mental health encounters is not new. Henry Stack Sullivan delivered a series of lectures in the mid-1940s under the title *The Psychiatric Interview*. These emerged following his death as the landmark treatise on this foundational clinical activity (Sullivan, 1954). Surprisingly, his unique contribution remains germane despite advancements and drastic revolutions within mental health settings. Early clinical encounters demand astute insight into the immediate human drama and discernment to apply professional knowledge.

The psychiatric interview is a special instance of interpersonal relations, and the term, as used here, does not refer exclusively to the meeting of a psychiatrist with his patient. The interview is characterized by the coming together of two people, one recognized as an expert in interpersonal relations, the other known as the client, interviewee, or patient, who expects to derive some benefit from serious discussion of his needs with this expert. The situation is designed to make clear certain characteristic patterns of the client's living with the prospect that such elucidation will prove useful to him. (Sullivan, 1954, p. ix)

One basic and unassumingly brilliant notion qualifies Sullivan's material as a definitive classic. Experts execute interviews to secure relevant information. Nevertheless, direct entry into interpersonal dialogue to gather these data entails active person-to-person engagement. Sullivan makes the case that the interviewer's role by necessity draws its expert power from a combination of functions, namely, that of external observer *and* immediate participant. Building on this premise, he issues a formidable challenge to maximize the potential of this unique position. Mental health practitioners strive to combine objective appraisal with subjective interpersonal experience to facilitate optimal evaluation, treatment insight, and therapeutic alignment.

Scientist-practitioner and participant-observer. Sullivan articulated his original analysis of the clinical encounter over a half century ago. Two dominant influences shaped mental health appraisal during that era. First, the premier and idealized model for this technical undertaking was that of a physician's medical examination: systematic, scientific, and predictable. Physicians listen to a chief complaint. Through methodical inspection they begin to gather functional data via direct examination and through an assortment of precise tests. They pursue informed hypotheses until one is ruled in or out.

Second, on all matters of psychological functioning there was the utmost regard for the dominant theoretical framework of psychoanalysis. Within that theoretical tradition, the therapist's role and function is that of a detached authority figure who hands down specialized insight. The patient learns to expect the clinician to offer mystifying and intoxicating interpretations in an effort to illuminate underlying intrapsychic processes.

For mental health specialists at that time, the objective in an initial encounter was to emulate a scientist-practitioner. This descriptive term reflects the research methodology approach interviewers brought to the clinical domain. Clinicians were taught to maintain sufficient distance from a patient during the interview to ensure objectivity. Remaining aloof and on a pedestal was important for establishing one's expertise and issuing curative pronouncements. The concerns of the patient were handled in much the same manner as a physician stitches up a wound or dispenses a prescription. The message essentially was, "Take this insight, trust that it will recalibrate your interior balance, and our interview will continue next week."

Sullivan does not abandon the essential role of scientist and human systems expert. Instead, he expands the role to include social relating, communication, and emotional expression in making contact. In this new portrayal, the interviewer leaps from the pedestal and plunges into an interpersonal exchange in which data flow to the surface and become available for consideration. That is, the patterns a patient exhibits or triggers within the therapist offer a direct and superior source of data critical to gaining insight into the patient's struggle.

It is best not to view Sullivan's new depiction of the interviewer role as pitting scientific objectivity against interpersonal association. Rather, the role of participant-observer complements that of scientist-practitioner. These hyphenated terms (not utilized by Sullivan himself) help emphasize the distinct priorities he articulated. Each role acknowledges the professional necessity to be engaged and impartial, actor and director, player and referee. This theme will carry forward into my recommendations for mental health professionals (MHPs) to engage with clients.

Formalities and becoming familiar. The initial intake takes on the format of an interview (Morrison, 2014). Unfortunately, the word *interview* dulls the senses to the interpersonal complexity involved. Interviewers formally pose questions and conduct an examination. But this is only the beginning. The desired outcome of a mental health dialogue runs much deeper than data acquisition. Rather, to use Sullivan's description of engagement, the helper combines the power of knowledge with active, supportive allegiance. The early encounter is a quest to become familiar with the ways a client's personality and relational style influence how they relate to others. The assumption is that the presenting concern stems from a combination of interpersonal patterns and current circumstances. Clinicians gather insights from the immediacy of the interpersonal exchange. In order to solve the multifaceted puzzle of a client's chief concern, MHPs apply structure to gather facts and make careful note of spontaneous nonverbal information, behavioral enactments, and relational patterns (Lukas, 1993). Thus, the matter of how therapist and client relate is of central interest.[1]

---

[1]The *Psychiatric Interview in Clinical Practice* (3rd ed.), published by the American Psychiatric Association, may be the contemporary heir to the early Sullivan proposal (MacKinnon, Michels, & Buckley, 2016). This expansive, encyclopedic volume dwarfs its ancestor by hundreds of pages and in its density of detailed application. There is valuable material in the comprehensive descriptions of how to identify, engage, and assess patients across the full range of psychiatric disorders according to recent diagnostic formulations. Chapters provide extensive coverage of specific patient presentations (e.g., the psychotic, antisocial, traumatized, cognitively impaired, and depressed patient, etc.). What is remarkable is the

Data resources. Counselors must attend to multiple domains during early clinical exchanges. The three main ones for consideration are content and process, introspective and inspective, and thought and affect (MacKinnon, Michels, & Buckley, 2016; see fig. 8.1). The most obvious material arises from the *content*— the facts and particulars shared directly through the verbal report of the client. Coherence between details and psychosocial insights are of special interest. Moving beneath the surface, the counselor's curiosity does not rest with the obvious. Every inflection of voice, word choice, nonverbal behavior, or omission is instantaneously ascribed value for understanding relational, motivational, and emotional dynamics. *Process*, or the relational communication between the interviewer and client, is critical. Subtle cues transmitted by the client become accessible in the interaction with the clinician. The counselor listens not only to what is said but to how the patient joins the conversation and reveals and withholds information. Process examination occurs in the relational "between." Is the client exhibiting an interpersonal style that is open, distant, arrogant, seductive, warm, optimistic, defensive, annoyed, or passive-aggressive? Material communicated via content and process represents a crucial dimension of the information gathering.

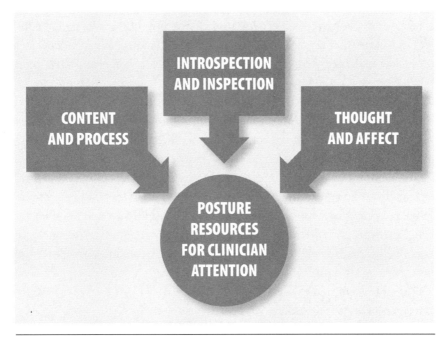

Figure 8.1. Objective and interpersonal dimensions for mental health assessment

continuity between the present-day, medical text and Sullivan's generic interview principles. The crux of the thesis remains familiar even as contemporary terminology portrays the resources to isolate data.

Building upon this beginning, counselors facilitate a client's *introspection*; that is, they help clients develop insight into their own experiences and emotions. Through this process, counselors gather descriptions of internal conditions, rationales for behavior, meaning attributions, and a client's understanding of the confluence of variables. This gives counselors a window into a client's inner state, thought patterns, and motivations. *Inspective* data, on the other hand, are gathered from close observation of any nonverbal but demonstrated feelings. These data are visible in tears, laughter, sweating, restlessness, and facial flushing. The attributes of voice, motor activity, and even silence yield clues about how a client perceives the self, others, and the situation at hand.

The third domain for clinician attention is *thought* and *affect*, both of which are evident in the client's present mental state. Unlike the first two domains, which focus on how a client interacts related to the area of concern, this domain examines the client's engagement in the interview. This dimension comes into view as the client reacts to the press of being evaluated. Clinicians observe clients' awareness, alertness, astuteness, and guardedness as each personal story takes center stage. They scrutinize thought sequence and development. They also monitor the quantity and quality of information, ease and rate of speech production, and the organizational structure of the narrative, or the lack of it. Attention is given to the topics selected, favored, and avoided. They note affect such as excitement, hope, joy, sadness, anger, shame, and frustration. In contrast, it is equally telling when signs of affect are absent around topics that would typically evoke it, or when the subject matter and the emotional display are incongruent. Finally, counselors also pay attention to internal patterns through descriptions and metaphors in response to queries, immediacy, or empathy statements.

The art of interviewing in mental health practice has been progressing for over half a century. Today, clinicians with appropriate training bring to an initial interview both the technical knowledge of a specialist and the interpersonal awareness of a perceptive participant. Both accomplished scientist and relationally attuned self are optimally present. This combination allows patterns of interaction associated with client problems to surface and then be subjected to sophisticated analysis. Clinicians are also able to recognize characteristics of certain disorders.

Different settings, from hospital to private practice to community clinic, will likely have different procedures for the first interview. These are customized to correspond with the purpose of the program, the orientation of its practitioners, and the scope of treatment. But despite the range of purposes, the merger of the roles of scientist-practitioner and participant-observer is exceedingly helpful.

COUNSELORS AS COMFORTED COMFORTERS

In addition to functioning as scientist-practitioner and participant-observer, Christian counselors have another role to bear in mind: comforted comforter. Paul captured this role well when he wrote:

> Praise be to the God and Father of our Lord Jesus Christ, the Father of compassion and the God of all comfort, who comforts us in all our troubles, so that we can comfort those in any trouble with the comfort we ourselves receive from God. (2 Cor 1:3-4)

Our personal relationship with the Lord and awareness of his grace toward our wounds motivate us to offer hospitality to others. Our bond to the Father of all compassion enables us to enter the life of another with compassion (Nouwen, 1979). A Christian helper comes alongside one bearing concerns and enters that person's spiritual journey. We operate under the conviction that the Great Comforter is already at work to accomplish his purpose in both us and the client (cf. Jn 14:16-18; 16:8-11). The helping effort only appears to begin with an interview; from a kingdom perspective, the Comforter has long been accompanying the client. Professional interpersonal activity is a human enterprise that strives to join with the Holy Spirit's ongoing convicting and re-creative work.

Establishing a counseling relationship and beginning a journey toward change demands expertise (Morrison, 2014; Murdin, 2005). We collect information that becomes the basis for comprehensive documentation within a case record. We organize observations, formulate a conceptualization of the client, evaluate person-situation-relationship dynamics, and target key issues for treatment. Beyond the technical work of analyzing a client's situation, it is important to develop a professional relationship that has a highly personal quality. Accomplishing both requires clinical expertise. Fortunately, the Christ-centered counselor can commit the entire exchange into our Lord's hands and rely on the ministry of the Comforter, the Holy Spirit. When we recognize that ultimate authority rests with the Lord, we are able to receive his perspective and participation.

In Christian counseling there is a broader agenda requiring a different form of expertise, in addition to technical and interpersonal skills. We discern the movement of the Spirit by attending to the client's motivation and where the winds of change are blowing. The scriptural metanarrative follows the good news of creation, fall, redemption, and restoration through Jesus Christ. Hearing the personal account of a particular client, we consider how the individual is uniquely crafted by the Creator and formed through the earthly forces of nature and nurture. We also see woven into this story brokenness caused by sin, the effects of which may fuel an internal drive to think, feel, and act in persistent rebellion or passive resistance to the directives of the Word or the Holy Spirit. No matter how extensive the client's bondage or pain, we pay attention to ways the God of all comfort may be at work to soothe, redeem, or restore the individual. The problem-solving dimensions of counseling combine with soul care to provide more holistic care.

RECOGNIZING SPIRITUAL ORIENTATION

As comforted comforters, we pay close attention to Christian identity and how this permeates the client's personal narrative. We observe the direction of thought, preferences, and interests related to spiritual themes within the client's story, beliefs, and passions. These are likely to appear naturally in conversation about the presenting concern. In this attuning, there are three dimensions that contribute to our understanding of Christian identity and that merit close monitoring. (See fig. 8.2.) These parallel the broad mental health domains previously described.

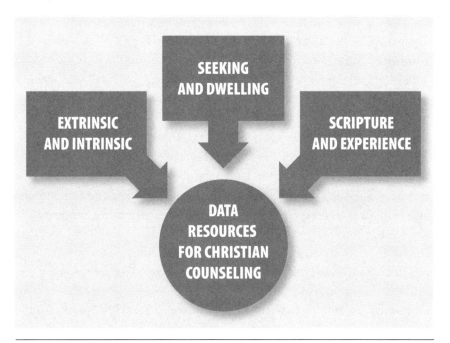

Figure 8.2. Indicators of spiritual state and faith development

The dimensions to consider are trends that display an extrinsic or intrinsic faith orientation, a preference for seeking or dwelling as a condition for faith development, and an emphasis on Scripture or experience in the discernment of truth to ground one's faith. It is imperative to realize that these categories are provided as organizational rubrics to fine-tune our listening; they are not discrete items for assessment. Instead, as we monitor content and process, introspection and inspection, and thought and affect, faith orientations are also visible. Consider these domains as you learn more about the client's personal narrative and spiritual journey.

Extrinsic or intrinsic faith orientation. The first area for attention is the extrinsic or intrinsic orientation of the client's account of his faith journey. The terms *extrinsic* and *intrinsic* have been in use for decades as a means to differentiate patterns of belief and personal practice (Allport & Ross, 1967). Religious orientation that is described primarily by one's membership ties, family background, organizational affiliations, and corporate identification is identified as external. This was once interpreted as self-serving and a sign that one's actions, beliefs, and individuality were more about belonging to a group than personal belief; group identification functioned as an external status symbol. In contrast, an intrinsic or privately defined faith experience was associated with a mature, internalized, and firm spiritual identity. Thus, in the bygone modernist era, when religious behavior and beliefs were not well respected by the psychiatric community, extrinsic religious tendencies were associated with limited ego strength and dependent psychological functioning.

My goal in this discussion is to portray the terms *extrinsic* and *intrinsic* as neutral and descriptive. This will remove any bias that elevates individualism over collectivism. This application is in keeping with contemporary portrayals where there is no disparity between the extrinsic or intrinsic options to classify spiritual and religious orientations (Hill & Pargament, 2017; Cohen & Hill, 2007). Religious motivation, a feature of one's identity, emerges from within the mutual framework encompassing the religious belief system and collective ideals. These tendencies are likely to be associated with cultural, ethnic, and social identification within a religious community. As presented here, an extrinsic or intrinsic faith orientation is not a sign of spiritual or psychological maturity. Instead, it is a means to recognize motivational forces within a person's faith narrative. We listen to discern what it means for the client to be in God's family and a member of a called-out community that is the bride of Jesus Christ.

A client demonstrates an extrinsic tendency when the client's spiritual journey reflects a high level of dedication to a specific denomination, religious tradition, or ethnic culture. There may be recognition of this leaning through a spoken dialect, specific terminology, loyalty to rituals that govern celebrations, or perhaps even a dress code or other visible symbols. Picture a client who staunchly carries a black-leather-bound King James Version of the Bible into sessions and places it conspicuously on a nearby stand. Even if it is never touched or read aloud, it makes a statement regarding conservative conventions and affiliations. Such a symbol would be a formidable presence in the room and a reminder of a distinctive church tie. Listen to accounts of events or life transitions. Note the people named who serve as models for morality, service, and spiritual maturity. They may be from a local church, family members, or recognizable historical figures in a particular religious movement. In such cases, the clients are drawing upon the spiritual capital from within their faith communities. If the measure of shalom is harmony within the faith community, the orientation is extrinsic. Faith practices conducted for and with others also reflect an extrinsic orientation.

An intrinsic focus is evident when the emphasis is on inner peace, private discernment, and how the Spirit is moving in the client's heart or inner being. In this orientation, the idealized criteria for faith may be a past or future level of personal engagement, giftedness, and Holy Spirit sensitivity. People whose faith has an intrinsic orientation look within to ascertain the presence of the Lord. When the measure of shalom is principally viewed as an interior state, the orientation is intrinsic. Finally, an intrinsic tendency is evident when a person prays routinely; when distressed, sits alone to read Scripture; or sings hymns or worships when there is no one but the Holy Spirit to notice the activity.

Consider these examples of extrinsic and intrinsic orientation:

- Extrinsic: My aunt and grandma have prophetic gifting. They serve with another woman as directors of our fellowship. As leaders, they pray in unison and without ceasing for me. They can sense darkness. They know that my marriage, which they once pronounced as blessed, is now under severe attack by the adversary.

- Extrinsic: The officer of our corps instructed me to speak with you about my battle with my old ways. I am now a cadet and have a responsibility to put old behaviors in the past. This is what it will take to be a leader in the Salvation Army.

- Extrinsic: As far back as I can recall, my large extended family spent Sundays within our own ethnic community. It was not a problem for me to leave home in order to go to college. Once I graduate, however, the expectation is for me to return and live with my family until I marry. This scares me to death.

- Intrinsic: My prayer life is dead. It is impossible to keep my mind from wandering. This is nothing like the prayer life I enjoyed when I first came to know the Lord! I would pray aloud, sing praise choruses with enthusiasm, and read my Bible for hours.

- Intrinsic: The stress at the office is ruining my health and in particular my sleep. Reading a psalm in my quiet time before bed helps me to rest more fully and prepare for a new day.

Seeking or dwelling faith orientation. The second dimension of the client's presentation deserving attention is the degree to which the client pursues spiritual growth. The terms *seekers* and *dwellers* are used in sociological research in reference to the shift away from association with established religious structures to a pursuit of a privatized spiritual journey (Wuthnow, 1998). Dwellers are those who submit to religious institutions, and seekers are those who pursue spiritual growth through spiritual experimentation. Seekers may disdain tradition and embrace novel or ancient practices. Dwellers identify with a place of worship, a congregation, and a pastor. Seekers favor a highly individualized approach and piece together elements that best suit their current objectives. In general, dwellers remain steadfast to longstanding religious authority while seekers value autonomy.

Here are several examples of the seeker and dweller orientations:

- Seeker: Our community church is so predictable and dull that I felt moved to dig deeper. I went on a weekend retreat with my new spiritual director. The presence of the Lord was palpable. She taught me new ways to meditate, and her prayers for me were so very personal.

- Dweller: Each time my pastor conducts a baptismal service, my eyes begin to tear up because it makes me recall my own commitment in baptism. I use the service to quietly renew my vows and intent to live as a disciple.

- Dweller/Seeker: The Lenten services my church offers are especially meaningful. The ministers give us specific ways to refresh our practice of several spiritual disciplines.

In counseling, the objective is to notice these themes in spiritual narratives. The effort is not to arrive at an accurate designation or to propagate stereotypes. The recommendation for counselors is use these categories as a filter to elucidate activity levels and practice preferences within a faith orientation. Notice a client's willingness to go solo after an innovative initiative, read challenging articles, hear provocative speakers, or take risks in the interest of Christian service. Is there an openness to cross-cultural mission experiences or to learning from other Christian traditions? Look for indications of allegiance to time-honored lifestyle choices and desires for rigid barriers between differing doctrinal positions. There may be evidence of a thinking pattern that applies black-and-white categories to outside people, movements, and activities. This is a signal that there is an embedded preference for dwelling within trusted categories.

Scripture or experience faith orientation. Finally, listen for ways that clients distinguish and ratify core beliefs. When convictions come under fire, how does the client authenticate a truth claim to bolster or revise a position? The two orientations in the last dimension are *Scripture* and *experience*. Is there evidence that the client attends on a regular basis to the teaching of Scripture? Is there correspondence between the viewpoints they hold, the values they espouse, and references to biblical passages, principles, parables, or accounts? This is not a matter of how often a client quotes a passage; rather, listen for openings where biblical metaphors, stories, and themes support decisions and choices made regarding life direction. There are followers of Christ who express solidarity with the Word of God yet tend to lean heavily on experience to give meaning to what Scripture teaches. Do matters become evident after energetic periods of prayer or an exceptional worship service? A client may make frequent reference to extraordinary activities, periods of spiritual fervor, miraculous signs, or how the Lord opens particular opportunities or instigates specific motivations. There may be appeals to heroic or inspirational stories from acquaintances, Christian celebrities, famous musicians, missionaries, or pastors.

Here are some examples of statements reflecting Scripture and experience orientations:

- Experience: As I was driving along, there was a sense of sadness and confusion. Suddenly, the Lord gave me a song on the radio that spoke directly to my heart.
- Scripture: The shift supervisor has been on my case to put in more hours, and this makes me so angry. But like it says in Proverbs (15:1), I answer

quietly, tell him the truth, and remember that "whoever walks in integrity walks securely" (Prov 10:9).

- Experience: There is so much to consider in this career decision, so I sought the Lord through fasting and prayer.

Now that these three ways to better understanding the spiritual life of a Christian have been described, a critical caveat must be mentioned. These are not experiences or themes to rank or locate on bipolar scales. They are not competing or opposing tendencies. Rather, they are frameworks to aid us in identifying priorities, preferences, and patterns in the spiritual life of a client. They may help surface existing resources that are being underutilized or identify resources that are no longer readily available.

For illustration, let's consider Vanessa, a sixteen-year-old adolescent who has a longstanding reputation for being an exemplary believer. She was known as an extroverted leader in her youth group and a musician who used her beautiful voice to honor the Lord. For eight months, her parents and teachers have observed an overall decline in mood, slipping grades, and a subtle but growing attitude of rebellion. When her physician picks up her parents' concern during a routine exam, she recommends they seek counseling. In the course of a mental health screening, there are ample indications of a heavy heart and possible depression. As she shares more about her faith story, certain noteworthy pieces of information surface.

Her extrinsic orientation is apparent as she recalls her experience as a leader in the youth group and the affirmation she has received for her singing. She then describes the death of her grandmother, who had lived with the family for eight years, as a particularly devastating loss. Vanessa is adamant that her grandmother's suffering is over and she is better off with Jesus. Less obvious is Vanessa dependence on her grandmother's consistent and adoring prayer for her faith. How could she sing in church if her grandmother wasn't there to pray before or praise her afterward? She expresses grief over the loss of her grandmother's references to Scripture, quiet encouragement, physical touches, smiles, and nods. Vanessa used to read Bible passages that her grandmother personally selected and gave to her; she did not open Scripture on her own. Without this quiet hero in her life, Vanessa is less inclined to pray, perform, or participate with confidence in her youth group. Once a bold risk taker who would seek opportunities to display her faith, Vanessa is now drained and depleted, like one who has lost contact with a guardian angel. Hearing her story opened the door to explore ways to revitalize her walk with the Lord.

What do we listen for to discern the way a client relates with the Lord? We attend to content and process, interpretation and inspection, affect and thought to understand the whole person. This does not break down functioning into discrete pieces. Rather, these are sources of data to satisfy both the objective scientist and interpersonal-relations expert in an effort to conceptualize a presenting problem while forming a holistic picture of the person. Likewise, we do not track extrinsic and intrinsic faith, dwelling and seeking, or Scripture and experience orientations to break a testimony down into neat components or clever observations. We proceed in the role of comforted comforter to pursue one overarching listening objective: how this follower of Christ relates to God the Father, Jesus the Son, and the Holy Spirit. These data can alert us to themes within the client's narrative. In Christian counseling, the spiritual life of the client must ultimately be understood not by a collection of spiritual experiences but by how the client's relationship with Creator and Lord is nurtured and sustained.

WISE IN HEART

There is merit in maintaining objectivity as a helper, particularly when undertaking assessment. This allows us to form a more accurate and comprehensive picture of a client's concern. With appraisal experience, the forces inhibiting a client's mental and spiritual well-being will become evident, and we are able to establish a reasonable explanation for the presenting problem and the contributing factors. The capacity for professional objectivity is advantageous.

Interpersonal experience can also provide helpful data. Like other tests, an interview by design collects a sample of behavior. Therefore, it's reasonable to expect that the interaction patterns in the interview may reflect how a client engages with others outside the office walls.

Counselors who partner with Christian clients must seek to develop skill in the execution of the traditional roles when interviewing but also strive to go further. Learning to sit with clients as a comforted comforter enables an even deeper level of discernment in the initial assessment. As the Holy Spirit has supplied comfort to us, counseling offers a divine opportunity for the Holy Spirit to touch others via a heart-to-heart connection.

A pair of proverbs set the tone and listening principles at the outset of this chapter. A third performs well as its conclusion: "The wise in heart are called discerning, / and gracious words promote instruction" (Prov 16:21). Clients long for helpers who are "wise in heart." This might be defined in contemporary terms as compassionate discernment. It is the ability of the helper to penetrate the veil of confusion, see the dynamic relational and spiritual factors at work, and communicate with warmth how to move forward in the way of the Lord. When we are wise in heart we are guided and empowered by the Holy Spirit to see into the core matters of a counselee's heart. Any words of instruction that follow will be sweet in flavor and eloquent in delivery, and will nurture with guidance (Walvoord & Zuck, 1983). When clients experience this quality in us, it opens the door for trust and safety.

REFERENCES

Allport, G. W., & Ross, J. M. (1967). Personal religious orientation and prejudice. *Journal of Personality and Social Psychology, 5*(4), 432-443.

Cohen, A. B., & Hill, P. C. (2007). Religion as culture: Religious individualism and collectivism among American Catholics, Jews, and Protestants. *Journal of Personality. 75*(4), 709-742.

Groth-Marnat, G., & Wright, A. J. (2016). *Handbook of psychological assessment* (6th ed.). Hoboken, NJ: John Wiley & Sons.

Hill, P. C., & Pargament, K. I. (2017). Measurement tools and issues in the psychology of religion and spirituality. In Roger Finke and Christopher D. Bader (Eds), *Faithful measures: New methods in the measurement of religion* (pp. 48-77). New York: New York University Press.

Lukas, S. (1993). *Where to start and what to ask: An assessment handbook.* New York: Norton.

MacKinnon, R. A., Michels, R., & Buckley, P. J. (2016). *The psychiatric interview in clinical practice* (3rd ed.) Arlington, VA: American Psychiatric Association Publishing.

Mears, G. (2016). Conducting an intake interview. In I. Marini & M. A. Stebnicki (Eds.), *The professional counselor's desk reference* (2nd ed., pp. 83-86). New York: Springer.

Morrison, J. (2014). *The first interview* (4th ed.). New York: Guilford Press.

Murdin, L. (with Erringon, M.). (2005). *Setting out: The importance of the beginning in psychotherapy and counseling.* New York: Routledge.

Nouwen, H. J. M. (1979). *The wounded healer: Ministry in contemporary society.* Garden City, NY: Doubleday.

Sullivan, H. S. (1954). *The psychiatric interview.* New York: Norton.

Walvoord, J. F., & Zuck, R. B. (Eds.). (1983). *The Bible knowledge commentary: An exposition of the Scriptures by Dallas Seminary Faculty* (new ed.). Wheaton, IL: Victor Books.

Wuthnow, R. (1998). *After heaven: Spirituality in America since the 1950s.* Berkeley: University of California.

CHAPTER NINE

CONNECTING IN INITIAL CONSULTATIONS

For I was hungry and you gave me something to eat, I was thirsty and
you gave me something to drink, I was a stranger and you invited me in.

MATTHEW 25:35

THEOLOGICAL THEME
Hospitality

FIRST CONTACT

Counseling ventures deserve a good start. In fact, START is my mnemonic for
the steps and outcomes involved in an early, pace-setting session (story, therapeutic alliance, assessment, recommendations, and treatment plan). Whether
the setting is pastoral or psychiatric, we face an ongoing challenge—our clients
graduate, and new partnerships commence.

All of us, from novices to seasoned veterans, know that initial interviews can
be intense, demanding, and overwhelming. Indeed, first counseling sessions
are akin to medical evaluations in emergency rooms or urgent care clinics.
Patients come recognizing their need for help, or someone close to that patient
is pushing them in the doorway. They feel the ache and know that what's happening is not the way it's supposed to be. The complete source of the discomfort
is unknown when they arrive, however, and there are critical obstacles at the
outset. First, no connection currently exists between the person in distress and
the professional about to deliver care. Strangers discover what it takes to unite.
The assessor must do an examination to gain insight into the client's unique
situation while also simultaneously demonstrating compassion (Marini, 2016).
The person in distress, in turn, must trust the professional enough to disclose

necessary information. Counseling necessitates that participants face unexplored interpersonal terrain and boldly enter the unfamiliar.

Second, the chaos that compels the client to seek help will naturally accompany him or her into counseling. This means that the session where first contact is made can resemble bushwhacking through an overgrown, shadowy, unfamiliar wilderness. The pair becomes a team by exploring together the turmoil that has brought about the meeting. This entails investigating the disruptions stirred by recent events or changes in relationships. We counselors do not get to be spectators in this process. Rather, we become active guides and supportive companions in whatever the travail may be, even while we also maintain a bird's-eye view of the circumstances to serve as critical commentators and quality advisers on the entire process.

Two extremes can drive a request for counseling care. On one end, a client may wish for relief from a crisis that is provoking sensations resembling a scorching fever. Situational uncertainty and relational upheaval are calling for urgent help. Inner stress meters are likely exhibiting readings in the danger zone. In contrast, on the other end of the spectrum a plea can emerge from a frigid state of interminable stagnation. The status quo is dysfunctional and so unpleasant that it is giving the client the chills. Surprisingly, these conditions have an exceedingly odd staying power. Clients can cling stubbornly to the familiar even when it perpetuates intolerable conditions. A client may also bounce between these opposing extremes. A recent crisis or an unfulfilled expectation may be enough to disturb the equilibrium and make the idea of change more palatable, or at least more appealing than the false comfort derived from persistent denial.

Identifying the motivational sources that need a revolution is a central task for helpers. We must detect what is pushing the temperature into an unbearably hot or cold range.

- Our marriage was running on fumes. Then we lost an income. The financial burden brought us to a dead stop. We can't bear to stay together, but can't afford to be apart.
- Our son began his unceasing string of behavioral incidents in kindergarten. Since the accident he had in third grade, his aggressive activity has shifted into overdrive.
- Conflicts with my idiot coworkers are disturbing. I mind my own business. After three months of constant pressure to fulfill higher quotas under my brainless supervisor, I found myself writhing in agony, tied

down in an ambulance, with excruciating chest pains. The ER doc had the nerve to suggest that this was nothing but anxiety!

The crisis may be as recent as an argument the client had in the parking lot before entering the building. Or it could be an irritation that has persisted for months or even years. Suddenly there's a snap. The entrenched configuration of roles, routines, and relationships becomes the change target when the existing state is no longer tolerable.

Whether the client is seeking relief from intense calamity or dull stagnation, we must exhibit courage, creativity, and proficiency to make the first appointment productive. Priorities need to be clear in the midst of conflicting demands. This chapter offers a generic map for hosting effective initial consultations that keep the building of productive connections as the highest priority. Specifically, we must (1) define the issue and identify where mutual understanding needs to be reached, (2) underscore motivation, (3) assess the extent of the problem, (4) recognize barriers to the therapeutic bond and work to gain rapport, and (5) outline an agenda for transformation. It is possible to accomplish these therapeutic tasks in a way that moves the relationship forward and begins building the framework necessary for a good-enough working alliance. We might even come to see first contact as both rewarding and intriguing!

HOSPITALITY: STRANGERS, GUESTS, AND FRIENDS

An ancient biblical premise offers a helpful perspective on this early clinical encounter. Recall that the Christian faith is rooted in the historical context of the ancient Near East. The God of Scripture made himself known to a chosen people who lived as sojourners in a land that was not their own. In that nomadic culture, a traveler journeying by caravan along primitive routes would regularly place his well-being in the hands of local inhabitants from whom he needed to obtain critical supplies, shelter, and protection. A host would function as an official representative of the entire community. Inhabitants of the community, however, were vulnerable to harm that outsiders might inflict. There was a delicate balance between the cultural necessity to extend benevolence to sojourners and the ultimate need residents had for homeland security. Prescribed steps were therefore followed to help nomads and community members become acquainted (Gen 18:1-19). The rituals, expectations, and gestures associated with the exchange of hospitality were no small matter (Ex 22:21; Job 31:32; Is 58:7). The welfare of a whole tribe would rest on the judgment of the host who welcomed a stranger on its behalf.

An ordinary definition of hospitality is the act of extending good will to a visitor. A sharper biblical portrayal tightens this definition and gives us a superb picture of our purposes in counseling. It is fair to depict hospitality in the ancient world as a threefold sequence to transform a stranger into an ally. The welcome ritual would commence with a basic conversation, which would screen the stranger, rule out the risk of danger, and determine if it was judicious to invite this stranger into the community as a guest. Next, the newly welcomed guest and host would visit, establishing cordial dialogue and fulfilling mutual responsibilities. Finally, the bond of friendship would form, and this person's status would be permanently altered. These former strangers would embrace as mutual, lifelong allies (Malina, 1985).

Should a visitor happen to show up with letters of recommendation from a recognized source, the steps of hospitality were streamlined or could be dispensed with altogether. Nevertheless, it was entirely proper and not in the least bit disrespectful to request that unknown travelers speak on matters of interest or make their intensions known. These inquiries tested the stranger's plausibility, authenticity, and intent. The host's best intuition and keen eye to note visual signs of conformity to cultural expectations were summoned for this crucial assignment. Close listening and careful scrutiny could reveal hostile motives. Watching behavior for instances of disrespect was a central means of recognizing evil lurking beneath the surface.

Once a stranger had made it through the initial conversations, a foot-washing ritual to cleanse away the dust of travel tangibly signaled that the stranger was now welcome as a guest. Another symbol of this transition was anointing the traveler's head with oil (Ps 23:5; Amos 6:6; Lk 7:46). When a stranger became a guest, that person would be honored under the patronage and protection of the host. This afforded newcomers prescribed privileges and freedoms while also requiring them to uphold certain obligations and responsibilities.

Following the stay, the host and guest, having formed a common understanding, would part as friends with lasting ties, conveying that both were open to future visits. If there was a violation of trust or honor during the probationary period while hospitality was being extended, however, the outlook for ongoing relations was bleak, and retribution was likely. If the relational status at the point of separation was that of enemies, there was no longer a social duty to extend hospitality.

In short, a customary sequence was in place for showing courtesy to complete strangers, incorporating them into one's household, and welcoming them to enjoy a safe stay. Upon departure, amicable relations would remain as an enduring resource—travel capital—for future journeys. The practice was a functional, reciprocal arrangement to facilitate commerce and build an extensive support network. Strangers became allies. The new affiliates would depart and widely praise the host elsewhere, as well as vigilantly look for opportunities to return the favor of hospitality.

Jesus was outspoken about his followers' duty to welcome strangers (Mt 25:31-46; Lk 10:29-37; 14:1-24). After all, he was a divine visitor who pitched his tent to wander among the very creatures made in his image. But the twist that Jesus, as divine sojourner, interjected into his message was shocking. He was saying that hospitality was no longer a social task meant to extend one's influence or to establish mutual connections between nobles or merchants of equivalent status and stature. Rather, followers of Jesus were to reach out in pure, unselfish, kingdom hospitality to the poor, rejected, lost, and undesirable (Pohl, 1999). Hospitality was to be a practice of love, administered with grace to those who were in no position to ever return the favor. A stranger was welcomed because it could be Jesus himself wandering about unannounced and incognito. The reward for hospitality would be the warmth of the welcome experienced as the host enters the kingdom feast of our Lord.

After the account of Pentecost (Acts 2) the New Testament elevates the practice of hospitality between fellow believers even more, making it an institutional requirement and symbol of kingdom alignment (Yong, 2008). Hospitality highlights the unity of believers, the bonds we're to have as the family of Christ, and our shared love of the Savior (Acts 16:15; Rom 12:13; Gal 6:10; Titus 1:8). Hospitality is the means by which Christ-followers publicly exhibit heavenly love and graciousness toward outsiders (Jipp, 2017). Openness to unknown sojourners has been the distinguishing hallmark of the church of Jesus Christ throughout the ages. Monasteries, convents, and church communities were the forerunners of our modern sanctuaries for healing, rest, and peace (e.g., hospitals, hostels, hospice, and hospitality; Pohl, 1999). Practicing hospitality in order to form lasting partnerships is the rationale behind the START perspective.

Christian counselors do well to pay close attention to the ways we welcome strangers as clients into care. We must be intentional and create routines that are accessible even for those who show up disoriented and weary. The aim is to enable the broken and distressed to find safety, nourishment, and shalom as our guests. When this happens, change can occur, the partnership can flourish, and clients might even leave ready to tell others where to find solace for their souls. This is not a counseling-practice expansion strategy to increase clientele.

Rather, the opening welcome is a kingdom initiative to incorporate New Testament priorities into contemporary counseling care customs.

AN UNDERLYING STRUCTURE FOR CLINICAL CONSULTATION

Being intentional about the initial consultation and addressing expectations builds rapport, displays competence, and eases anxiety. START is not a rigid arrangement or fixed question set that one pops out of the box for everyone who seeks help. Nor is it a packaged script to replace clinical creativity or limit the resourcefulness that is so indispensable to an inspiring opening session. Rather, START offers an underlying structure that helps map out the route we should use to aid client exploration and choose the best assessment options (see fig. 9.1). When implemented, this flexible grid can help us achieve the optimal blend of free-style conversation with probes needed to gather necessary data.

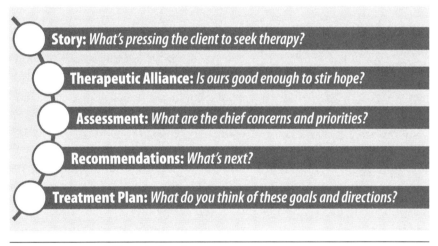

Story: *What's pressing the client to seek therapy?*

Therapeutic Alliance: *Is ours good enough to stir hope?*

Assessment: *What are the chief concerns and priorities?*

Recommendations: *What's next?*

Treatment Plan: *What do you think of these goals and directions?*

Figure 9.1. START model for early clinical encounters

The reality of first contact is that we are forced to make hard choices in rapid succession and on the fly. Each turn around a thematic corner heads us in a distinct direction. By default, there are good options that get left unexplored. The hourglass runs out. To achieve satisfactory results, we need a fluid agenda, an adaptable assessment grid, an effective way to determine priorities, an eye for opportunity, and a design that enables us to fill in all imperative blanks. START lays the groundwork for constructive therapy.

Groundwork is a key word here. The purpose of adopting an interview template for the initial consultation is not to produce a comprehensive psychiatric or psychosocial history. In settings where an itemized, sequenced, in-depth historical investigation is necessary, a blend of forms, technology, and dedicated face-to-face exploration can be used. In addition, the START opening will not spark an in-depth return to traumatic past events. First contact is not the moment for the client to lay bare the full range of intense turbulence from a marital relationship in severe distress. The main goal for this session and its surrounding activity is to complete an evenhanded synopsis that identifies the key people, influential events, and potent stressors now prompting the client to seek assistance. The START framework helps us determine the client's needs so that additional assessment techniques can be applied immediately and others can be identified to use as a follow-up. The face-to-face exchange yields information that can then be combined with insights gleaned from other assessment options. The finished comprehensive profile flows naturally into thorough exploration and a treatment plan. Once there is a sense of what needs to be addressed, the requisite exploration of past trauma can commence, marital distress can be unpacked, or behaviors needing adjustment can be approached.

For the sake of clarification, I will not be using the common term *intake* as the descriptive label for this early meeting. Rather, I call this an *initial consultation* (IC) that ponders how and if talk therapy should commence. This is not mere semantics. The designation *intake* implies that proceeding with counseling is a given. The dyad assumes future sessions. And, following an intake, inquirers become clients. This misses a decisive step. There is little to no value in customizing an assessment plan and walking through a range of getting-acquainted experiences when it is predetermined that counseling will commence. This downplays the central and immediate question: Is there potential in this unique helping relationship at this juncture and under these conditions to productively address the most pressing referral concerns? A mutual and critical decision must follow this session. The commitment to pursue counseling and to partner together is informed by what transpires in the consultation. The IC becomes a type of "trial therapy," after which it is imperative that a consensus be reached about the direction that needs to be taken before a genuine commitment to proceed can occur.

The immediate challenge is to discern if a conversational venture has merit as the means to reach the client's desired goals. This requires intentionality from the beginning. It is problematic when particular details on how to proceed are silently ignored as the pair moves aimlessly. A nondirective, gradual unmasking of concerns may appear to be client-centered and empowering, but simply letting the client share whatever comes into consciousness is actually not the optimal strategy to meet early assessment demands, and may fail to establish up front the helpful expectations that energize and ignite a therapeutic dyad. A clear welcome sequence at the outset can facilitate a determination of the best fit between persons, purpose, setting, and plan; from this base the counselor and client can take the next steps.

The initial consultation is forthright as it addresses questions such as these:

- Is talk therapy likely to be beneficial at this point in your life and under the conditions you are now facing?
- Is there good potential for this distinctive counselor and client combination to become a team that will contribute helpfully to the request expressed?
- Are there prerequisite experiences, evaluations, or support networks that would be advisable prior to therapy?
- What are the potential risks or adverse outcomes that could arise from therapy?
- Is there adequate time available for appointments, and are there financial resources to accomplish the agreed-upon purpose of this arrangement?
- Do the matter under consideration and the optimal change plan fit within the experience and practice scope of the counselor and therapeutic setting?
- Is there a reasonable expectation, based upon published literature, that the interventions to be applied can benefit a client with these concerns in the timeframe available?
- Is there a reasonable degree of mutual agreement on the anticipated outcomes of therapy to warrant moving forward?
- Are there ethical, moral, or spiritual layers to the request that need to be contemplated in further detail prior to the onset of counseling?

An initial consultation ponders the request, weighs the options, and tentatively canvasses the viability of the potential match between helper and client. This promotes an enlightened resolution on how to proceed and makes achieving informed consent something more than a legal or ethical formality. Other assessment activities will take place if further meetings are jointly determined to be feasible and beneficial. There is a legitimate possibility that constructive conversation may not be the wisest option at this moment.

There are also occasions when a one-session consultation is enough intervention to address the most pressing question. One-session therapy is possible and can be efficacious (Hoyt, 2011)! Viewing the initial consultation as having reasonable potential to be a stand-alone service can be advantageous. Again, an initial consultation considers not only how to proceed but if strategic dialogue is warranted, what direction would be most productive, and who in the role of helper would be ideally suited relationally or professionally to address the needs of the client. An intentional IC provides the opportunity for the client to explicitly commit to enter counseling to pursue growth. It is the moment when he or she must survey what is required, count the cost, and decide outright to continue into counseling with hope and determination.

After over two decades in my pastoral, counseling, and supervision career, I have given extensive consideration to the question of how to make the most of early contact to produce momentum toward change. The IC is a premium opportunity and a trendsetting encounter. Thus, I scrutinize every second, exchange, and ritual. Despite ample practice both conducting and supervising these sessions, I still feel personal internal angst regarding cold starts with new clients, even while I also convey a hopeful sense of expectation and excitement. Hosting this important initial consultation even to this day carries the weight of a significant responsibility. These sessions are never routine or mundane encounters. One is about to enter the chaos and confusion in another's life. Butterflies intrude during the quiet moments before I whisper to the Lord, push my chair back from the computer screen, open my door, and walk to the waiting room. If this is your experience as a novice or as a veteran, please hear that you are not alone. Use that emotional alertness as a reminder that clients themselves struggle to make these appointments. Each consultation represents a vast effort to confront the tangled behavior of human beings and take in the impact of creation groaning for redemption.

A familiar START structure contributes to us continually investing in these crucial sessions despite their inherent complexity. In the initial meeting, the goal is to establish a common rhythm, pace, and reason to be confident. The START framework can relieve the pressure to capture a wide range of details and help us make the most of this rare opportunity for a high-touch, meaningful interpersonal encounter.

The sheer number and magnitude of the decisions that rest on the IC make it imperative to blend data gathered via the initial interview with other assessment measures. Maximizing the benefit of extensive information early on can produce helpful gains for the client later (Groth-Marnat & Wright, 2016; Whiston, 2017). The following questions can be helpful:

- Do I need to issue a statement regarding a diagnostic impression, prognosis, or the suitability of the client for the agency's resources and level of service?
- Will the client be matched with a suitable therapist for this partnership?

- Is a basic treatment plan, even one subject to revision, the expected IC outcome?
- Is a consult with medical, educational, or social service personnel advisable?
- Do I need to authorize care with a third-party reviewer?
- Are there eligibility requirements at this particular site that require documentation?
- Is the client seeking generic help or desiring explicitly Christian counseling?

The answers to any combination of these related questions that might need to be answered early on define the informational and behavioral domains for the initial interview. This implies that the assessment strategy implemented can be improved by subjecting the IC to routine psychometric considerations, namely, the scrutiny of reliability, validity, and utility.

- Reliability: Will each and every IC consistently yield sufficient descriptive information and observations to address the list of standing questions?
- Validity: Do the sample of behavior and level of background detail acquired in the IC fulfill its assessment purpose?
- Utility: Will each discrete component of the consultation interview contribute added value to the quality of decisions and recommendations made in and following the session?

START makes optimal use of precounseling questionnaires, computer-administered social histories, symptom checklists, and even specialized instruments to enhance data collection in critical areas. These all extend information gathering beyond the face-to-face interaction. Since we know that additional assessment modalities will be employed, we can make informed decisions on how best to use the available contact time to capture a basic sample of therapeutic interactions.

Forms that clients complete in advance should be read with focused attention, not quickly scanned for completion. Glean as many background specifics as is possible. Develop forms that do not overwhelm but do capture what is needed to fill all of the expected demographic fields. They should give clients the chance to set the stage for what will come (Wiger, 2009; Zuckerman & Kolmes, 2017). These forms also aid us in determining what elements to include in the upcoming session to unpack the reason for referral. Demographic information places the client in relationship with other systems and within a developmental stage. The direction of the interview for a single, twenty-something female will differ from the direction we would take with a widow in her early sixties. Counselors use basic categorical data to tailor question sets to fit the client being seen. Agencies, supervisors, and counselors should routinely review the template for these entry forms in order to add items that could potentially generate useful responses without burdening the client with an overly lengthy questionnaire. Queries that are no longer relevant or that obtain answers replicated elsewhere should be cut. If the item makes no credible contribution to incremental validity, meaning that it adds little decision-making power, drop it in order to keep these templates lean and sharp.

The first moments. Begin an IC session by making the customary introductions. Acknowledge the timeframe and inform the client about what's coming. This establishes a direction and invites teamwork. The interviewer accepts the responsibility to lead the time together and vows to be as active as the client requires. This is indispensable with counselees who are exceedingly verbal or emotionally primed to unleash numerous tales. Clients enter anxious. As they hear what is about to take place, the unknown is demystified. The art in the exchange is to separate essential from nonessential details. The client, no matter how extroverted, cooperative, or insightful, cannot be expected to readily recognize what is crucial or what constitutes a successful counseling experience. Once the agenda and format are out in the open, see if there are any questions regarding expectations. If there are, deal with them immediately or make a definite plan to address a client's stated concerns.

Share the purpose of each phase so that the tasks, criteria for completion, and time allotment are reasonably transparent. It might look like the following:

> Welcome to this initial consultation. Our aim in this meeting is not to dive into all the features of your struggle or to review your entire autobiography. Our approach will be intentional. Let's identify priorities and establish a productive direction for change.
>
> Our time will be split to address three goals:
>
> - We want to become clear about what has brought you to the point of considering counseling now. I need to learn the extent and depth of the challenge you are facing.
>
> - We will review your specific concerns and symptoms that may accompany having this stressor in your life.
>
> - By the time we finish today, I will share what counseling might help you accomplish and offer recommendations on how to proceed.
>
> For about the next fifteen minutes, we are going to begin to explore your concerns, emotions, people in your life, and recent challenges. As your

counselor for this initial consultation, I will strive to listen and discern how to steer our time.

This session may feel different from counseling sessions you've had in the past and from those that are ahead. We have specific objectives to cover. I know what those are and will track our progress to get us to where we need to go. What's important is for me to hear the cry of your heart as unmistakably as I possibly can.

Where do you believe is the best place to capture what brings you here today? What do you need me to most appreciate about you and your story as we consider if counseling is the right choice for you?

Opening an IC with prayer is not typically the optimal way to begin. This holds even if prayer may be a legitimate option within the context, such as a church, ministry, or Christian university. Praying together is an intimate act of unity and mutual submission to the Lord. This is premature given that the client and counselor remain strangers. We can pray silently before the session. And we can determine or inquire as the partnership warms if a closing prayer of dedication is appropriate.

Once you've explained the agenda to the client, any lingering questions regarding informed consent should be addressed. It is wise also to briefly explain the limits to confidentiality. As soon as it is reasonably possible, move to explore the presenting concern within the client's story.

S is for capturing the client's "story." The counselor must respectfully secure a succinct outline of crucial people and events—in other words, identify the forces that brought the client to make this appointment. It is helpful to have a cache of potential kick-off questions. Ensure that each area is covered. Build your own interview set with words that are natural, fit your setting and clientele, and adjust easily to mirror client style, culture, tone, and intensity. These examples can help you build your repertoire:

- This is our opportunity to move directly into a very important story: yours. It is vital for me to understand what convinced you that the conditions were right to set this appointment. Would you briefly share your main concern and the factors that are now leading you to pursue counseling?

- This session will investigate if counseling is indeed a viable option to address your goals. Speak from your heart and in your own words about the main event or relationship that has made you aware that change is necessary.

- For the next fifteen minutes, let's work together to build a solid synopsis of the circumstances and relationships that have brought you here to share with me.

Clients need enough freedom to relay the dilemmas they face in their own terms and expressions. Still, unrestrained sharing will likely reveal their internal narrative without its pivotal turning points and perspectives exposed. You will need to encourage them to pause and prompt them to share aspects of the self not typically brought into the open in ordinary conversation. For example, you might break the story sharing momentarily not to clarify a fact but to empathetically help the client reflect on the emotion, injustice, or distress expressed and still bubbling up from beneath the surface. Or, it might be helpful to succinctly repeat a phrase for clarification that reveals an embedded belief. This consultation is meant to help you acquire a succinct abridgment of a longer tale. Reassure clients that there will be ample opportunities later on to look deeply and more fully at these important matters. The helper should provide adequate direction to enable the client to share an emotionally intense account of pressing concerns.

During a routine START consultation, dedicate approximately one-third of the session to hear the client's request, survey resources, and identify blocks that prevent resolution. Note, however, that the one-third guideline is a broad rule of thumb. Specialized treatment may require detailed inquiry into specific areas (e.g., a work history for a career assessment, a legal history for court-mandated treatment, crisis debriefing related to an unfolding tragedy, or a sexual- or substance-abuse history to tie with a specific request). Even so, you will need creativity to navigate the delicate balance of directing the client to expand on inner experiences or relational tensions without becoming overly intrusive. The general principle is this: experience tops facts. In other words, a client's outlook and distress is of greater importance than the precise particulars of what actually happened.

There are four categories you want the client to expand on as they share: (1) pressure surrounding central concerns, (2) crucial relational ties, (3) cognitive distortions and/or inconsistencies, and (4) the client's personal perspective on where change is essential. Too many facts can distract. The interview must uncover passions, hurts, dreams, visions, tensions, and the presence of pain. These are the core story ingredients.

Given that one desire of ours is to sense the potential leading of the Holy Spirit, listen for ways that the client exposes beliefs, values, and priorities that reflect a Christian worldview. Listen for an alignment with a community of faith. How does the client implement a daily walk with the Lord? In what ways does this person's identity as a Christian surface in the exchange? Counseling that fosters an identity in Christ is the overarching vision for faith-based counseling. (Specific options and ideas for spiritual life assessment will follow in the next chapter.)

T is for therapeutic alliance. When eliciting the client's story, be respectful, of course, but press in sufficiently to communicate empathy and to make emotional contact. The central charge in this formative phase is to discern the relational bond that will best facilitate the therapeutic work of this client. Even if the interviewer will not personally be the primary therapist, this session builds anticipation, awakens curiosity, and ignites hope. The key outcome is to have a sufficient collaborative alliance in place to foster a genuine commitment to the recommendations that flow from the consultation. If counseling is to be useful, such a commitment is indispensable.

You may feel a need to record good quotes or document certain descriptions while the client talks. Experts agree, however, that typing or writing constantly can distract us from exhibiting an open posture, making eye contact, and reading facial expression. One way to remain visibly accessible to clients is to have a START session record form ready for use *after* the session (see appendix two). Being familiar with the required items and fields on the form will help you attend to that information as it is disclosed, and then it can be readily documented afterward. A clipboard, tablet, or laptop may be picked up on occasion to record a metaphor, name, year, or language sample. But when it comes to taking notes, the risk of diminishing the relational connection is too high. Thus, it is best to restrict writing to the most imperative bullet points or quotes that are so distinctive that they have considerable therapeutic potential.

Connecting relationally can easily become lost amidst excessive cross-examination. This explains why mutual dialogue and open-ended exchange are so characteristic of the story phase while directive questions, along with checklists, behavioral ratings, and targeted symptom questions, are so characteristic of the assessment phase. When clients understand the purpose of these different interview approaches, they come to appreciate the support without viewing the approach or time limitations as a hindrance.

Counselors know that empathetic feedback facilitates a healing alliance. Therefore, as a counselee shares opening explanations, our job is to briefly offer encouragement, reflection, and transitional summaries. We are rightly eager to form the intimacy that will jump-start the therapeutic process. However, this is where the seasoned interviewer will be cautious and circumspect. In the IC, there may be numerous opportunities to assess the client's readiness to enter into a partnership and therapeutic dialogue, but the overriding purpose is to prepare the way for the conversations that lie ahead. Thus, in this first session, we should only pursue those client signals that point to a heart matter that can be better understood with immediate attention. Other areas can be highlighted as significant but left for another day. Not all emotive material that is lifted should be set apart for later exploration.

Within this immediate investigation, we can choose to approach two matters: (1) the agonizing upheaval that demands attention and (2) ambivalence about thinking, feeling, or acting differently. Making genuine affective connections in these two areas is a productive early therapeutic task. Put succinctly, we want to fashion a good-enough therapeutic bond to stimulate hope and inspire a willingness to continue. The promise of a helping partnership enables the client to take a step toward realizing change with a greater awareness of the potential cost.

A prognosis regarding the extent and features of the therapeutic alliance that might emerge later can be formed based on observations made during trial interventions. It is critical to note interpersonal cues such as defensiveness, vagueness, provocative behavior, emotional accessibility, cultural distinctiveness, and ease of communication. The investment in forging a basic alliance occurs throughout the entire session. It is not limited to any phase or task. As we share expertise, compassionate support is experienced by the client.

Finally, when ethically and therapeutically appropriate, a closing prayer may be an excellent choice to offer comfort and enjoy a personal moment together. Give thanks for the communication and connection that has occurred. This is a great point at which to recognize that the partnership that is about to proceed is not merely interpersonal but will also welcome the presence of the Great Comforter. When a brief prayer of dedication is welcome, it serves as a benediction—a personal blessing—and should conclude with a plea for wisdom. If it reflects the quality and focus of the initial consultation well, it can pave the way for clients to return to counseling and be enriched in their walk with the Lord through it. We call on the Lord to direct, bless, and empower what is about to take place.

A is for assessment. The START format dedicates the second phase of the initial session to formal and systematic inquiry. The actual content for this portion of the consultation should help you meet three goals: (1) appraise client functioning, safety, and readiness for counseling related to the reason for referral; (2) secure information for immediate decisions and documentation requirements; and (3) identify the problem in order to highlight potential treatment directions. Mixing specific inquiries into the story portion of the session is common and can become a counselor's default; if a story element stirs curiosity or raises a question, an immediate clarifying question is natural. When the spontaneity of a client's narrative is not interrupted, a blend of select probes in the story segment is reasonable.

However, the START format intentionally separates opened-ended exploration from direct informational requests. The reason for this is twofold. First, separating them establishes an explicit timeframe for both important sections. Second, it recognizes the uniqueness of this session for data gathering by building in a routine to make sure all critical matters are covered. By reserving the middle section of the IC for intentionally chosen, thoughtful question sets, the consistency and quality of your procedure is improved.

Consider the rationale for this as expressed in proper assessment terminology. First, apportioning a section of the interview for structured question lists increases the reliability of the consultation. In other words, the logical application of a data-gathering grid is akin to the item-selection procedure when constructing a psychological tool. Second, the format ensures that the conversation covers the matters necessary to make firm clinical decisions, which means the session fulfills its clinical purpose, thereby increasing validity. Thus, the recommendation for the mental health professional (MHP) to mentally and practically divide the interview into an intentional but loosely structured story section and a tightly executed symptom survey. You can separate the two sections with an explanatory transition such as,

- In this second section of our session, let's move into specific talking points to establish how recent events are shaping your everyday life; relationships with family, friends, and coworkers; and your physical health, mental health, and overall well-being.

- Many of the questions that we are about to cover are routine for this meeting. Please do not be embarrassed as we open up personal or unusual matters. Most important in our endeavor today is to understand the extent and intensity of your concerns.

Getting a proper list of the most troubling presenting symptoms with the requisite sample descriptions is important, as is clarifying contributing and complicating factors. Participation in a medical, third-party reimbursement plan will make this aspect of the interview automatic, as this is the part that establishes the foundation for a *DSM* (*Diagnostic and Statistical Manual of Mental Disorders*) diagnosis, if applicable. This section is also an assumed component of any professional counseling service. If brief therapy, life coaching, biblical counseling, or pastoral care is the appropriate service, there may not be a medical diagnosis, thereby making this level of assessment less necessary. However, since documentation standards generally require that the clinical record display how related conditions were ruled out and how the selected treatment approach was established, the use of targeted assessment to inform clinical decision making is a reasonable procedure.

A formal mental status exam and diagnostic interview may not be possible in the limited time available. Based on the preceding open-ended conversation, however, you might be able to fill in the outstanding items needed to report the results of a basic mental status examination. The next step is to inquire about distinctive symptoms that typically occur in conjunction with the presenting concern. For example, if anxiety or panic attacks appear to be central, you should utilize a question set that surveys triggers and systematically considers frequency, severity, and duration. Where more detail is needed, make a notation to follow up with a focused symptom checklist or domain-specific assessment measure, and then use the appropriate instruments immediately afterward or in the next scheduled session to further establish the diagnosis and behavioral baseline for the presenting concern.

Typically, item clusters are woven into the conversation to match the client's request or reflect the service priorities of the agency. For example, for a clinic that specializes in domestic violence, this is the principal opportunity to move through a set of critical items that probe lifestyle and relationships and uncover patterns that tend to surface with this population. If the possibility of alcohol abuse is indicated, extend the coverage by using a screening question set. The five items below, contained in the Rapid Alcohol Problems Screen (RAPS-L), would be handy to have available (Cherpitel, 2000).

1. R—During the last year have you experienced guilt feelings or remorse after drinking (remorse)?

2. A—During the last year has a friend or family member ever told you about things you said or did while you were drinking that you were not able to recall (amnesia or blackout)?

3. P—Thinking back over the past year, have you failed to do what was normally expected of you because of drinking (perform)?

4. S—Do you ever take a drink in the morning when you first get up (starter/eye-opener)?

5. L—Again, in the past year have you lost friends or girlfriends/boyfriends because of drinking (loss)?

Or, if there are any early indications that issues with eating may be a concern, drop in the question set from the SCOFF (Hill, Reid, Morgan, & Lacey, 2010; Luck et al., 2002):

1. S—Do you make yourself Sick because you feel uncomfortably full?

2. C—Do you worry you have lost Control over how much you eat?

3. O—Have you recently lost more than One stone (fourteen pounds) in a three-month period?[1]

4. F—Do you believe yourself to be Fat when others say you are too thin?

5. F—Would you say that Food dominates your life?

Given that the answers to question sets like these are tough for clients to disclose, it is useful to have pointed and focused questions for assessment in such tender areas. This does not need to open up a large exchange at this juncture. Rather, if the answers provided highlight the need for more information, make a plan to pursue this further in the next session. Follow-up in a particular area is one of the recommendations that will flow from this session.

In START interviews, no matter what the setting, clinicians need to decide in advance what questions will be standard and which item sets will be inserted when a need for them arises. For example, it is standard in most settings to inquire about thoughts of self-harm. So, be prepared to ask in a gentle, firm, and direct manner, with good eye contact and reasonable rapport, about the presence of thoughts to harm the self or others.

- Have you recently experienced any thoughts, entertained ideas, or made plans to harm yourself or another in any way? Do you now face a fear that you may actually do harm to yourself or someone else?

- Have you with intention cut, punctured, burned, scratched, or damaged the surface of your body in a way that has left a mark or drawn blood?

- Have you had thoughts of suicide? Have you made a plan to take your own life?

In certain settings, inquiries about sexual abuse, self-injury such as cutting or self-induced vomiting, and domestic violence might automatically need to be included. Or you may need to ask questions that help you rule in or rule out specific conditions, which can influence the self-report measures to be

---

[1]SCOFF did not originate in the United States; thus, stone is used as a weight category. The use of ten pounds as a general benchmark would be more common here.

administered as a follow-up. These are matters of such importance that a face-to-face, direct inquiry is the single most effective way to determine risk.

As a way to transition from this section to the next, a question that gives the client an opportunity to suggest additional areas for inquiry is useful. You might say something like:

- Thanks for being so descriptive and candid. More surveys or inventories may follow in our next session. For right now, is there an area that I have not covered related to your well-being or your visit today that you would like to mention?

- We did well making it through these important questions. Thank you. There may be topics that I have not covered but should. Please tell me if there is anything else important to you that I need to inquire about to know you and your situation better.

R is for recommendations. Providing reasonable and unambiguous recommendations related to the main request is the best way to bring the interview to a close. There must be a logical and obvious connection between what a client seeks and the proposal for remediation suggested by the counselor; the client needs to know you comprehend the client's dilemma. After only a brief interview and consultation, the recommendations are likely to be general, but they must be real and reflect the relational ground established in the session. You have worked to build trust in the session so that an important decision can now be made. In this third section of the IC, it is essential to make an unequivocal statement regarding the client's request and tie it to a recommendation on how to best proceed. Build the case for your recommendations by reviewing aspects of the initial interview. The goal is to create awareness and anticipation for the counseling work ahead, both of which are needed if such dialogue is likely to be beneficial in this specific situation and with this client. The following examples provide some ideas for how you might frame this section.

- Hearing your understanding of what's happening is so very helpful. You made the important decision about counseling because you desire to grow in the following ways . . .

- You have identified that this is a critical opportunity to become different in how you act, in the patterns you use to relate to others, and in the way you live out your faith convictions. You are to be commended for your readiness to address these life issues.

- Based upon the understanding we now have about what you shared with me, I will finish with three recommendations on how counseling and other supports may be beneficial to you. Let's focus on the next steps to realize change.

If the client has uttered a descriptive phrase, metaphor, or vivid example of the problem, it is ideal to revisit that here. Review the request for service, break it down into reasonable pieces, and use a summation to articulate general goals. As much as possible, make use of the client's actual terms and language. You cannot, of course, have thought through all possible solutions to the presenting problem at this point, as it is only partially visible after this consultation. You are simply stating what is called for at this junction. If you recommend an explicit task or homework assignment, keep it simple and not too demanding. The thrust of the recommendation is about direction and decision, not direct intervention. This is not the time to make a declaration on an off-the-cuff prescription to fix the chief complaint. The centerpiece of the recommendation is whether counseling should commence, what form it can take, and what priorities will be important to realize success. For example:

- Your friend and coworker, the one who gave you our number, knows and cares about you. You respect her. Now that you have acted on her advice, ask if she is willing to share specific qualities she sees in you that prompted her to make that recommendation. What does she see in you that could shed light on that "dark shadow eating away at your soul"? If she is willing to speak, you may gain insight into what others see in you and what they discern about how the Lord is at work.

- The communication blunders that happen so frequently in your marriage are disturbing. Unfortunately, relational dissatisfaction is not uncommon for parents of adolescents. There is ample evidence that this is indeed a stressful developmental period for the entire family, not only for the teen. Many couples find that marriage counseling can assist them in reducing tension, unpacking disagreements, and enhancing the effectiveness of communication. Marriage counseling does have the potential at this stage in your life to make a positive difference. Given your presence in this session, you both know what is at stake. It may get worse before it gets better, but it does make sense to proceed with counseling. Let's make a plan.

- Your move last spring to a high-pressure and demanding career position is a sure sign of accomplishment and your abilities. Living in a new location, away from friends and far from your former fellowship, has left you frequently feeling lonely and isolated. Unfortunately, this pattern is a recurring one in your life. There are signs in your sleeping, eating, and energy level that depression is setting in. A partnership that looks within, back, ahead, and between may sort out how to invest in sturdy, lasting relationships. This is worthwhile.

This is the optimal occasion to consider the demands, cost, and consequences associated with changing or not changing. If it is reasonable, identify a potential reward for the client for taking action. An effective recommendation will magnify motivation, establish a pathway to gain further detail, and open options for upcoming care. Once there is a decision to proceed, the next phase will develop a mutual treatment plan that holds promise and has clear objectives.

T is for treatment plan. As the consultation draws to a close, the outcomes, tasks, and actual approaches for counseling remain fluid. Naturally, more assessment will occur beyond this session. A detailed treatment plan will await the analysis of that data. But at this moment, the client may need you to show them how dialogue is going to realize a goal or resolve stubbornly rooted problems (Mears, 2016). Without hearing a basic outline of the unrefined treatment plan, clients can be reluctant to commit and take the next steps. And whether a client continues beyond the initial consultation should not be tied to desperation or even to the first impression of an insightful, kind therapist. The proposal of a broad outline of treatment enables a client to see what you see, and this conveys hope. It also clarifies how others may contribute to the growth process, such as physicians, pastors, relatives, and/or lay church leaders. In designing an initial plan, my prayer is, "Lord, what is it that you are seeking to accomplish in this client's life at this time?" The answer that the Holy Spirit provides in the moment determines how much is shared.

- You came today because the communication struggles and the outrageous conflicts in your marriage have become unbearable. Based upon our discussion, I recommend that we proceed to undertake a solid round of marital counseling. If you were to ask me how long this might take, I would have to admit that it is too early to speculate. Allow me to propose that you commit to an eight-week block, with a review of progress and expectations in week six. This way we will have two weeks to finish up or plan a second round. Our plan will include looking closely at how and when those communication distortions occur. Our next session will be built around the completion of a couple of assessments that tap into your distinct personality styles and target specific areas of marital distress. After we review those assessments, my approach will be to coach, rebuild connections, and develop skills to speak to one another in ways that revive the love you declare that you still have for one another.

- While you are fifteen, your parents are promising not to back off on those restrictions until your grades improve and life in your home becomes peaceful. You said that you're positive that as Christian parents, your mom and stepdad are committed to making your life miserable; "a living hell in Livingston" is how you described it. If counseling gets underway, we would first have to figure out what you could do to get them to lighten up. I might have a few tips on how to ask for what you want without having them explode. We could come up with a plan that makes sense to deal with the madness of your schoolwork. If we press hard into these three areas, we might have a chance to get you a life back.

Finally, there are occasions when the treatment plan offered after an initial consultation will outline steps for the client to take prior to the commencement of counseling. This has absolutely nothing to do with rejecting clients or dismissing the concerns that they have brought. It may be that the time they have available to invest in self-reflection and growth is too limited. Or conditions in their living arrangements, relationships, finances, or employment may make the risk of dropout or noncompliance too high.

- Finishing your fifth year as a waiter after two years of college is all the evidence you need to conclude that you are going nowhere. Getting high after work keeps you content in the dullness of the daily grind even though it forces you to wind down after a busy shift. The reality is that this late-night routine of self-medicating is ruining your day life, sucking the zest from your spiritual life, and killing your urge to get back into school. In summary, each time you get high, you are putting the dreams you once had for yourself further and further out of reach. In our approach to work together, we would include a systematic search of your interests and match those with plausible career options. The most difficult mountain to move will be to construct a no-nonsense accountability plan to cut back and eliminate that addictive pattern that you are admitting is out of hand and definitely outrageously hard to break. This will be rough—honestly, extremely rough. We can tap into proven community resources if you decide you want to take the next step. This two-prong plan is essential, and it doesn't make sense to do one without the other. It's your work. I'll partner on the planning if you decide to go forward. My recommendation is for you to take a week or so to ponder and pray over this. Let's schedule a second consultation to determine if this is the season in your life to make your big move.

When the clinician has confidence about and insight into the factors that need to come together to make counseling productive, it makes sense to declare a "plan" to make a plan. This will address motivational forces before a follow-up initial consultation is scheduled to assess if the timing, support, and stability are in place to get counseling off to a good start.

DEMONSTRATING THE ASSESSMENT CRAFT

Let's imagine this initial consultation approach as it flows through an actual session. The priority in any first encounter is to refresh the client with hope while evaluating the potential benefit of counseling services. My prayer, before the client even enters the room, is that the client will experience compassion in a way that conveys the love of Jesus Christ.

"Describe briefly the reason you are seeking counseling." This open-ended item appears on the personal information form that all clients complete prior to an initial consultation. Before our session actually begins, I notice that Cora (38) writes: "To rid myself of the depression and rage leftover from my childhood that constantly trashes my life." The request is both revealing and descriptive. It screams "hurt" as it points to a potential direction for psychotherapy that is well worth considering. Behind this statement about her past, there is a distinct likelihood that a recent event prompted her request for service. Childhood was decades in the past, so what makes it so pressing to dig up that pain now? What aspect of her life was recently "trashed"? Information available on the personal information form is examined to glean as much perspective as possible. In reading between the lines, my thoughts become oriented to the conversation that will follow. My imagination continues its work by making narrative connections based on the data reported on the form. I ponder curiosity questions such as these.

- What is it like to be a second child and the oldest female among nine siblings?
- Would her parents, now unfortunately deceased, have cherished all those grandchildren? Cora lists a tribe of nieces and nephews. How does Cora as a single woman with no children fit in this family system?

- Cora is college educated with an impressive career conducting management seminars for a global company. Extensive travel is a requirement for her job. Does that allow for local relationships? Thinking pragmatically, would her travel schedule permit attendance at routine counseling appointments?

- Her physical address indicates a residence in a quaint hamlet well outside the city. Might single life be conspicuous or lonely in a rural environment?

- Could her living location be making a statement? All family roots and ties plainly reflect urban addresses. With such a large family, what's the reason behind her isolation?

Cora states on her form that she has never been in therapy. It is a bold initiative to speak with a mental health professional. Clients request an appointment when facing a momentous adjustment or when provoked by a disturbance. Clients seek direction, relief, and support. Each concern tends to be accompanied by substantial pain. The circumstances that surround presenting problems are often formidable. After all, if the solution were within easy reach, the humbling plea for mental health services would never surface.

My impression is that Cora is in the midst of suffering. The apostle Paul writes that creation groans for the day of redemption (Rom 8:22-23). Scripture tells us that the physical realm is reeling under the influence of sin. The impact of sin against the Creator fuels restlessness, sorrow, and struggle. And the effects of sin not only press in from the outside; the most demanding disruptions of sin reside within (Jas 4:1-10). Sin pervades perspectives and limits the ability to contend with the challenges around us. Thus, for the client, the means to execute an effective response and successfully readjust are unclear. Hope begins to fade. Clients seek assistance when the future is as bleak as a blinding fog, energy is depleted, and the road ahead is obscure. Given these realities, I anticipate that there is much at stake for Cora or she would not consider becoming a client. As counselors, our mission is to greet seekers, inspire courage, instill confidence, invite disclosure, and organize a vast array of material. We accomplish all of this while continuously taking in a client's background, development, and spiritual maturity. With each predicament, the client's story unfolds from a void that lacks form and perhaps even a central theme. Tactical assessment is both a necessity and a priority.

As a client, Cora presents as an articulate management specialist who exudes outward success. During the early phase of the session, it is nearly impossible to recognize why she needs help. Her façade is impressive. Still, an inward and dangerous bitterness seeps out over longstanding loneliness. Emotion slowly surfaces as I repeat certain phrases or draw attention via empathy to the struggle within her. The story that Cora shares reveals stark disappointment. She now sees her seven-year, intermittent relationship with a married lover as destructive, unfulfilling, and terminal. Her remote residence was the place for their rendezvous, which were not as frequent as Cora would have liked. Hiding out in the country allowed for secrecy and escape. Her father's alcoholism and her eccentric, religious mother who enabled his drinking left her with many painful childhood memories.

This tale is gathered without difficulty through routine maneuvers. Once she displays her competency, Cora is ready to pour out her hurt. Two available but "unplanned" assessment question sets open the way for her to do this. One tool is the brief spiritual life interview (Plante, 2009), and the other is a substance-abuse screening approach known as CAGE (Ewing, 1984). These simple stock techniques prove to be pivotal. Cora's answers add import to the heart cry beneath her request.

I ask Cora about her desire for counseling with a Christian focus. This request is indicated by a box checked on our referral forms. Cora explains that her older sister had been to our agency and had strongly recommended it. This response appears straightforward enough. Nevertheless, the lack of a personal affirmation of faith prompts me to introduce several questions from a set of ten specific interview questions to tap into her spiritual resources and beliefs (Plante, 2009, p. 58). Questions such as, How were religious-spiritual discussions experienced within your family while you were growing up? Did your contact with the Christian faith come across as positive, negative, or a mixed bag? These questions aim to uncover how faith and religious background have helped or hindered in one's experience. Cora has a vast network of roots within a strict religious community. Currently, most family members are said to express vibrant Christian testimonies. Remarkably, the client's own internal spiritual experience is hollow and hidden by shame. Hope in a personal Savior, always a calming promise articulated by her mother, now resembles an unlikely and futuristic dream. Cora does not have confidence of being a new creature with a heavenly destiny or of belonging to a specially chosen family. Faith is like a silent wish that comes to mind when blowing out birthday candles. Her Christianity is primarily extrinsic, shame-based, and tied to her past dwelling in a conservative, Pentecostal church community. Perhaps the Holy Spirit is awakening an urge for renewal.

Further, a throwaway comment made by Cora during a rapid survey of current symptoms alerts me to include a substance abuse screening query known as CAGE (Ewing, 1984): Have you ever felt you should Cut down on your drinking? Have people Annoyed you by criticizing your drinking? Have you ever felt bad or Guilty about your drinking? Have you had an Eye-opener first thing in the morning to steady nerves or get rid of a hangover?

The answers not only bring tears to her eyes but also a forthright admission. Cora is facing her second charge of driving while intoxicated (DWI). The penalty could result in driving restrictions, which would seriously interfere with her employment. Her entrance into counseling is the result of a tough recommendation made by her defense attorney. This is not recorded anywhere on demographic forms, nor does it appear that Cora can readily reveal this embarrassing dilemma. Her bold self-portrayal is that of a wine connoisseur. There are enough reasons to wonder if this is a disguise for bouts of excessive drinking both in groups and when alone. In a moment of sheer transparency, after the disclosure of her problematic drinking, there is palpable sense of wonder as Cora surprisingly muses, "Maybe I've worked so hard not to become my mother that I've become a pathetic drunk like my father." It is evident that a plan to modify alcohol use will be an early treatment priority.

The assessment phase of the consultation not only brings transparency regarding symptoms, circumstances, and concerns; it fills in critical details to Cora's story. Her motivation for coming to counseling is a combination of terror over the threat of losing her driver's license and profound grief over the aspirations lost in a destructive relationship. These tentative observations are received with tears and gratitude, suggesting that the therapeutic alliance has appropriately formed. There is ample support for the recommendation that she enter therapy following participation in several additional assessments procedures. She is assured that while her desire to explore the toxic messages from the past will be honored, there is work to do in forging her identity in the present. Cora's career accomplishments and self-confidence are acknowledged as important strengths. The preliminary treatment plan will be to assess and address her substance abuse, revitalize hope in herself and others in light of her recent breakup, and unravel family/faith loyalties to restore bonds and overcome hurts. The possibility of a step group such as Alcoholics Anonymous (aa.org) or Celebrate Recovery (celebraterecovery.com) is mentioned as an option that will have to be carefully considered.

In short, within the semi-structured START interview, two uncomplicated assessment techniques are applied. Formal question sets were woven in to acquire a spiritual life history and to conduct a substance-abuse screening. In this instance, each option yields highly relevant pockets of information. The results contribute to the overall understanding of her clinical profile. This is a prime example of subjectively sensing an emotional vulnerability and responding with an objective yet empathetic investigation. In a follow-up session, standardized mental health measures are applied. The initial consultation accomplishes its therapeutic mission with Cora.

CUSTOMIZE YOUR START

START works best when it is full of interview items that fit your practice niche. Determine the essentials you will need to know in order to make informed decisions about treatment options and direction. Brainstorm with colleagues about how they do these consultations and collect their best queries. Review existing records to identify the range of issues that clients bring to treatment. Add, adjust, and eliminate questions/items so that every piece of data gathered during a START interview contributes toward the full picture needed for the mission of the setting. When a good sense of what needs to be assessed in an initial consultation is complete, the next step is to design or select a form to record the results of the session. Create a session template to accompany the START format such as the sample offered in appendix two. Software systems designed for electronic medical records (EMRs) have such built-in intake session forms. Whether you adapt or adopt, get a solid template that works for you, your clients, and the stakeholders who depend on your clinical documentation.

Note that the recording template for the IC must be customized to represent the range of personal issues that you are likely to see in clients. A ministry setting that energizes urban youth to stay invested in education or career training will have differing priorities from an outpatient mental health clinic. Identify heavy risk factors and place critical items in the START routine. Adjust the outcome expectations for the initial consultation by designing a template that will capture the results. The benefit of standardization is that it can produce tools to categorize and retell what happened in a complex session.

Unfortunately, there is a risk that recording templates can reduce us to robotic intake technicians. In this first contact we must resist projecting an unfeeling, insensitive manner, which does not fit the beautiful Christ-honoring mission we've been given to show hospitality to strangers—the theology that undergirds the rationale for defining best practice procedures to turn a stranger into a guest and eventually into an ally.

Also remember that it is possible to achieve a semblance of order in record forms and still describe a real and complex person. This is possible by mixing forced-choice and short-answer items with plenty of fields for open entries where descriptive and unique observations are charted. Sometimes it can feel like a large mass of information gets boiled down to neatly fit into checked boxes or nebulous, clinical phrases. Form filling can minimize the insights of the scientist-practitioner, muffle the voice of the participant-observer, and constrain recognition of the movement of the Holy Spirit in the comforted-comforter. Raw data are transferred but there is no communication about the heart of the person as revealed in the narrative. Regrettably, meaning is lost or obscured when there is no energetic attempt to convey the living dynamics and nuances felt via the interpersonal connection. Indeed, without extra commentary from us, it is impossible to warm to a client's passions, emotional turmoil, or unique spiritual gifting. Recording hardship and struggle in restrictive little check boxes will deplete the extraordinary satisfaction that coming together for a helping partnership can produce. Use forms that allow for checks, ratings, and free space, and use them to tell the story and start the healing conversation.

The solution is a recording template for START interviews that combines prompts, checklists, and reminders with ample narrative, quotes, examples, and commentary. Given the diversity of settings, one form cannot do it all. Customize the version of the START template provided for your own clinical and ministry purposes in appendix two. Record the information necessary to build a foundation for the best possible treatment decision. Set up a strategy to secure the necessary data, than share the imperatives that deserve attention.

Christian hospitality welcomes outsiders. In counseling, this will mean that others are brought into our personal space. There is so much more to a welcome that reflects our Christian values. The goal is to host well enough to make a heart-to-heart connection. This will not only refresh; it can also create an appetite for community. The purpose of a good START is to take strangers, entertain them as guests, and coach them through the work of becoming allies. As hosts, Christian helpers will bring hard matters to the surface for mutual protection, for refreshment, and to secure peace. The biblical picture for opening a modern-day counseling IC is the ancient practice of washing the feet of the weary sojourner. This is the precursor to embracing empathy and entering into dialogue for the sake of the kingdom.

REFERENCES

Cherpitel, C. J. (2000). A brief screening instrument for problem drinking in the emergency room: The RAPS4 (Rapid Alcohol Problems Screen). *Journal of Studies on Alcohol, 61*(3), 447-449.

Ewing, J. A. (1984). Detecting alcoholism: The CAGE questionnaire. *Journal of the American Medical Association, 252*(14), 1905-1907.

Groth-Marnat, G., & Wright, A. J. (2016). *Handbook of psychological assessment* (6th ed.). Hoboken, NJ: John Wiley & Sons.

Hill, L. S., Reid, F., Morgan, J. F., & Lacey, J. H. (2010) SCOFF, the development of an eating disorder screening questionnaire. *International Journal of Eating Disorders, 43*, 344-351.

Hoyt, M. F. (2011). Brief psychotherapies. In S. B. Messer & A. S. Gurman (Eds.), *Essential psychotherapies: Theory and practice* (3rd ed., pp. 387-425). New York: Guilford Press.

Jipp, J. W. (2017). *Saved by faith and hospitality*. Grand Rapids, MI: Eerdmans.

Luck, A. J., Morgan, J. F., Reid, F., O'Brien, A., Brunton, J., Price, C., Perry, L., & Lacey, J. H. (2002). The SCOFF questionnaire and clinical interview for eating disorders in general practice: Comparative study. *British Medical Journal, 325*, 755-756.

Malina, B. J. (1985). Hospitality. In P. Achtemeier (Ed.), *Harper's Bible dictionary* (pp. 408-409). San Francisco: HarperCollins.

Marini, I. (2016). Enhancing client return after the first session, and alternatively dealing with early termination. In I. Marini & M. A. Stebnicki (Eds.), *The professional counselor's desk reference* (2nd ed., pp. 99-104). New York: Springer.

Mears, G. (2016). Conducting an intake interview. In I. Marini & M. A. Stebnicki (Eds.), *The professional counselor's desk reference* (2nd ed., pp. 83-86). New York: Springer.

Plante, T. G. (2009). *Spiritual practices in psychotherapy: Thirteen tools for enhancing psychological health*. Washington, DC: American Psychological Association.

Pohl, C. D. (1999). *Making room: Recovering hospitality as a Christian tradition*. Grand Rapids, MI: Eerdmans.

Whiston, S. C. (2017). *Principles and applications of assessment in counseling* (5th ed.). Belmont, CA: Cengage.

Wiger, D. E. (2009). *The clinical documentation sourcebook: The complete paperwork resource for your mental health practice* (4th ed.). Hoboken, NJ: John Wiley & Sons.

Yong, A. (2008). *Hospitality & the other: Pentecost, Christian practices, and the neighbor*. Maryknoll, NY: Orbis.

Zuckerman, E. L., & Kolmes, K. (2017). *The paper office for the digital age: Forms, guidelines, and resources to make your practice work ethically, legally, and profitably* (5th ed.). New York: Guilford.

THERAPEUTIC ALLIANCE AND
THE SIGNIFICANT SELF

Therefore, with minds that are alert and fully sober, set your hope
on the grace to be brought to you when Jesus Christ is revealed at his
coming. As obedient children, do not conform to the evil desires you had
when you lived in ignorance. But just as he who called you is holy, so be
holy in all you do; for it is written: "Be holy, because I am holy."

1 Peter 1:13-16

The Call to Be Holy

ALLIANCE TRACKING: "HOW ARE 'WE' DOING?"

Ian is a counseling intern well along in his experience. One day in supervision
he expresses frustration. "Two appointments no-showed yesterday. I phoned
both. One told me that he was too busy to come anymore. The other did not
call back. My hours are not where they should be, and I really need those
clients." There was exasperation on his face and tension in his voice. Inconsistent
client compliance and dropout are typical with new counselors so Ian's supervisors routinely examine the state of the therapeutic alliance (Miller, Bargmann,
Chow, Seidel, & Maeschalck, 2016). Fortunately, the template Ian uses for
clinical documentation includes a prompt for reflection on the alliance following every session (see figs. 10.1 and 10.2). Ian recalls what he recorded in his
clinical notes.

Ian pauses when asked, "What has your client verbalized or enacted that
reveals how he regards the therapeutic partnership?" The realization emerges
that Ian has only his own impressions regarding his client's satisfaction,

Clinical Session Record *(Individual)*

Clinician: _____ Date: _____/_____/_____

Time Begun: _____:_____   Time Finished: _____:_____

Session with: _____

Session: #_____ of _____ through _____/_____/_____ (date)

Major Session Theme

Main Treatment Goal Addressed

Noteworthy Mental Status Observations

Medical/Medication Update

Therapeutic Alliance Observations

○ Strong   ○ Good   ○ Basic   ○ Strained   ○ Weak/Needs Attention

Comments

Plans for Next Session

Clinician Signature: _____ Date: _____/_____/_____

Clinician Credentials: _____

Figure 10.1. Clinical session record documentation template (individual). (Greggo, Stephen P. [2019]. *Assessment for Counseling in Christian Perspective*. Downers Grove, IL: InterVarsity Press.)

Clinical Session Record *(Couple)*

Clinician: _____ Date: _____/_____/_____

Time Begun: _____:_____ Time Finished: _____:_____

Session with: _____

Session: #_____ of _____ through _____/_____/_____ (date)

Major Session Theme

Main Relational Change Goal Addressed

Process Observations *(i.e., relational dynamics, communication patterns, emotional synergy)*

Progress Observations *(i.e., risk taking, creative initiative, care demonstrations, empathic connection)*

Therapeutic Alliance Observations

○ Strong ○ Good ○ Basic ○ Strained ○ Weak/Needs Attention

Comments

Homework Given/Plans for Next Session

Clinician Signature: _____ Date: _____/_____/_____

Clinician Credentials: _____

Figure 10.2. Clinical session record documentation template (couple). (Greggo, Stephen P. [2019]. *Assessment for Counseling in Christian Perspective*. Downers Grove, IL: InterVarsity Press.)

expectations, and evaluation. Ian's view is utterly subjective. He has no direct client comments or ratings with regard to the working relationship. In this regard, Ian's approach is no different from the vast majority of therapists across all ranges of proficiency. The reliance of clinicians exclusively on their own assumptions for gauging alliance security is stunning, especially given that there is extensive and compelling research on the correlation between the quality of the working relationship, treatment completion, and attainment of outcomes (Swift & Greenberg, 2015).

Assessment technology is available to track the quality of the alliance and surface tension. Using this technology Ian made a professional development plan to modify his client connection strategy that included incorporating an alliance measure into his everyday clinical work. If it's all about the partnership, why not take snapshots of how the relationship is going?

Counselors like Ian will benefit not only from a routine method to assess alliance strength but also from a comprehensive grasp of the basis of such a partnership. The natural way to build a relationship with another person is to uncover similarities. Discovering mutual interests in a sport, art, travel, culinary preference, or even a preferred style of worship can move people from strangers to acquaintances.

Likeness stimulates closeness, and similarities are not too difficult to locate. As common ground is discovered, smiles and laughter become spontaneous. Similarities help add motivation to the therapeutic journey. As clients share, counselors express empathy, which communicates to clients an understanding of their world. On the surface, forming a working alliance can appear to be all about finding similarities and communicating empathy.

WHOLENESS AND HOLINESS IN ALIGNMENT

Unlike our quest to find similarities with clients, the supreme God whom we worship is not entirely comparable to human beings. The holiness of God is a crucial and inescapable foundation of Christianity, and this feature can be disruptive and divisive. Scripture makes over nine hundred declarations about God's holiness. In Scripture the word for *holiness* means to cut, separate, consecrate, and purify (Carpenter & Comfort, 2000). The Lord God Almighty is pure, majestic, without blemish; he is holy, holy, holy (e.g., Ex 15:11; Lev 19:2; Rev 4:9). Throughout Christian tradition there have been different ideas of what holiness should look like in the lives of disciples; however, the belief that devoted followers are to move toward holiness has not changed. Holiness is essential to orthodoxy. If this were not so, there would be no necessity for the passion, crucifixion, or resurrection of our Lord.

Recall the moment that Jesus tenderly paused to instruct his disciples on the simplicity of prayer. He begins with "Our Father in heaven, hallowed [holy] be your name" (Mt 6:9). Jesus Christ, who overcame the infinite distance separating a holy God from his wandering creatures, taught his followers to speak openly and easily with his Father. At the same time, he acknowledged God's perfect and holy nature. His holiness is awe-inspiring. Thus, there is an element of separation from our Father, death and resurrection, the old becoming new, repentance and re-creation.

Counseling from within a Christian worldview reflects an agenda of separation from what is ordinary and movement by grace toward holiness. The restoration of health, a return to wholeness, and reconciliation of a relationship are all examples of outcomes that may result as we grow in holiness. Through repentance and re-creation we become more like the One whose image we bear. This process, called sanctification, is one of setting ourselves apart from sin, impurity, and brokenness. We seek renewal to honor the holy God that we love who calls us to "be holy, because I am holy" (Lev 11:44-45; 1 Pet 1:16). Counseling that is Christian lovingly speaks about the hardest of all matters: how hearts may be blind to distortions, selfishness, and sinful ways. This is not done by pointing fingers or boldly confronting the presence of sin. This may be an aspect of pastoral dialogue at times, but it is rarely productive in counseling. On the contrary, the partnership between counselor and client rests on the promise that the two will come together to face the effects of sin. Counseling conversations occur between allies who respond with a united voice to the call for consecration in accordance with treatment objectives and ongoing character formation.

COUNSELOR AND CLIENT: A WORKING ALLIANCE

What makes a therapeutic relationship unique when its goal is to imitate Jesus Christ and respond to the sanctifying work of the Holy Spirit? A comprehensive answer requires a detailed look at the relationship in terms of its parameters, assessment, and monitoring.

The counselor-client dynamic goes by several names: helping relationship, working alliance, therapeutic partnership. These terms describe this relationship positively (Horvath, Del Re, Flückiger, & Symonds, 2011). However, this hasn't always been the case. Over the past one hundred years, there has been a dramatic reversal in how this relationship is viewed. In the beginning, the interpersonal reality was viewed as an inconvenient nuisance, fraught with unconscious dynamics and inherent conflicts (e.g., transference/counter-transference; psychodynamics). Then it became a highly valuable, one-sided gift from the therapist to the client (e.g., unconditional positive regard; person-centered). In contemporary times, it has become a meeting place of collaboration and consensus building for therapist and client (e.g., mutual partnership; empirically supported relationship). The bond is recognized as a provisional attachment, filled with deeply rooted relational schemas, mystery, and emotion. Within the mainstream, the working relationship is one that receives dedicated attention and involves direct negotiation in therapeutic conversation, rather than unconscious pull. The therapeutic alliance is out of the shadows and in the spotlight.

The potency of a therapeutic alliance is measured by agreement in focus and regarding goals and mutuality. Counseling is a "partnership for change" conspiracy. The therapeutic alliance is recognized across theoretical helping models as perhaps the most important component in a client's healing. The working alliance is not to be confused with its superficial cousin, rapport—the general ease, flow, or familiarity within the conversation. Rather, it is the deep, tangible, comprehensible awareness of a goal-directed partnership. The general consensus surrounding this extensively researched relationship is that its prime elements include (1) a nurtured bond of affirmation (positive regard), (2) a cooperative approach to tasks (collaboration), and (3) transparent communication to establish an overall focus and outcome goals (consensus; Bordin, 1994; Norcross & Wampold, 2011). The therapeutic alliance has endorsement by theoretical models, evidenced-based support, and practical value (Stegman, Kelly, & Harwood, 2013).

The mental health field pushes hard to imitate the medical profession. This is particularly evident in the ongoing movement to employ evidence-based methods. The assumption is that counseling interventions function like medicine and that these procedures are effective regardless of who does the administering. But research raises serious doubt about such a naive view. There is little to endorse the plausibility that all benefit comes from the techniques themselves (Norcross, 2002). Research makes clear that therapist factors and the therapeutic relationship do matter (Castonguay & Hill, 2017). The self of the therapist is recognized as a central force in the healing process. Interventions are tools in the hands of craftspeople who apply them within an interpersonal context to achieve outcomes. The most effective counselors learn to use the alliance to its maximum potential; this is what the evidence supports.

An extensive meta-analysis investigated the relationship between the alliance and therapeutic outcomes using over two thousand research reports from literature across the globe (Horvath et al., 2011). This was actually the fourth of a series of similar research endeavors dating back to 1991. Each time the findings have become increasingly more convincing and more descriptive. Results strongly confirm that the strength of the alliance contributes heavily to the outcome of therapy. No matter what techniques or approaches are employed, the quality of the alliance is going to influence what clients actually accomplish and gain. The findings can be summarized as follows.

- Counselors and clients forge partnerships in the hard work of interpersonal dialogue. The alliance is built by executing the critical elements of therapy: assessment, treatment planning, therapeutic conversation, and evaluation. Alliances are not formed in mere amiable exchanges or informal excursions about nonessential matters.

- The alliance needs to be functional and secure to be therapeutic, not perfect or ideal. Research suggests that a "good enough" alliance is vital to keep clients engaged and to create the optimal climate conducive to the work.

- The therapist takes the initiative to build an adequate working alliance. This is accomplished by coordinating expectations, resources, priorities, readiness, and capacities. Further, the therapist may need to turn the conversation back on itself to address misunderstandings and examine ruptures.

- The alliance relies on mutual feedback. It benefits from active monitoring, maintenance, and repair. Being intentional in the collection and analysis of data helps therapists gain skill in facilitation because there is regular reflection on how to incorporate lessons learned.

COUNSELOR, CLIENT, AND HOLY SPIRIT: A TRIADIC ALLIANCE

The common term in Christianity that can be associated with the technical understanding of a working alliance is *faithfulness* (fidelity, allegiance, conscientiousness; Greggo, 2014). Striving to be faithful makes informed consent and transparency with clients a matter of not only professional importance but also Christian integrity. A counselor-client relationship displays qualities resembling a covenant (e.g., intimacy, security, privileged communication, informed consent, and mutual obligations; Elwell, 2000). Nevertheless, counseling relationships must respect the boundaries outlined in mental-health-professional

(MHP) ethical codes: counseling is a formal yet fluid agreement (i.e., temporary, adjunctive, time-limited, focused, and readily terminated).

The alliance literature has contributed to the movement toward spiritually integrated psychotherapy (Pargament, 2007). The discrepancies between generic spirituality and Christianity make it necessary to define terms and constructs in order to avoid confusion. For example, the phrase "sacred moment" has become common in therapeutic language. This refers to brief occasions in which a client has a deep inner experience. The surrounding reality appears to pulsate with life. Among the noted benefits of these moments are transcendence (an experience separate from the ordinary), ultimacy (a deeply inner stirring regarding truth or reality), boundlessness (exceeding the limitations of time and space), interconnectedness (perceptions of exceptional mutuality, compassion, and affirmation), and spiritual emotions (awareness of awe, humility, gratitude, mystery, joy, peace, and serenity; Pargament, Lomax, McGee, & Fang, 2014).

Ken Pargament, along with a team of researchers, conducted a groundbreaking study (Pargament et al., 2014) in which they examined the alliance between therapists and clients to identify sacred moments within counseling that went above and beyond what could be termed as important or pivotal occasions. In their study they found that clients and counselors were renewed by these intense experiences of relational connection. The researchers developed the Sacred Moment Qualities Scale (SMQS) to capture and quantify these striking interpersonal events (Pargament et al., 2014). The quite remarkable finding is that sacred moments tend to emerge from a strong therapeutic alliance in which there is openness, acceptance, active presence, and receptiveness. There are valuable implications here for how the therapeutic alliance is understood. As one commentator remarks with enthusiasm, this type of investigation demonstrates that, while scientific knowledge and evidence are invaluable, there is more to interpersonal therapeutic exchanges than what science can distill, explain, or contain in a treatment manual (Allen, 2014). At the same time, the study authors are abundantly clear that while "spiritual" terminology is applied, this research is intentionally psychological and not theological. "These perceptions do not speak one way or the other to the ontological reality of the sacred, higher powers, or God. They do, however, reflect on human character" (Pargament et al., 2014, p. 249).

Another term that can cause confusion is *sanctify*. In the language of clinical spirituality, this word describes the process of bringing the experience of the sacred into more and more of everyday life (Pargament, 2007)—of seeing more routinely through a sensitive and enriching spiritual lens. This process can increase the vibrancy of relationships and open the door for further spiritual experiences throughout life. Such outcomes move far beyond therapeutic interactions (Mahoney, 2013).

In the language of Scripture, sanctification involves maturing in our relationship with Jesus Christ and being responsive to the Holy Spirit. From a biblical perspective (i.e., separate from a purely psychological view), to sanctify is to transform a person by bringing that person into relationship with or closer to the likeness of the holy (Brower, 1996; Rom 6:19-22). In Christian counseling, the process of sanctification will separate past from future, old from new, sin from blessing, selfishness from sacrifice, and, in particular, self-exaltation from Christlikeness.

A psychological approach to the sacred yields insight into how the therapeutic alliance affects both counselors and clients. For Christian counselors, however, the term *sacred* refers to the movement of the Holy Spirit. The Spirit is on the move, calling those who believe to be reconciled to a Holy Father through his Son. The triune God is an eternal, holy, personal being who exists outside of his creation. This distinction alters our understanding of the therapeutic alliance. The counselor-client working alliance is the vehicle through which the Holy Spirit accomplishes his work of sanctification (i.e., progression in holy living) and transformation (i.e., renewal in the image of Jesus Christ).

Elsewhere I have made the case that redemptive interpersonal encounters are the most curative element of helping relationships (Greggo, 2007, 2011). These corrective emotional relationships (CERs) provide a context for clients to experience the grace of Jesus Christ. The phrase "corrective emotional relationships" recalls and paraphrases a powerful concept from the psychodynamic literature, the "corrective emotional experience" (Yalom & Leszcz, 2005). This is the experience of recalling, under more favorable conditions, emotional traumas that were once too much for the ego to bear. Through catharsis, what was once repressed by necessity is freed and flows to the surface, releasing pressure and resolving inner emotional turbulence. From the vantage point of the therapeutic alliance, it is not mere catharsis that is the curative factor. The relationship that receives the outpouring is the source of healing as it soothes the isolation and supports the crisis experience. Healing does not come solely from an intrapersonal release; it emerges from a disclosure that is received within an interpersonal (or transcendent) connection.

CERs are not exclusive to the domain of therapy; they can occur in normal life as well. Therapists, however, intentionally create conditions (i.e., nurture an alliance) where CERs are likely to develop. The CER is an example of the sacred moment discussed earlier. From a theological perspective, in this moment human beings break out of the ordinary through intersubjectivity to experience the extraordinary. This is the activity of the Holy Spirit breaking into human brokenness to offer a foretaste of heaven. The relational connection of Jesus Christ through the Holy Spirit is the source of healing, growth, forgiveness, and sanctification. A therapeutic alliance that is distinctively Christian is a triadic partnership between counselor, client, and the Holy Spirit.

TRACKING THERAPEUTIC PARTNERSHIPS

The sourcebook *Measures for Clinical Practice and Research* (Corcoran & Fischer, 2013) includes the classic thirty-six-item Working Alliance Inventory (WAI) by Adam Horvath.[1] This extensively researched measure has been used for over thirty years (Horvath & Greenberg, 1989) and still makes its way into clinical settings, primarily in its shortened form (WAI-SF; twelve items). The client rates statements such as

- [Therapist] and I agree about the things I will need to do in therapy to help improve my situation.
- [Therapist] and I are working toward mutually agreed upon goals.
- [Therapist] and I trust one another.

The hallmark of this instrument is its direct reliance on Bordin's model of the working alliance. Bordin's model defines the working alliance as the convergence of a relational bond, agreement on counseling tasks, and an openly negotiated plan to realize mutual goals (Bordin, 1994). A practical way to bring the WAI-SF into treatment would be to use it a couple of times during the first six sessions (e.g., after sessions one and three) and again later when conducting a review of progress. For Ian, the counselor mentioned at the opening of the chapter, this plan would be a reasonable professional development activity.

An important development in the area of therapeutic conversations is the immediate introduction of simple, straightforward, and discrete rating scales

---

[1]Permission for research and/or clinical use can be obtained from Adam O. Horvath, (http://wai.profhorvath.com/).

in the session to monitor counseling progress and strength of the alliance (Duncan, Miller, Wampold, & Hubble, 2010). This procedure becomes a major aspect of care to the extent that it literally becomes the therapy (feedback-informed treatment [FIT]) (Prescott, Maeschalck, Miller, 2017). The counseling skill of immediacy (i.e., talk about direct, present, interpersonal experience) moves from the wings to center stage as a helping technique. Considerable evidence exists to support the assertion that regular checks with clients on their perception of progress and their view of the therapeutic alliance can reduce dropout, increase satisfaction, and improve outcomes. The Session Rating Form (SRF) is a standard means to gather information using a scale that allows a client to rate the status of the relationship, agreement on goals/topics, and appropriate fit with the therapist's approach (Duncan et al., 2010).[2] The format is client friendly, and it contains only four items, making the SRF feasible to use in every session. This assessment practice shifts the focus from "Does counseling work?" to "How is this counseling partnership working to produce change?" The evidence suggests that this routine assessment can stimulate adjustments in attitudes and plan that foster greater effectiveness in talk therapy. Tracking alliance data is a way of maintaining attentiveness to the therapeutic alliance.

The Counseling Partnership Alliance Check (CPAC; see appendix three) is a measure that has been formulated to explicitly track the alliance in a manner that ties to the theological perspective depicted in this chapter. This is a three-item scale intended for use in Christian and pastoral counseling to track the quality of the counseling relationship. As with other alliance measures, the CPAC items tie to the elements known to constitute a productive therapeutic alliance. The "Hope for Change" item aims at the tasks by highlighting the activity in the session: "Reflect on the session themes, talking points, strategies and activities. Today I felt . . ." The "Hospitality and Connection" item reflects the bond between client and counselor with its mention of honesty, accountability, and mutual focus: "Consider the teamwork, common focus, honesty, and accountability in this session. Overall my experience was . . ." The final item, "Cultivating Character," taps into the goals at the core of personal development and spiritual formation: "Ponder the impact of this session in terms of how it might eventually strengthen your faith or shape you character. Today

---

[2]A license to utilize the Outcome Rating Scale (ORS) and the Session Rating Form (SRF) can be obtained from www.scottdmiller.com/performance-metrics/. There is currently no fee for individual practitioners. For ease of use, clinicians may opt for software to administer the SRS and the ORS on a portable device (fees apply): www.scottdmiller.com/fit-software-tools/.

my soul felt . . ." CPAC items were shaped with the priority of moving therapeutically in ways that are consistent with Christian maturation. Counseling
can stir disciples to become more like Christ. There is good reason to examine
the client's experience of hope, hospitality, and the teleological ideal of cultivating one's character.

The purpose of the CPAC is not merely to provide quantitative evidence of
the quality of the relationship. It is also an attempt to open the door to examine
expectations, approaches, and, ultimately, the client's experience of a CER.
Beyond the immediate benefit of this exploration, counselors who are Christian
know the potential of the helping relationship to assist clients in clarifying how
they're living out the Lord's vision for their personal identity. Here is a crucial
question to include in our prayers: How is the Holy Spirit at work in these
conversations and in this distinct restorative relationship to condition the heart,
stir canonical imagination, and prompt action that honors the Lord?

An alternative method to monitor how well the alliance is working is by
direct discussion. Plan to move into this question set at each juncture where
treatment progress is examined. This PACE (partnership, affinity, collaborative
conversation, and experience) outline serves as a model to guide the close examination of the alliance in action (fig. 10.3).

Partnership: *How are we doing as a team? How is our plan working?*

Affinity: *What does it feel like to be together right now?*

Collaborative Conversation: *Does our talk match our intent? Is our dialogue working?*

Experience: *Is there a felt transparency, saftey, and mutuality?*

Figure 10.3. PACE model for an alliance review

The PACE questions are recommended for use as the customary assessment
components of a formal treatment review. The backdrop to a PACE checkup
would be to provide realistic appraisal of how clients are addressing their
reasons for seeking care and how they are moving forward with their goals.

CHARACTER FORMATION: SANCTIFICATION AND THE SELF

Character formation, growing in conformity to the image of Jesus Christ, is the agenda for Christian counseling that is constantly operating beneath the surface. Grasping the implication of this requires an understanding of biblical anthropology. A Christian worldview asserts that the grand narrative of history is all about God's great drama of revelation and redemption. Human beings, by God's marvelous design, are created for community and to live in covenantal relationship (Vanhoozer, 2005). Going back as far as the womb, God had a role for us play that engages our uniqueness to portray his image. Our commitment and lifelong answer to him puts us in position to be a restored image bearer that brings him glory and honor.

Personality describes how human beings display unique patterns as embodied creatures in interaction with others. Our identity as a Christian shapes how our personality flows through our character and reflects our role in God's unfolding story. The Holy Spirit begins his re-creative work within the influential forces of biology, culture, intimate attachments, and even the desires of our own heart to further display our true character in Christ. The God who made us knows us; furthermore, he seeks to commune with us. Joining the Holy Spirit in a client's journey of identity gives resolve, meaning, and significance to therapeutic efforts (Greggo, 2014).

Counselors may find it helpful to visualize the direction of a client's change by adopting the model of a "significant" self. Significance is experienced as we respond to the wonder of God's creation and his work in our re-creation. The convention in the therapeutic field when referencing the inner world of identity construction, longing, and schema building is to use adjectives that qualify "self" such as *true, ideal, authentic,* or a*ctualized.* Each adjective depicts a future version of the self and captures the human urgency (i.e., self-agency) to mature, thrive, and flourish. However, these constructs, as prevalent as they are in counseling theories, do not easily line up with a biblical view of a disciple. Developmental processes drive our growth biologically, psychologically, and socially. Our internal narrative directs us to consistently make sense of the unfolding story of our lives (McAdams, 2013, 2015). The key difference between a general narrative theory of personality development and a Christian perspective is that a Christ-follower recognizes that the story of their identity development is not being written by them alone but is coauthored with the Holy Spirit as part of a theocentric drama.

As counselors, we need a framework to help us translate and interpret the human effort to increase mastery and further maturation that has an emphasis on grace, newness, and our heavenly destiny. I use the phrase "significant self" to refer to the disciple's ideal personal identity—the joining together of God's intent for a person and the person's experience of being who God envisioned. For convenience, consider this acrostic for significance (SIGN-IFICANT): Self In God's Narrative—Individuality in Fellowship with and Imitating Christ, Always reNewing Traits) (see fig. 10.4). For the Christ-follower, the "true self" derives definition and worth from being a reflection of the triune God of the Scriptures.

Figure 10.4. Sign-ificant self: self in God's narrative

Theologian Kevin Vanhoozer (2014) expands our understanding of the Scriptures and our place in God's redemptive drama. He warns of two prevailing misunderstandings regarding the self. These are depicted as counterfeit "sirens" who sing to lure humans away from the form the Creator spoke us to be. One extreme is the exaggerated and exalted self of modernity (self as idol)—the sovereign self (i.e., "I think therefore I am"). The other is the fragmented and dislocated self of postmodern thinking (self as toppled idol)—the shattered self (i.e., "I am whichever of my assorted selves I choose to be in this moment"). Vanhoozer points instead to the true self. "[This] is not the Cartesian *cogito* but the Christian *vocatio*: the self that God has called into existence from what did not exist (Rom 4:17), the self that is called by, and in turn calls on, Jesus Christ" (p. 116).

Our clients are custom-designed persons, born of fallen parents and raised in a cosmos that groans for renewal (Rom 8:22). In requesting therapy that nurtures Christian faith, clients are seeking self-coherence (security and stability) in dialogue with the Holy Spirit to best image the Lord of life. Christ-followers are committed to put the foolishness, tragedies, and relational severing caused by sin as far behind as is divinely possible (e.g., separate old from new self). Instead, Christians seek to actively give the Holy Spirit freedom to sanctify, redeem, and renew. Disciples answer, act, rejoice, and suffer as consecrated "icons." The formation focus in counseling is to stay with the client's request while keeping our eyes on character maturation. This implies turning, acting, speaking, and relating in ways that better reflect the light of Jesus Christ and thereby glorify the Father.

The gospel calls for an identity that is submissive and yielding to the Lord's perspective. God speaks his ways through his Word, the community he inhabits (i.e., the body of Christ), and his anointed messengers. This runs counter to the prevailing obsession in psychotherapy with autonomy, self-determination, and personal declaration. The portrayals of the sovereign and shattered self do not support a significant self, that is, a self who recognizes that "being real" is being in communion with the Lord. Unfortunately, broad worldview caricatures never have enough detail to be helpful in clinical conversations. Those who counsel clients toward being a significant self require descriptive verbs to portray priorities that can shape personality to God's intent. We need vivid descriptions to imagine the specific role each one plays and the unique ways they reflect Christ. The hope is to enable clients to enjoy the esteem of the Father by imitating the Son in the power of the Holy Spirit. This requires terminology that accounts for the forces of heritability, neuroscience, early life experience, trauma, and the critical influences of culture on one's immediate circumstances (Trull & Widiger, 2015).

For counseling, there are advantages to the alternative-personality model proposed in the *Diagnostic and Statistical Manual of Mental Disorders* (*DSM-5*; American Psychiatric Association, 2013; Krueger & Eaton, 2010; Samuel & Widiger, 2010; Trull & Widiger, 2013). Its dimensions are derived from the five-factor model (FFM) of personality (extroversion vs. introversion, agreeableness vs. antagonism, conscientiousness vs. carelessness, emotional stability vs. volatility, and openness vs. rigidity). The FFM is built on a lexical premise (Costa & McCrae, 2007). This means that its polarities are distilled from human language. Language is viewed as the "sedimentary deposit" for thousands of years of observations about how people think, feel, and act (Trull & Widiger, 2013, p. 136). Everyday phrases spoken about others capture personality patterns. A personality framework with deep footings in lexical studies is fitting. Human beings made *imago Dei* were given the capacity to communicate by a God who spoke to his creatures and who continues to speak to this day.

The *DSM-5* identifies the manifestations of psychopathology. Thus, it emphasizes the negative end of the FFM polarities. This alternative diagnostic framework narrows the options to six personality disorders, which correspond to severe expressions of a distorted self (borderline, antisocial, schizotypal, narcissistic, obsessive-compulsive, and avoidant; Trull & Widiger, 2013). This model conveys pathology as misalignment of personality characteristics that fall along a continuum (dimensional features), in contrast to the *DSM*-5, which relies on fixed, unipolar, maladaptive traits (categorical disorders).

The dimensional model has great potential for counseling with Christians. Counselors guide clients toward sanctification, wholeness, and character maturation by working on the management of personality characteristics that inhibit relating to others in love. Figure 10.5 provides a visual representation of this. (For ease of recognition, I have paired technical terms with ordinary language depictions.)

Counselor and client come together to consider the instincts, patterns, and preferences that make one distinct. Of course, the current challenge that has brought the client into counseling will reveal the aspects of the current pattern under pressure to change. For example, a client who may fit *DSM* criteria for borderline tendencies could be described using dimension language such as having a tendency toward anxiousness, depressivity, emotional lability, hostility, impulsivity, risk-taking, and separation insecurity (Trull, 2012). In building a working relationship, the counselor would do well to remain even tempered by tolerating and providing interpretation for mood swings. It would be ideal to keep direct imperatives to a minimum as the client may react against such control (Choca, 2004).

To use another example, the schizotypal client would be low on warmth, gregariousness, positive emotions, and order and high on openness to

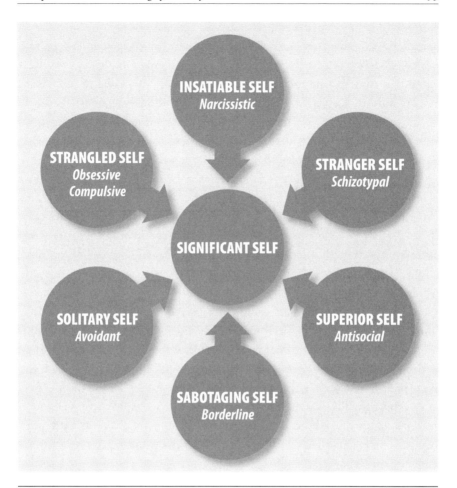

Figure 10.5. Common language self-patterns (unbalanced) to coach toward becoming a significant self

experience, anxiousness, and self-consciousness. Counselors working with such clients should allow more interpersonal distance in the alliance. Tasks become more critical than closeness. The priority in this case is to deal with practical problem solving and not to put pressure to deepen interpersonal relationships directly (Choca, 2004).

For both of these examples, the effort in counseling is to use the motivation to overcome a struggle to contemplate how autopilot personality actions might be moderated. The focus is on ways to reduce conflicts the person is experiencing, whether in relationships with others or internally. The case conceptualization has already identified targets for change. Bringing a Christian perspective into consideration does not necessarily add treatment goals.

Nor does it demand an explicit emphasis on spiritual formation using known spiritual disciplines. Rather, counselor and client come together as a team to notice behaviors and attitudes that will help remediate the chief complaint while also contributing to sanctification. There are no magic techniques to rapidly modify deeply rooted behavioral and relational schemas. These tendencies are biologically activated and became habit through steady interactions with others. Nevertheless, we look to offer a corrective emotional relationship as a means for the Holy Spirit to minister and foster maturity.

For Christ-followers, the counselor-client team prayerfully considers how a client's current personality preferences may be contributing to the symptoms experienced and how they might be inhibiting the ability to fulfill the role that the Holy Spirit is calling the client to fill. For example, the insatiable self (narcissistic) draws strength from the admiration of others without regard for mutuality or returning the gift of affirmation to others. The counselor in this case will need to word negative interpretations carefully and allow the client to set the pace. These clients will have difficulty expressing warmth, and they may unintentionally even communicate hostility. Extroversion and agreeableness are likely the personality dimensions to explore. It will be necessary to raise awareness about attention-seeking behavior that is apt to be one-sided, manipulative, and depleting for others. As moments of humbleness or openness occur, this formally unexamined pattern may be curbed in favor of acting to respect and honor the other. Counseling conversations coach the client toward being a significant self, a self that better images the triune God, by cultivating empathy toward others.

Another example is the solitary self (avoidant) who refuses to risk rejection by others to such an extent that the client remains entirely disengaged. The counselor here will need to build an alliance in a relaxed and easygoing manner that offers reassurance. This client type will grapple with characteristics related to introversion, close-mindedness, and low assertiveness. The preference for social withdrawal and inflexibility is to be considered in light of living out the role the client is called to.

The final example might be the strangled self (obsessive-compulsive) who is caught in the noose of pleasing others or performing rituals to the point of choking in the struggle to fulfill an impossible host of expectations. The counselor who notes these tendencies early on will attune to the client through recognizing the high value the client places on organization, deliberateness, and clarity. Such a client will need to eventually acknowledge how conscientiousness can morph into unrelenting perfectionism. Inflexibility may block communication and the ability to relate to others. Once again, the client imagines how personal traits, interpersonal patterns, and the thrust of the client's life narrative can be repositioned to represent the intentions and nudging of the Holy Spirit.

Counseling uses dialogue to bring awareness to how the self is currently being experienced. What does the Lord desire to see in our speech and action? The art of becoming a significant self requires responding to the Lord's loving call and practicing to be the best imitator of Jesus Christ. Retaining a holistic view is essential. Behaviors and personal characteristics emerge from a vast range of physiological, psychological, social, and ethical urges. The goal is to hear the voice of the Holy Spirit calling forth a new creation. No matter how the personality configuration currently leans, the charge for the significant self is to honor the Lord in thought, word, and deed.

THE UNIQUENESS OF A TRIADIC ALLIANCE

Christian counseling is a partnership for change that requires openness between counselor and client and to the Holy Spirit. As counselors, we rely on strategies research has shown to be effective in establishing, maintaining, and monitoring an alliance strong enough to further clinical work and character reformation. We acknowledge individuality and specific patterns that serve as strengths as well as those that inhibit the self from acting and speaking as the Lord directs. Individual differences are a product of God's design. They gain distinctiveness through our biology, psychosocial/cultural, and ethical domains. The challenge, mimicking the temptation of the fall, is that these unique traits can be used to increase autonomy or locate a hidden, self-fulfilling interior. Alternatively, our matchless personality features can position us to accept our calling and take our appointed place in the body of Christ, thus contributing to gospel progression.

A story about the sculptor Michelangelo provides a helpful metaphor for the work we do (Scigilano, 2012). As an artist, Michelangelo earned the reputation of being a perfectionist by mining his own blocks of marble from treacherous mountain quarries in Carrara, Italy, a task that involved tremendous risk and required extreme effort. In 1519 he was nearly killed when a chain snapped, dropping a huge column of the white marble nearly one hundred feet. Why go through such extraordinary exertion to secure a unique block of stone? Michelangelo knew that Carrara marble is not uniform; it has variations in color, grain, and veining. Imperfections such as discoloration, minerals, or cracks were prone to appear as the sculpting progressed. Michelangelo also knew that the most uncommon blocks are the ones that produce the most unique and beautiful art. The myth or remarkable reality is that Michelangelo could "see" his amazing design trapped inside the block that he carefully, lovingly, and with great pains extracted from the side of a mountain. He would chip away stone to release the beauty bound inside. His vision of the art caught within the marble resulted in the masterpieces we know today.

An additional piece of folklore about Michelangelo provides further inspiration for the work we do as counselors. While the *Pietà* and *Moses* were crafted from impeccable marble he mined himself, *David*—perhaps his ultimate masterpiece—was sculpted from an abandoned Carrara marble slab previously worked on and rejected by not one but two unsuccessful artists. *David* was stuck in that block for decades before Michelangelo partnered with the marble to complete his liberation!

Counselors use therapeutic conversation to develop a bond with clients that unites them around expectations of the change that the Lord will accomplish. The alliance is the crucible the Holy Spirit uses to bring forth an exceptional significant self. We may need to chip away deadness caused by trauma, imperfections magnified by anxiety, or even hardness of heart that has developed from experiences of loss or neglect. In our conversations we strive to set the client free by addressing issues of identity development that interfere with hearing and following the Holy Spirit.

It does not matter that our skills do not match that of Michelangelo. The Holy Spirit is the artist at work through our efforts. We submit ourselves and our counsel to the one whose innovative vision formed all raw materials from nothing. The alliance that becomes a cord of three strands is not quickly broken (Eccles 4:9-12). Assessment that tracks the quality of the alliance can help keep the connection with the client strong, the content on target, and both partners attentive to the Holy Spirit. The master craftsman knows exactly how to bring out the beauty of the human heart to act in God's drama for his glory.

REFERENCES

Allen, J. G. (2014). Beyond the therapeutic alliance. *Spirituality in Clinical Practice, 1*(4), 263-265.

American Psychiatric Association. (2013). *Diagnostic and statistical manual of mental disorders* (5th ed.). Arlington, VA: American Psychiatric Publishing.

Bordin, E. S. (1994). Theory and research on the therapeutic working alliance: New directions. In A. O. Horvath & L. S. Greenberg (Eds.), *The working alliance: Theory, research, and practice* (pp. 13-37). Oxford, England: John Wiley.

Brower, K. E. (1996). Sanctification, sanctify. In I. H. Marshall, A. R. Millard, J. I. Packer, & D. J. Wiseman (Eds.), *New Bible dictionary* (3rd ed., pp. 1057-1058). Downers Grove, IL: InterVarsity Press.

Carpenter, E. E., & Comfort, P. W. (2000). Holiness. In *Holman treasury of key Bible words: 200 Greek and 200 Hebrew words defined and explained* (p. 304). Nashville: Broadman & Holman.

Castonguay, L. G., & Hill, C. E. (2017). *How and why are some therapists better than others?: Understanding therapist effects.* Washington, DC: American Psychological Association.

Choca, J. P. (2004). *Interpretive guide to the Millon Clinical Multiaxial Inventory* (3rd ed.). Washington, DC: American Psychological Association.

Corcoran, K., & Fischer, J. (2013). *Measures for clinical practice and research: A sourcebook* (Vols. 1-2). Oxford, England: Oxford University Press.

Duncan, B. L., Miller, S. D., Wampold, B. E., & Hubble, M. A. (2010). *The heart & soul of change: Delivering what works in therapy* (2nd ed.). Washington, DC: American Psychological Association.

Elwell, W. A. (Ed.). (2000). *Baker theological dictionary of the Bible.* Grand Rapids, MI: Baker Books.

Greggo, S. P. (2007). *Trekking towards wholeness: A resource for care group leaders.* Downers Grove, IL: InterVarsity Press.

Greggo, S. P. (2011). Internal working model as heart: A translation to inspire Christian care groups. *Edification: The Transdisciplinary Journal of Christian Psychology, 5*(1), 4-13.

Greggo, S. P. (2014, November). *Theodramatic anthropology and the "significant" self: Implications for therapeutic relating.* Paper presented at the 66th Annual Meeting of the Evangelical Theological Society, San Diego, CA.

Horvath, A. O., Del Re, A. C., Flückiger, C., & Symonds, D. (2011). Alliance in individual psychotherapy. *Psychotherapy, 48*(1), 9-16.

Horvath, A. O., & Greenberg, L. S. (1989). Development and validation of the Working Alliance Inventory. *Journal of Counseling Psychology, 36*(2), 223-233.

Krueger, R. F., & Eaton, N. R. (2010). Personality traits and the classification of mental disorders: Toward a more complete integration in *DSM*-5 and an empirical model of psychopathology. *Personality Disorders: Theory, Research, and Treatment, 1*(2), 97-118.

Mahoney, A. (2013). The spirituality of us: Relational spirituality in the context of family relationships. In K. I. Pargament (Ed.), *APA handbook of psychology, religion, and spirituality: Vol. 1. Context, theory, and research* (pp. 365-389). Washington, DC: American Psychological Association.

McAdams, D. P. (2013). *The redemptive self: Stories Americans live by* (rev. ed.). Oxford, UK: Oxford University Press.

McAdams, D. P. (2015). *The art and science of personality development.* New York: Guilford Press.

Miller, S. D., Bargmann, S., Chow, D., Seidel, J. & Maeschalck, C. (2016). Feedback-informed treatment (FIT): Improving the outcome of psychotherapy one person at a time (pp. 247-262). In William O'Donohue and Alexandros, Maragakis (Eds.), *Quality improvement in behavioral health*. Cham, Switzerland. Springer International Publishing.

Norcross, J. (Ed.). (2002). *Psychotherapy relationships that work: Therapist contributions and responsiveness to patients*. Oxford, UK: Oxford University Press.

Norcross, J. C., & Wampold, B. E. (2011). Evidence-based therapy relationships: Research conclusions and clinical practices. In J. C. Norcross (Ed.), *Psychotherapy relationships that work: Evidence-based responsiveness* (2nd ed., pp. 423-430). New York: Oxford University Press.

Pargament, K. I. (2007). *Spiritually integrated psychotherapy: Understanding and addressing the sacred*. New York: Guilford Press.

Pargament, K. I., Lomax, J. W., McGee, J. S., & Fang, Q. (2014). Sacred moments in psychotherapy from the perspectives of mental health providers and clients: Prevalence, predictors, and consequences. *Spirituality in Clinical Practice, 1*(4), 248-262.

Prescott, D. S., Maeschalck, C. L., & Miller, S. D. (2017). *Feedback-informed treatment in clinical practice: reaching for excellence*. Washington, DC: American Psychological Association.

Samuel, D. B., & Widiger, T. A. (2010). Comparing personality disorder models: Cross-method assessment of the FFM and the *DSM-IV-TR. Journal of Personality Disorders, 24*(6), 721-745.

Scigliano, E. (2012). *Michelangelo's mountain: The quest for perfection in the marble quarries of Carrara*. New York: Simon & Schuster.

Stegman, R. S., Kelly, S. L., & Harwood, T. M. (2013). Evidence-based relationship and therapist factors in Christian counseling and psychotherapy. In Jamie D. Aten, Joshua N. Hook, Eric L. Johnson, & Everett Worthington, Jr. (Eds.), *Evidence-based practices for Christian counseling and psychotherapy*. Downers Grove, IL: InterVarsity Press.

Swift, J. K., & Greenberg, R. P. (2015). *Premature termination in psychotherapy: Strategies for engaging clients and improving outcomes*. Washington, DC: American Psychological Association.

Trull, T. J. (2012). The five-factor model of personality disorder and the *DSM-5. Journal of Personality 80*(6), 1697-1720.

Trull, T. J., & Widiger, T. A. (2013). Dimensional models of personality: The five-factor model and the *DSM-5. Dialogues in Clinical Neuroscience, 15*(2), 135-146.

Trull, T. J., & Widiger, T. A. (2015). Personality disorders and personality (pp. 601-618). In Mario Mikulincer, Philip R. Shaver, Lynne M. Cooper, & Randy J. Larsen (Eds.), *APA handbook of personality and social psychology, Volume 4: Personality processes and individual differences*. Washington, DC: American Psychological Association.

Vanhoozer, K. J. (2005). *The drama of doctrine: A canonical linguistic approach to Christian theology.* Louisville, KY: Westminster John Knox.

Vanhoozer, K. J. (2014). *Faith speaking understanding: Performing the drama of doctrine.* Louisville, KY: Westminster John Knox.

Yalom, I. D., & Leszcz, M. (2005). *The theory and practice of group psychotherapy* (5th ed.). New York: Basic Books.

CHAPTER ELEVEN

THE CUTTING EDGE OF SELECTIVE
THERAPEUTIC ASSESSMENT

Come to me, all you who are weary and burdened, and I will give you rest.

Take my yoke upon you and learn from me, for I am gentle and humble in heart,

and you will find rest for your souls. For my yoke is easy and my burden is light.

MATTHEW 11:28-30

THEOLOGICAL THEME

Healing Redemption

LIGHTENING BURDENS: BY THE POUND OR BY THE OUNCE

Leading productive initial consultations requires remarkable helping skills. So much occurs in those early dialogues to mold a mutual understanding of change. It takes amazing craftsmanship to track information, recognize multicultural factors, forge an alliance, and inspire hope. Beyond the skills required for clinical proficiency, Christians who counsel issue a special welcome in those formative conversations.

Consider this echo from an earlier chapter. Our intent is to humbly represent Jesus Christ as he issues his great invitation to the weighed down and weary. Counseling conversations are invitations to shed burdens and experience rest. The gospel offers freedom through a grace-filled relationship. Jesus makes an offer to provide a custom-fitted yoke to carry those earthy struggles. Included in his promise is release from the guilt of past transgression and eternal restoration for the soul (Mt 11:28-30). Mental health professionals (MHPs) enter helping relationships to set in motion the means to procure refreshment, ease struggles, and increase strength. In each initial encounter, we communicate a tangible extension of our Lord's compassion to those with burdens. The client's request and the organizational setting will determine if this message is expressed in spoken words. The essential element is extending the invitation of redemptive grace in Jesus Christ to arouse hope and vitality.

When client and counselor come together and the client's burden is identified, named, and changed, they find hope that relief is within reach. Consider how this inspires hope right from the outset of care.

- Aubrey pours out discouragement and apprehension. After fifteen years of marriage and three children, she has no confidence that her husband can curtail his substance abuse and turn around the family's downward financial spiral. She and her counselor come to this understanding: life may have to get worse before it gets better. For her family, this is the season to place full confidence in the Lord. Hard choices lie ahead, but so does the return of a genuine hope for the future.

- Carter, a college senior, is blindsided by a disabling haze of anxiety on his passage into adulthood. Talking with the therapist does not instantly restore vision. Still, the counselor's eyes suggest confidence that Carter can move forward, and that casts a contagious light.

- Collin was not naive about the demands of a church-building project on its pastor. But he couldn't have fathomed that the economy would fall so low or that his eldest son would get caught up with the wrong crowd or that the Lord would allow his spiritual well to run so desperately dry. Despite these real and acknowledged stressors, he resents the elders' mandate that he pursue psychological care. The counselor expresses a readiness to blend spiritual direction with therapeutic conversations to restrain the "black dog" biting at his heels. Pastor Collin softens under this appeal.

Jesus promises rest (Mt 11:28-30), and Aubrey, Carter, and Collin need the fulfillment of this promise. One biblical commentator draws out a fascinating contrast in the summons from the Lord to come and rest in his shalom (Robertson, 1933). Take time to compare these two phrases from the great invitation passage: "I will *give* you rest" and "you will *find* rest." So, which is it? Is the peace of the Lord experienced as a gift received or a lesson learned? Does one suddenly or gradually achieve new proficiency to remove and reallocate weight? If one listens well to the text, the message is that the rest from Jesus Christ is both given and found.

The images of receiving and pursuing contained in the great invitation complement each other. Like the apparent dichotomy of salvation by faith or works, receiving and pursuing are both indicated. Consider this in application to helping people. There are occasions when the experience of relief occurs during counseling conversations, like opening an intriguing gift. Hope breaks through with miraculous results as the gift of rest is openly received. For that moment, isolation yields to connection, shame fades, confession flows, rage defuses, and relationships are reinvigorated. The isolation, shame, and rage have not disappeared; they are present along with the hope and relief.

On the other hand, much work is often required before this gift is received. The challenges processed in therapy do not easily give way. Relief does not immediately take hold. However, this is no reason to become lost in disappointment. It only means another route is required. The alternate route may demand intense effort and discipline to relearn new patterns of behavior or thought. But because of his steadfast love, the Lord can provide ways to lighten loads and renew strength. Steady persistence is the necessary but not the sufficient condition to locate relief. It is only through the gracious presence of the Comforter that Jesus' pledge of rest and a customized yoke to bear burdens find fulfillment.

Assessment is a vital aid in this mission. It introduces a legitimate method for unpacking burdens and provides a sequence to quantify difficult subjective episodes that tend to defy verbal description. When one has precision in understanding, degrees of change can be defined. By making the pieces of a problem clear, it's possible to determine how to suitably prioritize what to reduce and remove. Exposing the divisions of a burden can assist a client in the throes of a struggle. Concrete depictions make it feasible to remove stressors at once or bit by bit. Either way, the right assessment strategy, completed at the optimal point in the therapeutic relationship, can ease a burden because clients are enabled to eliminate it piece by piece. This is highly practical when one's perceptive senses are blunted. Further, regular quantitative measurement can aid clients in discerning when a heavy load is actually becoming less arduous to bear. Assessment not only supplies a focus; it inserts a scale to mark progress. Good instruments magnify the increments of change so there is recognition of Jesus fulfilling his promise to lighten the load.

THE CASE FOR SCALE SELECTION

Early contact establishes a tentative therapeutic agreement in which the concerns to be addressed in counseling are broadly defined. This is the moment to pause and determine what and how further assessment will be implemented.

Let's contrast a routine counseling pattern with one that includes clinically targeted assessment to better realize outcomes.

Informal assessment. Counseling can naturally proceed by maintaining the dialogue already underway, and this is the ordinary progression. Standardized measures, assessment technology, or instruments with psychometric rigor are not usually introduced. Assessment remains conversational (e.g., interviewing) and informal. Verbal subjective appraisals arise solely from interpersonal exchange. Scaling questions may be employed in various forms; for example, "Carter, on a scale from one to ten with one being 'beach-blanket relaxed' and ten being 'gut-punching panic,' how would you rate your experience over the past twenty-four hours?" Occasional checks are casually conducted, and these are the only safeguards to keep the dyad on course. Any "measurements" taken are estimates via verbal inquiry. Accordingly, improvement cannot be measured because the change targets have not been clearly defined.

Regrettably, an instrument-free approach is too often ingrained in training. This trend prevails because on the surface it's perceived as paperless, convenient, and client friendly. The presumptions are as follows: Direct conversation is the optimal route toward insight and change. Assessment technology would create distance or dehumanize an authentic therapeutic relationship. As therapists we should maximize the message that we are with the client and not introduce methods that could imply we are operating on a patient; this hinders the dynamic by turning the client into a passive recipient of medical-style procedures (Othius, 2006).

Does it make good sense to interrupt the movement of an active alliance by inserting assessment? A recent, extensive survey was conducted on counselor use of standardized assessment treatments (Neukrug, Peterson, Bonner, & Lomas, 2013). In the survey, counselors acknowledged a working familiarity with many of the top one hundred standardized instruments. In their discussion, the researchers suggest that test administration behavior is undeniably distinct from the interpersonal interaction that counselors most readily enjoy. Thus, there may be a subtle resistance to adopt formal measures (i.e., measures that quantify frequency, severity, and duration) into routine practice since those examination-style undertakings are alien to dialogue. Many think psychological tests may pose a disruption or distraction. At best, they inflict an unnecessary complication.

Christ-followers in the mental health professions and pastors who counsel thrive on direct personal exchange and look forward to interacting with clients this way. For many of these people, gathering detailed data is perceived as scientifically high-tech but not suitably high-touch. If relating is curative, they reason, why get concerned about outcomes? However, exclusive reliance on interpersonal interaction becomes a detriment when direction and productivity are left unexamined.

Clinical assessment trends. Research on assessment trends in the counseling profession reveals a fascinating gap (Peterson, Lomas, Neukrug & Bonner, 2014). As mentioned earlier, mental health counselors have reasonable awareness of the leading formal assessment options. In fact, 73% of mental health counselors report that fluency with a wide array of assessment measures and data is expected in the performance of their role. However, routine direct application by counselors of standardized measures is reported on average to be rare to never. Thus, it appears unlikely that surveys, questionnaires, rating scales, or personality screenings are conducted with the typical client (Peterson et al., 2014). Counselors make use of assessment data when available or if there is exceptional pressure by an outside party to gather results. Otherwise, they do not appear to use instruments on a regular basis with clients. Assessment data are considered to be a means to speak about clients among peers or across disciplines; assessment is not seen as a therapeutic method to quantify behaviors related to one's presenting concern.

Several years ago there was a study done investigating the pattern of questions counselors asked at the beginning of a therapeutic relationship (Owen, 2007). The findings revealed a tendency to favor informal, interview-only assessment techniques. There is also evidence that counselors ask more questions that confirm their initial impressions than those that might yield conflicting information. In other words, counselors resist pursuing questions that might lower confidence in their original operational diagnosis (Owen, 2007). There is an unchecked inner drive to reach closure on case conceptualization. Moving rapidly can bypass the work of adequately securing sufficient data to conduct a thorough differential diagnosis.

Regrettably, this expedient and self-serving clinical tendency is encouraged by our culture's value of efficiency. Consequently, the early information released by clients can be incomplete, guarded, or biased. After all, their opening words are shared when the counselor is a mere stranger. Thus, it can be problematic when a clinician finalizes a quick hypothesis without further review of key assumptions. This pattern can lead to incomplete, impulsive, or biased diagnostic decisions (Beutler, Harwood, & Holaway, 2002). Misunderstanding can conceivably injure the therapeutic alliance. The client may lack confidence in the clinician's professional procedures and empathy.

Therefore, there is good reason to build in additional multifaceted checks on the case conceptualization. The information obtained can undergird the treatment planning that is underway.

Selective therapeutic assessment. The foundation is now in place to counter the prevailing convention of informal assessment. Assessment drawn from a range of established and semi-standardized instruments can produce creditable benefits in conventional practice. Thus, application of assessment technology ought not to be exceptional or extraordinary. Let me be clear: I am not arguing that we should swing the pendulum back to the outdated practice of conducting lengthy psychological evaluations on all those entering therapy. Instituting a blanket policy to automatically execute extensive and uniform psychological batteries to all clients would not serve clients or clinicians. Nor would it be financially feasible or clinically justified. A mechanistic approach is not the way of an artisan. One proficient with resources will decidedly reach for the best tool to accomplish the required task with a vision toward a quality result.

In selective therapeutic assessment, the restorative task of the clinician and the needs of the specific client are both embraced to establish the extent of the assessment. The desired outcome of therapy tailors the choice of instruments. The goal is to shed light on salient diagnostic concerns, discern a direction, and establish benchmarks for progress (Beutler, Harwood, & Holaway, 2002). For the Christian counselor, it can be advantageous to picture the application of formal assessment as a method to deepen understanding of a burden that the Lord is about to ease or adjust.

- Aubrey—a woman with deep faith convictions—has allowed herself to live for years under intolerable conditions. Even now, her desperate pleas about needing to change her marriage are not directed at her counselor; they are aimed at herself. She knows things must change for the sake of her children, yet she can't bring herself to act. Given this information, the counselor wonders about Aubrey's family exposure to substance abuse.

- Carter made this appointment because even he realizes he's beyond overwhelmed. The counselor hears his inner scream that life after college will be a miserable void. Still, there's the immediate concern to salvage what's left of the fall semester academically.

- Collin appears worn out. This pastor admits that the few hours he spends in bed are not filled with restful sleep. Nevertheless, he always delivers on his Sunday messages, and the membership has grown since the new sanctuary opened. Collin is gritting his teeth with inner frustration; it is sheer determination that keeps his ministry moving.

Rather than undermine the therapeutic alliance, the strategic use of well-matched measures can actually fortify it. This tactic communicates concern in a tangible manner. Imagine the experience of a client who is guided by well-ordered prompts to consider the broad impact of the presenting problem. Having a way to magnify factors and observe the consequences of an issue not previously considered sheds light on the path to change and yields hope. The client's experience of empathy is amplified as the clinician proficiently blends insights gleaned via structured assessment into the feedback that communicates understanding. Notice from the outset that implementing a data-driven approach is not to inform the clinician alone or protect clinicians from external liability threats. Nor is it for the benefit of the agency or to conform to the expectations of a third party. These are indeed potential related benefits. Still, at its core, selective assessment is intended to be for the client's insight; this is what makes it therapeutic.

The clinician demonstrates firsthand knowledge of the tools of the trade by using them with an explicit rationale and recognizable purpose. This is the way of an artisan. Counselors employ the right device to accomplish a task with finesse, precision, and a transparent plan. Assessment instruments brought skillfully to bear in counseling allow the therapeutic team to gain perspective from a source external to their immediate interpersonal connection. Picture assessment results as a consultation with a skilled researcher. The use of a research tool brings that expertise to one of the client's concerns. Applying an anchored measure enhances the focus and aligns expectations.

The descriptions that measures provide should never be viewed as the whole answer. Rather, each finding is placed under the expertise of the therapist, who merges these concepts into the explanations offered to the client. In other words, the counselor does not allow any labels or scores to override solid clinical impressions obtained via mutual exchange. Instead, the descriptions from the assessment are woven by the counselor into the ongoing conversation as a means to inform, stimulate, sharpen, and enrich. In fact, well-chosen measures create more available prospects for direct talk as less time is dedicated to establish a mutual understanding of the relevant details and contributing factors through dialogue alone.

Selection options. Based on the needs of the client and the parameters of the setting, an ideal time to introduce assessment tools and technology is immediately following the initial consultation (see fig. 11.1). The purpose is to extend the impact of counseling as a redemptive endeavor. As the treatment-planning phase commences, this is a prime moment to gather supportive and distinguishing information. Remember that any procedure introduced should maximize the benefit of counseling, not satisfy a hunch or curiosity. It is prudent to adopt a minimalist approach when it comes to instrument selection. In other words, administer only instruments that hold promise to yield tangible and immediately useful data.

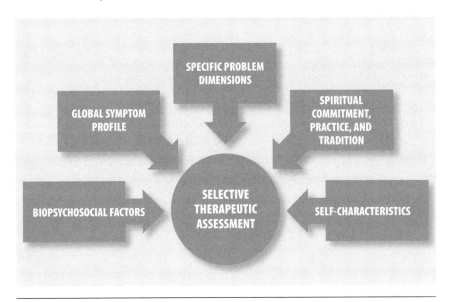

Figure 11.1. Domains for selective therapeutic assessment

In most counseling cases and settings, the outset of treatment is when it makes the most sense to organize a basic social/developmental/medical history and secure information regarding areas that may be relevant to the current request (bio-psycho-social factors). The intent of the selective assessment strategy is to gain details to tighten case conceptualization, further mutual goal formation, and produce an informed prognosis. This is also the optimal juncture at which to obtain a broad survey of potential concerns (global symptom profile). Once areas of need are identified, the most troubling ones can be pulled out for further investigation (specific problem dimensions). Exploring features of a specific problem can be a concrete way to respect the stated request of a client. Finally, it can useful to break down a known issue into discrete units to grasp the full extent of functional impairment.

Assessment procedures can help Christians invested in counseling to fulfill an ethical and therapeutic mandate. The differentiation of clients who want to invest in an openly Christian approach from those who desire spiritually sensitive therapy or who would prefer no explicit faith discussion is absolutely critical. Therefore, a robust assessment strategy to explore and document a client's spiritual tradition, current disciplines, affiliations both past and ongoing, and faith commitment is particularly important. Given the relevance of this domain for Christian counseling in the current practice climate, this will be given extensive consideration in chapter thirteen, "Gauging Religious Affections."

Finally, personality traits and patterns of relational interaction (self-characteristics) are worth screening. This can assist in ruling out or in the presence of a personality disorder. By itself, this is a justifiable reason to conduct personality screening, but there are other important rationales as well. Information about the longstanding characteristics of the client can contribute to a deeper case conceptualization, signal potential areas for Christian identity development, and influence how a therapist shapes the alliance (for more on this see chapter fourteen, "Calibrating the Contours of Personality"). There is also the potential to use broader personality surveys to explore the unique features of the individual who is actually going to have to implement steps to change. For a variety of reasons, to be addressed later, such measures are not tapped routinely by counselors. Counselors with a Christian orientation need to look beyond symptoms in order to see the person as *imago Dei* and anticipate the redemptive work that the Creator is going to accomplish. Incorporating useful instruments prevents counselors from becoming myopic and adopting a lens to see only pathology. In order to apply a strength-based approach, thinking holistically offers advantages.

The results from the selected instruments can contribute to the refining, modifying, or solidifying of an accurate diagnosis. The most beneficial impact is when the instruments directly influence treatment planning (Groth-Marnat & Wright, 2016; Jongsma, Peterson, & Bruce, 2006). The level, modality, and orientation of the primary intervention (e.g., inpatient/outpatient; individual/group; medical/ministry; situational/relational/existential; behavioral/insight-oriented/interpersonal/spiritual formation) are determined based on the severity, direction, and intensity of a struggle. Insight into factors requiring attention helps narrow the search for optimal treatment techniques. Recognition of personal strengths and dispositional traits can also help in selecting an intervention that matches not only the problem but the person.

Self-report measures ask clients to endorse statements about themselves. This is by far the instrument style most likely to dominate. These measures are concise, simple to administer, and offer the pragmatic advantage of face validity. However, given that self-report measures rely heavily on participant cooperation, we must use caution in using these tools when the client is mandated or enters treatment under duress. In such cases, instruments that have built-in mechanisms to monitor the response style of the client are preferable. Other assessment methods such as projective measures might be added if the clinician has the expertise to deliver these and if the results would add incremental validity. For the most part, though, projective methods are not generally used, with the exception of items like a mutual storytelling technique, house-tree-person drawing, or sand-tray play, all of which are valuable in understanding the perspectives of a child.

From symptoms to spiritual disciplines to self-characteristics, much headway can be made using standardized or semi-standardized instruments and global personality screening. Time restrictions pose a barrier, however. Certainly, a comprehensive mental health appraisal is necessary; yet this is a hefty challenge to accomplish while laying out the beneficial, motivational groundwork. Clearly some amount of potentially vital information must deliberately be left unexplored during a START consultation (story, therapeutic alliance, assessment, recommendations, and treatment plan). Despite this limitation, it's no reason to neglect crucial areas. The momentum to launch effective treatment continues to build as assessment forms and self-report instruments are applied. These supplement the information acquired via interview during that opening session.

The objectives of the START initial consultation model can be accomplished in a single session, but only when we anticipate that certain material will be systematically collected from other measures. The combined strategy of a START consultation followed by selective therapeutic assessment allows us to devote the precious face-to-face time to themes and complexities that are best investigated in person. The model here includes a face-to-face consultation interview plus choice instruments, procedures, and technology. This combination will assist both counselor and client in collecting a broader range of desirable information. This overall strategy yields ample benefits to set the therapeutic conversation on a solid platform.

- Aubrey is all too aware of how much is at stake. Signs of anxiety and depression are apparent. Two assessments are selected: (1) the Quickview Social History (QVW) with the Clinical Supplement to begin a dialogue on family background and to catalogue symptoms; and (2) the Millon Clinical Multiaxial Inventory-IV (MCMI-IV) to explore her presenting mental health concerns (state) and open discussion on personality patterns (traits) that must be addressed to realize change.

- Carter has immediate (academic distress) and intermediate concerns (future shock/career uncertainty). The Millon College Counseling Inventory (MCCI) or a career inventory would represent a reasonable choice. Instead, his counselor hones in on the present crisis to rebuild routine while assuring him that building an attainable life plan will follow. The Beck Anxiety Inventory (BAI) is put to use to get a handle on the scope and severity of his stress experience. The Procrastination Assessment Scale-Students (PASS) is applied to examine academic gridlock and to create language to discuss course load management (Solomon & Rothblum, 1984, as cited in Corcoran & Fischer, 2013).

- Collin may be uncomfortable with his board of elders pushing therapy. On the other hand, this does relieve questions about reimbursement for the financial cost; there's no necessity to rely on a health insurance benefit. This is ideal since Collin rejects that his being "down" is a medical concern. The Symptom Checklist 90 Revised (SCL-90-R) is administered to acquire a comprehensive baseline of distress. The 16PF Questionnaire (16 personality factors) is included to set the stage to consider how his personality inclinations contribute to his success and struggles.[1]

DSM-5: A DIMENSIONAL PERSPECTIVE AND THE CHARGE TO ASSESS

The appeal to combine an initial interview with select, succinct instruments to obtain quality diagnostic and treatment data is not unique. The assessment addition to the revised *Diagnostic and Statistical Manual of Mental Disorders* (*DSM*-5, American Psychiatric Association [APA], 2013) is a prime example. It firmly endorses the use of semi-standardized assessment (i.e., emerging measures) for this identical purpose (APA, 2013). Section three of the manual is

---

[1]There is a version of the 16PF called the PsychEval Personality Questionnaire (PEPQ) that would fit Collin's needs nicely. The PEPQ combines a basic mental health screening with a personality profile. The choice here to use a separate symptom screen represents a subtle crafting of selection. The stand-alone 16PF makes no reference to psychopathology. As a counselor, it is possible to recognize how factor combinations may contribute to his current plight. Further, the SCL-90-L would have good face validity for Collin as it is highly behavioral. This plan is designed to foster cooperation and to obtain results that can be shared directly with this educated pastor.

entirely dedicated to assessment. Whereas the global assessment of functioning was the one general scale included with the previous *DSM* system, there is now a collection of measures. In fact, to promote this combined interview/instrument approach, the American Psychiatric Association has free-access tools available to clinicians (psychiatry.org/practice/dsm/dsm5/online-assessment-measures).

Two related trends on diagnosis are making significant headway in the mental health field: (1) moving toward a dimensional view of diagnosis and (2) clinician adoption of a data-driven treatment approach. Both of these notions are conducive to the intentional mix of an interpersonal interview with anchored assessment measures.

The point of this dual approach goes beyond categorical recognition and accuracy. It allows us to look for the unique description of discrete symptoms with the means to track the frequency, severity, and duration of each. The thrust is to go beyond naming and embrace a plan to profile symptom patterns along a continuum in ways that can actively guide treatment. This is a definite departure from longstanding conventions where publication of detailed descriptions and criteria lists were there to enable the clinician to make the sharpest reasonable clinical judgment to match a client's problem to a particular diagnostic category. At the risk of oversimplifying a massive amount of historical development in the mental health field, assessment language provides a useful way to capture this progression in research, assessment, and treatment linked to diagnosis.

The *DSM* traces its origins to early statistical guides of institutionalized mental patients as far back as 1844 (APA, 2013). In the sixty years since World War II, there have been five major revisions of the *DSM*. There continues to be no shortage of controversies stemming from the political, ideological, economic, social, medical, and moral implications of this evolving disease-oriented organizational system. Setting these matters to one side, it is reasonable to point out that in each subsequent *DSM* ample gains were made in the reliance on epidemiological prevalence and incidence data. Given individual differences and the wide array of contextual variables, there is recognition that mental illness can manifest itself with nearly infinite variety. As clinicians habitually explain to patients, no two cases are absolutely identical. Thus, decades of ongoing research and revision to the *DSM* categorical system of diagnosis were conducted with the aim of assisting practitioners and researchers in adequately sorting and scrutinizing symptom clusters to discriminate between these varying disruptions in mental state. The immense enterprise to identify and classify mental illness has been a multidecade effort to increase consistency and accuracy in diagnosis. Using assessment terminology, the categories and supportive criteria were developed to establish the reliability of the *DSM* system. In order for the mental health field to gain respect within the medical sphere, it required a common language and sufficient operational precision to catalogue concerns. An essential rationale of the *DSM* was to increase inter-rater reliability. As this was realized, it became viable to tie diagnosis to specific evidence-based treatments. This follows the model of general medical practice. Accurate diagnosis is the means to implement best practice and access efficacious treatment.

As diagnosis consistency increased, strides in investigating pharmacological, behavioral, and psychological treatment options also advanced. Thus, an established and useful classification grid (reliability) led to the establishment of available diagnostically related treatment protocols (validity).

The introduction of an assessment framework that merges diagnosis with treatment in the most recent *DSM* is a means to move clinicians to gather symptom data beyond what is needed to establish the correct diagnostic category. Anchored measures allow clinicians to better ascertain the unique dimensions, severity, and functional impairment of the presenting issue. The challenge for us is to combine subjective and objective patient data to improve accuracy of diagnosis and to simultaneously establish a productive direction for treatment with built-in, recognizable benchmarks to evaluate progress.

The *DSM*-5 advocates the use of formal, abbreviated assessments. The approach it advocates is to get a reasonable amount of quantifiable data without overburdening clients or clinicians with extensive psychological test batteries. The assessment process begins with a broad Self-Rated Level 1 Cross-Cutting Symptom Measure (CCSM); there is one for adults, children ages eleven to seventeen, and parents/guardians of children ages six to seventeen. These are general and far-reaching, as twelve-symptom domains are surveyed in twenty-three to twenty-five items. The global measures are not intended to complete the assessment process. Rather, they capture enough data to identify crucial needs by establishing thresholds to mark a concern. These scores then inform the decision as to which level two crosscutting symptom clusters should be investigated next. The findings push the next assessment into a distinct area. The goal is to establish not only an overarching factual label but a quantifiable depiction of distress to launch treatment. In summary, a dimensional and data-driven diagnostic approach moves the focus of clinicians from broad labels that foster professional communication to discrete symptom levels that give both counselor and client a starting point to measure the success of their interventions.

This assessment model is now built into the *DSM-5*. Beyond the informal screening measures it provides, an extensive assortment of symptom checklists and problem identification scales are in use to conduct similar screening. Selecting measures that are psychometrically sturdy for clinical use has multiple benefits. In terms of immediate impact, these results can contribute to point-in-time descriptions that aid in the formulation of treatment goals. The right measures assist in making good choices about where to direct change efforts and how to quantify results. Then, ongoing measurement can detect and track progress by degrees.

GLOBAL SYMPTOM SCREENING

Broad symptom measures separate functional difficulties into discrete categories. The identification of troublesome symptoms in plain black-and-white terms is a powerful way to communicate personalized care. Listing an intensity level for those concerns can provide strategic language to communicate with one another about the delicate matter of how the helping process itself is influencing adjustment. Unraveling the tangle of physical, medical, and mental health issues is a challenge. This effort can pay off in terms of identifying the most direct route to reduce suffering. The following suggestions will serve as reasonable starting points. New measures are constantly being developed and current ones revised. Once counselors are convinced that such tools add value, they will be motivated to seek out those that are the optimal fit for their style and setting.

Symptom Checklist 90 Revised (SCL-90-R). This state measure is a widely recognized instrument for initial evaluation of problems and the securing of a current symptom snapshot of psychopathology (pearsonclinical.com). One valuable feature is its extensive historical legacy going back to the notable early self-report checklists such as the Woodworth Personal Data Sheet (1918), the Cornell Medical Index (1948), and the Hopkins Symptom Checklist (1968; Derogatis, 2017). Currently it's a frequently applied measure for research. It also has extensive applications in primary care settings as a mental health screening tool and available full psychometric reviews (Pauker & Payne, 1985). Clinicians grounded in the fundamentals of assessment can rapidly gain the proficiency necessary to implement this tool in their counseling practice.

Designed for adolescents over thirteen and adults with at least a sixth-grade reading level, this ninety-item checklist captures symptom severity ratings and groups them into a dimensional report in less than fifteen minutes. While paper-and-pencil administration is available, along with efficient hand-scoring templates, computer administration and reporting make this instrument most appealing for clinical use. The graphic depiction of findings is a readily accessible and convincing profile. Nine primary symptom dimensions are assessed, and three global ratings yield definite impressions of overall distress (somatization, obsessive-compulsive, interpersonal sensitivity, depression, anxiety, hostility, phobias, paranoia, and psychoticism). Beyond the handy scales for the common issues, the hostility and interpersonal sensitivity dimensions have distinct utility in counseling. These dimensions are difficult to rate objectively during an initial interview, so in this area, the measure offers a picture of something hard to discern face-to-face. The Global Severity Index is useful to show clients, in a candid way, the level of life disruption evident during the recent past. If computer technology is readily available and the cost for subsequent administrations can be absorbed, the SCL-90-R progress report feature that graphs successive administrations is handy. Counselors using this measure will learn to discern clinically meaningful change, which is not synonymous with statistical significance.

The Brief Symptom Inventory (BSI) compresses the SCL90-R by about 50% but maintains its nine dimensions. There is also the highly compact BSI-18, which reduces the total dimensions to three (depression, anxiety, and somatization). Due to its brevity, the BSI-18 is finding its way into primary care settings where these three mental health concerns are the most relevant. These briefer screens certainly have a place, but for counseling, the added items and extra minutes give the findings a depth that make it worthwhile to use the full SCL-90-R. Critical items related to threats of self-harm are a useful check even though these would repeat queries required in a direct interview. There are occasions when clients reveal to a computer what they are not ready to speak aloud.

Based on practical use and a review of technical features, the SCL-90-R is recommended to counselors who hold firm to a Christian worldview. There are no explicit items or spiritual themes covered, so the potential for faith distortions is small. The main threat to faith that could arise from this measure would apply to any checklist that catalogues and counts symptoms. Symptoms are not to be confused with the actual problem; they are a signal that something is wrong. Reducing a life concern to its physical and emotional manifestations would be a clinician error and is not a liability embedded in the instrument itself.

Quickview Social History (QVW). The Quickview Social History is a computer-administered screening tool based on Ronald Giannetti's self-report

for a wide range of social, psychological, and physical problems (pearsonclinical
.com). The Quickview Basic report is a 130-item form that gathers social history
information across a number of spheres (e.g., developmental, family of origin,
educational, marital, occupational, financial, legal, and military). For counseling
applications, it makes the most sense when using the QVW to include administration of the Clinical Supplement. This adds 105 items to collect information
on physical and psychological distress. Thus, in one measure that takes about
twenty to forty-five minutes to complete, the clinician has a generic but
adequate social history along with a symptom profile.

The end product is a readable, standardized report. The symptom screen
portion appears in list form with notification of critical items. Severity levels
are not detailed or readily apparent. This is the simplest type of checklist
without any dimensional reporting options. Therefore, a follow-up clinical interview is absolutely essential. This should always be the plan when the QVW
is put to use. In fact, the report generated by the QVW presents a starter list of
items for the clinician to explore. A best practice protocol would be to use the
QVW as a supplement to the initial consultation. The clinician then reviews
the results, generates pointed questions for follow-up, and poses these during
the next clinical session. This communicates that the clinician has invested
effort in learning about the client's story and symptoms. The clinical note that
follows can customize the standardized report to bring out relevant details
about the uniqueness of the client's background. Used appropriately, the QVW
demonstrates a synchrony between face-to-face and standardized assessment.
It can accomplish quickly what would take a clinician much more time.
However, if the QVW is used as a stand-alone instrument, there will most
certainly be significant gaps in background information. It is a supplement that
organizes themes. When applied, this can give the clinician a reasonable
head start.

The QVW is efficient and practical. However, one downside of this measure
is that it is bare bones and plain, particularly given the capabilities of our
current technology. As published reviewers have stated, it simply does not
make sense that this measure has gone so long without an extensive update and
upgrade (Dixon & Starr, 1998). Other items could expand its scope, and more
importantly, the use of interactive technology would allow for different item
sets to be administered as needed.

DSM-5 Self-Rated Level 1 Cross-Cutting Symptom Measures (Adult and Child).
These two measures are recent additions to the self-report symptom checklist
arsenal. The design lends itself to use in psychiatric settings, which is

appropriate since these are included in *DSM*-5. The APA makes these available to clinicians on the web so that more extensive clinical and research use can be generated. In field trials conducted before their release, not all reliability data were optimal, although findings were reasonable enough to support release (Narrow et al., 2012). Still, further refinement is anticipated. The cost-free use of these tests (available at psychiatry.org/dsm5) certainly makes them appealing, and scoring information is readily available in the brief instructions contained on the forms.

The adult measure has twenty-three questions that cover all the domains relevant for a psychiatric interview (depression, anger, mania, anxiety, somatic symptoms, suicidal ideation, psychosis, sleep problems, memory, repetitive thoughts and behaviors, dissociation, personality functioning, and substance abuse). Respondents are asked to consider only the past two weeks and to indicate the frequency of experience related to each item (0-none at all to 4-nearly every day). Not every patient will be open to being totally candid on these items since they pointedly request disclosure on inner experiences and behavior (e.g., "Feeling detached or distant from yourself, your body, your physical surroundings, or your memories?" "Drink at least 4 drinks of alcohol in a single day?"). A score of mild (2) or greater warrants further inquiry by the interviewing clinician. For children ages six to seventeen, parents or guardians are given the instrument with twenty-five items. This survey covers similar dimensions as the adult one.

For clinicians seeking to communicate with medical professionals, these cross-cutting measures may be particularly useful. Should this be the exclusive symptom checklist provided to patients, it's important to recognize that by design and intent, the tone of these measures tends to place the experience of symptoms in medical terms. Given the origin and intended use, this comment is not intended as a critique. But for those who wish to explore a holistic view of presenting symptoms, this perspective would need to be expanded during an interview.

SYMPTOM SCREENS IN CHRISTIAN CONVERSATIONS

Christian counseling boldly strives to achieve an eternal impact. Still, investing effort to measure immediate, temporary symptoms must not be described as superficial or less spiritually relevant. Making troubling symptoms clear enables us to better know how to relieve burdens and secure rest for clients. The relief that can flow from counseling is similar to the refreshing movement of the Holy Spirit. He may move like the wind that "blows wherever it pleases" (Jn 3:8), but one can see him passing. Reducing disruptions in physical, emotional, and relational domains reflects the Spirit's activity and the Lord's soothing.

Furthermore, displaying success in plain black and white communicates a sense of competence. Get the symptom picture to establish a definitive baseline of distress at the outset. Then make objective assessment of progress a priority at routine intervals. Symptom profiles are an example of assessment that contributes to consistent, reliable counseling services. Christian counselors honor the Lord by keeping their word to those God allows them to serve.

The value of Christian counseling is that life challenges are confronted with an open acknowledgment of the Creator, his values, and his eternal perspective. Yet in the midst of such lofty spiritual priorities, we never trivialize or ignore symptoms. We cultivate trust by attending to a client's pain in the moment.

- Aubrey, thanks for those questionnaires you completed. Your responses helped me to recognize that the discouragement and disappointment in your life is very familiar because it's been a part of your life for years. Recently though, as you are building your courage to press for change, the signs of stress in your emotions and body are on the rise (those eight to ten times per week when your heart pounds, you feel apprehensive, and you get shortness of breath and that extraordinary muscle tension). As you commit to making tough decisions for a better future, we'll look for ways to help you soothe those symptoms so that you don't get discouraged and give up.

- Carter, it's refreshing to sense the hope God has instilled in you for the future and how the daily problems that once weighed you down when we began are now a lighter burden. There are now fewer times that your mind goes blank; you are getting to classes. And while concentration is still not coming easy, it's on the rise.

- Collin, it is remarkable how you are fulfilling your responsibilities to honor the Lord and your calling. Sleep hygiene is going to be an area of focus for us in the short term. The checklist you completed also lets me know that there is an edge of hostility bubbling out of you that's not comfortable because it's not part of your "A" game. You struggle to toss aside negative comments and take into yourself the disappointments of others.

Selective therapeutic assessment does not end with symptom management. There are numerous instruments with therapeutic value to provide insight into specific problem domains, personality patterns, and even a client's spiritual life.

Let's continue this exploration of how to bring research measures into clinical sessions. The goal is to expand the use of screening instruments and rating scales to aid clients not only in securing relief but in building new habits to realize the abundant life (Jn 10:10).

REFERENCES

American Psychiatric Association. (2013). *Diagnostic and statistical manual of mental disorders* (5th ed.). Arlington, VA: American Psychiatric Publishing.

Beutler, L. E., Harwood, T. M., & Holaway, R. (2002). How to assess clients in pre-treatment planning. In J. N. Butcher (Ed.), *Clinical personality assessment: Practical approaches* (2nd ed., pp. 76-95). New York: Oxford University Press.

Corcoran, K., & Fischer, J. (2013). *Measures for clinical practice and research: A sourcebook* (5th ed., Vol. 2). Oxford, England: Oxford University Press.

Derogatis, L. R. (2017). SCL-90-R and BSI Tests: The Derogatis Checklist Series. Pearson Clinical Assessment Webinar (Nov. 15, 2017). Retrieved November 28, 2018, from https://downloads.pearsonclinical.com/videos/111517-SCL90R-BSI/SCL-90-R-and-BSI-Tests-111517.mp4

Dixon, D. N., & Starr, E. R. (1998). Review of the Quickview Social History. In J. C. Impara & B. S. Plake (Eds.), *The thirteenth mental measurements yearbook*. Lincoln, NE: Buros Institute of Mental Measurements. Retrieved from Mental Measurements Yearbook with Tests in Print database.

Groth-Marnat, G., & Wright, A. J. (2016). *Handbook of psychological assessment* (6th ed.). Hoboken, NJ: John Wiley & Sons.

Jongsma, A. E., Peterson, L. M., & Bruce, T. J. (2006). *The complete adult psychotherapy treatment planner*. Hoboken, N.J.: Wiley.

Narrow, W. E., Clarke, D. E., Kuramoto, S. J., Kraemer, H. C., Kupfer, D. J., Greiner, L., & Regier, D. A. (2012). *DSM*-5 field trials in the United States and Canada: Part III. Development and reliability testing of a cross-cutting symptom assessment for *DSM*-5. *American Journal of Psychiatry, 170*(1), 71-82.

Neukrug, E., Peterson, C. H., Bonner, M., & Lomas, G. I. (2013). A national survey of assessment instruments taught by counselor educators. *Counselor Education and Supervision, 52*(3), 207-221.

Othuis, J. H. (2006). With-ing: A psychology of love. *Journal of Psychology and Theology, 34*(1), 66-77.

Owen, J. (2007). The nature of confirmatory strategies in the initial assessment process. *Journal of Mental Health Counseling, 30*(4), 362-374.

Pauker, J. D., & Payne, R. W. (1985). Review of the Symptom Checklist-90-Revised. In J. V. Mitchell, Jr. (Ed.), *The ninth mental measurements yearbook*. Lincoln, NE: Buros Institute of Mental Measurements. Retrieved from Mental Measurements Yearbook with Tests in Print database.

Peterson, C. H., Lomas, G. I., Neukrug, E. S., & Bonner, M. W. (2014). Assessment use by counselors in the United States: Implications for policy and practice. *Journal of Counseling & Development, 92*(1), 90-98.

Robertson, A. T. (1933). *Word pictures in the New Testament* (Mat 11:29), (Vol. 1, pp. 94-95). Nashville: Broadman Press.

Solomon, L. J., & Rothblum, E. D. (1984). Procrastination Assessment Scale-Students (PASS). As reproduced in K. Corcoran & J. Fischer, (2013), *Measures for clinical practice and research: A Sourcebook* (5th ed., pp. 626-631). Oxford: Oxford University Press.

CHAPTER TWELVE

OUTFITTING THE CLINICIAN'S TOOLBOX

Offer hospitality to one another without grumbling. Each of you should use whatever gift you have received to serve others, as faithful stewards of God's grace in its various forms.

1 PETER 4:9-10

STEWARDSHIP AND ACCOUNTABILITY

Counselors begin assessment by gathering the central story, seeking out the source of symptoms, and fortifying courage in clients to conquer change. The next phase in treatment planning is to expose explicit features of the presenting request while uncovering available resources. The aim is to form a common understanding, establish objectives, and examine adjustment in greater depth and detail. The healthcare climate places high value on transparency in the treatment planning and on results. Accountability in a conventional sense implies that mental health professionals (MHPs) have an obligation as healthcare providers to deliver effective services and to employ methods that help clients feel their investment was warranted (Corcoran & Fischer, 2013). As professionals we have responsibilities to multiple stakeholders (referral sources, third-party payers, etc.). Of course these obligations do not diminish the priority of duty to our client. Given the obligation to deliver effective service, we do well to work with clients to form goals and reach pivotal outcome markers.

Our ultimate desire as counselors with Christian conviction should be to honor the Lord. The privilege to come alongside a person in distress and guide change unites a professional career and ministry calling. Given the complexity of role obligations, the merger of these vocations and aspirations requires exceptional clarity. To do this, we must adopt the posture of a faithful steward of God's grace (1 Pet 4:10). This reprises the Lord's intent for Adam as expressed in Genesis 2:15. Human beings are placed in the garden not to draw a living from it but to invest in, care for, and enhance the wonder of what God provided. Peter's epistle gives Christians the parallel charge to use our lives, gifts, and artistic creativity to distribute God's provisions in service to others. In biblical terms a steward is a project overseer or household manager. The role can include the promise of an inheritance. The most cherished steward is one who fulfills the master's purpose and exhibits proficiency in bringing together available assets, shrewd insights, and reliable people (Gen 43:19; Mt 20:8; Lk 16:2-3; 1 Cor 4:1-2). Christians who counsel accept this stewardship office as a serious yet joyous honor. Counselors oversee a client's personal change project. Christian counselors recognize that a client's request may incorporate an overarching goal of developing a more consistent identity in Christ. In these cases, *therapeutic restoration can be spiritual revitalization.* Client and counselor can choose to make themselves accountable not only to one another but to the Holy Spirit.

In today's practice climate, there is an effective means to demonstrate acceptance of this stewardship role—namely, we counselors can enter helping relationships bearing our assessment toolboxes furnished with a respectable array of useful measures to assist clients.

In order to implement this stewardship perspective, one should employ three mental activities. First, cultivate a farsighted vision. This requires the ability to see the layers of what needs to be resolved or addressed and allows us to set the direction. We can then select quantitative measures to unpack attitudinal and behavioral patterns related to a client's request. Second, apply measures that assist in the detection of faith convictions and concerns. This can help in forming spiritually related objectives. In order to achieve a faith-enhancing plan, discipleship and Christian identity should be treated as a distinct treatment domain. Determining which instruments to use entails evaluating the redemptive validity of quantitative measures that tap into spirituality and religiosity. Third, develop a plan that smoothly blends a variety of measures into conversations that enhance the progression of the entire change effort. The intent here is to outline a stepwise approach where high-quality rating scales are combined with a progressive interview approach. In order to bring assessment more to the center of the therapeutic process, counselors need versatile measures to function well in a stewardship capacity. It's time to stock the toolbox.

ASSESSMENT TO OPERATIONALIZE TREATMENT OBJECTIVES

Exposure to the *ACA Code of Ethics* in traditional graduate courses that examine psychological tests instills an unambiguous ethical mandate: "Counselors carefully consider the validity, reliability, psychometric limitations, and appropriateness of instruments when selecting assessments" (American Counseling Association, 2014, para. E.6.a). Professionals make decisions for or about clients based on the findings of standardized psychological assessments. I have already argued that safeguards for the development and application of these measures are imperative to ensure fairness, justice, and appropriateness. Only credible measures—that is, those with convincing psychometric properties and extensive validation procedures—are appropriate for use with clients. Unfortunately, instilling stark appreciation for the risks of these instruments to harm, can inadvertently make counselors hesitant to pursue elective assessment for collaborative and therapeutic purposes. They may develop the view that formidable "power tools" should only be called upon when absolutely necessary to appraise functioning, make a diagnosis, determine medical necessity, or justify eligibility for placement in a treatment program.

The rigor and investment required for test development is extensive. Given this, it is no surprise that the cost to acquire and implement instruments can be considerable. Administration and scoring technology is another consideration. Add the expense to attain advanced training to remain current on the use of psychological measures, and the time and financial costs can be substantial. This is all prior to the time demands and cost of actual administration. Yet despite these hindrances, utilization of leading instruments and commercially available products is often worthwhile. If the cost barrier is too high, there are options to consider that are affordable and accessible, but they are not likely to be published by psychological appraisal companies.

In clinic and ministry settings, assessment procedures inform the approach and define attainable outcomes. This is not a way to make decisions for clients; it's a two-way and open exploration with clients. This does not reduce the requirements regarding a clinician's obligation to bring only suitable, accurate, and reputable measures into the process. Still, the shift to share responsibility in decision making does open possibilities. It may be fitting to include less sophisticated behavioral and attitudinal measures that clarify a client's perspective. There are scales that were built to describe, educate, and inform via quantification without the explicit intent to formally categorize. Clinical application is about using these measures according to their original purpose, that is, to conduct research investigations. The difference is that the inquiry is not academic or theoretical; it is clinical. In the helping process, counselor and client join forces as field researchers to bring about change. Measures can "operationalize" a portion of a client's presenting problem or interpersonal pattern. It is paramount to ascertain where change would be valuable and to generate a way to objectively reveal results.

This brings our assessment focus to a decisive climax. A good steward of change will adopt comprehensive strategies to maximize influence. This is the direction that leading proponents of assessment applications in counseling are now heading. The clinical dyad must gather sufficient detail on the presenting problem in light of how it extends from a client's global behavioral and interpersonal patterns. Measures that quantify and qualify patterns are essential.

> The therapist practices under a premise that fosters imprecise clinical reasoning when patients are treated without consideration of the accumulation of factors that affect treatment efficacy. The blind application of therapies and other interventions solely as a function of the therapist's proclivities and familiarity, without regard to the suitability of the patient's unique characteristics and problems to those procedures, is wrong—wrong for the patient because substandard services are provided and wrong for mental health professionals because it wastes precious resources and is professionally irresponsible. (Beutler, Harwood, & Holaway, 2002, p. 80)

It is important to examine problem severity, complexity, distress, and expectations, along with patient characteristics, to lay essential groundwork for productive therapeutic conversations.

There is an acute demand for affordable measures that can be employed on a routine basis to monitor progress. Clinicians entering the field should expect to practice in a progressive and technically advancing marketplace. Measures not only launch care but contribute to continuous improvement of the assistance provided. The breadth of counseling services will expand to add value to the lives of a broader clientele seeking to realize an even wider range of outcomes. Even as more people avail themselves of counseling, coaching, and behavioral health consultations, efforts to contain costs will continue to be vigorous. Professionals with assessment savvy can position themselves and their clients to face these trends by outfitting their assessment toolbox with an assortment of ready-to-apply measures.

DEFINING AND ACCESSING RAPID ASSESSMENT
INSTRUMENTS (RAIS)

Best practice procedures now include infusing helping dialogues with ways to calculate movement. Measurement is a routine expectation when treating pathology from depression and anxiety to eating disorders, attention deficit hyperactivity disorder (ADHD), posttraumatic stress disorder (PTSD), or schizophrenia (Baer & Blais, 2010), and counselors can apply clinical rating scales, known as Rapid Assessment Instruments (RAIs), that offer accessibility, efficiency, and effectiveness (Corcoran & Fischer, 2013). One category of measures that we can put to use is composed of screening devices that rule out or in the presence of a condition, disorder, or impairment. A second category contains domain-targeted clinical rating scales that quantify symptom extent and severity. A recent edited handbook of measures for psychiatry and mental health lists thirty-six scales and denotes those from designated areas that have obtained "gold standard" status (Baer & Blais, 2010).

As already mentioned, Christian counselors have to consider the prudence of use or neglect of measurement. Ponder this implicit message. The field has enough confidence in these tools to identify select ones with gold-standard rankings. Is it justifiable to ignore an assessment trend that has such a robust research base?

The *DSM*-5 cross-cutting instruments narrow the symptom focus (levels 1 and 2) or quantify symptom severity in specific disorder domains. These RAIs are available for immediate use and yet they continue to evolve (American Psychiatric Association, 2013). Norms are still undergoing formulation. In addition, these measures combine questions from previous scales with newer items to reflect recent refinements. Trustworthy items to investigate features of a concern are adopted into convenient, easy-to-score forms. In sum, there is a demonstrated history and adequate psychometric evidence available to warrant further usage as long as the adopting clinician appreciates that these scales remain provisional and are open to ongoing modification.

The "anchoring" feature reflects how these scales directly serve clients. The scales establish benchmarks that are uniformly understood. A measurement anchor designates a navigation point regarding current behavior or emotion (i.e., quantifies a point-in-time experience of frequency, duration, and intensity). This authenticates a fixed marker. Movement in treatment can then be evaluated clearly. In a clinical context the interest is to monitor change within the client, not necessarily to compare the client to an external population.

Because the *DSM*-5 cross-cutting and disorder-specific severity measures are available online for instant access at no charge, they are ideal for client use throughout treatment.

Similar RAI measures for cooperative clinical practice and outcome tracking have been in use for several decades (Corcoran & Fischer, 2013). An RAI is a semi-standardized measure that provides a concise, convenient, and credible means of capturing discrete data on an indicator related to the broader presenting concern. RAIs do not replace other assessment methods but rather complement them. They can supplement behavioral observations, interviews, client logs, individualized ratings scales, physiological measures, or commercially available self-report questionnaires (e.g., NEO Personality Inventory-3, the Millon Clinical Multiaxial Inventory IV, or the 16PF [personality factors] Questionnaire). The Corcoran and Fischer two-volume sourcebook (2013) gathers such measures for clinical and research use. Hundreds of scales have been reproduced and reviewed. One volume covers measures for couples, families, and children. Its companion volume centers on adults.

The divide between RAIs and more highly recognized measures is a matter of focus, pragmatics, and availability of normative data. Generally, RAIs quantify observations but may not produce scores that fall along a normal distribution curve for comparison with an extensive normative sample, though there are exceptions. Certain RAIs offer rudimentary norm-referenced features and tables. RAIs are short, quick to complete, transparent in focus, and easy to score. In concise terminology, these are client/clinician friendly self-report measures. The rule of thumb is that RAIs can take less than five minutes but no more than fifteen minutes to complete. Additionally, RAIs are pragmatic and global as opposed to unilateral in their theoretical orientation. Finally, RAIs have been reviewed by experts and piloted in research, which gives them an edge over clinician-devised question sets. Ultimately, RAIs provide a structured opportunity to collect data to define an issue, quantify an experience and make comparisons.

Corcoran and Fischer (2013) classify RAIs as standardized, without the modifier *semi* that I have inserted. These instruments have uniform items, a prescribed procedure for scoring, and a general template for administration. Essentially, "standardized," according to Corcoran and Fischer, indicates that the measure is applied in the same manner each time it's put to use. They do differentiate this regularizing feature from the general expectation that there will be a wealth of supportive and technical information available in a manual since there is an abundance of literature that typically accompanies a standardized measure. Such background adds depth to the story of its development, purpose, interpretation, reliability, validity, and norming population. There are statistical charts, tables, and delineated scoring guidelines. Corcoran and Fischer make the case that the lack of extensive technical information in RAIs does not disqualify them as standardized because there is consistency of presentation. Certainly these experts are resting on firm psychometric conceptual footings. Nonetheless, it seems to make good common sense to recognize and separate the level of development sophistication using ordinary language. Commercially available, fully "standardized" measures developed for wide usage are sophisticated and have extensive support in the literature. RAIs, in contrast, are piloted and then roughly polished for research purposes. Thus, for ease of communication among clinicians, who are already squeamish when it comes to scientific linguistics, I will continue to use the term *semi-standardized* here as a clarifying concession.

Regardless of the terminology, these are measures that have proven to be useful in research. RAIs have a definitive design and aim to yield quantifiable data according to an operational definition of a construct. Here is the key distinction for clinicians. On a standardized, commercial measure the developer asserts how and when the measure is appropriate for use. For semi-standardized RAIs, it is the counselor who forms the acceptance criteria and assumes the role of decision maker as "local" researcher serving a specific client.

For illustration, let's recall Carter, the college student mentioned in the previous chapter with a severe case of "senior panic." The Procrastination Assessment Scale-Students (PASS) was selected to obtain behavioral/attitudinal details to inform his treatment plan. This limited, targeted measure was pulled from the RAI sourcebook (Corcoran & Fischer, 2013; Solomon & Rothblum, 1984). The PASS poses sixty-six items to explore the prevalence of procrastination across six areas of academic functioning, the reasons for procrastination, and interest in change. A similar scale, the Procrastination Scale (PS) was also reviewed with interest. The PS defines procrastination as the absence of self-regulated performance and use of self-control to put off or avoid an activity (Tuckman, 1991). These operational definitions and quantifiable data could be useful in treatment planning. Despite its range of activities and clarity of focus, the PS was ultimately rejected because it did not have sufficient face validity for Carter due to its lack of an exclusive academic orientation. The Perfectionism Inventory (PI) was also given consideration because it offers a comprehensive and multidimensional view of its central construct (concern over mistakes, need for approval, organization, rumination, striking for excellence, etc.; Hill et al., 2004). Therapeutic conversations could readily flow with Carter once differences were picked up concretely on the related perfectionism subscales.

In the end, the purpose of assessment with Carter at the earliest phase of treatment directed instrument choice. The instrument needed to capture a quick look at the activities where Carter was horribly stuck and spinning his academic wheels at this critical point in the semester. Thus, the PASS was selected. Notice that this choice is not about which measure is the strongest psychometrically or most conceptually robust but about which measure was best suited to stimulate conversations within this clinical scenario.

The overarching label of procrastination may not in point of fact become the leading frame for the case conceptualization. Rather, inner apprehension over an uncertain future would be the main identified issue that takes that point position. Procrastination and perfectionistic tendencies, aggravated by heightened anxiety due to his uncertainty over the future, are problematic for Carter at this point in time since these give rise to the behavioral pattern most evident to others. Thus, the PASS gives counselor and client detailed material to reveal the contours of the terrain surrounding coursework management. This is where Carter needs immediate traction to get out of the rut where he is stuck. These areas become short-term targets for immediate intervention planning and focused prayer. A counselor familiar with the assessment options offered by Corcoran and Fischer (2013) indeed has a flexible and functional set of instruments.

A comparable collection of RAIs by Simmons and Lehmann (2013) pulls together an assortment of instruments that are strengths-based at their core. A strengths measure places the spotlight on assets and flourishing while pathology, problems, and deficits are left in the shadows. The categories for these measures range from happiness and subjective well-being to acceptance, mindfulness, and humor to social supports, relationships, and emotional intelligence. The scales are reproduced in their entirety and a straightforward review is provided.

Consider the Flourishing Scale (FS), a subjective well-being measure, as a basic example (Diener et al., 2009). This is a succinct eight-item statement collection coupled with a common seven-point, agree/disagree Likert scale. The client supplies agree/disagree ratings to prompts such as: "I lead a purposeful and meaningful life"; "I am engaged and interested in my daily activities"; and "I am optimistic about my future." In total, this activity would demand only a few minutes of a client's time and could be completed before or after a clinical session. The alternative approach would be to secure the resulting perspective on life with stimulating interview questions, but consider the effort and investment it would take to use an interpersonal interaction approach. If one were to begin to explore the topic of the meaning of life, there would be no surprise should this take extended session time! In the end, dialogue alone would not yield any tangible score. The style of measure represented by the FS would generate a marker of a client's perception of psychological existential resources early in treatment that could be readily reassessed along the way. The clinical discussion picks up once a commitment to a quantified perspective is declared.

Another typical type of RAI comes from a radically different domain. The Pinney Sexual Satisfaction Inventory (PSSI) is a twenty-six-item inventory. Like many other RAI tools, this one was initially developed for research (Pinney, Gerrard, & Denney, 1987). The PSSI is exclusively for women and contains items to collect information regarding two main factors: general sexual satisfaction and satisfaction with the woman's partner. Illustrative items would be: "I am satisfied with the amount of time that my partner(s) and I spend together when we make love," "I am satisfied with my ability to make my physical needs known to my partner(s)," and "I wish my partner(s) and I were more loving and caring when we make love." Conventional Likert ratings are applied.

I highlight this particular instrument here for a reason. From the samples just listed, it is clear there are redemptive validity (RV) implications (Greggo & Lawrence, 2012b). It is difficult to miss or overlook the gender neutral term *partner* over the more common terms in ministry circles, namely, *spouse* or *husband*. The plural reading option makes a nonjudgmental statement on the issue of multiple partners. Consider both the value and liability of this approach. For a researcher or clinician looking for a general-use measure, this open stance would be appropriate and respectful. However, these stylistic elements convey an underlying worldview perspective, evident in contemporary culture, regarding sexual practices. This is apparent in the items themselves and would surface in an RV consideration related to content validity. It is reasonable that many clients and counselors with Christian convictions would see this as directly counter to scriptural teaching on exclusivity in marital relations (e.g., Ex 20:14; 1 Cor 6:18; 1 Thess 4:3). We need to account for this perspective when evaluating an instrument's potential for clinical use. Further, the PSSI's open perspective could make it an offensive measure for a client who has requested that her counseling be Christ-honoring and biblically congruent. Therefore, when selecting an RAI, it should be evaluated not only for its psychometric strength, clinician appeal, targeted domain, or population applicability but also for its use with a particular client. This is not a matter of mere face validity, for it touches on a more central point. An RAI is deemed appropriate for collaborative counseling if it has potential to further the therapeutic alliance by clarifying treatment tasks. Thus, any potential RV obstacles within the PSSI would have to be addressed prior to use (e.g., an advanced orientation/explanation regarding the measure's general applicability or item modification).

There are alternate measures that address similar attitudes. At the same time, there could well be a presenting concern that would make it relevant and meaningful to explore this sensitive topic of general sexual and partner satisfaction with a client. In such a unique case, completing an inventory such as the PSSI, with its explicit items on intimacy expectations and disappointments, might accomplish its purpose and bring valuable information into therapeutic conversation. The inventory could well be a highly empathetic means to employ the least threatening approach.

It can be far less intrusive for a client to complete an inventory to give the counselor access to these details than to answer a series of questions in a face-to-face discussion. Indeed, it may not be realistic to expect a client in pain to express satisfaction or disappointment in sexual intimacy so candidly to a stranger early in treatment. After all, if there was no rationale for inhibition when discussing these matters, it's less likely that this domain would need to be explored with an RAI. If a measure like the PSSI helps a woman locate a way to communicate to her husband, it makes a vital connection. The power is not in the technology itself but in how the information is harnessed by the therapist to help the client change.

In each of these RAI collections cited, not all of the measures cited and reproduced are available for instant use. Many are accessible for clinical applications without significant financial charge. Others require that clinicians take an additional step to contact the author for permission to use. Given the demands of practice, this correspondence expectation may indeed present an obstacle. Realistically, this would be the customary practice whenever a scale is deemed useful for a research investigation. Should a professional or doctoral candidate wish to apply that scale in another project or bring it into the clinical setting, the practitioner would need to obtain the consent of the lead author, whose contact information is regularly included in the published article for this very reason. This courteous and ethical step applies even if there is no plan for extensive reproduction, publication, or internet posting. In these published RAI collections, email addresses for authors are supplied in the review to facilitate this process.

Recognizing that busy counselors may be reticent to take on this "permission of the author(s) procedure," Sandberg, Richards, and Erford (2013) assembled a collection of free-access instruments. These have no restrictions for immediate clinical use. The measures themselves are not reproduced in their entirety in this convenient handbook. Instead, this resource neatly tackles two matters. First, it points clinicians to instruments on the web covering the full range of common counseling concerns (anxiety, mood disorders, addictions, impulse control, schizophrenia/autistic spectrum, eating disorders, and trauma). Second, over and above its directory features, this guide reviews these instruments. It offers the measure's background that would not likely be discussed in the usual resources that clinicians would access (i.e., tests in print; *Mental Measurements Yearbook* [*MMY*]).

Here are two examples of measures reviewed that are available in the public domain: the Hamilton Anxiety Rating Scale (HAM-A) and the PTSD Checklist—Civilian Version (PCL-C).[1] The HAM-A is a veteran of multiple research studies and is one of those measures that has earned the gold standard designation (Marques et al., 2010). These measures are available from reputable government-funded agencies and are downloadable in a format that is ready to print and use. Regardless of the source, there are no posted manuals. One could dig around for more information but that would require access to published resources. Without further investment, the counselor would not automatically be prepared to competently put either of the measures into use.

Applying a measure based on accessibility and reputation alone would not be judicious on the part of the counselor. What about its purpose, limitations, psychometric features, and research pedigree? This is where the reviews offered by Sandberg, Richards, and Erford (2013) become invaluable. Armed with enough detail to grasp the features and/or limitations of the measure, and having current access links, these RAIs are ripe and ready to serve in sessions. This offers busy clinicians a way to responsibly furnish an assessment toolkit on a budget. Even a ministry-funded counselor can afford these measures and have the added benefit of knowing how it stands among the best available. As more instruments become available via free access, selective clinical assessment can be applied even in low-resource mental health settings (Beidas et al., 2015).

---

[1]The Hamilton Anxiety Rating Scale (HAM-A) can be found at https://dcf.psychiatry.ufl.edu /files/2011/05/HAMILTON-ANXIETY.pdf. The PTSD Checklist—Civilian Version (PCL-C) is available at http://www.mirecc.va.gov/docs/visn6/3_PTSD_CheckList_and_Scoring.pdf.

IN SEARCH OF RAIS FOR EXPLICIT USE IN CHRISTIAN FORMATION

RAIs make it possible to meet contemporary clinical accountability standards by aiding in the fine-tuning of treatment objectives. Counseling within a Christian framework is not exempt from this practice expectation. Thus, when a client's openly stated yearning for change fits with a domain that an RAI can define and quantify, counselors are admonished to apply a suitable instrument. Optimal measures for use in Christian counseling are ones that blend seamlessly with a Christian worldview, establish markers to evaluate growth in the desired change area, and add benefit to counseling by encouraging faith maturation. Fischer and Corcoran's (2007) two-volume RAI collection with 471 measures for children, adults, and families on diverse issues for treatment did not include a single RAI for spirituality or religiousness. The more recent edition (Corcoran & Fischer, 2013) has 473 measures, but only two relate directly to spirituality. The Intrinsic Spirituality Scale (ISS) is a six-item functional measure of spirituality that considers how spirituality influences thought and behavior. The Jewish Religious Coping Scale (JCOPE) is a sixteen-item scale to examine the use of Jewish customs, beliefs, and practices to cope with stressful situations. These volumes by Corcoran and Fischer offer a wealth of clinical measurement resources but still neglect tools that address religious and spiritual matters. *Spirituality* and *religion* are not even terms appearing in the index. This missing domain would appear odd given the interest in these themes in clinical practice.

In light of the paucity of measures that address faith concerns in these major collections, a colleague and I conducted a review of suitable RAIs for use in counseling (Greggo & Lawrence, 2012a). The goal was to identify RAIs with potential for application in counseling that incorporate a faith maturation component consistent with traditional Christian portraits of sanctification (Mic 6:6-8; Rom 6) and bearing spiritual fruit (Gal 5:22; Col 1:10).

Christian counseling can be a service called on for help in overcoming a prevailing sense of inertia in spiritual growth. The use of spiritually oriented assessments can facilitate the identification of clients with a clinically significant religious impairment (CSRI). A CSRI is the reduced ability to perform religious activities, achieve religious goals, or experience religious states due to interference by the presence of a psychological disorder (Hathaway, 2003). Surfacing a CSRI makes an explicit link between spirituality and a mental health diagnosis. Beyond identification of a specific faith-related problem, there is considerable evidence that clients with under-lying faith values and traditions tend to invest more in counseling services when the goals align with their spiritual journey narrative (Hook et al., 2010; Worthington, Kurusu, McCullough, & Sandage, 1996). Spiritually oriented assessments, which acknowledge and use the faith resources of the client, are likely to be appreciated by clients with Christian convictions. This can contribute to positive therapeutic outcomes.

Regrettably, Christian counselors who tend to underutilize standardized psychological assessment may also resist use of semi-standardized RAIs. They may be suspicious about the validity of these measures with a population dedi-cated to traditional Christian values. In terms of evaluating outcomes, Scripture teaches that spiritual formation is exclusively under the domain of the Holy Spirit and that gains are indications of divine grace (Gal 5:22-26). The protest may then follow that an objective measure is, at best, a human work but at its worst is judgmental, intrusive, condescending, and arrogant.

It is important to face such concerns with an explicit rationale and detailed review procedure. Earlier I defined and demonstrated redemptive validity (RV) in conjunction with the selection of measures for depression. RV looks at what a measure can surface (behavior, attitudes, experience, etc.) and how it can contribute insight to living in conformity with Scripture. RV addresses the false dichotomy that spiritual formation is Spirit-led while assessment is human-led. By actively bringing the Holy Spirit into assessment selection, implementation, and interpretation, Christian MHPs can adopt both standardized and nonstan-dardized measures of spirituality into customary clinical practice.

Research has produced credible measures to examine spiritual and reli-gious themes (Hill & Kilian, 2003; Hill, Kopp, & Bollinger, 2007; Hill & Pargament, 2008; Standard, Sandhu, & Painter, 2000). The literature tends to define religion and spirituality in discrete ways (Worthington, Hook, Davis, & McDaniel, 2011). Religiosity tends to be associated with a declaration of al-legiance to a known belief and practice system within a traditional organiza-tional structure. Spirituality is more inner focused and is often defined as the sensation of feeling close and connected to the sacred. When it comes to Christianity, there is an expansive heritage of religious traditions as well as sets of disciplines that promote personal spiritual experience. The majority of instruments measure religiousness and spirituality throughout the lifespan and across traditions and cultural and ethnic communities. These instruments are intended for use by research participants who may hold individualistic or syncretistic conceptions of transcendence and moral experience. Many instruments are inclusive and have broad religious applicability. We sifted through extensive listings to cull measures with adequate promise for use in explicitly Christian counseling. Through this process we located twenty-two measures of spirituality and religiousness with reasonable psychometric qualities. For reference, the full list is reproduced in table 12.1 (Greggo & Lawrence, 2012a). Alternative lists and recommendations are located in Gold (2010), Hill et al. (2007), Hill and Hood (1999), and Plante (2009).

Table 12.1. Comprehensive list of measures of spirituality and religiousness for Christian counseling

Measure	Description
Attitudes Toward God Scale-9	A 9-item functional measure to quickly appraise attachment to God as a source of security along with struggles in this relationship by combing two subscales: Positive Attitudes Toward God and Disappointment and Anger with God.
Brief Multidimensional Measure of Religiousness/Spirituality	A 38-item multidimensional measure of both dispositional and functional religiousness/spirituality, evaluating domains such as community or denominational affiliation, public and private practices, values and beliefs, coping and social support.
Daily Spiritual Experiences Scale	A 16-item measure of dispositional religiousness/spirituality, which specifically evaluates spiritual maturity through ideas such as perceived relationship with and experiences of God, peace and harmony, and compassion.
Duke Religion Index	A 5-item measure of functional religiousness/spirituality that assesses three religiosity subscales: organizational/public, nonorganizational/private, and intrinsic.
Faith Maturity Scale	A 12-item measure of dispositional religiousness/spirituality, focused on the evaluation of spiritual maturity via behavior, and vertical and horizontal relationship domains.
Intrinsic Religious Motivation Scale	A 10-item measure of functional religiousness/spirituality, evaluating religious motivation through extrinsic/intrinsic framework.
Mysticism Scale	A 32-item measure of dispositional religiousness/spirituality focused on the evaluation of mystical experiences through two subscales: general mysticism and interpretation of mystical experiences.
Religious Commitment Inventory-10	A 10-item measure of dispositional religiousness/spirituality that assesses religious commitment via consistency between religious belief and practice.
RCOPE	A 105-item measure of functional religiousness/spirituality that evaluates religious coping via 17 factors.
Brief RCOPE	A 35-item brief version of the RCOPE, measuring religious coping through two domains, positive and negative coping.
Religious Background and Behavior Scale	A 3-item measure of functional religiousness/spirituality focused on the assessment of religious behaviors and practices.
Religious Doubts Scale	A 10-item measure of dispositional religiousness/spirituality, which evaluates individual religious doubt.
Religious Problem-Solving Scale	A 36-item measure of functional religiousness/spirituality that assesses religious coping through identification style of approach (i.e., active vs. passive) and attribution (i.e., internal vs. external).
Religious Support Scale	A 21-item measure of functional religiousness/spirituality, assessing religious support through three dimensions of support: religious community, church leader, and God.

Measure	Description
Revised Religious Orientation Scale	A 14-item measure of functional religiousness/spirituality, evaluating religious motivation using extrinsic and intrinsic subscales.
Santa Clara Strength of Religious Faith Questionnaire	A 10-item measure of dispositional religiousness/spirituality, assessing general depth of religious faith.
Spiritual Assessment Inventory	A 54-item measure of dispositional religiousness/spirituality that measures spiritual maturity using an object relations and attachment theory framework. The SAI examines two primary dimensions: awareness of God and quality of the vertical relationship.
Spiritual Experience Index-Revised	A 23-item measure of dispositional religiousness/spirituality, evaluating spiritual maturity using two subscales: spiritual support and spiritual openness.
Spiritual Transformation Inventory 2.0	A standardized assessment tool that evaluates spiritual development using a relational model. The STI 2.0 contains 31 scales within the five domains of Hall and Edwards' Connected Life model.
Spiritual Well-Being Scale	A 20-item measure of dispositional religiousness/spirituality that assesses spiritual well-being through two well-being subscales: existential and religious.
Springfield Religiosity Scale	A 35-item measure of functional religiousness/spirituality that evaluates participation in a religious community or organization.
Ways of Religious Coping Scale	A 40-item measure of functional religiousness/spirituality, specifically assessing religious coping through two subscales: internal/private and external/social.

We then took the identified measures through an intensive utility screening procedure with four general considerations in mind: (1) instrument fit with the parameters of an RAI, (2) acceptability to favorable psychometric properties, (3) availability and accessibility, and (4) compelling RV potential for application with a population that holds a Christian worldview. RV is not a characteristic of the measure itself. Instead, it is a method to weigh the client experience, addressing the items as well as the language, underlying values, and data obtained by the measure against the gospel story of creation, fall, redemption, and restoration.

In order to sharpen the focus on construct validity and increase appreciation for the distinct purpose of each instrument during the selection procedure, we applied a categorical grid from an earlier research review (Hill et al., 2007). This grid clarifies what each of the measures intends to accomplish. Eight dimensions of religiousness and spirituality fall under two overarching headings that essentially mirror the customary trait (long-term) and state (current experience) designations common in assessment discussion. *Dispositional* measures aim to uncover persistent patterns and leanings. The following are subdimensions under this heading: general scales, commitment inventories, and measures of developmental spiritual maturity. *Functional* measures capture everyday coping mechanisms, behaviors, and feelings. Five subdimensions with a temporal focus follow: religious motivation, social and faith community participation, spiritual private practices, religious support, and spiritual coping. Each of these eight categories is represented by at least one measure presented here.

Those with hobbies requiring any kind of tools will be familiar with the concept of a starter kit. This is an elementary assortment of essentials without which your toolbox would be incomplete and you wouldn't be able to practice your hobby. Here is a description of eight RAIs of spirituality and religiousness that would make an excellent starter kit for Christian counseling: Santa Clara Strength of Religious Faith Questionnaire (SCSRFQ), Religious Commitment Inventory-10 (RCI-10), Brief RCOPE, Attitudes Toward God Scale (ATGS-9), Springfield Religiosity Scale (SRS), Religious Support Scale (RSS), Duke Religion Index (DRI), and Spiritual Assessment Inventory (SAI). These instruments reflect diverse operational definitions. Each measure sets out to quantify complex, emotionally charged, multidimensional phenomena of religious and spiritual experience. Thus, despite the pre-selection, each clinician must gauge the best fit for the population being served, the particular client, and how the clinician expects to blend results into treatment.

Santa Clara Strength of Religious Faith Questionnaire (SCSRFQ). The SCSRFQ is a ten-item general scale that quantifies a client's faith intensity (Freiheit, Sonstegard, Schmitt, & Vye, 2006; Plante, 2009; Plante & Boccaccini, 1997a, 1997b). The full version would be brief enough for most clinical situations. Still, there is an option to use only five designed items while retaining reasonable validity. (Storch, Roberti, Bravata, & Storch, 2004) The SCSRFQ rates the declaration of religious faith to anchor one's identity. It has relatively few items that address everyday practice. Given its brevity and directness, the SCSRFQ is a choice method to discern whether a client is both suitable and amenable to counseling that explicitly incorporates a Christian worldview and spiritual resources.

The SCSRFQ quickly supplies a self-report on one's depth of faith. Given its inclusive language, minimalist style, and ease of scoring, it could certainly blend easily into initial paperwork. Administration can be repeated down the road to track faith intensity as an outcome. The beauty of this tool is simplicity. Unfortunately, it may not be an ideal choice for highly committed evangelicals. There is limited opportunity to express one's highest priorities, degree of devotion, and cherished practices. It is a great fit for a religiously affiliated college setting where students might display a wide range of faith commitment.

Religious Commitment Inventory (RCI-10). The RCI-10 is an understandable and unassuming commitment yardstick. It provides a quantified score for the degree of adherence between internalized religious beliefs and daily faith practice (Worthington et al., 2003). It is a prototypical RAI because it has a single target, ease of scoring, and plain interpretation. The RCI-10 has research depth. An extensive psychometric study to operationalize the commitment construct reduces the item count from sixty-four to a mere ten. Normative data are available to differentiate low/high religious commitment using means and standard deviations. It is possible to compare scores with a range of populations, including clients in Christian counseling agencies.

One objective of the RCI-10 developers was to create a psychometrically valid measure with utility for religiously committed clients (Worthington et al., 2003). Given its narrow target, uncomplicated format, and normative data, it offers considerable potential for clinical application in Christian settings. It does not appear that any specific item would cause difficulties with an evangelical Christian population. However, the frequent use of *religious* might be less than ideal given the recent rejection of this term by evangelicals who prefer descriptors such as *faith* or *spiritual journey*. In regards to interpretation, a low score might indicate individuals who lack a faith tradition and reject religious beliefs or individuals with low consistency between reported convictions and behavioral commitments. Thus, the RCI-10 does yield data useful to identify clients with CSRI, even though the reasons for a low score require further investigation.

The RCI-10 measures the degree to which an individual puts faith into action (Jas 2:14-26). After clarification of the meaning of a low, midrange, or high score, it provides identifiable material to ground faith interventions that could increase the link between belief and action (fellowship, tithing, prayer, worship, etc.). The RCI-10 provides a snapshot of only one spiritual dimension—consistency between belief and routine activity. Nonetheless, having a concrete, quantified sample of such behavior could readily result in productive conversations with clients who desire an authentic walk with Jesus Christ.

Springfield Religiosity Scale (SRS). The SRS is a functional measure that aims to ascertain participation in a religious community or organization (Hill et al., 2007). The SRS originally took shape as a research measure for use with a geriatric population. Based on the existing published information, the generalizability of the SRS is questionable given its nearly exclusive use with geriatric clients. At face value, this is an apparent strike against the measure for general practice. Developers set out to form a measure that would find a warm reception in a population associated with Judeo-Christian traditions and where 90% of users were either Protestant or Catholic (Koenig, Smiley, & Gonzales, 1988). By design the instrument visibly reflects Christian beliefs and activities.

The dimensions of religion included in the SRS are beliefs, rituals, experiences, knowledge, communal participation, spiritual well-being, and intrinsic religiosity. Unique to the SRS is the association of religious belief with Christian orthodoxy. The measure contains four items to assess core positions on one's concept of God, the divinity of Jesus Christ, biblical authority, and the existence of the devil.[2] This feature regarding soliciting a response to doctrinal matters alone increases its RV with the target population. Overall, the SRS provides clinicians with a multifaceted portrait of Christian spirituality. It is suitable for adoption, with item updating, as a formalized questionnaire. The SRS functions admirably as a conversation starter with discrete items as topics for consideration. In order to gain maximum benefit from its factor structure, modification would be necessary to specify and streamline scoring procedures.

Attitudes Toward God Scale (ATGS-9). The ATGS-9 is a functional measure of religious support and coping. It investigates one's relationship with God from the perspective that this experience can be both a fundamental resource and an immediate stressor (Wood et al., 2009). It was developed to facilitate research into the complexities of a relationship with God due to its attachment qualities. The construct underlying its scales and items is the premise that an attachment bond with the divine can be maintained but can be a source of strain when one experiences disappointment. The ten-point rating scales, nine items, and two scales makes it sensitive enough to identify subtle shifts in one's attitude toward God.

The ATGS-9 went through an extensive standardization effort as an abridgment of an existing research tool designed to gather data on religious comfort and strain. A series of six studies with nearly three thousand participants yielded psychometric data to form the basis for its reliability, internal consistency, and construct validity. Despite its brevity, it is a commendable RAI. Factor analysis supported two scales. The Positive Attitudes toward God (PAG) subscale correlates with religious commitment and the personality trait of conscientiousness. Disappointment and Anger with God (DAG) surfaces disruption in this relationship that spurs distress and withdrawal from faith-based activities and inhibits religious coping. Given the attitudes tracked and the common therapeutic conversations in Christian counseling, this measure has potential for initial assessment and ongoing evaluation.

---

[2]I used the SRS as an RAI in clinical practice with select clients and added an item on the Holy Spirit to round out the doctrinal section. I also updated media references (radio, television religious programming) to reflect contemporary technology and delivery options.

Religious Support Scale (RSS). The RSS, with its twenty-one items, succinctly measures a single aspect of spiritual distress, namely, religious support (Lazar & Bjorck, 2008; Plante, 2009). The item arrangement taps into three prime sources of support: religious community, spiritual leadership, and divine intervention. The language is intentionally inclusive, but no phrases appear troublesome for a conservative-oriented population.

The target construct of religious support would be practical for clients with clinical issues that isolate or for those in life transitions that disrupt natural supports (e.g., depression, isolation, or social anxiety; career shift, divorce, or childbirth). Thus, with its pointed application, this measure may be a best fit when applied to cases where an increased perception of social/spiritual support is an identified outcome in the treatment plan. The support aspect of faith, though critical and essential, may not be broad enough to warrant adoption of the RSS as a routine assessment tool. This is the beauty of a good toolbox though; there are measures well suited to identifiable client needs.

Duke Religion Index (DRI). The five-item DRI, designed for large-scale epidemiological research, rapidly captures estimates of three religious dimensions: organizational (one item on frequency of attendance at religious services); nonorganizational (a single item on prayer and religious study); and intrinsic (three items from Hoge's [1972] Intrinsic Religiosity Scale measuring one's experience of the presence of the divine). The psychometric evidence is solid and extensive (i.e., one hundred published studies; availability in ten languages). It has been the key method to catalogue religious data on thousands of research participants across the entire span of adult development (Hill, 1999; Koenig & Bussing, 2010; Storch et al., 2004). The authors caution against calculating a total score, although alternative scoring methods can generate a composite score. For clinical use, the preferred approach would be to follow the authors' recommendation and look at each of its three scales separately. Use the first item to ascertain organizational participation, the second to gauge private devotional activity, and combine the last three to capture how the client merges faith into life as a whole. Given the brevity of the measure, it would be reasonable to collect results down the road to evaluate change following counseling intervention and prior to discharge planning.

The language on this measure is broadly compatible with Christian traditions. Still, when applied in an explicitly evangelical setting, the phrase "private religious activities" could be supplemented with "spiritual disciplines" to better capture an individual's solitary engagement in prayer, Scripture reading, and personal worship. Given its survey use design, the DRI could be tied to demographic forms and other information-gathering techniques prior to the initial consultation or near the outset of the intake process. The clinician could then explore responses in an early interview. This compact tool is up-to-date and efficient and shows promise as a basic objective method to ground further discussion regarding spiritual history and present experience.

Brief RCOPE. The Brief RCOPE is a fourteen-item abridgement of a comprehensive measure of religious coping that addresses five faith functions: search for meaning, control, spiritual comfort, spiritual intimacy, and life transformation (Pargament, Koenig, & Perez, 2000). This measure applies to the aftermath of an adverse event or significant season of illness or stress. An important assumption within the measure is that clients may demonstrate positive religious coping (PRC) or negative religious coping (NRC). Research has dispelled the myth that all spirituality and religious activity are constructive and healthy. This measure, like its longer predecessor, identifies the dark side or dysfunctional forms of religious coping such as feeling punished or abandoned by God, attributing an experience to the devil's control, or questioning the power of God.

In terms of RV, the Brief RCOPE has much to offer for clients who are in the midst of spiritual distress. Specifically, either low scores on PRC or a high score on NRC identifies spiritual distress. This may indicate lack of dependence on or attachment to the Lord or ignorance of biblical truths (forgiveness, the character of God, etc.). The specific source of distress will have to be explored via dialogue—highlighting the value of an RAI can contribute to counseling. The Brief RCOPE has a definitive functional aim since it assumes adversity or suffering, so it is not appropriate for all clients.

Spiritual Assessment Inventory (SAI). The SAI examines spiritual maturity by considering two primary dimensions: quality of relationship with God and awareness of God (Hall & Edwards, 1996, 2002; Hall, Reise, & Haviland, 2007). It achieves a portrait of psychospiritual development through five subscales: awareness, realistic acceptance, disappointment, grandiosity, and instability. Using theoretical concepts from object relations and attachment theory, the SAI looks at spiritual maturation by investigating one's relationship with God. The norming population leans heavily on religiously committed college students, yet psychometric investigation supports its structure and items (Tisdale, 1999).

The measure comprises fifty-four items and would be relatively easy for a client to complete. On the other hand, the effort and time a clinician would have to invest to calculate subscale scores and responsibly interpret the measure are more demanding. Upon close examination, it is perhaps misleading to classify the SAI as an RAI. With its theoretical underpinnings, complexity, and impression management scale, the SAI is a notch above the typical RAI. It is not a pick-up-and-go style instrument—the hallmark feature of an RAI. However, given its unique construct (quality of relationship with God), it may be well worth the learning curve and additional assessment effort.

Nevertheless, Hall and Edwards (1996) developed the SAI from a Judeo-Christian perspective with specific New Testament themes in mind. Its biblical relational view, based on the *imago Dei* (Gen 1:26), is its underlying theological and theoretical premise. The authors build on the theme of love based on the Great Commandment in Mark 12:28-31. These Christian doctrines and priorities at its core dramatically impact the value of the SAI for Christian counseling. Therefore, the information gathered from the SAI is likely to be more informative concerning an individual's spiritual status, particularly in terms of the security of attachment with the Lord. This is a measure to apply when the therapeutic relationship is blending in spiritual formation and relational themes. Its value may be evident in settings where therapy extends beyond brief crisis intervention and basic cognitive behavioral approaches.

RAI IMPLEMENTATION AS A STEWARDSHIP ACTIVITY

A straightforward recommendation for those who aspire to do Christian counseling would be to get to know a half-dozen religious and spirituality scales well enough to put them into use with clients. Selecting from the ones reviewed here would make a reasonable starter kit for the assessment toolbox.

There are limitations and reminders regarding the use of an RAI. (1) Most RAIs lack detailed directions for interpretation. The responsibility for any explanation of content falls on the counselor. (2) RAIs are transparent assessment measures. There is concern over potential response style distortions common to all self-report measures (faking good/bad; making a positive impression, etc.). The clinician's judgment is the only check for whether the assessment results are a valid representation of the individual. (3) The normative data for RAIs are limited. Sample populations are characteristically small, and diversity ratios are not likely to coincide with recent census data. This raises a concern especially when these RAIs are put to use with racially and ethnically diverse clients. Developing local norms is a good procedure, as well as remaining vigilant to the expression of cultural differences. (4) Finally, Christianity has a wide range of distinctive formulations, cultural expressions, and ethnic traditions. Clinicians build skills to blend spiritual matters ethically into counseling, especially when the spiritual/faith background of the client is not an identical match with the clinician. This is likely to be the case more often than not.

In conclusion, assessment is indeed an essential aspect of quality mental health service. Despite the dependence of Christian helpers on the movement of the Holy Spirit and the experience of divine grace, there is no reason to avoid the use of instruments that increase understanding and clarify behavioral change. Frankly, the effort to locate and use good instruments displays good stewardship of resources. These measures can help tailor treatment goals to issues that matter most to clients. RAIs collect information in an efficient fashion and pave the way for counselors to move with greater precision into the helping conversations that follow. As counselors we display good stewardship when we apply ethical principles to select the very best measures possible and use them to serve clients. This begins as a technical process to explore psychometric strength and clinical utility. It reaches fulfillment in Christian counseling when clients are encouraged and blessed in their spiritual journeys.

REFERENCES

American Counseling Association. (2014). *ACA code of ethics: As approved by the ACA Governing Council.* http://www.counseling.org/resources/aca-code-of-ethics.pdf

American Psychiatric Association. (2013). *Diagnostic and statistical manual of mental disorders* (5th ed.). Arlington, VA: American Psychiatric Publishing.

Baer, L., & Blais, M. A. (Eds.). (2010). *Handbook of clinical rating scales and assessment in psychiatry and mental health.* New York: Humana Press.

Beidas, R. S., Stewart, R. E., Walsh, L., Lucas, S., Downey, M. M., Jackson, K., Fernandez, T., & Mandell, D. S. (2015). Free, brief, and validated: Standardized instruments for low-resource mental health settings. *Cognitive and Behavioral Practice, 22*(1), 5-19.

Beutler, L. E., Harwood, T. M., & Holaway, R. (2002). How to assess clients in pretreatment planning. In J. N. Butcher (Ed.), *Clinical personality assessment: Practical approaches* (2nd ed., pp. 76-95). New York: Oxford University Press.

Corcoran, K., & Fischer, J. (2013). *Measures for clinical practice and research: A sourcebook* (5th ed., Vols. 1-2). Oxford, England: Oxford University Press.

Diener, E., Wirtz, D., Tov, W., Kim-Prieto, C., Choi, D., Oishi, S., & Biswas-Diener, R. (2009). New well-being measures: Short scales to assess flourishing and positive and negative feelings. *Social Indicators Research, 97*(2), 143-156.

Fischer, J., & Corcoran, K. (2007). *Measures for clinical practice and research: A sourcebook* (4th ed., Vols. 1-2). New York: Oxford University Press.

Freiheit, S. R., Sonstegard, K., Schmitt, A., & Vye, C. (2006). Religiosity and spirituality: A psychometric evaluation of the Santa Clara Strength of Religious Faith Questionnaire. *Pastoral Psychology, 55*(1), 27-33.

Gold, J. M. (2010). *Counseling and spirituality: Integrating spiritual and clinical orientations.* Upper Saddle River, NJ: Pearson Education.

Greggo, S. P., & Lawrence, K. (2012a). Clinical appraisal of spirituality: In search of rapid assessment instruments (RAIs) for Christian counseling. *Journal of Psychology and Christianity, 31*(3), 253-266.

Greggo, S. P., & Lawrence, K. (2012b). Redemptive validity and the assessment of depression: Singing songs to heavy hearts. *Journal of Psychology and Theology, 40*(3), 188-198.

Hall, T. W., & Edwards, K. J. (1996). The initial development and factor analysis of the Spiritual Assessment Inventory. *Journal of Psychology and Theology, 24*(3), 233-246.

Hall, T. W., & Edwards, K. J. (2002). The Spiritual Assessment Inventory: A theistic model and measure for assessing spiritual development. *Journal for the Scientific Study of Religion, 41*(2), 341-357.

Hall, T. W., Reise, S. P., & Haviland, M. G. (2007). An item response theory analysis of the Spiritual Assessment Inventory. *International Journal for the Psychology of Religion, 17*(2), 157-178.

Hathaway, W. L. (2003). Clinically significant religious impairment. *Mental Health, Religion & Culture, 6*(2), 39-55.

Hill, P. C. (1999). Duke University Religion Index (DUREL). In P. C. Hill & R. W. Hood, Jr. (Eds.), *Measures of religiosity* (pp. 130-132). Birmingham, AL: Religious Education Press.

Hill, P. C., & Hood, R. W., Jr. (Eds.). (1999). *Measures of religiosity.* Birmingham, AL: Religious Education Press.

Hill, P. C., & Kilian, M. K. (2003). Assessing clinically significant religious impairment in clients: Applications from measures in the psychology of religion and spirituality. *Mental Health, Religion & Culture, 6*(2), 149-160.

Hill, P. C., Kopp, K. J., & Bollinger, R. A. (2007). A few good measures: Assessing religion and spirituality in relation to health. In T. G. Plante & C. E. Thoresen (Eds.), *Spirit, science, and health: How the spiritual mind fuels physical wellness* (pp. 25-39). Westport, CT: Praeger.

Hill, P. C., & Pargament, K. I. (2008). Advances in the conceptualization and measurement of religion and spirituality: Implications for physical and mental health research. *Psychology of Religion and Spirituality, 1*, 3-17.

Hill, R. W., Huelsman, T. J., Furr, R. M., Kibler, J., Vicente, B. B., & Kennedy, C. (2004). A new measure of perfectionism: The Perfectionism Inventory. *Journal of Personality Assessment, 82*(1), 80-91.

Hoge, D. R. (1972). A validated intrinsic religious motivation scale. *Journal for the Scientific Study of Religion, 11*(4), 369-376.

Hook, J. N., Worthington, E. L., Jr., Davis, D. E., Jennings, D. J. II, Gartner, A. L., & Hook, J. P. (2010). Empirically supported religious and spiritual therapies. *Journal of Clinical Psychology, 66*(1), 46-72.

Koenig, H. G., & Bussing, A. (2010). The Duke University Religion Index (DUREL): A five-item measure for use in epidemiological studies. *Religions, 1*(1), 78-85.

Koenig, H. G., Smiley, M., & Gonzales, J. A. P. (1988). *Religion, health, and aging: A review and theoretical integration.* Westport, CT: Greenwood.

Lazar, A., & Bjorck, J. P. (2008). Religious support and psychosocial well-being among a religious Jewish population. *Mental Health, Religion & Culture, 11*(4), 403-421.

Marques, L., Chosak, A., Simon, N. M., Phan D. M., Wilhelm, S., & Pollack, M. (2010). Rating scales for anxiety disorders. In L. Baer & M. Blais (Eds.), *Handbook of clinical rating scales and assessment in psychiatry and mental health* (pp. 37-72). New York: Humana Press.

Pargament, K. I., Koenig, H. G., & Perez, L. M. (2000). The many methods of religious coping: Development and initial validation of the RCOPE. *Journal of Clinical Psychology, 56*(4), 519-543.

Pinney, E. M., Gerrard, M., & Denney, N. W. (1987). The Pinney Sexual Satisfaction Inventory. *Journal of Sex Research, 23*(2), 233-251.

Plante, T. G. (2009). *Spiritual practices in psychotherapy: Thirteen tools for enhancing psychological health.* Washington, DC: American Psychological Association.

Plante, T. G., & Boccaccini, M.T. (1997a). Reliability and validity of the Santa Clara Strength of Religious Faith Questionnaire. *Pastoral Psychology, 45*(6) 386-437.

Plante, T. G., & Boccaccini, M. T. (1997b). The Santa Clara Strength of Religious Faith Questionnaire. *Pastoral Psychology, 45*(5), 375-387.

Sandberg, K. M., Richards, T. E., & Erford, B. T. (2013). *Assessing common mental health and addiction issues with free-access instruments.* New York: Routledge.

Simmons, C. A., & Lehmann, P. (2013). *Tools for strengths-based assessment and evaluation.* New York: Springer.

Solomon, L. J., & Rothblum, E. D. (1984). Academic procrastination: Frequency and cognitive-behavioral correlates. *Journal of Counseling Psychology, 31*(4), 503-509.

Stanard, R. P., Sandhu, D. S., & Painter, L. C. (2000). Assessment of spirituality in counseling. *Journal of Counseling & Development, 78*(2), 204-210.

Storch, E. A., Roberti, J. W., Bravata, E., & Storch, J. B. (2004). Psychometric investigation of the Santa Clara Strength of Religious Faith Questionnaire—short form. *Pastoral Psychology, 52*(6), 479-483.

Storch, E. A., Roberti, J. W., Heidgerken, A. D., Storch, J. B., Lewin, A. B., Killiany, E. M., . . .Geffken, G. R. (2004). The Duke Religion Index: A psychometric investigation. *Pastoral Psychology, 53*(2), 175-181.

Tisdale, T. C. (1999). Spiritual Assessment Inventory. In P. C. Hill & R. W. Hood, Jr. (Eds.), *Measures of religiosity* (pp. 367-371). Birmingham, AL: Religious Education Press.

Tuckman, B. W. (1991). The development and concurrent validity of the Procrastination Scale. *Educational and Psychological Measurement, 51*(2), 473-480.

Wood, B. T., Worthington, E. L., Exline, J. J., Yali, A. M., Aten, J. D., & McMinn, M. R. (2009). Development, refinement, and psychometric properties of the Attitudes Toward God Scale (ATGS-9). *Psychology of Religion and Spirituality, 2*(3), 148-167.

Worthington, E. L., Jr., Hook, J. N., Davis, D. E., & McDaniel, M. A. (2011). Religion and spirituality. *Journal of Clinical Psychology, 16*(2), 204-214.

Worthington, E. L., Jr., Kurusu, T. A., McCullough, M. E., & Sandage, S. J. (1996). Empirical research on religion and psychotherapeutic processes and outcomes: A 10-year review and research prospectus. *Psychological Bulletin, 119*(3), 448-487.

Worthington, E. L., Jr., Wade, N. G., Hight, T. L., Ripley, J. S., McCullough, M. E., Berry, J. W., . . .O'Connor, L. (2003). The Religious Commitment Inventory-10: Development, refinement, and validation of a brief scale for research and counseling. *Journal of Counseling Psychology, 50*(1), 84-96.

PART 4

RESULTS AND

INTERPRETATION

CHAPTER THIRTEEN

GAUGING RELIGIOUS AFFECTIONS

The person without the Spirit does not accept the things that come from the Spirit of God but considers them foolishness, and cannot understand them because they are discerned only through the Spirit.

Brothers and sisters, I could not address you as people who live by the Spirit but as people who are still worldly—mere infants in Christ. I gave you milk, not solid food, for you were not yet ready for it. Indeed, you are still not ready.

1 Corinthians 2:14; 3:1-2

THEOLOGICAL THEME

Discerning Convictions

IT'S COUNSELING: DOES THEOLOGICAL TRADITION MATTER?

Two unique clients, Charles and Carlos, make the identical request to the receptionist: "I need counseling that's Christian." Yet as you meet with them you discover that what they want is actually quite distinct.

"It's really important that the counselor does not contradict the beliefs of my church," Charles stammers. "My pastor teaches a special way of salvation that my whole family follows. He preaches that if a so-called Christian is not living for the Lord when he dies, that person will suffer for eternity in hell." The client inquires openly about the therapist's convictions on what it means to be a follower of Christ and, in particular, about the notion of "once saved, always saved." Charles makes an outright declaration. He has an aversion to the doctrine of eternal security. The doctrine essentially teaches that when God grants salvation by grace, the Holy Spirit moves within to provide a guarantee or "seal" of heavenly citizenship; thus the convert cannot abandon the saving faith that God has gifted. For Charles, and for those from his tradition, salvation status is dependent on evidence displayed in one's walk. Charles explicitly warns that any effort to promulgate a soft "false assurance" on him would be misguided.

As Charles talks, his story begins to unfold. This socially awkward, timid young man has a three-generation legacy in a holiness congregation that's quite at home in the rural countryside. His grandfather, once a preacher, is buried on the hill behind the hundred-year-old, white clapboard building. Charles is engaged to a woman from the same religious background. Although his intense reluctance to enter therapy is obvious, he is convicted that he must overcome a compulsive and shameful sexual fetish. Charles desires deliverance and relief. His acting out was recently discovered, and an embarrassing confrontation ensued. Only a select few know of his dark secret. Professional treatment is now a pastoral mandate. Beyond loyalty to his cherished denomination, a twisted belief holds strategic power. He is convinced that without the scorching threat of burning in hell for all eternity, he has no power to cease his disgraceful behavior. Fortunately, he has never abused or directly harmed anyone. By his own recognition, his actions invade the privacy of women and must immediately cease. For Charles, doctrine really matters.

Carlos brings a different story as a young urban survivor. He relays a tale of a bad beating by thugs. This happened nearly a year ago, in his girlfriend's apartment where he continues to live. The hospital stay lasted one night, the bruises for weeks, the physical pain for months, and his anguish from the memory is ongoing. He has been unable to return to any gainful employment since that terrible night. Carlos describes acute anxiety symptoms: tightness in his chest, dizziness, difficulty falling asleep, restlessness. In fact, he remains awake for a good part of the night. His demand is that his counselor be "biblical." This therapist responds with sincere reassurance. "Each clinician in this practice honors the authority of Scripture, is ready to convey a born-again testimony, and is active in a local ministry to mature in Jesus Christ."

Despite direct attempts to address his request, the session sputters and stalls. Lifestyle choices surface that are not consistent with his insistent appeal for a counselor who adheres strictly to the Bible. Carlos admits to getting high daily. If medical marijuana were legal in this state, he would not be looking for a counselor but a medical cannabis access card. He lives with his girlfriend and her daughter. He harbors anger over the suggestion made by the cops to his girlfriend that his beating may have been drug or money related. Her ultimatum: Carlos must cease getting high, never be under the influence when caring for her daughter, and begin to pull his financial weight or leave. The clinician pauses to further explore Carlos's faith perspective.

Carlos explains that his "holy-roller" grandmother made the stipulation regarding the faith perspective of his mental health professional (MHP). The counselor is to be a believer in Jesus Christ who trusts in the Scriptures and the power of the Spirit to heal. She told him exactly what to ask based on a radio program she hears every day. This condition must be fulfilled before she will fund his copay. He unabashedly discloses his assumptions: Christian counseling is cheaper, a spirit-filled therapist will be sympathetic to his plea to obtain permanent disability, and it will take a miracle for his girlfriend to allow him to continue living in her apartment! His request for a helping professional who whole-heartedly embraces Christianity is tied to pragmatic, simplistic, egocentric, and magical ideations. His own aspirations for faith development are barely a fleeting thought. Still, Carlos makes this confession with softness in his voice and eyes that grow damp with tears. His Pentecostal grandmother, with her eccentric and over-the-top religious babble, is a gracious and steadfast supporter. "My *abuelita* [grandma] gets me."

When sitting with clients such as Charles or Carlos, Christian helpers need to implement processes for conducting spiritual and religious assessment. One critical ethical imperative must be targeted: does the client earnestly desire to further Christian identity development? This question is vital in order to specify a client's faith tradition, document commitment, and discern readiness to venture into Christian-oriented counseling. We do this for reasons I will describe below. In addition, the Christian tradition encourages those within it to consider orthodoxy (right beliefs), orthopraxy (right conduct), and orthokardia (a true heart). Discernment in these areas occurs through the ministry of the Holy Spirit. Toward that end, rapid assessment instruments (RAIs) can surface meaningful perspectives.

COMPETENCY IN FAITH ASSESSMENT

There is ample evidence that clients with strongly held religious commitments obtain greater benefits in counseling (e.g., symptom reduction and spiritual growth) when treatment makes use of faith language and practices (Hook et al., 2010). Counselees with a distinct Christian heritage and a personal faith bring both resources and restrictions into helping dialogues. Once expressed, a client's certitudes and routines regarding spirituality can be successfully blended into psychotherapy. Recognizing perspectives that flow from a religious background or stance can be useful. More importantly, this is a professional ethical expectation. Before a Christian or pastoral approach can be therapeutically introduced with Charles, Carlos, or any client for that matter, we must conduct a proper spiritual/religious assessment.

Across the range of MHP ethical codes, there is a central thrust that can be summarized as keeping the client's welfare as the chief priority, demonstrating respect for diversity and self-determination, and achieving fully informed consent (Gold, 2010). Classic ethical terms continue to serve as guiding pillars: *beneficence* (clinicians work for the benefit of the client), *fidelity* (clinicians are faithful to the interest of the client), *nonmaleficence* (clinicians avoid doing harm), *autonomy* (the client determines the outcomes/orientation for care), and *justice* (approaches and procedures are fair, transparent, and nondiscriminating; Beauchamp, Walters, Kahn, & Mastroianni, 2014). We can explain our own cherished theology, theory, or technique, but what actually takes place in any given session must be guided by the client; he or she is in the primary position to set the direction, tone, and boundaries for how spiritual material is brought into a session (American Counseling Association, 2014). We must strive with great intentionality to comprehend what clients desire.

It is essential to be just, particularly when the common phrase "Christian counseling" is evoked. For MHPs, ethical guidelines and principles must consistently be applied. The faith emphasis does not bypass ethical obligations. The word *just* conveys being morally right, even-handed, and fair. It is deliberately applied here according to the charge issued in Micah 6:8:

> He has shown you, O mortal, what is good.
>   And what does the LORD require of you?
> To act justly and to love mercy
>   and to walk humbly with your God.

Clients who hold to Christian tradition may unequivocally express an open request for mental health services that contribute to faith maturation. Nevertheless, there is considerable diversity within Christianity and a wide range of idiosyncratic adaptations. We must be cautious, unassuming, and informed; we cannot impose theological views or recommendations that lie outside of a client's comfort zone or beyond the expressed request.

For clergy who are not bound as MHPs to an explicit ethical code, these remain good principles to apply in pastoral counseling. This is frequently what clients actually anticipate based upon ordinary conventions within the culture. It would be a best practice procedure not to assume that each counselee is aware that clergy are in a position of community trust. This implies that when clergy are functioning in a pastoral capacity and role, direction may come from the Word as understood in the doctrines, traditions, and values expressed in one's ordination and commission. Explaining the influence of Christianity on the counseling process and content is best accomplished within a reasonable orientation provided by the pastoral counselor. The National Association of Evangelicals adopted a recently established code of ethics for pastors in 2012 (Neff, 2012). A pastor can voluntarily adopt this. Consider how the classic principles are consistent with the broad points related to trustworthiness, fairness, and accountability (https://www.nae.net/code-of-ethics-for-pastors/). Thus, prior to referencing a particular faith tradition, making use of a general evangelical frame, or blending in Christian interventions, it is imperative to identify and confirm a client's beliefs, hopes, and intentions.

When it comes to raising theological premises, biblical principles, or spiritual outcomes in counseling praxis, there are standards within the training curriculum, prescribed role expectancies, and evidence-based techniques (i.e., ACA, 2014; Council for Accreditation of Counseling & Related Educational Programs, 2016; Pargament, 2007). There are also specified and measureable counselor competencies (e.g., culture and worldview, counselor self-awareness, human and spiritual development, communication, assessment, and diagnosis and treatment; Association for Spiritual, Ethical, and Religious Values in Counseling [ASERVIC], 2009; Dailey, Robertson, & Gill, 2015; Hathaway, 2013; Robertson, 2010; Sauerheber, Holeman, Dean, & Haynes, 2014). The assessment task is to ascertain the peculiarities of the client's faith identification and spiritual story. It is essential to specify the meaning of religious terms, surface underlying motivation, and identify preferred pathways to spiritual enrichment. For example, which (if any) of these reasonable targets fits the objective of the client: achieving spiritual health (adaptability and optimal functioning), movement toward sanctification (progression in holy living), or advancement in Christian maturation (increased conformity to the image of Jesus Christ)?

Clinicians who reference religious themes and resources will attend to the explicit statement offered under "Assessment" by the Association for Spiritual, Ethical, and Religious Values in Counseling (ASERVIC), a division of ACA (Gill, Harper, & Dailey, 2011):

Competency 10. During the intake and assessment processes, the professional counselor strives to understand a client's spiritual and/or religious perspective by gathering information from the client and/or other sources. (ASERVIC, 2009)

This prerequisite for blending faith perspectives into treatment is well established across the literature. Gill et al. (2011) list five areas of benefit derived from this best-practice strategy:

1. Worldview comprehension. A client's belief system is the starting point for any bridging of mental health interventions with spiritual resources. Therapists make every effort to apply assessment and active listening skills to grasp the complex and contextual dimensions of a client's inner, social and cultural, spiritual, or religious views.

2. Spiritual or religious issues. The helping request itself may be primarily centered on a crisis of faith. Given the presenting concern, there may be tight links to religious beliefs, spiritual domains, or faith communities. If so, will these be a resource or a hindrance to the change that the client seeks to realize?

3. Strengths, opportunities, & resources. The counselor attends to the client's inner spiritual world and structural supports for security, hope, healing, and soothing.

4. Interventions. Spiritual practices may be ready-made pathways to generate adjustment and transformation (i.e., rituals, prayer, reading, meditation, and forgiveness).

5. Self-exploration. Frequently, the need to enter counseling arises from a developmental transition or situation crisis that is stirring up an examination of identity, direction, and purpose. This is a prime opportunity to pause to reflect on one's spiritual history, values, and beliefs in relation to a sacred core.

In our pluralistic culture, MHPs who serve the general public naturally anticipate a diversity of faith perspectives. Thus, having a procedural and strategic practice to seek out ways to empathize and embrace the whole person, including religious influences, is entirely reasonable. Despite a growing curiosity regarding a client's spirituality, most MHPs have not generally adopted a systematic protocol to gather religious information (Plante, 2009). In ministry or church-affiliated clinics that are transparent about operating under a particular faith umbrella, it is easy to assume without asking that clients come in seeking services that incorporate that faith. Or, counselors may publicly explain or issue detailed documents making it evident that a particular emphasis will appear in the service provided. Delivery of information about the agency or the agent is all well and good. It does not, however, secure the right to launch into a particular style of faith-based counseling.

The goal of this chapter is to reflect on how to obtain ample personal information and faith perspectives directly from the client. Counselees do often come looking for care with the plain statement that they are seeking Christian-oriented counseling. This may be accompanied by a word of testimony. Certain clients may even name a special class of techniques associated with a well-known author or speaker. Such direct indications will open avenues for further discussion, but they do not constitute sufficient grounds to proceed with a faith-anchored approach. The cases of Charles and Carlos are reminders that it is our duty to apply competency in assessment to realize the benefits of a helping approach anchored in faith.

In Christian counseling, there is a need to discern the range, depth, and commitment level of a client's beliefs and practices. We are past the era when a generic religious label, announcement of a denominational affiliation, or even naming a home church can accurately portray a client's belief system, standards of spiritual maturity, or community-based behavioral practices. The global descriptor *Christian* requires a precise location within a doctrinal tradition and identifiable community. Not only is one's background in a denomination relevant, but rejections, migrations, and returns are often even more revealing. Is the client from a megachurch with multiple sites, technology, and a contemporary approach? Or is there a preference for liturgical worship, longstanding rituals, and time-honored language? Learning about a client's private spiritual experience, preferences, and commitments is a critical priority. Talk therapy with the stated intent of being overtly religious necessitates a thoughtful elucidation of differences in perspective between the counselor and the client. Assessment will contribute to precision and mutual understanding in this conversation.

Accordingly, a professional counselor needs to document in a patient's record that reasonable attempts were made to achieve a mutual, educated decision on treatment direction and any methods employed. To ensure ethical compliance, practitioners adopt procedures such as policy statements, patient education, and direct exploratory negotiation. When intervention options will be considered in conjunction with a joint counselor-client commitment to honor a theological worldview, it is essential for us to discern a patient's unique faith parameters, priorities, and particulars. We do well to display due diligence when becoming familiar with a patient's spiritual history and theological framework. This is how to honor worldview and reach agreement on a moral foundation. Learning the nuances of a client's faith journey and priorities prior to launching a counseling conversation where value-based decisions will be front and center is of utmost concern (Greggo, 2010).

This assessment task will be the platform to illustrate the benefit of using brief, objective assessment measures (RAIs) to unpack the dimensions of specific problems and the elements of a spiritual history (quantitative). Assessment procedures in the early phase of a helping relationship can also make use of semi-structured assessment techniques. The intent is to implement a multi-faceted assessment strategy that results in the establishment of a common understanding of the patient's presenting concerns. Beyond securing details on a particular problem, screening tools and self-report surveys can help streamline and guide the formulation of a spiritual history, surface theological commitments, and specify faith practices (Gold, 2010). The result is a robust bio-psycho-social-spiritual foundation upon which to build treatment priorities that reflect the client's spiritual journey. Combining assessment procedures and faith-based conversations joins patient and clinician in a faith-enhancing endeavor. "Do two walk together / unless they have agreed to do so?" (Amos 3:3).

Christian counselors have ample tools available to them to explore the dimension of beliefs, spiritual health, and, perhaps, the inclinations of the soul.

EXPLORING SPIRITUAL LIFE STORIES

It is important to acknowledge that there can be an expanded agenda in Christian counseling. You can set a goal within a therapeutic relationship of enhancing faith. In such scenarios the helper steps into the role of pastor, prophet, and priest. This occurs even when partnering with local clergy or spiritual leaders, or when the client brings treatment concerns before a spiritual mentor. Clinicians and clients need to be clear on where mental health and faith maturation are better separated. The spiritual formation sphere requires merging doctrinal attentiveness with the technical and interpersonal requirements. The counselor looks to discern the movement of the Spirit.

Spirituality can be described as a combination of values (passions and moral convictions), vision (mission, calling, and purpose), and lived experience (subjective and emotional states) shaped and stimulated by an awareness of a transcendent force that may or may not include a distinct deity (Aten & Leach, 2009; Wiggins, 2011). Spirituality includes themes of searching (attempts to identify, articulate, maintain, or transform) and the sacred (refers to a divine being, force, or object; Hill et al., 2000). Religion is associated with a recognizable tradition and social context with common beliefs, rituals, and experiences (Young & Cashwell, 2011). The distinguishing factor between religion and spirituality rests on institutional, structural, and creedal aspects. Religion and spirituality can often be viewed as being in opposition. Spirituality can be viewed as intrinsic while religious affiliation is seen as extrinsic. In fact, research has demonstrated that, in terms of how ordinary people practice, these can be overlapping descriptions with religion comprising a search for the sacred in association with a group of people (Hill et al., 2000). Using the terminology introduced in chapter eight on interviewing, *seeking* is more commonly associated with spirituality while *dwelling* connects to established religious routines, liturgies, and places of worship (Wuthnow, 1998). For the sake of providing categories for assessment, consider potential ways of applying these labels to those who identify with Christianity (Gold, 2010; Young & Cashwell, 2011).

- Religious and spiritual clients. These clients speak about individual spiritual life activities and experiences as well as the influence of and participation in an identifiable community, fellowship, or denomination. This is a combination of dweller and seeker.

- Spiritual but not religious. There is an overt tone of spiritual commitment without any clear association with an identifiable fellowship or faith tradition. There is more conversation about one's conversion, spiritual journey, or formation and less about a local church, organization, or membership. This fits the seeker profile.

- Religious but not spiritual. There is greater emphasis on participation in group rituals or practices with a high level of loyalty to a known community. This need not be merely extrinsic or about conforming. Rather, these clients show a preference for spiritual experience by participation with others, dwelling in a familiar sacred place or treasured denomination.

- Religiously accepting but passive. This may fit the common language of agnosticism or nominal Christianity. The client has no ardent opposition, and religion adds no value to a client's identity or well-being. The client doesn't espouse any value to religion as a whole while possibly conceding that a sense of the sacred and transcendent could be helpful for others. Going to a worship service on a special occasion with friends and family can be a pleasant, "entertaining" experience, but it contains nothing vital or existentially stirring.

- Religiously antagonistic. There is a range of clients who fit into this category. On the one end is the client who is bitter and hostile to organized religion or spiritual nonsense. This extreme is the tradition of atheism. This can also describe a client who was once involved in spiritual or religious pursuits but now is burned out and alienated.

If theological principles are going to influence treatment decisions, the client's religious-spiritual history, religious orientation, and recent spiritual habits are important. These categories lie on a continuum and can help us visualize a client's underlying religious-spiritual orientation. Information on explicit features of the client's faith narrative can be systematically gathered via background forms, interview questions, and assessment measures.

There are mnemonics to direct a basic interview sequence for gathering such information. One can pursue a tactic known as FICA—faith, importance, community, and address (Puchalski, 2006). Do you consider yourself to be a person of *faith,* and how do you describe your faith tradition? What *importance* does your faith have in your life? Are you participating in a *church* or faith *community*? How would you like me to *address* these spiritual matters in your care? An alternative acronym is FACT: What is your *faith* or belief? In what ways are you *active* in your spiritual community, and how does your faith community support you? How are you *coping* with your medical, social, and psychological situation? How does your faith enable you to cope? Based on the responses to these questions, offer a spiritually enhancing *treatment* plan. Both of these question sets have potential for standardization and ease of use.

Gill et al. (2011) offer two other sets of questions that may function as comforting or challenging probes. These can be applied creatively and have considerable potential.

- When have you had the experience of feeling the most alive?
- What vision or dreams do you have about what your legacy will be?
- What gives you strength and comfort during stressful or difficult times?
- Tell me about what awakens a sense of gratefulness and gratitude within you.
- Describe what you hold most sacred.

The next set requires a reasonable level of trust. These probes raise emotion, so counselors do need to proceed with caution because they could easily be experienced as intrusive when there is not a readiness to share. Consider the benefits of these when approaching a request related to persistent grief, pain, and struggle. In the right moment with a ready client, these could be an ideal invitation to say exactly what they came to say.

- What stirs the greatest suffering in you?
- This event (loss, trauma, or tragedy) has brought you to take a hard and profound look within. What have you discovered that is almost too disturbing to say out loud?
- Can you identify and speak about any deep regrets?

These semi-structured interview question sets can generate insight regarding a patient's values, faith, legacy, and spiritual resources.

The spiritual genogram method takes a step away from interviewing and has the potential to bring productive material to the surface (Gill et al., 2011; Gold, 2010; Willow, Tobin, & Toner, 2009). This can be a rather natural assessment exercise for clinicians who routinely do basic genograms or for those who already make use of genogram software. The basic technique is to place before the client and yourself a standard, graphic genogram that includes at least two generations. A variety of free-access genogram forms are available online. Instruct the client that this is an exercise to reflect on one's spiritual heritage. Move through each person and generation to religious influences and the legacy passed along. Take time to go back through a survey of relatives to recall who was a mentor, teacher, inspiration, or model of a saint. Who would be placed in the client's spiritual hall of fame (cf. Heb 11)? What was that family member's source of spiritual authority or inspiration? Are there Scripture passages, poems, or books that were cherished? Was there a special pilgrimage, conversion, or awakening? Is there a sadness connected to how the "sins of the father" affected future generations? Some clinicians get artistic and use colors to code religious affiliations. Pictures and symbols can add visual clarity and meaning. This activity tends to produce more of a response in those who have remembrance of one or more family members with a tremendous heart for worship or spiritual growth. While a scarcity of such memories can stir grief, this can also bring the client's spiritual longings into sharper focus.

A less graphic but parallel spiritual resource inventory can be accomplished using newsprint, a whiteboard, or whatever is handy for creating a list. Draw a simple cross to divide the surface into four quadrants. Label these as people, places, messages, and moments. In the first quadrant have the client list people who have been spiritual examples or mentors. Move on to list places where they recall acquiring lessons of faith (e.g., bedroom stories, vacation Bible school, summer camp, baptismal service, wilderness adventure, worship experience).

Next have the client list messages, books, or sermons that stand out as formational. Finally, take a slow and careful inventory of memorable moments of prayer, worship, service, or grace where the presence of the Lord was vibrant or palpable. After this inventory is conducted, take an opportunity to revisit it a week or so later to see if the dialogue brought other influential memories back to the present tense. The after-session impact of this process is often enlightening.

Unfortunately, interviewing with a set of questions, plotting genograms, or taking a spiritual inventory may require ten to thirty minutes. Certainly efficiency is not the main priority in grasping the intricacies of another's spiritual journey. Such activities can be conducted after the initial assessment phase of treatment and can serve as intervention activities since there is so much to accomplish at the outset of treatment. A practical system and standardized approach to ensure that enough detail regarding spiritual life and history are in hand as a treatment plan is established. Choice instruments and methods can reduce interview time and increase the precision of the information obtained.

As outlined in the previous chapter, an assortment of brief and credible measures exist to aid in investigating the dimensions of spiritual/religious themes and experience within a client's story (Hill & Pargament, 2008; Stanard, Sandhu, & Painter, 2000). If we believe a comprehensive assessment of a client's spiritual journey is necessary to gain the requisite understanding to make counseling formative, it makes sense to establish a standard means to accomplish this. A multimethod assessment strategy can achieve this objective through a blend of guided listening (e.g., the dimensions of faith orientation), direct interview questions (e.g., FICA or FACT), and use of select instruments (e.g., RAIs of spirituality).

APPLIED SPIRITUAL LIFE ASSESSMENT TO DETECT THEOLOGICAL ORIENTATION

For illustration, I survey a systematic procedure for detecting interest in a Christian orientation for treatment planning. This approach has been piloted by the counseling practice I am affiliated with (ccahope.com). This agency was founded forty years ago by a cross section of area evangelical ministries who continue to refer to this day. Thus, it has an ongoing partnership with local ministries as it supplies mental health, spiritual formation, and coaching services.[1] The reputation and vision of the agency shape the assessment rubric. The

---

[1]For clarification, many clients utilize medical insurance when available and applicable to cover psychotherapy (i.e., medically necessary services). Sessions supplied outside of the medical framework are either ministry supported or are an elective choice by clients.

agency does not regulate assessment choices to the extent that the general plan overrides client interest.

Given the emphasis on the spiritual-life assessment depicted in this chapter, it would be logical to assume that this is the main appraisal effort. However, this is most certainly not the case. Rather, each step is a small but important piece of the overall process for collecting and organizing client data (request, history, story, symptoms, and personality features) in the early phase of care. Spiritual assessment blends seamlessly into an overall information-gathering procedure. Results inform the immediate process and set the groundwork for what follows. Clinicians can tailor the therapeutic relationship and establish benchmarks for treatment planning.

These steps portray a prototype strategy, not a definitive script. This routine has continued to evolve over decades. Ongoing forces of change in the dominant culture, the church climate, and the healthcare environment certainly have implications for the assessment of faith perspectives. For example, there was an era in days gone by when the client was pointedly invited to share a word of personal testimony or to relay pivotal aspects of one's spiritual journey. This open-ended approach requires more contact time than can be carved out during a multifaceted mental health assessment. Further, in a contemporary climate this prompt is not likely to be understood and welcomed by a widely diverse population of clients. Thus, the illustration outlined here begins with a broad, inclusive approach to spirituality and becomes more narrowly focused on a particular faith perspective along the way. Allow this example to provoke more imagination than imitation. How might a realistic, client- and practice-friendly protocol be devised for the unique setting where you practice?

Step 1. The collection of spiritual life information begins with the demographic form. This is completed prior to clinician contact and occurs when a client makes a request for service. A question regarding the referral source will often suggest that the passage toward care began with a conversation with a pastor, fellow Christian, or former agency client. Clergy and members of the congregation refer many counselees. There is a basic item that asks clients to indicate if they have an association with a local fellowship and how frequently they attend functions such as worship or study groups. Beyond these two benign queries, the demographic form includes a dispositional, spirituality-focused RAI. This is embedded right into the personal information profile. These results automatically become part of the permanent record. Brief statements ask clients to rank faith-related interests, routines, and priorities. This seemingly innocuous insert is actually a decisive opportunity to tie the client's request for mental health services with their own preferences regarding a spiritually integrated approach. If a client does not make known an interest in cultivating their Christian identity, counseling services are likely to proceed without faith-oriented accommodations.

Several RAI instruments would be well suited for this purpose (Greggo & Lawrence, 2012), but I have chosen the Duke Religion Index (DRI). Due to the generic design of the DRI and its longevity in the field, I implemented minor wording changes for use in our application. The wide application of the DRI on national surveys lends it credibility. Its quick, five-item format makes it efficient. Its three subscale categories offer a neat bridge to key topics when taking a spiritual history. Thus, even before clients enter into conversation with an MHP for the first meeting, data are available on organized/non-organized religious activities as well as intrinsic religious motivation. Further, by responding to these items on the demographic forms, clients are prepped to pursue these matters in upcoming communication if this is of interest to them. These demographic forms are concise and request the typical information regarding primary complaint, family relationships, contact preferences, and insurance coverage.

Step 2. The next step in the assessment sequence takes place during the initial consultation (IC). This is included in the START model outlined earlier (story, therapeutic alliance, assessment, recommendations, and treatment plan). If the client includes a faith perspective or a Christian testimony in any of the opening comments, the clinician notes this on the START form. During the assessment phase of the IC, semi-structured interview questions such as the sets mentioned in this chapter build on the information supplied by the demographic form. If further clarification of faith orientation is necessary and there is available time, the clinician is encouraged to use the FICA/FACT questions at this juncture. One or two inquiries about religious upbringing and current spiritual life practices are ordinarily the norm, particularly if this does not flow from spontaneous conversation. A typical question might be to inquire about what influenced the client's decision to seek services at an agency that openly identifies itself as Christian. This inquiry would transfer easily to a church clinic or Christian university setting. The clinician documents regular spiritual enhancement activities (devotional reading, retreats, worship music, Bible study, etc.) and exceptional involvement in a local ministry. Since a computer-administered social history does follow, there is minimal discussion regarding family background during the IC session.

Step 3. The third step requires a clinical decision and only occurs in select cases. Still, at present, this is completed for the majority of incoming clients. Nonetheless, this step does represent a choice tied to the client's already announced preferences. A second RAI is selected for use. The DRI on the application form is intentionally succinct and provides a general picture. The next faith survey measure will capture different information and is matched to the client. It will be administered alongside a standard symptom checklist, an automated social history, and a global personality screen. The clinician makes the selection from available RAIs. There are four main preferences, and each contains ten items or fewer. This step takes only minutes. These are administered electronically through forms produced in house or, in rare cases, could be given in a paper/pencil format.

1. The Springfield Religiosity Scale (SRS) is an older RAI that was designed for use with aging adults. Thus, it leans on traditional theistic language and Christian categories (Koenig, Smiley, & Gonzales, 1988). It contains items to detect the respondent's doctrinal stance on the Trinity, the divinity of Jesus Christ, the authority of Scripture, and the existence of Satan. Our agency employs an abbreviated SRS version containing those doctrinal items with an additional item added regarding the Holy Spirit. This RAI option is appropriate for those who are not in the slightest degree ambiguous about desiring a Christian perspective. It gives these folks the opportunity to weigh in on matters of theological alignment that are important to them. A high score is indicative of a mainstream evangelical doctrinal position.

2. The Religious Commitment Inventory (RCI-10) is a good choice to follow the DRI because it obtains additional information on practical life commitments related to external religious behaviors. No modifications are necessary as it functions well as offered by the authors (Worthington et al., 2003).

3. The Attitudes Toward God Scale (ATGS-9) picks up on one's prevailing stance regarding enjoyment, disappointment, or alienation from God (Wood et al., 2010). This RAI is selected when clients suggest that there has been a drift away from a prior season of robust faith. This scale yields information on positive attitudes toward God as well as anger at God. Therefore, it immediately sets the groundwork for therapeutic applications and/or exploration.

4. The Santa Clara Strength of Religious Faith Questionnaire (SCSRFQ) is a short measure with casual, laid-back language. Thus, it is used with youth or young adults to secure similar material to that of the RCI-10.

Step 4. The fourth procedural step occurs as clients participate in a formal orientation to the agency, called the orientation and assessment session (O&A). This includes a brief explanation of services/fees, general and crisis policies, and psycho-educational instruction on how to get the most from our counseling services. The key component of this session is to move systematically through expectations, emergency procedures, risks, and responsibilities. The general agency informed-consent form has already been signed and returned prior to the initial consultation. However, this is an opportunity to stop, reiterate key elements, and explore any questions. At this juncture, the client is transitioning from inquirer to committed participant. The O&A is a formal exchange that highlights explicit features regarding informed consent. This ensures that a client has not blindly signed the form to get treatment underway as quickly as possible. The interaction creates a designated pause to openly consider the suitability of the match between a patient's preferences and our policies, staff, and perspective. Following the orientation, any selected formal measures will be administered.

Step 5. The fifth step is an abbreviated structured interview. It is included at the completion of the O&A session. This results in a separate clinical note for the chart that details a spiritual life assessment (SLA) summary. The clinician does a deliberate examination of the results from both RAIs as well as the spiritual life information from the demographic forms and the START interview. Following this review, the clinician may pose one or all three of the following questions.

1. Name any one item from the faith questionnaires that caused you to pause and ponder. Would you appreciate the opportunity to explore this item with your counselor?

2. Given the importance of your personal faith and walk with Christ, our counselors want to know the hopes or expectations that you have for our counseling efforts. Name one feature of your spiritual life/faith journey that you hope counseling will affect.

3. Have you given thought to what distinctively Christian counseling will look like as we work on your particular concerns? In other words, how would you like your faith incorporated in the counseling process?

In conclusion, as clinical services commence, the therapist has clarity on a client's spiritual history and commitment to a Christian worldview. When there is intentionality to arrive at a reciprocal understanding of Christian commitment, the relationship is in a place in which treatment concerns and outcomes can be plainly discussed. The use of objective assessment tools and techniques contributes to a definitive documentation trail and establishes that the client explicitly and without undue influence sought out mental health services that would contribute to a more fervent and mature faith experience. At this point clients are ready to join with counselors who can affirm theological convictions, faith practices, and growth in the Holy Spirit.

ASSESSING THEOLOGICAL ORIENTATION
FOR TREATMENT PLANNING

Establishing a Christian worldview as the basis for a helping partnership is a weighty challenge in an age of pluralism, radical individualism, and privately construed spirituality. For pastors and counseling professionals who seek to guide disciples in ways consistent with orthodox Christianity, it is essential to explore a client's spiritual history and desires prior to launching any discussion on matters where theological views will guide counseling options. Counseling tends to focus mainly on orthopraxy, but this is grounded on a mutual understanding of a client's theological worldview. The aim of spiritual life assessment in the initial phase of care is to reach the place where client and counselor together can jointly assess the most vital matter, orthokardia, the inner temper and affections of the heart (Clapper, 2013).

On matters regarding the essence of heart religion, two well-known spokespeople representing diverse theological traditions were remarkably united. Jonathan Edwards (1703–1758) was the premier early American theologian associated with the Puritan movement and Reformed theology. John Wesley (1703–1791), an Anglican evangelist and theologian, is best known for launching the Methodist movement. These great contributors to modern Christian thought converge in the way that each depicts the heart as the source of affections and the center of spiritual vitality. Consider these words from John Wesley.

> May every real Christian say, "I now am assured that these things are so; I experienced them in my own breast. What Christianity (considered as a doctrine) promised, is accomplished in my soul." And Christianity, considered as an inward principle, is the completion of all those promises. It is holiness and happiness, the image of God impressed on a created spirit, a fountain of peace, and love springing up into everlasting life. (Wesley, as cited in Clapper, 2013)

This focus on heart experience may appear to promote pure interior spirituality, but this is not so. Wesley was unyielding in his commitment to an outward Christian community and the beauty of fellowship. The evidence for this is his extraordinary effort to form bands, classes, and societies where hearts of devotion could be mutually edified. The point is that faith is more than beliefs and practices; it is ultimately a dependence on, trust in, and bond with the Lord of the universe. This is spirituality and religion.

Turning to Edwards, he views the heart as the seat of inclinations:

> From hence it clearly and certainly appears, that great part of true religion consists in the affections. For love is not only one of the affections, but it is the first and chief of the affections, and the fountain of all the affections. From love arises hatred of those things which are contrary to what we love, or which oppose and thwart us in those things that we delight in: and from the various exercises of love and hatred, according to the circumstances of the objects of these affections, as present or absent, certain or uncertain, probable or improbable, arise all those other affections of desire, hope, fear, joy, grief, gratitude, anger, [etc.]. From a vigorous, affectionate, and fervent love to God, will necessarily arise other religious affections; hence will arise an intense hatred and abhorrence of sin, fear of sin, and a dread of God's displeasure, gratitude to God for his goodness, complacence and joy in God, when God is graciously and sensibly present, and grief when he is absent, and a joyful hope when a future enjoyment of God is expected, and fervent zeal for the glory of God. And in like manner, from a fervent love to men, will arise all other virtuous affections towards men. (Edwards, 1746/1959, pp. 107-108)

For Edwards, keeping the commandments as summarized by Jesus Christ is bound in the yearnings and affections of the heart.

Why am I turning to the heart at the close of this exploration of spiritual and religious assessment? Addressing matters of the heart is where counseling with Christian conviction moves with the will and wishes of the client toward the kingdom of God. When one's affections are drawn to God, the counseling dialogue is jointly turned over to the ministry of the Holy Spirit. The counselor and client begin to inwardly pray in phrases such as these: "O Lord, we now look for what you will do throughout this change process. Quicken our hearts to sense the moving of the Holy Spirit. By our obedience, may Jesus Christ be glorified."

Mental health counseling looks to spirituality and religion as a resource to promote health and well-being. Counseling that is Christian does not ignore these good benefits but may well turn its gaze on to transcendent matters.

When counselor and client are invested in conditioning the heart toward kingdom interests, the conversation on therapeutic issues will be geared toward enriching one's spiritual walk and affections for the Lord.

For a client like Charles, the beliefs of his church related to holiness and sanctification are invaluable. Charles will not be deterred from his doctrinal viewpoint. His heart will be given exercises to meditate on the nature of God's love, beauty, patience, and kindness. It would not be conducive to right worship, service, or even the betterment of his martial covenant if Charles can only picture a punitive and vengeful God.

For Carlos, who does not express personal faith convictions, a counselor would proceed with caution by avoiding faith-based language and spiritual development interventions. It may turn out that the prayer and devotion of a genuinely invested grandmother will prove to be a resource beyond measure (Jas 5:16). If Carlos commits to getting clean of substances, he will eventually be on the lookout for a "higher" power. His counselor does not by role or necessity take on the role of evangelist. Rather, the counselor waits calmly to sense how the Holy Spirit will enter this moment of personal and relational crisis to minister to the fear as well as emptiness inside his heart.

Armed with the results of a robust spiritual assessment and having an awareness of a client's theological orientation, we can develop treatment goals that foster sanctification and Christian identity development. Planned treatment outcomes will connect to the chief clinical concerns. Each can be formulated to be consistent with biblical behavioral prescriptions. Here's a general rule of thumb: for clients who desire to grow as disciples, one of the three main treatment goals should have a uniquely targeted, faith-enhancement objective. Specific findings from these assessment procedures will sensitize clients to the need for change. This provides counselors with multiple options. Consider these sample outcome goals:

- Increase the sense of supernatural support that I experience from God the Father, Son, and Holy Spirit to deal with the difficulties in my life
- Expand and deepen my friendships with others in my faith community
- Explore ways to recognize and express gratitude for how I experience God's intervention in my life in concrete and personal ways
- Seek out, commit to, and utilize realistic accountability partnerships

It is worth noting that each of these goals builds directly on a scaled item lifted from one of the RAIs mentioned earlier. Direct assessment of spiritual commitments lays the groundwork for incorporating faith-anchored goals into the treatment plans.

In conclusion, for patients and professionals who self-identify as disciples of the Christian faith, the most important person to include in the assessment process is the Holy Spirit (2 Cor 3:17). How can the helping partnership seek to hear the Spirit? Will there be openness to attend deliberately to how the Holy Spirit would like to speak into life dilemmas? The use of contemporary assessment procedures and protocols is recommended to establish a mutually agreed upon theological platform to commence counseling. Once that common faith perspective is established, the feasibility of a biblically informed, theologically relevant, and spiritually meaningful treatment plan becomes realistic. Counselors work cooperatively within a client's faith tradition to respond to the Holy Spirit, increase adherence to the Word of God, and transform identity in Jesus Christ. Essentially, this brings counselor and client into a partnership that will attend the affections of the heart toward God, others, and self.

REFERENCES

American Counseling Association. (2014). *ACA code of ethics: As approved by the ACA Governing Council.* http://www.counseling.org/resources/aca-code-of-ethics.pdf

Association for Spiritual, Ethical, and Religious Values in Counseling. (2009). Competencies for addressing spiritual and religious issues in counseling. Retrieved April 2, 2018 from https://www.counseling.org/docs/default-source/competencies /competencies-for-addressing-spiritual-and-religious-issues-in-counseling .pdf?sfvrsn=8

Aten, J. D., & Leach, M. M. (Eds). (2009). *Spirituality and the therapeutic process: A comprehensive resource from intake to termination.* Washington, DC: American Psychological Association.

Beauchamp, T. L, Walters, L., Kahn, J. P., & Mastroianni, A. C. (2014). *Contemporary issues in bioethics* (8th ed.). Boston: Wadsworth/Cengage.

Clapper, G. S. (2013, November). *John Wesley's theology in the language of the heart: How Wesley's version of Christianity, and recent thinking about emotion, can help counselors and pastors facilitate healing and wholeness.* Paper presented at the Evangelical Theological Society (ETS) 65th Annual Meeting, Baltimore, MD.

Council for Accreditation of Counseling & Related Educational Programs. (2016). 2016 CACREP standards. Retrieved June 5, 2018 from https://www.cacrep.org /for-programs/2016-cacrep-standards/

Dailey, S. F., Robertson, L. A., & Gill, C. S. (2015). Spiritual Competency Scale: Further analysis. *Measurement and Evaluation in Counseling and Development, 48*(1), 15-29.

Edwards, J. (1746/1959). *Religious affections.* New Haven, CT: Yale University Press.

Gill, C. S., Harper, M. C., & Dailey, S. F. (2011). Assessing the spiritual and religious domain. In C. S. Cashwell & J. S. Young (Eds.), *Integrating spirituality and religion into counseling: A guide to competent practice* (2nd ed., pp. 141-162). Alexandria, VA: American Counseling Association.

Gold, J. M. (2010). *Counseling and spirituality: Integrating spiritual and clinical orientations.* Upper Saddle River, NJ: Merrill.

Greggo, S. P. (2010). Applied Christian bioethics: Counseling on the moral edge. *Journal of Psychology and Christianity, 29*(3), 252-262.

Greggo, S. P., & Lawrence, K. (2012). Clinical appraisal of spirituality: In search of rapid assessment instruments (RAIs) for Christian counseling. *Journal of Christianity and Psychology. 31*(3), 253-266.

Hathaway, W. (2013). Pathways toward graduate training in the clinical psychology of religion and spirituality: A spiritual competencies model. In K. I. Pargament (Ed.), *APA handbook of psychology, religion, and spirituality: Vol. 2. An applied psychology of religion and spirituality* (pp. 635-650). Washington, DC: American Psychological Association.

Hill, P. C. & Pargament, K. I. (2008). Advances in the conceptualization and measurement of religion and spirituality: Implications for physical and mental health research. *Psychology of Religion and Spirituality, 1,* 3-17.

Hill, P. C., Pargament, K. I., Hood, R. W., Jr., McCullough, M. E., Swyers, J. P., Larson, D. B., & Zinnbauer, B. J. (2000). Conceptualizing religion and spirituality: Points of commonality, points of departure. *Journal for the Theory of Social Behaviour, 30*(1), 51-77.

Hook, J. N., Worthington, E. L., Jr., Davis, D. E., Gartner, A. L., Jennings, J., & Hook, J. P. (2010). Empirically supported religious and spiritual therapies. *Journal of Clinical Psychology, 66*(1), 46-72.

Koenig, H. G., Smiley, M., & Gonzales, J. A. P. (1988). *Religion, health, and aging: A review and theoretical integration.* Westport, CT: Greenwood.

Neff, D. (2012). Why the NAE issued a clergy code of ethics: An interview with Luder Whitlock. *Christianity Today.* http://www.christianitytoday.com/ct/2012/juneweb -only/nae-clergy-ethics-code.html

Pargament, K. I. (2007). *Spiritually integrated psychotherapy: Understanding and addressing the sacred.* New York: Guilford Press.

Plante, T. G. (2009). *Spiritual practices in psychotherapy: Thirteen tools for enhancing psychological health.* Washington, DC: American Psychological Association.

Puchalski, C. M. (2006). *A time for listening and caring: Spirituality and the care of the chronically ill and dying.* New York: Oxford.

Robertson, L. A. (2010). The Spiritual Competency Scale. *Counseling and Values, 55*(1), 6-24.

Sauerheber, J. D., Holeman, V. T., Dean, J. B., & Haynes, J. (2014). Perceptions of counselor educators about spiritual competencies. *Journal of Psychology and Christianity, 33*(1), 70-83.

Stanard, R. P., Sandhu, D. S., & Painter, L. C. (2000). Assessment of spirituality in counseling. *Journal of Counseling & Development, 78*, 204-210.

Wiggins, M. I. (2011). Culture and worldview. In C. S. Cashwell & J. S. Young (Eds.),
Integrating spirituality and religion into counseling: A guide to competent practice
(2nd ed., pp. 43-69). Alexandria, VA: American Counseling Association.

Willow, R. A., Tobin, D. J., & Toner, S. (2009). Assessment of the use of spiritual genograms in counselor education. *Counseling and Values, 53*(3), 214-223.

Wood, B. T., Worthington, E. L., Exline, J. J., Yali, A. M., Aten, J. D., & McMinn, M. R.
(2010). Development, refinement, and psychometric properties of the attitudes
toward God scale (ATGS-9). *Psychology of Religion and Spirituality, 2*(3), 148-167.

Worthington, E. L., Jr., Wade, N. G., Hight, T. L., Ripley, J. S., McCullough, M. E., Berry,
J. W., . . .O'Connor, L. (2003). The Religious Commitment Inventory-10:
Development, refinement, and validation of a brief scale for research and counseling.
Journal of Counseling Psychology, 50(1), 84-96.

Wuthnow, R. (1998). *After heaven, spirituality in America since the 1950s*. Berkeley:
University of California Press.

Young, J. S. & Cashwell, C. S. (2011). Integrating spirituality and religion into counseling:
An introduction. In C. S. Cashwell & J. S. Young (Eds.), *Integrating spirituality and
religion into counseling: A guide to competent practice* (2nd ed., pp. 1-24). Alexandria,
VA: American Counseling Association.

CHAPTER FOURTEEN

CALIBRATING THE CONTOURS
OF PERSONALITY

Consider it pure joy, my brothers and sisters, whenever you face trials
of many kinds, because you know that the testing of your faith produces
perseverance. Let perseverance finish its work so that you may be mature
and complete, not lacking anything.

James 1:2-4

THEOLOGICAL THEME

Christian Maturity

PERSONALITY: CONTOURS AND CONFLICTS

Alex (48) and Sharon (47) are heading for that anniversary where tradition would suggest a gift of china, but given the turbulence and conflict in their lives, it might be best to opt for an item a little less fragile. They may not even reach that celebration of twenty years of Christian marriage. Perhaps residing with three teenagers makes it too tough to live with one another. Or maybe the Lord never meant for them to come together. Those are thoughts Alex and Sharon bring to their counselor.

The couple was referred to a veteran pastor for their marital counseling. His intent is to instruct the couple on how to love one another as followers of Christ and to overcome parenting conflicts surrounding their second born, a fourteen-year-old son who seems unmotivated to do just about anything. Alex is awfully tired of the constant, high-pitched tension between his wife and son. Home is not a fun place to be. Of course, when she is on a verbal roll, Sharon points out the similarities between Alex and his apathetic adolescent clone. Sharon has also accused Alex of showing interest in a recently divorced female coworker on his division's team. Alex does not attempt to deny her accusation, though there is no outward unfaithfulness, deceptiveness, or indiscretion in question. In her typical, no-nonsense style, Sharon has rushed them in to speak with their pastor before any acute damage is done.

Three sessions of pastoral wisdom, admonition, and prayer has done little to encourage or to slow down the steady progression toward an irreparable break. So their trusted pastor makes a referral to a professional counselor who picks up the effort. The counselor hears examples of the history of the marital conflict and how it has begun to manifest itself in intolerable ways over recent months. In fairness, Alex has agreed to enter counseling and expresses determination to improve communication all around. He wants peace. At the same time, Sharon is pulling out all the stops to fight for her family's well-being. This is a scenario in which it is not hard for the counselor to say with empathy that Alex and Sharon are both giving and doing the best that each knows how to do.

Despite the cooperation of the couple during the initial consultation, the counselor is aware that a mediation tactic will only contain the fire, not extinguish it. Compatibility, differing perspectives, and the drift away from oneness need to be faced. The orientation session focuses on the marriage and gathers further assessment information with computer-assisted administration. Before diving into the first treatment session, the counselor is able to sit down and examine the results of the 16PF (Personality Factors) Couple's Counseling Questionnaire, which combines the core 16PF with items regarding relational history, satisfaction, and concerns. The counselor systematically studies the graphic depiction of a visual comparison between Alex and Sharon on numerous personality factors (16pf.com). The relational satisfaction ratings point out that increasing "care and affection" is the highest priority for Sharon while for Alex "problem-solving communication" needs the most intensive remediation.

On most factors, their personalities appear closely matched. One of the scales often skipped during similar reviews actually stands out. Reasoning (factor B) displays identical scores at the low end of this bipolar scale. This couple reports a firm preference for concrete, practical, and down-to-earth ways of solving problems. The counselor no longer wonders why Pastor Dave's "customized preaching for two" hit the proverbial brick wall. Dave is known to be a highly credible pastoral counselor who is an extreme bibliophile. He is prone to push "good reads" from his list of favorites. This pastor also has a tendency to relay lengthy anecdotal stories, unfortunately without always including a succinct delivery of the bottom line, moral, or maxim. This couple is likely to prefer a helper who can focus on practical strategies that have an immediate, recognizable, and direct application.

There are four personality factors where Alex and Sharon display meaningful differences. These are telling, and stir the counselor's thoughts about treatment. Sharon spikes high on being forceful and assertive (Dominance, Factor E) whereas Alex moves modestly toward cooperation while avoiding conflict. Sharon tends to be naively straightforward and trusting. This makes her disappointment all the more intense when those close to her (i.e., her husband and son) do not live up to their word on house rules. Alex prefers to keep matters private and does not enjoy putting the family laundry out for public display (Privateness, Factor N). This might explain his relief and willingness to accept the professional counseling over pastoral intervention. Alex identifies Pastor Dave as a friend and is embarrassed about all the dirt that Sharon discloses so bluntly and harshly. Alex shuts down before any admonishment can be delivered.

The sharpest personality-factor divide mirrors the main complaint. Alex has an extreme score in the low direction that points toward flexibility, a tolerance for disorder, and little interest in rules (Perfectionism, Q3). On the very same factor, Sharon is high. She strives for organization and applies self-discipline to the point of being a perfectionist—and she's proud of it. No wonder Alex tends to shy away from Sharon's intensity in regard to raising their son and executing the directives of a Christian home. He has no longing to be in a household with the sterility of a hospital, particularly when he's the prime patient. In fact, he'd rather be elsewhere.

The counselor readily recognizes how this information regarding explicit features of Alex's and Sharon's personality profiles will be useful as counseling gets underway. How long would it take via dialogue alone to obtain a description of these engrained patterns as crisply? The counselor develops an upfront plan for an early clinical session that will include frank discussion regarding several of these trends with Alex and Sharon. This should encourage them to ponder what to expect of one another and to sharpen the outcome expectations for treatment. For this couple in particular, the opportunity to recognize their struggle in the graphic comparison of personality factors should be a plus. Having a visual picture of "fit" on one succinct report gives them concrete and neutral terminology to discuss what keeps them stuck and feeling worlds apart. In fact, this particular couple's version of a 16PF report is designed exactly for this purpose.

Contemporary marital counseling often looks for ways to move rapidly toward a discrete focus. For instance, it can be helpful to apply the brief therapy strategy of naming, visualizing, unpacking, and objectively tackling the chief presenting complaint. There is merit in taking a solution orientation on the more serious issues and drilling down on these problems as if each were an alien invader or insipient disease. On the downside, the rush to locate a unifying focal point can inadvertently be a distraction. The "problem" becomes the enemy to defeat. Counselors must learn to help their clients recognize that reality is not always simple and is often best depicted under the general heading of interactive effects. The "problem" does not enter counseling; people do. Thus, while the emphasis of the therapeutic conversation centers on a struggle that needs to be resolved or diminished, the clinical target for change is typically tagged at the intersection of one's preferences and the challenging scenario. It may be that the enemy's secret weapon is actually staring at us from the other side of the mirror (Jas 1:22-23).

Clients display symptoms and strains in response to stressors. The counselor develops a case conceptualization that places presenting concerns into one of three overlapping categories: (1) a mismatch between personality traits and the demands of the present circumstances, (2) a conflict between one's personality and others, and (3) personality features exhibited in excess as an automatic reaction to perturbation (i.e., doing more of what one does best in response to an uncomfortable disturbance in the status quo; Karson, Karson, & O'Dell, 1997). The target for change lies at the point where the counselee's personality is being rubbed raw against a life scenario, a social demand, or a sense of self out of order. Tactics for growth involve narrowing the distance between the person and the problem. More often than not, these are inseparable. Counseling is an effort to increase a client's skill, ability, and relational fluidity to better deal with these incongruities. This facilitates adjustment and adaptation to meet the dysregulation challenge. In terms of how the initial assessment uncovers these targets, clues emerge in response to queries such as, "What has changed that made you decide that this is the opportune time for counseling?" For example, Alex and Sharon have long been at odds over how to handle their son. The strain certainly has been getting worse. Still, it's the hint, however remote, that Alex may be wavering in his loyalty to the marriage, sending shock waves through the security of nearly twenty years of responsible coping with unique personality styles.

Personality can be described as distinctive individual tendencies (i.e., traits, preferences, dispositions, etc.) on display in patterns of thinking, feeling, behaving, and relating with others. When a pattern is predictable, it becomes associated with a personality factor. This general explanation blends together the more sophisticated theories of underlying dispositional traits (e.g., biological nature as genetically or physiologically hard-wired) and characteristic adaptations (e.g., nurtured tendencies via culture, family, and intimate attachments; Bayne, 2013; McAdams & Pals, 2006). Psychopathology—behavioral dysfunction, social disorganization, or the experience of mental health symptoms— can be pragmatically described as personality under stress (i.e., state, disorder, mental illness). For counselors who strive to note strengths over failures or brokenness, a reasonable working assumption is that each unique mix of personality factors comes with its advantages and limitations. Concerns arise, complaints surface, and symptoms emerge when one's ordinary stylistic presentation is disrupted to the extent that it is no longer adaptive to meet current demands or inner ideals (Choca, 2004).

From the vantage point of cultivating spiritual growth, those who counsel within a Christian framework have interests beyond self-discovery or facilitating more adaptive functioning. Our interest is to hear and collaborate with the Holy Spirit as he calls those who follow after God's own heart to become more closely fitted to the image of Jesus Christ. Alex and Sharon will seek ways to reduce the intensity and frequency of conflict, parent more proficiently with a united front, and preserve their marriage by respecting one another. As such goals come into sharper focus, each will face profound choices about how much they love the Lord and who they are ready to become to honor that devotion.

For convenience and accuracy, I will employ a useful division between personality and character. This difference is typically blurry within present-day language. These two words commonly run together and are virtually interchangeable. Dictionaries actually list them as synonymous, except in the case that *character* is used to refer to an odd or unusual aspect of personality. The moral and values dimension of these terms has faded. For the sake of this conversation, I am using the terms as follows. *Personality* references our basic, default, or automatic patterns of thinking, feeling, relating, and doing. *Character* speaks to how we willfully, intentionally, and sacrificially express or alter these patterns to fulfill a higher purpose and realize virtue. Using terminology from a comprehensive personality theory, one is not bound to "dispositional traits" or "characteristic adaptations." Self-identity is expressed in an enduring self-narrative (i.e., self-awareness, self-concept, self-theory) that guides choices for living so that there is coherence between our internal, integrative life narrative and how personality is displayed (Mayer, 2005; McAdams, 2015; McAdams & Pals, 2006).

Thus, for a Christian, personality assessment yields ready access to useful descriptions and natural (i.e., default) preferences. A personality profile is like having a self-portrait of these patterns. It opens a panoramic view that allows for reflection and deliberation. A focus on character—living as the person we seek to be—is the point at which a counseling partnership turns to Scripture for direction. Our temperament may pull us toward particular emotional expressions, behavioral activities, or interpersonal rituals. Our faith convinces us that our will is now surrendered to the calling of a loving Creator. One who has been raised with Christ walks in new ways (Col 3:7). The Holy Spirit is operating to redeem and reshape how our embodied self commonly displays integrity of heart. There is intentionality to redirect the limits and boundaries of our personality as we interact with others. Obedience to the Great Commandment means adopting the priority to act in love. This takes precedence over doing what habit would ordinarily dictate (Mt 22:37-40). Counselors calibrate the normal contours of personality to consider how unique urges, when yielded to the Holy Spirit, can produce spiritual fruit (Gal 5:16-23; Col 3:12).

A personality profile is a rough sketch of the form that one's behavioral and attitudinal patterns tend to take. Assessment produces an outline to observe how we do or do not fit with others. The term *contour* is derived from the turning and cutting of an object by the use of a lathe, similar to the carpentry tool that places curves and grooves into wood as it is spun. Counseling as artisanship makes use of any abrasive and painful conflicts that are interfering with one's means of self-expression. Environmental challenges, the pace of life, and oppressive forces may have a client spinning as if on a lathe. Role demands from family or career may exert pressure to the point that the individual needs to adjust his or her expression of emotions and behavioral preferences. This is an opportunity to shape the contours of personality into character.

I don't offer this perspective as a trite platitude tossed glibly into therapeutic conversation. Rather, this is a profound recognition of a long-term theological conviction (e.g., eschatological; Phil 1:6, 9-11). Using biblical language, trials or temptations faced squarely and boldly can bring about maturation through perseverance so that the marvelous fruit of the Spirit is revealed (Jas 1:1-3). It is no surprise that while the book of James leads off with its declaration on the process of maturation, it moves on to explore great themes such as humility (Jas 1:19-21), self-reflection (Jas 1:23-25), justice (Jas 2), taming the tongue

(Jas 3), expectations and submission (Jas 4), patience in affliction (Jas 5:1-12), and personal renewal or healing within Christian community (Jas 5:13-20). Perseverance and maturation in these areas may be operating well below the surface; the effects can be seen in nearly every counseling session.

PERSONALITY SCREENING: THE "NEW" ORDINARY

The application of personality instruments for treatment planning is an under-utilized opportunity. The use of such measures by counselors is not only per-missible; it can be viewed as a critical aspect of the assessment phase (American Counseling Association [ACA], 2014, sec. E introduction, para. E.1.a; Cashel, 2016). Counselors are acquainted with suitable measures (e.g., MBTI, MMPI; 16PF; MCMI-IV, etc.; Peterson, Lomas, Neukrug, & Bonner, 2014), but despite familiarity, direct implementation by nonpsychologist mental health professionals (MHPs) tends to be soft. Broad-based personality appraisal is not a common clinical technique. In a recent investigation into the hands-on use of commercial standardized assessments by counselors, average use ratings fell between rare and never. This is based upon rating a list of ninety-eight assessment instruments of which fourteen were personality and twenty-two clinical/behavioral. In addition, whereas the Myers-Briggs Type Indicator (MBTI) and the Minnesota Multiphasic Personality Inventory (MMPI) were ranked as five and six in terms of familiarity by mental health counselors, other such prominent measures were well down the list. School and career coun-selors may review assessment findings with more regularity.

Counselor deficiency in the regular handling of personality measures only feeds the ongoing controversy regarding professional parameters in terms of access and privilege to use all levels of psychological instruments (Dattilio, Tresco, & Siegel, 2007). These usage ratios may explain why 67% of states have restrictions on the administration of psychological testing by nonpsychologists. It may well be that a lack of expertise, confidence, and motivation inhibits actual use of the very tools that counselors would find most advantageous. There is a reasonable way to confront this professional dilemma and dispute over "tool" turf.

Achieving proficiency and competence in this area is not all that difficult. Perhaps on this particular assessment frontier, those in Christian service are in a prime position to lead the way. Linking personality trends with reflection on ways to honor God as a means of spiritual formation is not a huge conceptual leap. When it comes to capable use of the best instruments for a task, there is no better method to advance craftsmanship than routine practice. This is particularly the case when it comes to recognizing correlations between a configuration on a personality profile and the dynamics contributing to a clinical concern. Thus, what follows is an attempt to establish a compelling rationale for counselors to move beyond familiarity toward proficiency in the use of select personality measures. Field conditions are ripe to make the application of personality assessment the new ordinary during the initial phase of counseling.

Earlier, I recommended employing rapid assessment instruments (RAIs) as a technique to heighten awareness of symptom severity and increase insight into factors that contribute to the presenting concern. Taking that first step with RAI implementation will raise the bar on assessment as a method to identify specific client concerns and track treatment progress. The next initiative is to turn around the underutilization of formal personality measures in therapeutic counseling. MHPs would do well to adopt personality screening early in the course of care. Obtaining a picture of personality contours as displayed in persistent patterns of thinking, feeling, and behaving is in the best interest of clients (Butcher, Bubany, & Mason, 2013; Butcher & Perry, 2008).

Personality appraisal conducted with a strategic objective facilitates alliance building, narrows the range of attainable outcomes, and contributes to technique customization. Notice that this assertion is not bound to a purely diagnostic procedure (e.g., assess to improve diagnostic precision). This is not a method to chase after personality disorders or to increase diagnostic complexity. Rather, personality assessment is a built-in method to inform the interpersonal process of trust building. Knowing a client well focuses the delivery of care and encourages client-fitted interventions. We also acquire insights that aid us in case conceptualization. However, the priority when using personality assessment within an intake battery is to ignite mutual conversation regarding intra- and interpersonal patterns. This serves the purposes of client education and empowerment (Berman & Song, 2013).

Early recognition of a client's ingrained personality tendencies can deepen the counselor's perception of the client. The intensity of therapeutic dialogue moves quickly to an advanced level. Increased self-awareness can translate into greater client satisfaction. It is generally agreed that those who seek out professional services on their own for psychological, career, or interpersonal problems are accessible and highly motivated to discover more about themselves (Butcher & Perry, 2008). This opens the door to build a mutual partnership, guide treatment toward character development, and address matters of self-worth.

Several decades ago, a procedure termed "client-centered assessment" was developed similar to what I'm advocating here (Costa & McCrae, 2008). Open discussion of personality results with clients can be compared to therapeutic assessment, in which the consultation for psychological testing *is* the intervention, for the purpose of raising self-awareness (Hilsenroth, Peters, & Ackerman, 2004; de Saeger et al., 2014). The emphasis can be on strengths without ignoring aspects of self that are magnifying tensions.

The strategic use of a global self-report measure at the outset of care has multiple benefits. Consider these advantages:

1. An objective personality screen can reduce distortions arising from a compressed subjective interview. Or it may provide confirmation of a counselor's subjective experience of the client.

2. The self-report format offers an alternative method of self-disclosure. This allows clients a means to communicate personal tendencies and ideals that might not at first glance be recognized as relevant to the counseling request.

3. Awareness of personality attributes can improve the counselor's grasp of distinct client qualities and provide terms to bring these out in immediate feedback.

4. Early awareness of the counselee's preferred mode of thinking, feeling, and behaving assists in tailoring one's interpersonal approach, thereby improving the working alliance.

5. Helping strategies are not one size fits all. Early consideration of personality characteristics informs decisions surrounding goal setting and treatment planning (Edwards, Holleran, & Beutler, 2016).

6. Having a framework and an explicit language to describe enduring traits can contribute to the dyad's deliberation on how the Holy Spirit may be cultivating character and fostering maturity by re-creating habits in the form of virtues.

Investigating personality gives the counseling relationship an indispensable advantage. Admittedly, this approach can be painted as controversial. Several legitimate concerns have inhibited the expansion of this practice and may explain why it is not more widespread. We will consider a few of these risks here.

Cost effectiveness. In the not too distant past in psychotherapy, it was common for a comprehensive psychological evaluation to be completed at the outset. The combination of a broad cognitive-ability measure with a detailed exploration of personality was viewed as a way to determine amenability to treatment and to uncover underlying conflicts within the personality structure (e.g., id, ego, and superego). This full evaluation was accomplished through a formal investigation using a blend of interviewing, projective testing, and standardized measures. Afterward, a full-scale report was generated, and that material became the foundation for the lengthy process of personality reconstruction via nondirective psychotherapy. This admittedly was a cumbersome and costly procedure that might require five or ten—or more—hours of specialized psychological expertise.

The stance that only those clients with average or above intellectual capacity are capable of benefiting from psychotherapy has disappeared. Assumptions regarding the unconscious aspect of personality persist but are no longer as prominent. Thus, extensive assessment was rapidly eliminated from the therapeutic intake during the managed-care revolution. This type of intensive evaluation required advance authorization for reimbursement. Social service agencies, hospitals, educational institutions, and larger clinics do continue to refer clients for full psychological evaluations as a gateway procedure to obtain or define service. The rationale for this type of undertaking can be made for specific referral questions or in settings where such a global evaluation contributes to an adjudication regarding the direction of care. It is also worth noting that evaluation referrals on the contemporary scene are most likely to focus on essentials regarding neurological functioning (e.g., brain processes and disabilities) over interior personality structure (e.g., unconscious processes and wayward defense mechanisms).

The recommendation I'm making here is nothing close to the revitalization of those extensive and expensive full-blown evaluations. Rather, I'm advocating the application of streamlined, cost-effective, self-report tools. Given the ease of administration, scoring, and reporting results thanks to digital technology, numerous self-report personality measures have become accessible, user friendly, and efficient. This may require less than an hour of professional time for interpretation and documentation. A general rule of thumb when it comes to including personality screening as an element of treatment planning is that it is both beneficial and cost effective to include a personality measure when counseling is likely to run beyond three to five sessions.

Treatment-targeted assessment. When a personality measure is included prior to beginning treatment, I refer to that as a personality screening, not as a full-blown psychological evaluation. This distinction is not trivial, nor a mere matter of terminology. This is also not an attempt to sidestep any ethical principles pertaining to the limits of professional territory. On the contrary, this proposal embraces a potential assessment division between psychologists and other MHPs. This is not so much about access to instruments as it is about the purpose for which these measures are applied. Such a role distinction makes absolute sense given the number of assessment courses and experiences built into the typical training sequence for each mental health profession.

My proposal joins the initial consultation (a semi-structured interview) with an additional session that gathers data (orientation and assessment [O&A]). This will include appropriate RAIs to explore symptoms and spirituality. It may also include an automated or paper-and-pencil social history. The assessment phase is rounded off with a self-report measure that produces a robust personality profile. This constitutes a therapeutically targeted, client-oriented mental health appraisal. The client commissions the request and consents to these steps with the sole objective of obtaining relief and achieving a breakthrough in personal/spiritual growth. The purpose of assessment is to give therapy an optimal, preliminary push that improves the quality of care and shortens its duration. Its exclusive aim is to prepare a mutually informed, realistic plan to launch treatment and realize change. For the sake of contrast, this is not a multimeasure, multisource, comprehensive psychological evaluation to generate an objective report for the clinician, the clinical record, or any outside party.

The use of a targeted personality screen is not solely to produce a diagnostic formulation. Such a narrow aim at diagnosis could result in premature closure on a limiting clinical perspective. This can unwittingly contribute to the unfortunate use of destructive adjectives outside of formal clinical formulations (e.g., *borderline, narcissistic, socially inhibited, social butterfly, impulsive*). This risk can be mitigated with supervision and clinical experience. The purpose of personality assessment is not to locate a determinative cause within the individual seeking help. Rather, it is a means to establish working hypotheses on what will be immediately and ultimately helpful. These formulations are gleaned from instruments that identify patterns and are woven together with the client's own language and empathy and a holistic therapeutic lens on the part of the clinician. Personality information obtained in this way contributes to a creative, collaborative, and hopeful case conceptualization. Clinicians who include this step need to make an explicit plan to use any finding as part of the feedback loop to the client. Speak directly to your clients using words that make sense to them. In fact, the most useful comments are ones that integrate pieces of the client's story with a fair appraisal of strengths and blind spots. This will inevitably point to where exploration should proceed and is a safeguard to ensure openness to new perspectives.

Informed consent for assessment. These outlined assessment procedures should not be expanded to facilitate the accomplishment of any separate evaluative purpose. Simply put, this procedure is exclusively for the client's therapeutic gain during a period of personal upheaval. During the discussion on informed consent, the nature and purpose of the screening should be explained (ACA, 2014, paras. E.3.a-b). Clients are best served when they receive feedback that is practical and uses terminology and illustrations they understand.

It is conceivable that at a later juncture in therapy or perhaps after discharge a client may request a written mental health report. This could be for a purpose other than the development of a treatment plan, such as an employment/ educational evaluation or for a forensic matter (e.g., court mandate or custody hearing). Should the counselor be prepared and have the experience to switch roles from therapist to evaluator, I believe, based on the ethical principles of informed consent, that new assessment data should be collected. This is not an attempt to contest or undermine the stability of traits. Rather, it an outward procedural recognition that clients come to treatment to address discomfort stemming from a personality in distress.

The temptation can be great to compromise and use the screening information conducted for therapeutic purposes for other purposes. There is the practical desire to save time and cost, and to remove the uncertainty of working with another professional. The client may naively consent or make this request without realizing the inherent contradictions. Remember, the counselor retains the professional awareness that a therapeutic appraisal is built on the cooperative and confidential agreement between therapist and client. The clinician must align completely with the client and not do anything to blur this relationship or put that therapeutic trust at risk by later allowing assessment information to be applied for any other purpose.

Consider this scenario. A woman (37), married for seven years, seeks treatment to relieve acute depression in compliance with a referral from her primary-care specialist. Following hard-won gains, she invites her husband to join her for conjoint therapy to address relevant marriage issues. As treatment reaches a productive conclusion, the couple determines that they will pursue the route of adoption to expand their family. The agency they choose requires a complete psychological evaluation. Funds are tight. The client inquires if the counselor can write a report and release her treatment records to the agency. This may indeed be the client's prerogative. Still, her counselor is always looking out for the client's best interest (ACA, 2014, paras. B.6.g, B.7.b, E.3.b). The counselor has numerous options and must keep a clear view of what is at stake for the client. He might decide to prepare a summary recommendation or a brief letter reviewing the therapeutic outcomes. However, an outright forwarding of the entire clinical record that could conceivably contain a computer-generated personality or symptom report or other mental health screening may or may not be in the client's best interest. A counselor can cooperate with the request and support the client without forwarding every single item in the clinical file. After all, the initial data contained in the file was collected at the point in time when this client's depression was raging at its worst. The client was attentive to her physician and voluntarily sought counseling. The evaluation procedure contributed to the treatment plan that now has her feeling optimistic about the future and the dream of a family. This all served the very resolution that the client hoped for. The assessment conducted at the outset of care did not focus in any way on the client's amenability to parent or readiness to adopt.

Forensic or formal psychological evaluations for outside parties are best contracted separately. Any such examination to explore global psychological functioning would optimally be completed by MHPs with special training in forensic-style reporting (psychologists), systematic family histories (social workers), or diagnostic psychiatric evaluations (psychiatrists or psychiatric nurse practitioners). Counselors should be cautious and wise about conflating the role of therapist/advocate with that of objective consultant or evaluator. Those with sufficient supervision and experience may develop the expertise to conduct this type of assessment and generate reports. MHPs who major in offering therapy on a day-to-day basis should consider assessment, treatment planning, and implementation of counseling to be a specialty in itself.

Finally, it would not be in the client's best interest to report symptom data and personality leanings collected during a difficult season of life for any purpose other than that which was explained to the client when the assessment was conducted. The initial consultation and mental health screening provide counselors and clients an organized process to secure accurate information to form and achieve therapeutic goals.

The strong rationale for the regular use of personality assessment actually lies beyond its immediate clinical benefit. A joint awareness of personality traits, patterns, and trends can favorably impact coaching regarding discipleship and Christian maturation.

SELECTING AND APPLYING GLOBAL PERSONALITY INSTRUMENTS

The central thrust of this chapter is to encourage the inclusion of choice personality measures specifically for treatment-plan development. Novice clinicians and supervisors will do well to set out a professional development plan that fosters clinical acuity in one, two, or several measures such as these. Develop this practice habit early. Be a pioneer. Explore how clients respond as the insights gained are brought to bear on the areas where they are seeking to grow. Studying how availability of personality information can improve the attainment of outcomes and client satisfaction would be an ideal area for advanced research. At the clinical level, it is important to consider the utility for clients and the setting. Counselors can adopt a comprehensive evaluation process that includes steps such as these:

1. Only bring a psychological instrument into contact with clients after completing a full psychometric review.

2. Evaluate the norming population to ensure that your clients with diverse cultural backgrounds will be fairly represented and gain relevant insights.

3. Counselors with clients looking to explore change from within a Christian worldview need to progressively address redemptive validity in relation to a measure's content, constructs, and criterion. The Clinical Assessment Instrument Christian Evaluation Form (CAICEF) provided earlier is intended as a guide so that clinicians can complete this necessary review.

4. Read reviews in the Mental Measurement Yearbook Database. Access is available through most university or hospital libraries or directly for a fee (buros.org/mental-measurements-yearbook).

5. Consider how each measure is featured within a familiar counseling assessment text (e.g., Erford, 2013; Hays, 2017; Whiston, 2017).

6. Consult with other MHPs or supervisors who know the preferred measures. It is ideal to confer with a clinician who foresees the value for client self-understanding.

7. Following these preparations, make an instrument determination and secure the necessary materials for administration, scoring, and interpretation.

8. Digest the manual.

9. Pilot the instrument during the initial phase of assessment with a limited pool of clients. Use peer supervision or professional consultation to

improve skill in interpretation and to make ties to treatment plan development.

10. Create a feedback loop. Share insights gained, and blend these into clinical conversations. A formal summary early on is beneficial. Yet spontaneous use of the information on a regular basis tends to be an effective way of showing clients how to be more self-aware as they make deliberate use of personality trends.

11. Record a brief entry in the clinical record for documentation. This should capture your interpretation of the results and how these may be useful in treatment.

12. Revisit these assessment findings as counseling care comes to a close. Look for ways that the client can make use of strengths or wisely adjust by acquiring supports to account for areas of challenge. Be explicit about how the Holy Spirit is at work in sanctification and formation.

This personality screening assessment is conducted for clients and treatment planning. No formal report is prepared for external use. Therefore, it is necessary to design a routine method to document findings in a standard client file. A good practice is to adopt a template to record clinical insights (see fig. 14.1). Many clinicians will decide to place a graphic profile or table of the results in the record. This should be signed and dated to signify clinician review. Even if this type of information is formally incorporated into the clinical documentation, it is most helpful to have a brief narrative regarding what clinical benefit was derived. Writing this as a formal entry is not only expected; it is realistic preparation to later blend these ideas into counseling communication. This provides summary material for reference throughout the client's care. If a computer-generated report narrative is produced, the clinician's entry filters and determines what is actually transposed into the enduring clinical record. Computer-generated narrative reports are provided purely as a consulting resource to clinicians. Boilerplate reports, no matter how insightful, are best left out of clinical documentation without endorsement and careful review by the clinician. Phrases and observations can be made part of the clinician's notes. The critical notion is that assessment results and interpretations enter treatment records exclusively through the oversight and deliberate decision of a clinician. The use of a template such as the one provided gives clinicians a viable routine to take responsibility for results and record clinical impressions. A good tip is to review these findings again during the closing phase of treatment. Client strengths and preferences can be incorporated into the aftercare plan, and there can be an open celebration of gains made along the way.

Clinician Review of Personality Screening Results

Date of Review: _____/_____/_____   Screening Tool: _____

Date of Administration: _____/_____/_____

Clinician/Staff Overseeing Administration: _____

Behavioral Observations/Client Comments

Review of Validity Indicators

Noteworthy State (Recent), Symptoms, and/or Mental Health Concerns

Outstanding Trait Features (Long-Term), Strengths, Preferences, and Vulnerabilities

Impressions on potential links between presenting concerns and assessment findings:

Summary/Conclusion

Clinician Signature: _____ Date: _____/_____/_____

Clinician Credentials: _____

Figure 14.1. Clinical record personality assessment documentation template. (Greggo, Stephen P. [2019]. *Assessment for Counseling in Christian Perspective*. Downers Grove, IL: InterVarsity Press.)

SAMPLE PERSONALITY INSTRUMENTS: REDEMPTIVE VALIDITY

As this chapter concludes, four measures will serve as examples. Certainly there are additional comparable measures that may be an ideal fit for population service. Counselors are challenged to develop competency in using one, two, or perhaps several of these. The NEO Personality Inventory-3 (NEO-PI-3) and the Sixteen Personality Factors Questionnaire (16PF) are long-established, highly practical instruments for building a profile of personality strengths and tendencies in comparison to the general (normal) population. In contrast, the Millon Clinical Multiaxial Inventory (MCMI-IV) and the Minnesota Multiphasic Personality Inventory-2 Restructured Form (MMPI-2-RF) are designed for use specifically with those seeking services within mental health settings where diagnosable concerns are quite likely to be present. All four of these self-report measures have earned an overall reputation for psychometric validity and clinical utility, and each has longevity of implementation in its favor.

This selection represents a reasonable short list of recommendations for further investigation. There is considerable published information and critique available on each of these tools. Major assessment textbooks offer complete summaries. Sample reports of common reporting options from computer applications are available for downloading on publisher websites. Thus, the comments here are limited to clinical utility and redemptive validity.

One obvious omission from this short list is the noteworthy Myers-Briggs Type Indicator (MBTI; www.myersbriggs.org). The MBTI is not only utilized in counseling; it is a frequent choice for consulting situations to promote self versus other awareness. Based on Jung's personality concepts, it has been in service for nearly a hundred years and has earned its place in the assessment toolbox. One reason for its popularity is also the basis for the rationale to exclude it from these selections. The MBTI generates no good, bad, or unpopular score combinations. This remarkable asset makes it conducive for group work within teams where interpersonal safety is essential. In counseling, where the aim is to highlight how the contours of one's personality are rubbing up against others, this rare feature becomes a liability. The MBTI may promote self-insight and group consideration of the distinctive contribution of its members. It is relatively low in clinical utility since it does not by its own design highlight aspects of personality that may have an uncomfortable bite.

NEO Personality Inventory-3 (NEO-PI-3). This is one of several in a family of measures established to assess the five-factor model (FFM; Costa & McCrae,

2008; McCrae & Costa, 2010). From face validity to interpretation, this is a straightforward, intuitive, and transparent tool. Each of the five scales has forty-eight items that yield six facet subscales for each of the Big Five domains (see table 14.1). The agree/disagree Likert scale format is readily understood by clients, and they are generally able to complete this measure in less than thirty minutes. The NEO-PI-3 measure relies heavily on the cooperation of the client since its validity scale is minimal. The transparent and sensible items are an asset.

Table 14.1. Domain and facet scales for the NEO-PI-3

DOMAINS	Neuroticism	Extroversion	Openness to Experience	Agreeableness	Conscientiousness
FACETS	Anxiety	Warmth	Fantasy	Trust	Competence
	Angry Hostility	Gregariousness	Aesthetics	Straightforwardness	Order
	Depression	Assertiveness	Feelings	Altruism	Dutifulness
	Self-Consciousness	Activity	Actions	Compliance	Achievement Striving
	Impulsiveness	Excitement-Seeking	Ideas	Modesty	Self-Discipline
	Vulnerability	Positive Emotions	Values	Tender-Mindedness	Deliberation

The appeal of the NEO-PI-3 in terms of redemptive validity can be summarized in three ways. First, based on extensive research around the globe, it is fair to list the FFM as a gold standard for a broad and practical assessment of normal adult personality (McCrae & Allik, 2002). This measure is built on personality descriptions in current use within everyday language. It lends itself to an emic (inductive/insider) over etic (deductive/outsider) approach to investigate personality. In other words, instead of simply translating this measure into other languages, it is readily geared toward building the measure anew from the ground up using the primary language of the culture. Ministry today is multicultural. It is useful to develop proficiency with a measure that places its assumptions under the scrutiny of cross-cultural investigation. Second, its linguistic foundation gives this measure construct validity that readily transfers into Christian applications. As people of the Book, we are accustomed to focusing on speech, narrative, and communication in words and deeds. The lexical approach is grounded in how ordinary people use language to make sense of each other. This theory of personality description stimulates the least controversy in terms of worldview. Finally, this model includes neuroticism (N; i.e., high scores indicate emotional vulnerability or turbulence while low scores signal self-confidence and ego stability). For the believer, both sides of this factor are reminders of the presence of sin. There is considerable evidence that those who score high on N tend to be more susceptible to mental health disturbances. On the surface, being free of neurotic conflicts (low N) certainly has appeal, for this does contribute to overall health. But this high score can manifest itself as self-sufficiency or insensitivity to the convicting work of the Holy Spirit. The neuroticism factor is thus consistent with a view that while human brokenness and inner conflicts are not God's intent or our ideal, we are disposed to struggle when relating to others, God, self, and the world.

The measure lends itself well to training MHPs. Its ordinary language and common-sense notions make the transition from measure interpretation to self-reflective conversations relatively smooth. The inclusion of the neuroticism scale with polarities that most find less attractive keeps discussion real and requires communicating with empathy. However, when considering the gradients of FFM (emotional vulnerability to stability), it does not take long to turn attention from what flows from the inside to the outside, and this is where character can be demonstrated. There are novel and deliberate ways to express emotions and preferences.

The NEO-PI-3 is highly conducive to career counseling, team building, and other interpersonal applications. Thus, developing proficiency with this measure will yield a versatile counseling and consulting skill. It lends itself to consultations that place emphasis on strengths. There is a downside to the NEO-PI-3 in clinical settings. As a measure dedicated to uncover long-term traits, it does not gather information about current states that may be of diagnostic interest. However, given the emphasis within the counseling profession on doing preventative work with a normal adult population, this limitation is not problematic in many settings. A literature search of research publications would suggest that the NEO is now getting more extensive attention globally.

Sixteen Personality Factors (16PF) Questionnaire. This measure has been making a major contribution to personality assessment for over seven decades (Cattell & Mead, 2008). The current adult edition has 185 items in the core 16PF Questionnaire, and most clients complete these in thirty-five to forty-five minutes. Built on empirical evidence from its inception, the 16PF demonstrates the benefits of factor analysis in test development. The 16PF is also tied to language samples that name personality traits. Its hallmark distinction is the structure that reports sixteen personality factors in a hierarchical order. In this feature, the 16PF makes every attempt to portray clearly its underlying research evidence. Not all factors influence personality in equal amounts. In keeping the emphasis on sixteen factors, each with high and low dimensions, there is an outstanding opportunity to consider how these factors converge to form the nuances that color one's personality (warmth, reasoning, emotional stability, dominance, liveliness, rule-consciousness, social boldness, sensitivity, vigilance, abstractedness, privateness, apprehensiveness, openness to change, self-reliance, perfectionism, and tension). As an additional feature, the 16PF produces scores on its own version of the five factors (extroversion/introversion, low anxiety/high anxiety, tough-mindedness/receptivity, independence/accommodation, self-control/lack of restraint). These combination factors are established by combining relevant scores from its sixteen scales.

The learning curve for both clinicians and clients on this measure is extremely comfortable (Cattell & Schuerger, 2003). While earlier 16PF editions were so tightly bound to research conventions that this measure was once cumbersome to absorb and awkward to use, this is no longer the case. In fact, the factors are so readily identifiable that the potential for career coaching, for counseling adults or adolescents, and in relational enhancement for couples is immediately evident. It has been gratifying to observe numerous interns grow swiftly in confidence using this measure with training and supervision to the extent that personality assessment early on becomes a preferred way of launching treatment. For twenty years, one objective of my counselor education assessment courses has been for students to achieve rudimentary-level competency to use the 16PF for self-exploration with clients.

The 16PF is paired by the developer with other custom measures to accomplish specific assessment tasks (16pf.com). For example, there is the option to combine the 185 questions that comprise the core 16PF with 140 additional questions that look into the current experience of pathology. This results in a reasonably comprehensive, general-purpose screening for personality and problematic patterns of behavior. Counselors should note that this combined measure has a broad purpose for personnel screening, vocational direction, and relational compatibility. It may contribute to and assist a mental health screening as a starting point. This is very much a measure to investigate personality factors and adjustment as these present in the normal range.

This chapter began with Alex and Sharon, who completed the 16PF Couple's Counseling Questionnaire, the combination of the core 16PF with items regarding relational history, satisfaction, and concerns. It is in these combined measures that the clinician discovers that learning one tool well can be useful for several purposes. On the down side, its fifth edition has been around for a couple of decades even though the norms were updated in 2002. The new publisher reports that a new sixth edition is forthcoming. On the positive side, the 16PF has a considerable international presence.

Minnesota Multiphasic Personality Inventory-2 Restructured Form (MMPI-2-RF). This is admittedly an unusual measure to include on a short list for MHPs. This dominant force in the assessment world since the 1930s may have *personality* plainly in its title, but its reputation is primarily related to its uncovering of psychopathology in relation to personality (Greene, 2011). The two previous recommendations (NEO-PI-3 and 16PF) are all about describing traits; the MMPI-2-RF combines state and trait into one do-it-all measure. This raises the bar several notches in terms of the skill necessary to interpret results. Further, including its nine scales dedicated exclusively to investigate the client's attitude toward taking the test (e.g., tendency to under- or overreport), the MMPI-2-RF yields an incredible 51 scales from its 338 items (Ben-Porath, 2012). This makes it an extremely multifaceted measure. Such breadth and intricacy requires advanced training and supervision to bring the MMPI-2-RF into clinical use. The substantial blow that would appear to disqualify it for inclusion is that it focuses heavily on psychopathology and dysfunction. Findings from the MMPI-2-RF are not "client friendly" and require considerable translation before there is beneficial insight to communicate back to the client. As suggested by its "C" user-level qualification listed by the publisher, this measure demands a high level of expertise in test construction, implementation, and interpretation.

What then is the explanation for placing this measure in this chapter? Notice that the well-known, traditional MMPI-2 is not on the list. That particular version remains very much in use and has vast popularity. Unfortunately, there are features that make it troublesome for applications in counseling. There are concerns in terms of its clinical utility (disconnected from the *Diagnostic and Statistical Manual of Mental Disorders* [DSM]) and redemptive validity (an apparent antireligious bias). The more recent version of the classic, the MMPI-2-RF is geared to assess major symptoms, personality characteristics, and behavioral tendencies in a way that is comprehensive, unique, and current. The RF version is more targeted and relevant and involves less subjectivity in interpretation to make use of its findings. The impressive and deep research history of the MMPI has finally caught up to provide what those in clinics need to address. There is no necessity to untangle an intricate range of code types or to figure out how to discount scales that reflect antiquated categories of psychopathology. These restructured scales have the benefit of factor analysis, are more unitary and sensible, and have credibility for therapeutic purposes beyond their diagnostic value. There are still psychometric questions that arise. For example, so many scales are derived from one item pool, and this restructured version continues to use previous norms (i.e., from the MMPI-2 1989 revision). Researchers are candid about the restructuring process and the limitations of each scale (Ben-Porath, 2012).

Counselors have sufficient educational training to pursue mastery of this revised instrument through additional workshops, independent study, and supervision. For the MMPI-2-RF the learning curve is steep. Nevertheless, given the momentum this innovation has achieved, this measure is worth considering as a potential tool for treatment planning purposes. Technology for administration and reporting has become more accessible (pearsonclinical.com).

It is likely that counselors in the years ahead will move from educational and community services to invest careers in medical, correctional, criminal justice, substance abuse, and psychiatric settings. Medical clinics are increasingly blending behavioral counseling into healthcare. This type of measure may be indispensable for full counselor participation on multidisciplinary treatment teams. The average MHP may not find an immediate reason to plunge into the training regimen necessary to get up to speed on the MMPI-2-RF. At this juncture, it is reasonable to raise awareness that this measure is well positioned for further advancement and resurgence of use in the not too distant future. Christian counselors may need to give this next generation MMPI-2-RF renewed attention and respect.

Millon Clinical Multiaxial Inventory IV (MCMI-IV). This fresh release of the extremely popular MCMI-III ties closely to the *DSM*-5. In keeping with the advantages of the previous Millon Clinical measures, test results on the IV point directly to prevailing diagnostic categories and terminology (Choca, 2004). In part, the correlation is due to how these measures and Millon's evolutionary theory of personality have been instrumental in contributing to the data gathered for the *DSM*. Counselors will find this measure useful when they see clients who display signs of a mental health disorder and are likely to meet the criteria of "medical necessity" (i.e., a disease, illness, or health condition exists and healthcare services are indicated to foster recovery). It is important to note that while the MCMI-III would lean toward detecting personality disorders, the IV views personality more on a continuum (Weiner & Greene, 2017). The MCMI-IV is efficient: in less than thirty minutes of the client's time, we receive a considerable depth of information regarding the client's symptoms (state) and personality (trait). Given Millon's view that psychopathology grows directly from maladaptive personality patterns, this instrument produces a personality screen, though admittedly through a narrow clinical lens.

The MCMI-IV is constructed using an entirely different method of score generation from the customary pattern familiar on other instruments. This is not a norm-referenced measure, and therefore the MCMI-IV does not provide standard scores that indicate normally distributed traits. Thus, MHPs who use this measure must become familiar with its psychometric distinctiveness in terms of "base rates" and "hit rates" as well as true positives and negatives to ensure that the results are clearly placed into the specific context. The MCMI-IV does not compare clients to a normal population, only to a clinical one. The administrative assumption is that the test taker has made a request for mental health services and has a presenting complaint. The instrument brings to the surface early in the treatment relationship what underlying motivations and experiences are contributing to the reason for entering therapy. Its most significant contribution is to display the relationship between personality styles or disorders and the experience of clinical symptoms. The MCMI-IV is a measure that draws out psychopathology. This inherent feature makes the inexperienced user prone to misapply findings and overdiagnose. This tool should only be applied with its intended population, that is, those who are requesting mental health services and who are suspected of having an actual disorder (Hays, 2017). There are other similar measures within the Millon inventory group that are fitting for medical, college, or human resource settings (pearsonclinical.com).

The Millon inventories have grown in popularity among counselors in mental health agencies that interface with third-party payment systems. The reason is easy to grasp. These measures aid in diagnosis and treatment planning. Further, early detection of how personality style may contribute to the reason for referral has immediate benefit. Recognition of deep-seated personality patterns enables the clinician to proceed with caution and awareness of the pitfalls in relating to the client in ways that provoke tension. In addition, taking a magnified look at dominant personality patterns using its main scales, along with more descriptive features that appear in the Grossman Facet Scales, offers the clinician material that can be very valuable to treatment planning. In the right setting and in capable hands, the MCMI-IV is valuable. This endorsement comes from extensive use with Christian clients, many of whom have not done well with lay-level helpers, pastoral counselors, or support ministries. These clients enter therapy with doubts that professional services will make much difference. Should the MCMI-IV results reveal a pattern that suggests problematic ways of relating to the environment, others, or themselves (e.g., self-defeating), the informed helper can work with this prevailing personality pattern right from the outset.

There are several critical concerns with the MCMI-IV for Christian MHPs who wish to adopt this measure. First, it is necessary to gain a sufficient understanding of the Millon personality theory to recognize, navigate, and compensate for its worldview assumptions. A theological anthropology drawn from Scripture needs to be considered in light of its deterministic and evolutionary assumptions. Second, the embedded depictions of personality disorder and categories cannot be automatically carried over into clinical conversations. It takes fluency in these constructs to rephrase the caustic descriptions into palatable concepts. In practical terminology, MCMI-IV results do not flow easily into a feedback loop to the client. It may be tempting to leave its benefit at the level of informing the clinician. With experience and skill, behavioral descriptions drawn from the client's life examples can make those personality patterns useful to clients.

Finally, the advantage of the MCMI-IV comes from the opportunity to allow the measure to provide a perspective on a client through the lens of Millon's personality theory. This specialized "consultation" made possible through an accessible personality measure and technology is only productive to treatment when applied with reason, compassion, and astute awareness of what it suggests. Damage can be done to the therapeutic relationship if sufficient expertise and care are not applied. When a clinician relies too heavily on computer-generated narratives or leans exclusively on the MCMI-IV results to determine a diagnosis, clients will not be well served. Therefore, the learning curve to implement use of the MCMI-IV should be viewed as steep and ongoing.

Consider this nontechnical illustration that borrows from medical terminology. Think of the MCMI-IV as a powerful instrument that provides a point-in-time personality-in-distress (PID) scan. The tool is applied with the assumption that a mental health problem is already present. Using a client's responses along with information on statistics of prevalence and incidence, the MCMI-IV attempts to find similarities between your client and others known to be in need of clinical or psychiatric care. This PID scan is not uncovering the design of the Creator or the destiny of the client. Rather, it displays the struggle of an individual who is pressing back against adversities, systematic sin, and brokenness on several levels. The Christian receives this PID scan as a helpful consult with an expert in psychopathology. Simultaneously, the counselor makes a request of the Holy Spirit: "Lord, by your Spirit and by your mercy, grant me vision to see your unique character-under-development

[CUD] perspective. Help me to begin to see and encourage the potential you see as you gaze with love and grace at the concerns this client is bringing into counseling." The efforts of counseling are to move forward with an awareness of the past and empathy for the present. Our hope is in what the Holy Spirit is still bringing to completion through sanctification and Christian maturation. This theme of hope for renewal will be explored further in the next chapter.

In summary, these are four tools for counselors to consider bringing into their care for clients at the very beginning. The MCMI-IV and MMPI-2-RF are sophisticated psychological screening measures that require advanced training and clinical experience. These are worthwhile investments of a clinician's energy and effort when dealing with populations that will benefit from the insights each can provide. For those with aspirations of helping clients move toward spiritual maturity, it will require thought, prayer, and intentionality to move past the mere diagnostic application of these tools to bring the insights gained into the mainstream of the clinical conversation. In contrast, the NEO-PI-3 and the 16PF are instruments that surface insights into personality traits that are readily carried over into counseling conversations. The benefit of assessment is realized when our clients can see themselves as works in progress under the re-creative genius not of us as stellar counselors but of the Great Comforter. It is his maturation efforts that counselors seek to join.

REFERENCES

American Counseling Association. (2014). *ACA code of ethics: As approved by the ACA Governing Council*. http://www.counseling.org/resources/aca-code-of-ethics.pdf

Bayne, R. (2013). *The counsellor's guide to personality: Understanding preferences, motives and life stories*. Hampshire, UK: Palgrave Macmillan.

Ben-Porath, Y. S. (2012). *Interpreting the MMPI-2-RF*. Minneapolis: University of Minnesota Press.

Berman, M. I., & Song, S. L. (2013). Assessment of personality in counseling settings. In K. F. Geisinger (Ed.), *APA handbook of testing and assessment in psychology: Vol. 2. Testing and assessment in clinical and counseling psychology* (pp. 406-426). Washington, DC: American Psychological Association.

Butcher, J. N., Bubany, S., & Mason, S. N. (2013). Assessment of personality and psychopathology with self-report inventories. In K. F. Geisinger (Ed.), *APA handbook of testing and assessment in psychology: Vol. 2. Testing and assessment in clinical and counseling psychology* (pp. 171-192). Washington, DC: American Psychological Association.

Butcher, J. N., & Perry, J. N. (2008). *Personality assessment in treatment planning: Use of the MMPI-2 and BTPI*. New York: Oxford University Press.

Cashel, M. L. (2016). What counselors should know about personality assessments. In I. Marini & M. A. Stebnicki (Eds.), *The professional counselor's desk reference* (2nd ed., pp. 299-303). New York: Springer.

Cattell, H. E. P., & Mead, A. D. (2008). The Sixteen Personality Factor questionnaire (16PF). In G. J. Boyle, G. Matthews, & D. H. Saklofske (Eds.), *The Sage handbook of personality theory and assessment: Vol. 2. Personality measurement and testing* (pp. 135-159). Los Angeles: Sage.

Cattell, H. E. P., & Schuerger, J. M. (2003). *Essentials of 16PF assessment.* Hoboken, NJ: John Wiley & Sons.

Choca, J. P. (2004). *Interpretive guide to the Millon Clinical Multiaxial Inventory* (3rd ed.). Washington, DC: American Psychological Association.

Costa, P. T., Jr., & McCrae, R. R. (2008). The revised NEO Personality Inventory (NEO-PI-R). In G. J. Boyle, G. Matthews, & D. H. Saklofske (Eds.), *Sage handbook of personality theory and assessment: Vol. 2. Personality measurement and testing* (pp. 179-198). Los Angeles: Sage.

Dattilio, F. M., Tresco, K. E., & Siegel, A. (2007). An empirical survey on psychological testing and the use of the term *psychological*: Turf battles or clinical necessity? *Professional Psychology: Research and Practice, 38*(6), 682-689.

De Saeger, H., Kamphuis, J. H., Finn, S. E., Smith, J. D., Verheul, R., van Busschbach, J. J., . . .& Horn, E. K. (2014). Therapeutic assessment promotes treatment readiness but does not affect symptom change in patients with personality disorders: Findings from a randomized clinical trial. *Psychological Assessment, 26*(2), 474-483.

Edwards, C. J., Holleran, L., & Beutler, L. E. (2016). Integrative treatments come of age: Systematic treatment selections (STS). In U. Kumar (Ed.), *The Wiley handbook of personality assessment* (pp. 285-301). Malden, MA: John Wiley & Sons.

Erford, B. T. (2013). *Assessment for counselors* (2nd ed.). Belmont, CA: Brooks/Cole.

Greene, R. L. (2011). *The MMPI-2/MMPI-2-RF: An interpretive manual* (3rd ed.). Boston: Allyn & Bacon.

Hays, D. G. (2017). *Assessment in counseling: Procedures and practices* (6th ed). Alexandria, VA: American Counseling Association.

Hilsenroth, M. J., Peters, E. J., & Ackerman, S. J. (2004). The development of therapeutic alliance during psychological assessment: Patient and therapist perspectives across treatment. *Journal of Personality Assessment, 83*(3), 332-344.

Karson, M., Karson, S., & O'Dell, J. (1997). *16PF interpretation in clinical practice: A guide to the fifth edition.* Champaign, IL: Institute for Personality and Ability Testing.

Mayer, J. D. (2005). A tale of two visions: Can a new view of personality help integrate psychology? *American Psychologist, 60*(4), 294-307.

McAdams, D. P. (2015). *The art and science of personality development.* New York: Guilford Press.

McAdams, D. P., & Pals, J. L. (2006). A new big five: Fundamental principles for an integrative science of personality. *American Psychologist, 61*(3), 204-217.

McCrae, R. R., & Allik, J. (Eds.). (2002). *The five-factor model of personality across cultures.* New York: Kluwer Academic.

McCrae, R. R., & Costa, P. T., Jr. (2010). *NEO inventories: Professional manual.* Lutz, FL: Psychological Assessment Resources.

Peterson, C. H., Lomas, G. I., Neukrug, E. S., & Bonner, M. W. (2014). Assessment use by counselors in the United States: Implications for policy and practice. *Journal of Counseling & Development, 92*(1), 90-98.

Weiner, I. B., & Greene, R. L. (2017). *Handbook of personality assessment* (2nd ed.). Hoboken, NJ: John Wiley & Sons.

Whiston, S. C. (2017). *Principles and applications of assessment in counseling* (5th ed.). Belmont, CA: Cengage.

CHAPTER FIFTEEN

GRADUATION AND RECOMMENDATIONS

In all my prayers for all of you, I always pray with joy because of your
partnership in the gospel from the first day until now, being confident
of this, that he who began a good work in you will carry it on to
completion until the day of Christ Jesus.

PHILIPPIANS 1:4-6

THEOLOGICAL THEME
Partnership in God's Good Work

THERAPEUTIC GRADUATION: PARTING CAN BE SUCH SWEET SORROW

Therapists are not likely to have a trophy case on display. We do not have a shadow box with medals of recognition to pull out on special occasions and share with friends. Still, we possess a collection of treasured communication hidden away in a secure folder or drawer and a cache of notes, cards, and small mementos that clients leave behind to express gratitude as they solidify gains and counseling nears completion. Parting creates "sweet sorrow" moments that turn tears into testimonies of courage. It is an opportunity to express appreciation.

Going to extra measures to communicate parting words well and with perceptiveness is worth the effort. The final exchange between client and counselor can leave meaningful impressions and echo long in the heart. You may want to keep a supply of blank notecards or fine stationery on which to write words of admiration and encouragement or favorite Bible passages to send with departing counselees. Messages need not be glowingly positive or filled with unconditional praise. If the counseling process has been genuine, then risks, disappointments, and challenges can all be openly recognized. Ambivalence, confusion, disappointment, sadness, and perhaps anger may be mixed into the departure. This is whole body-and-soul communication that requires one's face, voice, and personal intensity. For a rare few, an expressive picture, symbol, or oft-cited phrase may instantly capture a hope-fortifying memory. Most clients, however, will fumble with words to express feelings typically excluded from ordinary conversations.

Blake, a young child client, made an unusual request as we finished our final session of brief therapy. He was a quiet and intense little guy who was prone to anxiety and dramatic bursts of emotion, so our short therapeutic journey had searched for self-soothing behaviors to help him and his parents get a better handle on an assortment of uncomfortable fears that had become far too disruptive. Besides his phobic, panicky meltdowns, however, his overall life was pleasant. There was no known trauma to address or separations to appease. Blake decided that he only wanted the two of us in the room for his fun, yet tender closing session. After I had given him my special card, he surprisingly asked if I could leave him alone in my office! When he invited me back in, his father joined us. Blake had set up a puppet we'd spoken through several times as a display on the small play table. The whiteboard behind it had a block-letter message written in his small hand: *Thank you for helping my fear.* That experience was a precious and moving occasion. A photo was snapped of his handiwork, and the recollection continues to stand as one of my favorite symbols of the joy of therapeutic celebration. Here Blake's sensitive side came through as an interpersonal treasure.

Bonnie was a veteran fourth-grade teacher with a family of her own. She had sought out treatment during a prolonged season of lapses into infuriation and discouragement, brought to the surface by the loss of her mother. There were twists in that relationship that took heroic efforts to untangle. Several sessions set the stage for our partnership to come to a fitting conclusion. There were no longer replays of uneasy recollections from the distant past. Instead, Bonnie would share exciting recent episodes involving students in her class, laughter from the dinner table, and a renewed spark in her marriage. Life was bright again. Bonnie revealed resilience and resourcefulness. Her parting gift was an embroidered bookmark. When I notice it even now, I hear the voices of fourth graders whom I never met basking in the energy that Bonnie poured over them with love.

Not all counseling journeys reach such a crescendo during closing visits, but remembrances like these make the chaos of initial consultations an occasion for hope. We can see at the beginning what the client does not—a successful graduation from the therapeutic process, with stories and emotions to reflect on and enjoy, which flow from gains made within a trusting partnership that confirms progress along the way.

Closing sessions emphasize once again the subjective side of the interpersonal alliance, but, similar to the initial consultation, a comprehensive closure sequence can be enhanced by the thoughtful use of assessment results. Using assessments from the beginning of the relationship means that now you can revisit key quantifiable and qualitative information, which is a productive way to unpack and distinguish what has actually occurred. This also allows for a straightforward appraisal of what's better, what's not, and how to ensure that the gains made keep heading in the right direction.

Assessment will not be as formal during these final dialogues as it was in the initial sessions. Appraisal at discharge is highly personalized, distinguishing counseling in the real world from research in the laboratory. There is no straightforward pretest-posttest. Repeating a screening measure from earlier in treatment may reveal a different pattern of scores but not a higher total score. This can be discouraging until you learn to move ahead to conversation, where the results are compared with the client, which will reveal how the recent ratings indicate a deeper grasp of the matter and how they are now dealing with it. Progress is reflected in a client's growth in perception. The actual total scores on a rapid assessment instrument (RAI) may or may not reflect this.

Again, a return to significant items on early symptom scales, RAIs, or a customized tracking measure can be helpful. However, a full repeat screening is most often not necessary. Target only those items that were marked for change and check the current status of those points in a tangible way. Take a close and objective look at the distance traveled. This will make recalling the effort that has been invested even more rewarding. In addition, data may inform aftercare recommendations in important ways.

PARTNERSHIPS FOR GRADUATION, NOT TERMINATION

The prevalent and longstanding clinical expression for bringing a therapeutic relationship to a conclusion is *termination*. It remains especially common in psychoanalytic forums, where it has roots. Even the *ACA Code of Ethics* makes use of it: "Counselors terminate a counseling relationship when it becomes reasonably apparent that the client no longer needs assistance, is not likely to benefit, or is being harmed by continued counseling" (American Counseling Association, 2014, para. A.11.a). "Termination" comes about when the counselor and the client come to a joint understanding that it is time to bring the therapeutic relationship to an end (Maples & Walker, 2014). The last few clinical sessions before termination usually focus on the emotions arising as the interpersonal relationship closes, as well as on helping the client plan for how to navigate circumstances as this explicit support is removed. The latter is ideally complemented by tangible appraisal of behavior and attitude changes in other areas.

Still, it is difficult to cast a positive spin on the term *termination*. In ordinary language, the word connotes death, grief, or an unwanted ending. Perhaps the use of *termination* was justifiable in reference to the completion of a long-term, dependent psychoanalytic arrangement. However, the majority of helping relationships in mental health settings do not come to a forceful and problematic ending, and have not for quite some time. Termination was actually labeled a lost metaphor nearly two decades ago (Quintana, as cited in Maples & Walker, 2014), but movements to replace it are sporadic and tend to lack traction. *Consolidation* is a recent replacement proposal. This would be a far better label, as it conveys the idea of a planned and productive finish to an advantageous counseling effort.

The term that I have long commended in training and supervision for the close of therapy is *graduation* or *commencement*. These terms signify an anticipated milestone in development that is celebrated, not mourned. And the images of new adventures, fresh beginnings, and an earned achievement in status that are commonly associated with graduation are fitting for the short-term, targeted treatment common in mental health care today.

Graduation is a particularly apt term in counseling that is Christian, where the therapeutic relationship is optimally viewed as a temporary or adjunctive one, similar in some ways to the role teachers and professors play in the lives of students. The therapist should be seen as a collaborator, not a novel authority figure who replaces a parent, pastor, or even the Holy Spirit (though these role associations could apply in particular helping relationships). We are meant to be a provisional support. And by design, a moment of transition will come in which a client who is a disciple of Christ will recognize that fellowship within the local church is the key source of supportive relationships that bring about healing, growth, and further steps toward holiness (e.g., Acts 2:42; Eph 1:22-23; Col 1:18; Jas 5:14). In addition, Christian clients are ideally constantly cultivating an increasingly intimate relationship with the Lord of the universe. The therapeutic alliance is a means to arm clients with the tools they need to engage readily in active spiritual formation. Therapeutic graduation is therefore a transition that should give way to enduring interpersonal and transpersonal resources.

There are further advantages in portraying the end of counseling as graduation. First, graduates are free to return for occasional visits to refresh their learning or recall the support they once experienced. This is not a sign of regression or failure. On the contrary, it is beneficial routine maintenance. The understanding from the outset of the counseling relationship is that the habits, resources, and supportive networks brought together during treatment—like the knowledge students gain in school—facilitate attitudinal, behavioral, and interpersonal adjustments that can be the new normal even after graduation. A desire to check in occasionally with the person or people who helped bring about those changes is natural. It may make sense to actually build a three- or six-month visit into the aftercare plan to assess how gains have solidified or moved forward. Second, additional coursework postgraduation might be valuable. The previously productive therapeutic partnership can be revived to take on additional assignments. Last, just as it is entirely normal in an educational venture to assess comprehension and achievement of outcomes along the way, it is natural in a counseling setting to utilize continual assessment and feedback-informed treatment in preparation for commencement (Lambert, 2010, 2013; Patterson, Matthey, & Baker, 2006). If an assessment check signals that remedial help is needed, additional coursework or a change in plan can be readily undertaken.

Michael Lambert (2013), a notable expert in the area of practice-based evidence, makes a crucial case built on clinical research that certain clients can achieve gains earlier than anticipated and in fewer sessions than most clinicians might estimate. The prevailing expectation amongst therapists is that 75% of clients will utilize fifty sessions. However, when the mental health concern that brought a client to treatment is monitored regularly via assessment, a sizable number of clients (17-40%) will demonstrate dramatic and sustainable gains well before that one year. The implication is that therapists and clients do well to look at the change trajectory within the partnership. It may end up being entirely reasonable to issue a diploma and host graduation earlier rather than later. Abbreviated treatment due to goal attainment in a key outcome variable is much preferred to the client losing motivation and ending therapy by attrition, rationalization, or failure to show.

The most extraordinary benefit of regular assessment during the course of treatment is that it can alert unsuspecting therapists to an increasing risk of treatment failure (i.e., dropout, in a school context; Lambert, 2010). Premature discontinuation occurs when a client ends care before it is mutually agreed upon and prior to making therapeutic gains that are reasonably attainable (Swift & Greenberg, 2015). In other words, clients (1) cease treatment before the prescribed number of sessions, (2) do not finish the treatment protocol or fail to make gains in the anticipated direction, or (3) stop showing up for appointments. Therapists may also determine that client compliance and cooperation has reached the level where it constitutes treatment failure (Swift & Greenberg, 2015). Estimates of dropout range from an extraordinarily low 5% to as high as 70%. The mental health setting, service population characteristics, and treatment specialty all influence the attrition rate. A general rule of thumb is to use a one in five (20%) ratio as a rough estimate of the number of clients who may fail to complete treatment. An even better strategy is to establish a baseline rate for a clinic as well as for each clinician. With these kinds of benchmarks in place, you can set realistic goals and monitor monthly/quarterly stats to improve results along the way.

Note that practice-based evidence and investigations into abandonment of treatment have been extremely productive in uncovering what tends to go amiss and in noticing warning signs (Lambert, 2010; Shimokawa, Lambert, & Smart, 2010). It is possible to predict when treatment failure will occur and what can be reasonably done to keep care heading in a productive direction. You can utilize procedures involving direct assessment of clients' immediate experiences to manage motivation and ensure that they gain relief for their chief complaints (e.g., symptom reduction, return to functional capacity, relational restoration, etc.) and reach graduation. A plan and a partnership brought to completion is quality care.

In clinical supervision, it is reasonable to define successful graduation as reaching a mutually determined end that includes dedicated time to process that conclusion (i.e., at least one graduation theme session). There are numerous ways that counselor and client can finish admirably. For our reflection and supervision as counselors, these retrospective questions might be considered:

- Did the client complete the course of therapy as originally recommended?
- How were the initial plan and the intended outcomes evaluated to prepare for the client's departure at this point in time?
- What contributed to the client's exit plan, and were there recognizable gains? Was this a mutually agreed upon decision to graduate from therapy?
- Even if this was an abrupt or unpredicted ending, was sufficient session time dedicated to finishing well (e.g., consolidating gains, discussing aftercare and risks of regression, considering how to know when to restart or return to therapy, etc.)?
- What evidence (objective/subjective) is available to establish how successfully the client was implementing change strategies as treatment came to a close?

- How can the state of the therapeutic alliance (i.e., bond, goals, and tasks) best be described?
- What themes surfaced in regard to the client's expectations for spiritual growth and maturation as the graduation was underway?

A mnemonic to begin therapy was offered (START: story, therapeutic alliance, assessment, recommendations, and treatment plan). Next, a means to conduct a progress review was recommended (PACE: partnership, affinity, collaborative conversation, and experience). Figure 15.1 offers a model to guide therapy toward a credible CLOSE. The agenda can be shared with clients as the counselor and client together assess what has been accomplished. This is a mutual reflection, so it is best not to turn these into questions posed to the client. Counselors should review the entire clinical record with keen attention to assessment findings as a way to prepare for this meaningful exchange. The observations we share are part of the gift of therapy.

- Change in chief concern(s). What is the change status of the chief concern(s) that once brought the client into therapy? Explore growth in terms of behaviors, beliefs, expectations, relationships, and even spiritual maturation.
- Lessons learned. Describe the major lessons learned along the way. What makes these memorable, and how deep is the client's confidence that the habits now in place are likely to continue?
- Openness to others. What was experienced in the therapeutic relationship that can be applied to an openness to others? Express how relationships can look, feel, and be intentionally different. Recall the interpersonal skills cultivated and character decisions made along the therapeutic journey. How will this new openness to others create resources in Christian fellowship, family, and valued friendships?
- Spiritual practices. Identify renewed or recently discovered spiritual practices (e.g., worship, fellowship, Scripture reading, etc.). How can growth in discipleship continue so that the ongoing renewal of individual traits becomes associated with spiritual gifts? How are these practices equipping the client to better reflect the Lord's light and glory?
- Alternative: Support networks & behavior.[1] Identify new or recently renewed relationships. Reflect on the instrumental and inspirational

---

[1]Obviously, the focus on spiritual practices is particularly suitable for clients who actively sought a Christian perspective. When doing regular counseling without a Christian emphasis, the S in CLOSE would best be depicted as Support.

benefits that flow from these interpersonal connections. Describe routines and habits that are likely to support the gains achieved.

- Expectations. Look ahead to short- and long-term challenges and opportunities. What risks may be around the corner? Where is there an image of hope of refreshment? Spend a moment enjoying memories that inspire a sense of accomplishment and success.

More than a simplistic ending, graduation is the inception of movement toward reaching a client's new expectations for personal, relational, and spiritual growth.

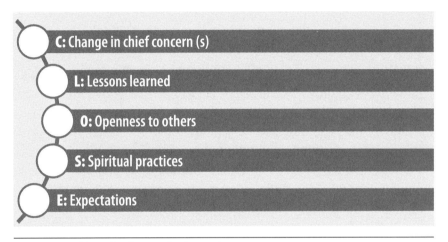

Figure 15.1. CLOSE outline for a graduation session

PRESERVING ALLIANCES UNTIL THERAPEUTIC GRADUATION

Swift & Greenberg (2015) in *Premature Termination in Psychology: Strategies for Engaging Clients and Improving Outcomes* make the case for eight tactics to use to reach a treatment graduation worth celebrating. Their conclusions, based on a thorough examination of extensive research, provide a suitable structure for reviewing assessment concepts. The strategies below expand on Swift and Greenberg's summation points to show how their recommendations highlight the assessment techniques covered in the previous chapters along with the various theological themes. Each recommendation supplies the means to demonstrate craftsmanship in applying techniques within a consequential therapeutic connection.

Extend hospitality and prepare clients for treatment success. Research tells us that clients are less likely to drop out of treatment if they have been given adequate role induction. Clients must become familiar with productive expectations for themselves and the therapist, and specific features of the treatment regimen. The assumption might be that an informal and automatic acclimation happens naturally along the way, but this is a flawed conjecture and has a high cost. For those clients who do not adjust to the service process, the risk of dissatisfaction and disillusionment leading to noncompletion is too severe. The prevention recommendation is to utilize well-honed methods to both prepare clients and establish a productive counseling dyad that is poised to experience progress.

In Christian counseling, "role induction" translates easily into the notion of extending hospitality and creating an open way of welcoming clients into healing conversations. In any gesture of hospitality, the conveniences and refreshment offered are carefully selected to communicate a particular mood, attribute, or implication. For this reason, we do well to outfit a toolbox with well-chosen assessment measures that can be surveyed to find the ones that are a good fit for the population being served and for the growth area that must be addressed. Mental health professionals are to bring instruments that meet the highest level of psychometric precision available (see Clinical Assessment Instrument Christian Evaluation Form [CAICEF], appendix one), and we must be familiar with the assets and disadvantages to any measure employed with clients. Further, we need to contemplate the conceptual contribution of a measure in terms of its incremental validity (additive value) and redemptive validity (restorative and re-creation potential). Remember, clinicians are the ones who assess redemptive validity; it will not be discussed by instrument developers. We examine the effectiveness of an assessment measure for providing insight into wise living as described by our Creator and for increasing insight around what it means to be crucified and risen with Christ (Greggo & Lawrence, 2012). Then we are prepared to introduce each assessment step in the early phase of care with a vision for its potential to contribute to a better understanding of where the client desires to be at the close of the healing journey. Assessment in counseling is more about discharge than diagnosis.

The START (story, therapeutic alliance, assessment, recommendations, and treatment plan) framework for use in initial assessments offers a flexible method to unite crisp and effective assessment techniques with a high-touch relational approach. Using select instruments outside of the interview (before and after) also expands the range and depth of information gathered as it frees up precious face-to-face space for dedicated interpersonal dialogue. The concept of an initial consultation followed by a formal orientation and assessment session offers clients and therapists alike a solid reading on where to begin and how to proceed.

This is role induction in action. The opportunity is wide open to discuss how this partnership will become all that it can be to further counseling objectives. Assessment done well conveys professionalism. When we are confident that our adopted launch procedures will address the coverage and documentation demands of today's mental health environment, we can be courageous and respectful in meeting clients where they are. This is the optimal therapeutic climate in which to invite the Holy Spirit to be active in the journey ahead.

Hear a client's heart, hopes, and expectations. Researchers advise incorporating a client's preferences into every possible aspect of the treatment decision-making process right from the start. Selective assessment is an intentional and coordinated effort to bring those unique preferences to the surface. It is advantageous to have actual scores that depict levels of concern or describe patterns of response (Mours, Campbell, Gathercoat, & Peterson, 2009; Reese et al., 2014). These can be brought with compassion directly into conversations with clients.

Assessment findings are for both the clinician and the client. Results are explored as a way to enlighten the client about his or her needs, options, and reasonable objectives. Of course, the counselor is responsible to limit results to what the client is ready to hear and use. Raw labels, psychological jargon, or disconnected assessment data is never to be tossed around to dazzle or impress. Advocacy requires that new insights are returned as feedback with empathy, sensitivity, and comprehensibility. Assessment relies on client disclosure that is received with honor and appreciation. The assessment instrument does not discover anything that the client does not give. Clients share sensitive experiences with a therapist as a demonstration of trust. These exchanges become the basis of the alliance. Good inquiries, fair answers, constructive synthesis, and considerate communication set the pace for the work ahead.

Christian counselors understand this notion of "joining" with a client's preferences as seeing the orientations of the client's heart. In Scripture, the heart is the central metaphor to describe attitudes toward the self, others, and the Lord. It operates as the relational hub from which originate our motivations and apprehensions. Thus, we are to listen not merely to uncover preferences; we are to attune to a client's heart. This implies becoming familiar with the uniqueness of the one being served, along with their qualities, resources, and special divine purpose. Mental health counseling seeks solutions to dilemmas and resolution of symptoms. When Christian spirituality is incorporated, counseling will consider how the Lord is accomplishing his work of sanctification and formation. By mutual agreement, a search for wisdom becomes the defining purpose for this therapeutic partnership.

We have a professional obligation to be responsive to a client's convictions and worldview. This is why I outlined assessment tactics earlier to help you determine if and how earnestly a client may desire counsel that adheres to a particular Christian tradition. Before counseling that is deliberately Christian can begin, a client's religious affections must be gauged. Taking these measures and asking key questions equip us to recognize spiritual traditions, leanings, and pathways that fit a particular client of faith. Bringing these valued discoveries back to clients provides verification that counseling is actually going to make use of their heritage, hope, and longings of the heart.

Plan for a good ending right from the beginning. Experts in improving the quality of treatment make the case that clients need to be aware of the criteria that will eventually determine readiness for discharge, and should be active in setting the level of functioning or goal achievement that is reasonable. These key aspects of treatment planning are not for the therapist alone, no matter what level of expertise we have regarding the presenting concern. We should always talk with the client about the behavioral baseline, what getting better might be like, and how the ultimate best can be achieved beyond therapy.

Treatment goals can be shaped around items on symptom checklists or RAIs. For example, if you're going to address clients' experiences of anxiety, items sensitive to their unique situations can be adopted to create customized treatment goals. This way, clients can know that they are getting close to finishing when the frequency, severity, and duration of an experience are occurring at a level that they believe is better, tolerable, and even desirable. For example, if item three from the Severity Measure for Generalized Anxiety was enlightening for a client ("during the past seven days, I have had thoughts of bad things happening, such as family tragedy, ill health, loss of a job, or accidents"), the dyad can track weekly the occurrence of thoughts related to bad things happening (American Psychiatric Association, 2015). And the entire measure could be reapplied during the course of treatment since it is only ten items. To sharpen the therapeutic focus, however, it is good to locate single items that are most salient and turn those into criteria to track client progress.

There are two other useful ways to create more precision in this process with clients. The first is to build a customized Subjective Units of Distress Scale (SUDS). Most people are familiar with this kind of scale because it is used so frequently in medicine (e.g., "on a scale of one to ten, rate your pain, with one meaning you have no pain whatsoever and a ten meaning the pain is unbearable and you believe you are about to pass out"). For this scale to be useful in a mental health context, you will need to establish "anchors" that nail down what the discrete steps of the scale mean. Record descriptions of what a two, four, six, and eight mean on the client's customized SUDS scale. These anchors give clients and clinicians a shorthand method to express recent discomfort as well as improvement. For example, you might have a client count the number of times on a given day that his or her experience of anxiety was greater than six on the individualized SUDS scale. Eventually, they may report a count of six-plus episodes for the week or less than once per day—a dramatic improvement.

A second concrete method to establish expectations in specific areas is to build a Goal Attainment Scale (GAS). A GAS is useful once clients have a defined notion about what they desire to change (e.g., reducing the number of conflicts with coworkers during the week, increasing the number of satisfying social outings they have in a week, or soothing fears and apprehension through the use of prayer and biblical meditation). A personalized GAS starts with a key problem area, which is followed by five questions that help the client predict what will happen within a range of potential outcomes:

- (0) What would be expected at the end of intervention?
- (+1) What would be expected if the outcome of treatment is somewhat better than expected?
- (+2) What would be expected if the outcome of treatment is much better than expected?
- (-1) What would be the outcome if it is somewhat less than expected?
- (-2) What would it be like if it is a lot less than expected?

Personalized scale building is a helpful way to shape joint expectations. It is also useful in exploring how clients picture improvement in one, two, or six months, and when they believe that they would be able to move from individual counseling support to other networks such as community self-help systems, church fellowship, or a pastoral-care small group. Hosting an imaginative consideration of what "better" is going to be like and how gains can be maintained will give clients a more reasonable outlook on how long treatment will last and what they can do to move the process to completion.

Predict patterns and count the cost of change. A closely related factor to contemplating the look of change is helping the client recognize that achieving growth is not typically a steady movement forward. In other words, it's important for clients to know that how change will look is not identical to when it will be realized (Norcross, Krebs, & Prochaska, 2011). Motivation is subject to ebbs and flows. In fact, relief can actually decrease the urge to persist. Basic psycho-education regarding the stages of change can keep clients in the game and help them avoid surprise when the going slows down.

Precontemplation is the stage when clients do not have an inner awareness that change involves them. In other words, they know that a problem needs attention and that they need guidance from others, but they don't necessarily see that they have a role to play in bringing about change. *Contemplation* is when they have clarity that self-investment will be necessary to overcome the pervasiveness of their problems. *Preparation* is when counseling really gets moving, with clients taking small steps in the direction they need to pursue. *Action* is the most dramatic stage because energy, effort, and time are dedicated to make change happen. *Maintenance* is the stage in which the new experience becomes the new normal. Helping clients understand how motivation cycles back and forth among phases allows them to anticipate how the intensity, pace, and progress within counseling might occur.

Assessments can aid in this process because of how they quantify an experience and increase consciousness of its component features. Counselees can use data as feedback to count the cost of remaining in the status quo against the benefits of proceeding on a course toward another way of living. Further, when the challenge to keep going becomes intense or living differently feels awkward, the baseline descriptions help them remember what it was like to remain in interminable contemplation.

For the Christ-follower, the pace and destination of change can be sustained or quickened by listening for the Great Comforter as he communicates via worship, prayer, Scripture reading, and fellowship. We can educate clients early on to recognize this spiritual input and guide them to be in the right settings and engage in formation practices where they can hear his voice. They likely have already been asking the Lord to lighten a burden, provide strength, or help them rest. We can remind them of the full range of resources available that can help them maintain motivation, persistence, and readiness for change.

Patterns from a personality screening can also enhance a client's grasp of how change is likely to unfold. Indeed, we should seek to blend a client's personal attributes into any discussion on motivation for change. Understanding how personal characteristics like extroversion, openness to experience, agreeableness, conscientiousness, and emotional stability interact with symptoms will provide deeper insights for the dyad. When we name these individualized dynamics during sessions, clients will have stronger incentive to lean further into the alliance.

Stimulate hope in a constructive START. The research on therapy and successful completion suggests that strengthening hope early on sets a tone of confidence. Three closely related assumptions support a client's commitment to stay in treatment: (1) a belief in therapy, (2) belief in one's therapist, and (3) sufficient self-efficacy to sustain hope in transformation. Thus, experts agree that counselors who are proficient in completing treatment with clients plant and nurture these conventions in those tentative initial discussions.

If you recall, the START model prompts therapists to be up front about the recommendation to enter therapy to pursue a definitive outcome (R). This affirms that the talking cure and a general treatment plan (T) have the potential to bring growth in the client's area of need. This in turn inspires hope not only in a generic process but also in an immediate application. The therapeutic alliance (T) is nurtured at the outset to raise confidence in the strength of the match between the counselor and client. This all ties together as the client's story (S) is heard with empathy and the presenting concerns are assessed (A) in ways that demonstrate that the counselor has a strategy to initiate and deliver quality care.

Christians who counsel can also draw on a client's faith to support the therapeutic relationship. Our faith rests on beliefs in a supreme loving Creator who empowers the helping process. In fact, early on we can assure clients of faith that compatible theological tradition, theocentric convictions, and formation practices will be shared. This amplifies a client's hope from the outset in ways that make graduation not only appealing but also attainable. They are reminded that the journey will not be a solo or even just a dyadic effort. The Lord will oversee his sanctifying and strengthening work within his beloved child. And Christian clients can ask trusted members of their faith community, such as a pastor or Bible study leader, to pray with them about entry into counseling. This creates firm groundwork for a future commencement.

Embrace and enhance motivation. Simply put, the counseling conversation begins with the client's understanding of what it means to pursue change. Clinicians who finish well begin by communicating to clients a sense of acceptance and empathy regarding the tension between the comfort of staying one's course and the hope of a novel adventure. Using motivational interviewing (Miller & Rollnick, 2013) to do this is strategic. At root, this technique involves implementing a collaborative conversational style that draws out a client's own motivations and commitment level to change. The literature on premature termination indicates that without attention to motivation levels from start to finish, counseling is prone to getting off track.

This brings us back to the central recommendation that counselors apply assessment in ways that make an advocacy role obvious. The goal of assessment is not to manipulate, control, impress, exploit, or label. Rather, it provides a form of measurement for the benefit of clients and helps establish the counseling partnership more deeply. Discussions about ratings and results along the way are never about revealing failure. This is where the graduation metaphor could potentially be misleading. Tracking progress is all about adjusting strategies and aligning the relationship. Measurement is a means to enhance the collaborative potential of a helping partnership.

Foster a therapeutic and triadic alliance. Evidence shows that a good-enough therapeutic alliance is built around agreement on the goals and task of treatment within a stable interpersonal bond. The hope of graduation diminishes when breaks, strains, or ruptures in the partnership are left unattended and unaddressed. Examining and repairing a helping relationship is not going to be natural for a client unless permission is given for it and a prototype introduced. This is where tracking the strength of the alliance through the use of an explicit instrument as a customary session activity can seamlessly and powerfully interrupt a client's inclination to drop out. Take time along the way to check in about whether the relationship is meeting expectations. Clarify misunderstandings, recognize a client's feelings or concerns, and preserve the partnership.

The concept of a triadic alliance—inviting the Lord's presence into the immediate counseling conversation—is an intense, mysterious, and powerful one. Broadening the alliance in this transcendent direction places both client and therapist in a submissive position where they can hear and discern how the Holy Spirit is leading. This can foster a joint dependency and worshipful posture that secures wisdom and can help clients reap the benefits of a relationship with the Lord and with fellow believers. These healing relationships can become the norm within families and the family of God. And when trauma, tragedy, or distorted thinking has its way in a person's heart, a therapeutic alliance can help restore a client's openness and readiness to enter into the beauty of fellowship.

Celebrate progress with simplicity and gratitude. The field of psychotherapy is starting to see monitoring outcomes and using feedback from clients on a regular, even weekly, basis as a helpful practice. The availability of apps and in-session short forms makes it easier than ever. Again, because clients who are making progress are more likely to continue onward to graduation, regular progress checks are a powerful tool that can help us improve treatment completion rates.

Recognizing and celebrating progress, even in small ways, has obvious therapeutic benefits. It can also fulfill biblical exhortations to notice the grace of the Lord and become an opportunity to mutually give thanks (Phil 4:8; Col 3:15; 1 Thess 5:17-18; Heb 10:24-25). Imagine how powerful it can be for a client to recognize progress in behavior, interpersonal relations, or spiritual maturation during a session and take that knowledge into a worship service including the Lord's Supper. Gratitude turns from conversation to a divine-human, heavenly Father–spiritual child occasion of celebration. Even when rating scales reveal low levels of movement toward change, be thankful for this awareness and for the opportunity to revise your approach. This is prudent and wise.

POSTGRADUATION PLANNING: AFTERCARE

That special juncture when a client is ready to separate from regular counseling sessions and prosper with natural supports is a prime moment for you both to express appreciation while debriefing the twists and turns of this series of counseling sessions. Review promotes consolidation of gains.

It's also a key time for discussing aftercare plans. At graduation, clients must be prepared to self-monitor how they are doing on key behavioral and relational fronts. They can take away a mindset of assessment, by which they understand how to make a goal concrete by breaking it down into smaller, manageable pieces and how to recognize change on their own in incremental ways. Progress checks can become self-checks, or other accountability partners can be brought into the conversation. We can equip them with an assessment procedure that they can apply periodically to recognize signs of regression or a return to risky situations involving problematic people, places, or things. You could even have a client take an RAI home with them and then come back to see you, bringing their RAI, six or twelve weeks later. Assessment in counseling care becomes an aspect of the client's pursuit of health and further growth after counseling.

Using feedback as a technique to keep a relationship vital and productive is not the easiest skill to bring directly into other relationships, beyond the counseling dyad. It would not feel normal for most people to hand a tablet over to a friend and ask the person to rate the relationship in terms of goals, tasks, and bonds! However, by the time a client graduates, the two of you have likely talked through session experiences where awkward relational and procedural matters existed. After all, in counseling, the focus is not only on the content of the conversation but also on how the relationship itself is fostering mutuality and common ground. These communication skills as well as the interpersonal boldness required to be transparent, clear, and emotionally alive are transferable to other relationships. In fact, practicing ways to increase the intensity of communication with others prior to graduation is a fairly common therapeutic undertaking. This sets the stage for a client to maintain personal gains in behavioral terms while enjoying greater relational fluidity—the ability to bring one's awareness of being a significant self (SIGN-IFICANT: Self In God's Narrative—Individuality in Fellowship with and Imitating Christ, Always reNewing Traits)—to promote genuineness and mutuality with others.

Christian fellowship is about loving one another in ways that highlight the love of our triune God. Contained in that is the ability to recognize how individuals are each becoming a better reflection of the image of Jesus Christ. Aftercare planning for disciples involves foreseeing how deeper, authentic, mutual involvement with others will continue. There were reasons that brought the client into counseling. Therapy stirred forces of redemption and renewal into motion. Counselor and client imagine together how this progression can be sustained and blessed by the Lord.

TECHNIQUES IN SERVICE OF CONNECTION

Assessment embedded within the entire counseling process is a means to gain insight, gather feedback, and keep momentum strong toward reaching the objectives of the partnership. But there is more to this thesis than it being a persuasive plea to adopt scientific techniques and standardized ways of gathering meaningful information via well-implemented measurement.

The social philosopher Jacques Ellul (1964) once drew attention to the decay that accompanies the blind adoption of novel techniques and refined ways of conducting tasks in the name of progress. He recognized the pitfalls of technology in an age when everyone is striving to do all things with improving skill and higher efficiency and productivity. His prophetic warning is principally to beware of the continuous quest embedded in standardization to improve methods only to reach carelessly examined ends. Is that what the premises I've set before you—the importance of applying credible and precise instruments that offer insight into the human relational encounter known as counseling and of seeing that soul care and spiritual formation may be guided by good assessment strategies—will lead to? The risk is real if the key objective is lost. Thus, let's recall the intent and goal of the application of quality assessment instruments to the helping relationship.

The goal in counseling that has a Christian foundation is to honor the Lord and to assist in the equipping of the client to obtain the mind of Christ in all things. Clinicians are to apply psychological instruments as artisans utilize tools to artistically shape objects of value. A craftsperson is one with "wisdom" in his or her hands. A counselor sets out to secure wisdom to understand and strengthen the affections of the human heart. The connection formed in the counseling relationship becomes a catalyst for change and further relational connection. Assessment of the alliance itself helps us make adjustments to ensure that the relationship is fostering growth toward the expected outcome. The good achieved becomes a means to bring glory to the Lord.

In terms of serving the Lord and our clients, our mission is to enable human beings to better reflect the image of the Creator in all that they do in ways that only their uniqueness can display. Connecting with others, the self, and the Lord is the work of artisans. As we carefully attend to our clients and their requests, our techniques may reflect best clinical practice and human ingenuity without being earthly or selfish or seeking dominance and autonomy. The Holy Spirit's presence and participation assure us that the wisdom produced will emerge from above. This is partnership in God's good work.

> But the wisdom that comes from heaven is first of all pure; then peace-loving, considerate, submissive, full of mercy and good fruit, impartial and sincere. Peacemakers who sow in peace reap a harvest of righteousness. (Jas 3:17-18)

REFERENCES

American Counseling Association. (2014). *ACA code of ethics: As approved by the ACA Governing Council.* http://www.counseling.org/resources/aca-code-of-ethics.pdf

American Psychiatric Association. (2015). Severity measure for generalized anxiety disorder—Adult. Downloaded April 29, 2015 from http://www.psychiatry.org/practice /dsm/dsm5/online-assessment-measures#Disorder

Ellul, J. (1964). *The technological society.* (John Wilkinson, Trans.). New York: Knopf/ Random House. (Original work published in French in 1954)

Greggo, S. P., & Lawrence, K. (2012). Redemptive validity and the assessment of depression: Singing songs to heavy hearts. *Journal of Psychology and Theology, 40*(3), 188-198.

Lambert, M. J. (2010). *Prevention of treatment failure: The use of measuring, monitoring, and feedback in clinical practice.* Washington, DC: American Psychological Association.

Lambert, M. J. (2013). Outcome in psychotherapy: The past and important advances. *Psychotherapy, 50*(1), 42-51.

Maples, J. L., & Walker, R. L. (2014). Consolidation rather than termination: Rethinking how psychologists label and conceptualize the final phase of psychological treatment. *Professional Psychology: Research and Practice, 45*(2), 104-110.

Miller, W. R., & Rollnick, S. (2013). *Motivational interviewing: Helping people change* (3rd ed.). New York: Guilford Press.

Mours, J. M., Campbell, C. D., Gathercoal, K. A., & Peterson, M. K. (2009). Training in the use of psychotherapy outcome assessment measures at psychology internship sites. *Training in Education in Professional Psychology, 3*(3), 169-176.

Norcross, J. C., Krebs, P. M., & Prochaska, J. O. (2011). Stages of change. *Journal of Clinical Psychology, 67*(2), 143-154.

Patterson, P., Matthey, S., & Baker, M. (2006). Using mental health outcome measures in everyday clinical practice. *Australasian Psychiatry, 14*(2), 133-136.

Reese, R. J., Duncan, B. L., Bohanske, R. T., Owen, J. J., & Minami, T. (2014). Benchmarking outcomes in a public behavioral health setting: Feedback as a quality improvement strategy. *Journal of Consulting and Clinical Psychology, 82*(4), 731-742.

Shimokawa, K., Lambert, M. J., & Smart, D. W. (2010). Enhancing treatment outcome of patients at risk of treatment failure: Meta-analytic and mega-analytic review of a psychotherapy quality assurance system. *Journal of Consulting and Clinical Psychology, 78*(3), 298-311.

Swift, J. K., & Greenberg, R. P. (2015). *Premature termination in psychotherapy: Strategies for engaging clients and improving outcomes.* Washington, DC: American Psychological Association.

APPENDIX 1

CLINICAL ASSESSMENT INSTRUMENT CHRISTIAN EVALUATION FORM (CAICEF)

Name of the assessment instrument:

PURPOSE

According to the manual, what is the purpose of the assessment instrument?

Does this purpose align with the clinical needs of my client base?　❏ YES　❏ NO

TEST DEVELOPMENT

Is the assessment instrument *norm-referenced* or *criterion-referenced?* (check one)

❏ *Norm-referenced*

Is the size of the norming population adequate?　❏ YES　❏ NO

Does the norming population adequately represent the demographics and relevant characteristics of my client base? (i.e., age, gender, race)　❏ YES　❏ NO

Rate the overall appropriateness of the norming population:

❏ Very Inappropriate　❏ Inappropriate　❏ Average　❏ Appropriate　❏ Very Appropriate　❏ Not Applicable

Explain any norming population concerns:

❏ *Criterion-referenced*

Rate the overall appropriateness of the criterion:

❏ Very Inappropriate　❏ Inappropriate　❏ Average　❏ Appropriate　❏ Very Appropriate　❏ Not Applicable

Criterion concerns:

ITEM ANALYSIS

Consider the items of the assessment instrument.

Multidimensional evaluation

Does the assessment instrument contain items that evaluate physiological distress? ❏ YES ❏ NO

Does the assessment instrument contain items that evaluate psychological distress? ❏ YES ❏ NO

Does the assessment instrument contain items that evaluate social distress? ❏ YES ❏ NO

Does the assessment instrument contain items that evaluate spiritual distress? ❏ YES ❏ NO

Faith-sensitive items

Does the assessment instrument contain any faith-sensitive items? ❏ YES ❏ NO

If yes, please specify:

Given the belief system of my client base, rate the probability that these faith-sensitive items will skew the results of the assessment instrument:

❏ Very Low   ❏ Low   ❏ Average   ❏ High   ❏ Very High   ❏ Not Applicable

PSYCHOMETRICS

Reliability

Rate the acceptability of each of the following types of reliability:

Test re-test reliability: Is individual performance on the first administration consistent with performance on the second administration?

❏ Very Unacceptable ❏ Unacceptable ❏ Average ❏ Acceptable ❏ Very Acceptable ❏ Not Applicable

Alternate or parallel forms: Is individual performance consistent between the two forms?

❏ Very Unacceptable ❏ Unacceptable ❏ Average ❏ Acceptable ❏ Very Acceptable ❏ Not Applicable

Internal consistency: Is the assessment instrument internally consistent?

❏ Very Unacceptable ❏ Unacceptable ❏ Average ❏ Acceptable ❏ Very Acceptable ❏ Not Applicable

Inter-rater reliability: Is there sufficient evidence that the scoring is consistent among raters?

❏ Very Unacceptable ❏ Unacceptable ❏ Average ❏ Acceptable ❏ Very Acceptable ❏ Not Applicable

Rate the overall acceptability of reliability:

❏ Very Unacceptable ❏ Unacceptable ❏ Average ❏ Acceptable ❏ Very Acceptable

Reliability concerns:

Validity

Rate the acceptability of each of the following types of validity:

Face validity: Based on the appearance and style of the assessment instrument, are items likely to invite reasonable client responses, particularly from clients with Christian faith convictions?

❏ **Very Unacceptable**   ❏ **Unacceptable**   ❏ **Average**   ❏ **Acceptable**   ❏ **Very Acceptable**

Content relevance and structure: Does the assessment instrument cover a representative sample of the specified skills and knowledge? Does factor analysis support the subscales, the precision of the measure, and its freedom from distracting embedded variables?

❏ **Very Unacceptable**   ❏ **Unacceptable**   ❏ **Average**   ❏ **Acceptable**   ❏ **Very Acceptable**

Redemptive validity: Does the instrument reveal aspects of a client's self-narrative that have implications for Christian identity and/or spiritual development? Do items raise awareness on matters that may invite reflection from a gospel lens (i.e., creation, fall, redemption, consummation)?   ❏ **YES**   ❏ **NO**

Construct representation: How well does the assessment instrument reflect and measure the intended construct?

❏ **Very Unacceptable**   ❏ **Unacceptable**   ❏ **Average**   ❏ **Acceptable**   ❏ **Very Acceptable**

Redemptive validity: Does the assessment instrument contribute to a more detailed understanding of the central condition of the human heart or reveal ways that core affections (i.e., attachment, ethical motivation, awe, hope, etc.) may need to further rest in the grace of God?   ❏ **YES**   ❏ **NO**

If yes, please specify:

Concurrent validity: Is the assessment instrument systematically a good indicator of a condition, and is there evidence that it does it as well or better than other measures?

❏ **Very Unacceptable**   ❏ **Unacceptable**   ❏ **Average**   ❏ **Acceptable**   ❏ **Very Acceptable**   ❏ **Not Applicable**

Redemptive validity: Does the assessment instrument provide insight into life issues or existential matters that reveal personality concerns (patterns of thinking, feeling, and acting) that indicate areas for potential growth in spiritual development? Does the measure point to a character matter that the Holy Spirit may also be addressing?   ❏ **YES**   ❏ **NO**

If yes, please specify:

Does the assessment instrument measure behaviors, attitudes, or beliefs that Scripture directly addresses or reveal areas where an increased dependency upon the Creator for wisdom is warranted?   ❏ **YES**   ❏ **NO**

If yes, please specify:

Rate the overall acceptability of validity:

❏ Very Unacceptable   ❏ Unacceptable   ❏ Average   ❏ Acceptable   ❏ Very Acceptable

Explain any validity concerns (e.g., construct underrepresentation or construct-irrelevance):

Rate the overall acceptability of redemptive validity:

❏ Very Unacceptable   ❏ Unacceptable   ❏ Average   ❏ Acceptable   ❏ Very Acceptable

Redemptive validity concerns:

ADMINISTRATION, INTERPRETATION, AND SCORING

User qualifications

User qualification level required for administration and interpretation: ❏ A   ❏ B   ❏ C

Based upon the criteria of this user qualification level, am I competent to administer and
interpret the test results of this assessment instrument?   ❏ YES   ❏ NO

Administration procedure

Is the administration procedure outlined in the manual compatible with the overall
logistics and procedures of my organization?   ❏ YES   ❏ NO

Potential conflict areas:

Scoring

The assessment instrument requires: ❏ Hand-scoring   ❏ Computerized scoring

Overall ease of scoring:

❏ Highly Complex   ❏ Complex   ❏ Average   ❏ Easy   ❏ Very Easy

Scoring concerns:

Interpretation

Does the manual provide sufficient information to appropriately interpret the results
of the assessment instrument?   ❑ YES   ❑ NO

Does the manual provide sufficient information to assist in communicating results to
clients in ways that will facilitate understanding of behavioral, internal, interpersonal, or
spiritual areas in need of restoration and redemption?   ❑ YES   ❑ NO

Overall ease of interpretation:

❑ Highly Complex   ❑ Complex   ❑ Average   ❑ Easy   ❑ Very Easy

Interpretation concerns:

UTILITY

Is there a significant additional investment in time, resources, and training for my
organization if this assessment instrument is adopted for us?   ❑ YES   ❑ NO

If yes, please specify:

What information, benefit, risk reduction, or new efficiency is likely to be gained from the application of this
assessment instrument?

If this assessment instrument is adopted by my organization, what supplemental questions should be asked in
order to improve my conceptualization of the distress from a spiritual perspective?

Utility concerns:

TOTAL EVALUATION

Based on the information and concerns above, rate the overall appropriateness of assessment instrument:

❏ Very Inappropriate   ❏ Inappropriate   ❏ Average   ❏ Appropriate   ❏ Very Appropriate

Provide a brief narrative summary, evaluation conclusion, and recommendations or qualifications for use:

Greggo, Stephen P. (2019). *Assessment for Counseling in Christian Perspective*. Downers Grove, IL: InterVarsity Press.

APPENDIX 2

START INITIAL CONSULTATION REPORT

STORY

Referral source:

Reason for referral

What has motivated the client to come?

Presenting problem

Focus on one or more of the following: trigger/why now?, behavioral/functional problems, precipitating factors, developmental stage/social clock, role change, services sought, previous experience, conditions when problem improves/worsens, duration, etc. *NOTE: Record level of severity next to abnormal findings—1 (mild), 2 (moderate), or 3 (severe); use "X" if normal finding.*

Stressors		Birth of a child		Change of residence		Child leaving		Chronic health problems
		Death of a family member		Divorce		Financial problems		Major illness/disability
		Parent-child problems		Separation		Unemployment		Workplace change
		Marital problems						
Duration		Temporary		Permanent				
Frequency		/day		/week		/month		/year
Locus of control		Internal		External				

Client expectations

What does the client hope to gain from counseling?

Relevant family factors

Family dynamics, rules, values, discipline, boundaries, early development, and/or anything unusual regarding family relationships, communication, and/or family medical history:

Career/educational highlights:

Spirituality/religion:

Does the client express willingness to incorporate faith into counseling?   ❏ YES   ❏ NO

Present religious affiliation:

Spiritual/religious upbringing or practices (denomination, patterns, rules, experiences, etc.):

Current spiritual/religious commitment:

Spirituality/religion	Unable to rate	None	Minimal	Some	Moderate	Significant	Potential level at termination
Importance	0	1	2	3	4	5	
Influence on daily activities & life	0	1	2	3	4	5	
Practice of spiritual discipline	0	1	2	3	4	5	
Spiritual maturity	0	1	2	3	4	5	

THERAPEUTIC ALLIANCE

Initial session rating		Strong		Average		Strained		Weak		None
Client self-disclosure		Strong		Average		Minimum		Initial		None
Client resistance		Strong		Average		Minimum		Initial		None
Therapeutic alliance		Appropriate		Defensive		Dependent		Domineering		Evasive
		Hostile		Passive		Seductive		Other		

List one to three client strengths evident in this session.

1.

2.

3.

List characteristics or attitudes that may impact the alliance or counseling progress.

ASSESSMENT

Current functioning

Categories	IMPAIRMENT LEVEL (select one)					Impairment Level After Treatment
	None	Mild	Moderate	Marked	Extreme	
Marriage/relationship/family/ job/school/performance	1	2	3	4	5	
_____ Disability leave _____ Job jeopardy	1	2	3	4	5	
Friendships/peer relationships	1	2	3	4	5	
Financial situation	1	2	3	4	5	
Hobbies/interests/play activities	1	2	3	4	5	
Physical health	1	2	3	4	5	
Activities of daily living (personal hygiene, bathing, etc.)	1	2	3	4	5	
Eating habits Weight loss _____ lbs. Weight gain _____ lbs Current weight _____ lbs.	1	2	3	4	5	
Sleeping habits _____ Difficulty falling asleep _____ Difficulty staying asleep _____ Early morning awakening	1	2	3	4	5	
Sexual functioning	1	2	3	4	5	
Spiritual/religious activities	1	2	3	4	5	
Ability to concentrate	1	2	3	4	5	
Ability to control temper	1	2	3	4	5	

Elaboration:

Symptoms

Record level of severity next to abnormal findings—*1 (mild), 2 (moderate), or 3 (severe); use "X" if normal finding.*

Physical ■ N/A	Aches & pains	Chest pain	Dizziness	Fatigue
	Headaches	Heart palpitations	High blood pressure	Panic attacks
	Pregnancy	Frequent illness	Sleeping problems	Trembling
Cognitive ■ N/A	Distractibility	Disorientation	Recurring thoughts	Other (specify)
Emotional ■ N/A	Grief	Guilt	Hopelessness	Insecurity
	Loneliness	Mood shifts	Phobias/fears	Worrying
	Apathy			
Behavioral ■ N/A	Antisocial	Avoiding	Eating disorder	Hyperactivity
	Impulsivity	Learning disability	Speech problems	Withdrawing
Cultural ■ N/A	Conforming	Dissonance	Resistance & immersion	Introspection
	Integration awareness			
Coping ability	Normal	Resilient	Exhausted	Overwhelmed
	Deficient supports	Deficient skills	Growing	Other (specify)
Skill deficit	Normal	Intellect/education	Communication	Interpersonal
	Decision making	Self-control	Self-care	Other (specify)
Risk factors ■ Assessed ■ Legally Reportable	Child neglect	Elder neglect	Poverty	Domestic violence
	Physical abuse	Sexual abuse/molestation	Verbal/emotional abuse	
Substance use/abuse ■ N/A	Tobacco	Caffeine	Drug	Alcohol
	Early partial remission	Early full remission	Sustained full remission	Sustained partial remission

Elaboration:

Medical History

Medications (include medical, psychiatric, over-the-counter/herbal):

Previous therapy (purpose, counselor/psychologist/pastor, when, duration, outcome):

Recent physical exam & results:

Hospitalization (when, reason, duration):

Mental status exam

Record level of severity next to abnormal findings—

1 (mild), 2 (moderate), or 3 (severe); use "X" if normal finding.

General observations	Appearance	Well groomed	Unkempt	Disheveled
	Build	Average	Thin	Overweight
	Demeanor	Average	Hostile	Mistrustful
		Withdrawn	Preoccupied	Demanding
	Eye contact	Average	Avoidant	Intense
	Activity	Average	Agitated	Slowed
	Speech	Clear	Slurred	Rapid
		Pressured		
Thought content	Delusions ☐ None reported	Grandiose	Persecutory	Somatic
		Bizarre	Nihilistic	Religious
	Other ☐ None reported	Autistic	Obsessional	Phobic
		Guilty	Ideas of reference	Preoccupied
		Guarded	Other:	
	Self-Abuse ☐ None reported	Suicidal	Intent	Lethal
		Self-mutilation	Means	Plan
	Aggressive ☐ None reported	Homicidal	Intent	Lethal
			Means	Plan
Perception	Hallucinations ☐ None reported	Auditory	Visual	Olfactory
		Gustatory	Tactile	
	Other ☐ None reported	Illusions	Depersonalization	Derealization
Thought process	Logical	Circumstantial	Tangential	Loose
	Racing	Incoherent	Concrete	Blocked
	Flight of ideas			
Judgment	Normal	Street-smart	Naive	Impaired
Mood	Euthymic	Depressed	Anxious	Angry
	Euphoric	Irritable		
Affect	Full	Constricted	Flat	Inappropriate
	Liable			
Behavior	Cooperative	Resistant	Agitated	Impulsive
	Oversedated	Assaultive	Aggressive	Hyperactive
	Restless	Loss of interests	Withdrawn	
Cognition	Impairment of ☐ None reported	Orientation	Memory	Attention/concentration
		Judgment	Insight	Ability to abstract
Intelligence estimate	Well below average	Below average	Average	Above average

Social History

Support			
Family	Friends	Partner	Membership
Relatives	Neighbors	Professionals	Coworkers
Pastoral staff	Mentor		

Interpersonal maturity			
Dependent	Impulsive	Irresponsible	Isolated
Responsible	Self-centered		

Elaboration:

Initial Diagnostic Impression:

RECOMMENDATIONS

Session length	30 minutes	45 minutes	60 minutes	Other (specify)
Frequency	twice weekly	weekly	twice monthly	monthly
Format	Individual	Family	Marital/relational	Group
Classification	Primary	Secondary	Tertiary	Other
Model of therapy	Crisis management	Consultation	Medical evaluation	Prevention
	Psychodynamic	Person-centered	Existential	Adlerian
	Gestalt theory	REBT	Behavioral	Cognitive
	Reality	Family therapy	Other (specify)	
Support groups	12-step program	Alcoholics Anonymous	Narcotics Anonymous	
	Gamblers Anonymous	Overeaters Anonymous	Other (specify)	
Psycho-educational groups	Assertiveness	Anger management	Child management	Communication skills
	Divorce care	Finance management	Grief care	Parenting skills
	Premarital counseling	Stress management	Women's issues	Other (specify)

Referrals for continuing services	Advocacy	Alcohol-drug treatment program	Education on medications & compliance	Educational/vocational services
	Hospitalization	Intellectual evaluation	Legal services	Nursing care
	Occupational/physical therapy	Outpatient therapy	Offender program	Parochial services
	Personality evaluation	Physical medical care	Psychological evaluation	Psychiatric evaluation
	Psychotropic evaluation	Victim support	Vocational/career counseling	Other (specify)

Elaboration on recommendation(s):

TREATMENT PLAN (Initial)

Complex Treatment Issues:

☐ One or more acute admissions in past year

☐ Prior treatment attempts without success

☐ Suicidal/homicidal behavior

☐ Medical co-morbidity

☐ Multiple family members in treatment

☐ Disorder keeps child out of school

☐ Psychiatric disability

☐ Prescription medication

☐ Multiple providers

☐ Agency involvement

☐ Community support services

☐ Arrests and/or incarcerations

☐ Treatment noncompliance

☐ Out-of-home placement in past year

☐ Disorder related to sexual trauma

Elaboration:

Behavior(s) to be changed/observable indicators of improvement:

Interventions:

Questionnaires/handouts/assignments given:

Summary:

Clinician's Signature: _____ Date: _____

Greggo, Stephen P. (2019). *Assessment for Counseling in Christian Perspective*. Downers Grove, IL: InterVarsity Press.

APPENDIX 3

COUNSELING PARTNERSHIP ALLIANCE CHECK (CPAC)

Reflect and focus on your most recent session. Please provide three candid ratings for these categories. Immediate feedback can foster communication and contribute to a productive counseling partnership.

Hope for Change

Reflect on the session themes, talking points, strategies, and activities. Today I felt . . .

DOUBTFUL 〈 ☐☐☐☐☐☐☐☐ 〉 CONFIDENT

Hospitality and Connection

Consider today's teamwork, common focus, honesty, and accountability. Overall, my experience was . . .

DISTANCING 〈 ☐☐☐☐☐☐☐☐ 〉 WELCOMING

Cultivating Character

Ponder how today's work might eventually strengthen your faith or shape your character. Today I felt . . .

DOWNCAST/DISCOURAGED 〈 ☐☐☐☐☐☐☐☐ 〉 BLESSED/REFRESHED

Client ID: _____ Session Date: _____

Greggo, Stephen P. (2019). *Assessment for Counseling in Christian Perspective*. Downers Grove, IL: InterVarsity Press.

AUTHOR INDEX

SUBJECT INDEX

CAPS
INTERNATIONAL

An Association for Christian Psychologists,
Therapists, Counselors and Academicians

CAPS is a vibrant Christian organization with a rich tradition. Founded in 1956 by a small group of Christian mental health professionals, chaplains and pastors, CAPS has grown to more than 2,100 members in the U.S., Canada and more than 25 other countries.

CAPS encourages in-depth consideration of therapeutic, research, theoretical and theological issues. The association is a forum for creative new ideas. In fact, their publications and conferences are the birthplace for many of the formative concepts in our field today.

CAPS members represent a variety of denominations, professional groups and theoretical orientations; yet all are united in their commitment to Christ and to professional excellence.

CAPS is a non-profit, member-supported organization. It is led by a fully functioning board of directors, and the membership has a voice in the direction of CAPS.

CAPS is more than a professional association. It is a fellowship, and in addition to national and international activities, the organization strongly encourages regional, local and area activities which provide networking and fellowship opportunities as well as professional enrichment.

To learn more about CAPS, visit www.caps.net.

The joint publishing venture between IVP Academic and CAPS aims to promote the understanding of the relationship between Christianity and the behavioral sciences at both the clinical/counseling and the theoretical/research levels. These books will be of particular value for students and practitioners, teachers and researchers.

For more information about CAPS Books, visit InterVarsity Press's website at www.ivpress.com/christian-association-for-psychological-studies-books-set.

Finding the Textbook You Need

The IVP Academic Textbook Selector
is an online tool for instantly finding the IVP books
suitable for over 250 courses across 24 disciplines.

ivpacademic.com